CooL LISTENING

3

DARAKWON

저자 선생님

조금배
- Hawaii Pacific University TESL 학사 및 석사
- 서강대학교 대학원 영어영문학과 언어학 박사 과정
- 〈Hot Listening〉, 〈Cool Grammar〉 시리즈 등 공저

백영실
- 미국 Liberty University 졸업
- 〈Hot Listening〉, 〈절대어휘 5100〉 시리즈 등 공저

김정인
- 캐나다 Mount Saint Vincent University 영어교육학 석사
- 현 캐나다 온타리오주 공인회계사 (CPA)

영어듣기 모의고사

저자 조금배, 백영실, 김정인
펴낸이 정규도
펴낸곳 (주)다락원

초판 2쇄 발행 2024년 1월 25일

편집 안혜원, 정연순, 서정아
디자인 구수정, 정규옥
삽화 권순옥
영문 감수 Michael A. Putlack

다락원 경기도 파주시 문발로 211
내용문의 (02) 736-2031 내선 532, 501, 503
구입문의 (02) 736-2031 내선 250~252
Fax (02) 732-2037
출판등록 1977년 9월 16일 제406-2008-000007호

ISBN 978-89-277-8022-9 54740
　　　978-89-277-8016-8 54740(set)

http://www.darakwon.co.kr

다락원 홈페이지를 방문하시면 상세한 출판 정보와 함께 MP3 자료 등의 다양한 어학 정보를 얻으실 수 있습니다.

영어듣기 모의고사

CooL

LISTENING

3

STRUCTURES & FEATURES
구성과 특징

TEST
실전 모의고사

CooL LISTENING 시리즈는 시·도 교육청 영어듣기평가를 비롯한 다양한 듣기 시험 문제 유형을 분석·반영한 실전 모의고사 20회를 수록했습니다. 다양한 유형의 실전 문제와 실생활에서 사용하는 주제들로 대화 및 담화가 구성되어 있어 실전 감각을 키우고 듣기 실력을 향상시키는 데 도움이 될 것입니다.

QR코드로 음원 바로 듣기

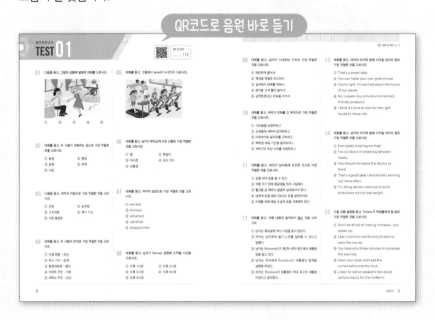

DICTATION
받아쓰기

중요 어휘·표현 및 헷갈릴 수 있는 발음을 점검하고 학습할 수 있도록 받아쓰기를 구성했습니다. 모의고사 전 지문의 받아쓰기를 통해서 대화 및 담화 내용을 한 번 더 익히고, 중요 표현을 복습할 수 있습니다.

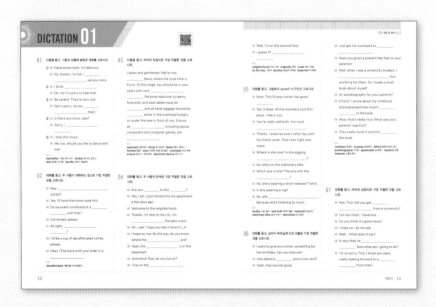

REVIEW TEST
리뷰 테스트

모의고사에서 나온 중요 어휘와 문장을 복습할 수 있는 리뷰 테스트를 수록했습니다.
어휘를 듣고 어휘 및 우리말 뜻 쓰기와, 문장 빈칸 채우기를 통해서 핵심 어휘와 표현을 확실하게 복습할 수 있습니다.

ANSWERS & SCRIPTS
정답 및 해석

한눈에 들어오는 정답 및 해석으로 편리하게 정답, 대본, 중요 어휘를 확인할 수 있습니다.

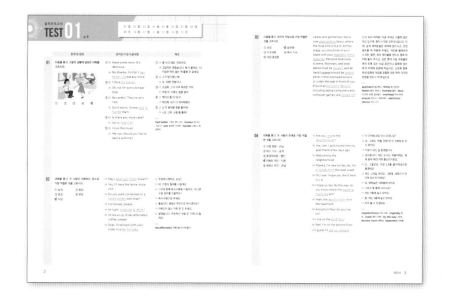

온라인 부가자료 www.darakwon.co.kr
다락원 홈페이지에서 무료로 부가자료를 다운로드하거나 웹에서 이용할 수 있습니다.
- 다양한 MP3 파일 제공: TEST별(0.8배속 / 1.0배속 / 1.2배속) & 문항별
- 어휘 리스트 & 어휘 테스트

CONTENTS
목차

TEST
실전 모의고사

MY SCORE

········· / 15

01 다음을 듣고, 그림의 상황에 알맞은 대화를 고르시오.

① ② ③ ④ ⑤

02 대화를 듣고, 두 사람이 대화하는 장소로 가장 적절한 곳을 고르시오.

① 농장   ② 빵집
③ 공장   ④ 부엌
⑤ 식당

03 다음을 듣고, 여자의 직업으로 가장 적절한 것을 고르시오.

① 선장   ② 승무원
③ 구조대원   ④ 택시 기사
⑤ 식당 종업원

04 대화를 듣고, 두 사람의 관계로 가장 적절한 것을 고르시오.

① 서점 점원 - 손님
② 버스 기사 - 승객
③ 환경미화원 - 행인
④ 아파트 주민 - 이웃
⑤ 세탁소 주인 - 손님

05 대화를 듣고, 그림에서 Janet이 누구인지 고르시오.

06 대화를 듣고, 남자가 부모님께 드린 선물로 가장 적절한 것을 고르시오.

① 꽃   ② 목걸이
③ 자서전   ④ 감사 카드
⑤ 상품권

07 대화를 듣고, 여자의 심정으로 가장 적절한 것을 고르시오.

① excited
② envious
③ ashamed
④ satisfied
⑤ disappointed

08 대화를 듣고, 남자가 Denver 공항에 도착할 시각을 고르시오.

① 오후 1시경   ② 오후 2시경
③ 오후 6시경   ④ 오후 8시경
⑤ 오후 9시경

09 대화를 듣고, 남자가 사과하는 이유로 가장 적절한 것을 고르시오.

① 예민하게 굴어서
② 책상을 연필로 두드려서
③ 실내에서 담배를 피워서
④ 음악을 크게 틀어 놓아서
⑤ 금연하겠다는 약속을 어겨서

10 대화를 듣고, 여자가 전화를 건 목적으로 가장 적절한 것을 고르시오.

① 사은품을 요청하려고
② 신제품에 대하여 문의하려고
③ 아르바이트 일자리를 구하려고
④ 백화점 세일 기간을 알아보려고
⑤ 세탁기의 무상 수리를 의뢰하려고

11 대화를 듣고, 여자가 남자에게 조언한 것으로 가장 적절한 것을 고르시오.

① 돈을 써야 돈을 벌 수 있다.
② 여행 가기 전에 항공권을 먼저 구입해라.
③ 물건을 살 때마다 꼼꼼히 살펴보아야 한다.
④ 남에게 돈을 빌리기보다는 돈을 빌려주어라.
⑤ 미래를 위해 매일 조금씩 돈을 저축해야 한다.

12 대화를 듣고, 대화 내용과 일치하지 않는 것을 고르시오.

① 남자는 목요일에 역사 수업을 듣지 않았다.
② 여자는 남자에게 필기 노트를 빌려줄 수 있다고 말했다.
③ 남자는 Roosevelt가 제2차 세계 대전 때의 대통령임을 알고 있다.
④ 남자는 여자에게 Roosevelt 대통령의 업적을 설명해 주었다.
⑤ 여자는 Roosevelt 대통령이 역대 최고의 대통령이었다고 생각한다.

13 대화를 듣고, 여자의 마지막 말에 이어질 남자의 말로 가장 적절한 것을 고르시오.

① That's a smart idea.
② You can make your own greenhouse.
③ You're right. I'm worried about the future of our planet.
④ No, I usually buy only environmentally friendly products.
⑤ I think it's time to look for the right house to move into.

14 대화를 듣고, 남자의 마지막 말에 이어질 여자의 말로 가장 적절한 것을 고르시오.

① Everybody is telling me that!
② I've cut down on snacking between meals.
③ You should introduce the doctor to them.
④ That's a good idea! I should start working out more often.
⑤ Try doing aerobic exercise to build endurance and to lose weight.

15 다음 상황 설명을 듣고, Tommy가 학생들에게 할 말로 가장 적절한 것을 고르시오.

① Don't be afraid of making mistakes. Just speak up!
② Learn common words and phrases to pass the course.
③ You have only three minutes to complete the exercise.
④ Open your book and read the conversation silently once.
⑤ Listen to native speakers talk about various topics for the midterm.

DICTATION 01

01 다음을 듣고, 그림의 상황에 알맞은 대화를 고르시오.

① M Have some more. It's delicious.

W No, thanks. I'm full. I _____ _____ _____ eat any more.

② M I think _____ _____.

W Oh, no! I'm sorry to hear that.

③ M Be careful. They're very rare.

W Don't worry. I know _____ _____ _____ them.

④ M Is there any more cake?

W Sorry. I _____ _____ _____.

⑤ M I love this music.

W Me, too. Would you like to dance with me?

●●
had better ~하는 편이 낫다 **broken** 망가진, 고장 난
rare 희귀한, 진귀한 **handle** 다루다, 취급하다

02 대화를 듣고, 두 사람이 대화하는 장소로 가장 적절한 곳을 고르시오.

M May I _____ _____ _____, ma'am?

W Yes, I'll have the home-style chili.

M Do you want cornbread or a _____ _____ with that?

W Cornbread, please.

M All right. _____ _____?

W I'd like a cup of decaffeinated coffee, please.

M Okay. I'll be back with your order in a _____ _____.

●●
decaffeinated 카페인을 제거한[줄인]

03 다음을 듣고, 여자의 직업으로 가장 적절한 것을 고르시오.

Ladies and gentlemen! We're now _____ Seoul, where the local time is 9 a.m. At this stage, you should be in your seats with your _____ _____ _____. Personal television screens, footrests, and seat tables must be _____, and all hand luggage should be _____ either in the overhead lockers or under the seat in front of you. Ensure all _____ _____, including laptop computers and computer games, are _____ _____.

●●
approach 접근하다 **firmly** 꽉, 단단히 **fasten** 매다, 채우다
footrest 발판 **stow** (안전한 곳에) 집어넣다 **overhead** 머리 위에
ensure 반드시 ~하게 하다 **electronic device** 전자 기기

04 대화를 듣고, 두 사람의 관계로 가장 적절한 것을 고르시오.

W Are you _____ to the _____?

M Yes, I am. I just moved into my apartment a few days ago.

W Welcome to the neighborhood.

M Thanks. I'm new to the city. I'm _____ _____ the east coast.

W Oh, I see. I hope you like it here in L.A.

M I hope so, too. By the way, do you know where the _____ _____ are?

W Yeah, the _____ _____ is in the basement.

M And which floor do you live on?

W I live on the _____ _____.

M Well, I'm on the second floor.

W I guess I'll _____ _____

_____.

05 대화를 듣고, 그림에서 Janet이 누구인지 고르시오.

W Wow. This fitness center has great

_____.

M Yes, it does. All the members love this

place. I like it, too.

W You're really well built. You must

_____ _____ _____.

M Thanks. I exercise every other day with

my friend Janet. That's her right over

there.

W Where is she now? Is she jogging

_____ _____ _____?

M No, she's on the stationary bike.

W Which one is she? The one with the

_____ _____?

M No, she's wearing a short-sleeved T-shirt.

W Is she wearing a cap?

M No, she _____ _____ _____

because she's listening to music.

06 대화를 듣고, 남자가 부모님께 드린 선물로 가장 적절한
것을 고르시오.

W I want to give my mother something for

her birthday. Can you help me?

M How about a _____ and a nice card?

W Yeah, that sounds good.

M Just get her a present to _____

_____ _____.

W Have you given a present like that to your

parents?

M Well, when I was a university student, I

_____ _____ _____ buy

anything for them. So I made a small

book about myself.

W An autobiography for your parents?

M Kind of. I wrote about my childhood

and expressed how much I _____

_____ in the book.

W Wow, that's really nice. What was your

parents' reaction?

M They really loved it and still _____

the book.

07 대화를 듣고, 여자의 심정으로 가장 적절한 것을 고르
시오.

M Hey, Tina. Did you get _____

_____ from a university?

W Let me check. I have one.

M Do you think it's good news?

W I hope so. Let me see.

M Well... What does it say?

W It says they've _____ _____

_____. Now what am I going to do?

M I'm so sorry, Tina. I know you were

really looking forward to a _____

_____ from them.

DICTATION 01

W I was. Now I have to think about what I'm going to do with my life. I _____ _____ _____ some time _____ now.

reject 거절하다 **application** 지원, 신청 **response** 응답, 대답

08 대화를 듣고, 남자가 Denver 공항에 도착할 시각을 고르시오.

M Hi, Martha. It's Mike. I am at the airport _____ _____ _____ _____.

W What time is your flight?

M It leaves at _____ o'clock in the afternoon.

W I see. You _____ _____ very _____ from your long trip. Did you have fun?

M Oh, yeah. I am just a little hungry, but everything is fine with me. It was a wonderful trip. By the way, is Mom or Dad there?

W No, _____ _____ _____ now. But don't worry. They know you will be here today. We will be waiting for you at Denver Airport.

M What a relief! I thought they had forgotten about my return. Do they know _____ _____ _____ _____ there?

W I think so. It only _____ _____ _____ from there, right? Just in case, I will call them now.

M Thanks.

flight 비행편 **forget** 잊다 **just in case** 만약을 위해서

09 대화를 듣고, 남자가 사과하는 이유로 가장 적절한 것을 고르시오.

M Would you mind _____ _____ _____ _____ on the desk? It's irritating me.

W Sorry. I didn't realize I was doing that.

M And your _____ is very _____. The sound is quite annoying.

W I had no idea I was doing that either.

M Look. Let me apologize. In fact, I'm trying to _____ _____, and it has made me very _____.

W I understand. It's hard to quit cigarettes.

M This is my _____ _____ at quitting. I'm determined to do it this time.

W You need a strong will to do it. Good luck.

tap (가볍게) 두드리다 **irritate** 짜증나게 하다 **realize** 깨닫다 **breathing** 호흡 **apologize** 사과하다 **quit** 그만두다 **attempt** 시도 **be determined to** ~하기로 결심하다 **will** 의지

10 대화를 듣고, 여자가 전화를 건 목적으로 가장 적절한 것을 고르시오.

M GL Electronics Service Department. This is William Smith. How may I help you?

W Hi. I _____ _____ _____ _____ from your company, but now it's broken.

M When did you buy the machine, ma'am?

W Just three months ago.

M In that case, it should still be _____ _____.

W That's what I figured. You'll fix it _____ _____, right?

12

M Yes, but you'll need to show _____

_____ _____.

W That's no problem.

M Then we'll send you a _____ soon.

W Thank you very much.

●●
under warranty 보증 기간 중인 **figure** 이해하다
proof of purchase 구매 필증 **repairman** 수리 기사

11 대화를 듣고, 여자가 남자에게 조언한 것으로 가장 적절한 것을 고르시오.

M Hey, Gina, you look like you're going somewhere. What's the suitcase?

W I'm _____ _____ _____ _____ France for a vacation.

M Are you serious? How can you afford that?

W Well, I spend a lot of time thinking about _____ _____ _____ money and actually saved some.

M _____ _____ _____ _____ to Europe?

W Yes.

M I can't believe it. How could you do that?

W It's important to save a little for the future each day.

M You are my inspiration.

W I have to go to the airport now. Goodbye.

●●
inspiration 영감

12 대화를 듣고, 대화 내용과 일치하지 <u>않는</u> 것을 고르시오.

M I didn't go to history class on Thursday. Did you go?

W Yes, and I can _____ you _____ _____ if you want to look at them. We talked about the _____ _____ of the USA, Franklin Delano Roosevelt.

M I know he was the president during World War II, right?

W That's correct. Amazingly, Roosevelt did a lot of things _____ _____ _____ _____ his legs.

M What do you mean?

W He was disabled by polio, which _____ his legs _____ _____, and he spent most of his life in a wheelchair.

M I didn't know that. How do you think he compares to other presidents?

W I think he was the best president ever. And _____ _____ continue to _____ him as one of the three or four greatest American presidents of all time.

●●
president 대통령 **disabled** 불구가 된, 장애를 가진
polio 소아마비 **useless** 쓸모 없는 **compare to** ~와 비교가 되다
historian 역사가 **regard** 간주하다, 여기다

13 대화를 듣고, 여자의 마지막 말에 이어질 남자의 말로 가장 적절한 것을 고르시오.

W I can't stand this hot weather.

M You're not the only one. I _____ _____ _____ _____.

W Why is it so hot?

M My teacher told me that it _____ _____ _____ _____ the greenhouse effect.

W I've heard about that. Doesn't that come from all the carbon gases from factories?

M It sure does. Besides all the factories, so many cars _____ _____ the _____ _____. Heat trapped in the atmosphere makes it hotter and hotter.

W I think that's scary.

M You're right. I'm worried about the future of our planet.

greenhouse effect 온실 효과 **carbon gas** 탄소 가스
factory 공장 **contribute to** ~에 일조하다 **trap** 가두다
atmosphere 대기

14 대화를 듣고, 남자의 마지막 말에 이어질 여자의 말로 가장 적절한 것을 고르시오.

W Have you _____ Mark _____?

M No, I've been so busy.

W Do you know he has gained 10kg since he _____ _____ three months ago?

M Really? His wife must be a _____ _____.

W Yes, she is. But she's gained 15kg, too.

M _____ _____ _____!

W I think they should do something to lose weight.

M I think so, too. I know a doctor who has a _____ _____ _____ at his clinic.

W You should introduce the doctor to them.

15 다음 상황 설명을 듣고, Tommy가 학생에게 할 말로 가장 적절한 것을 고르시오.

Tommy lives in Chicago and teaches an English course. There are 20 students in his class. They are all _____ _____. Most of them _____ _____ _____ _____ speaking English. They don't like to make mistakes when they speak English. They are shy and _____ _____. Yet they should realize that mistakes improve their English. A shy student has _____ _____ to practice English than a confident one. So Tommy wants to _____ shy students to be _____ _____. In this situation, what would Tommy most likely say to them?

Tommy: Don't be afraid of making mistakes. Just speak up!

mistake 실수 **improve** 향상시키다 **opportunity** 기회
confident 자신감 있는 **active** 적극적인, 활동적인

A 다음을 듣고, 어휘와 우리말 뜻을 쓰시오.

① _____ _____   ⑦ _____ _____

② _____ _____   ⑧ _____ _____

③ _____ _____   ⑨ _____ _____

④ _____ _____   ⑩ _____ _____

⑤ _____ _____   ⑪ _____ _____

⑥ _____ _____   ⑫ _____ _____

B 우리말을 참고하여 빈칸에 알맞은 단어를 쓰시오.

① I'm _____ from the east _____.

저는 원래 동부 해안 지역 출신이에요.

② Ensure all _____ _____ are turned off.

모든 전자 기기의 전원을 반드시 꺼 주십시오.

③ I'm really looking forward to a(n) _____ _____ from them.

나는 그들에게서 긍정적인 응답을 얻기를 정말로 기대하고 있어.

④ I know _____ _____ _____ them.

나는 그것들을 다루는 법을 알아.

⑤ The _____ _____ is in the _____.

세탁실은 지하층에 있어요.

⑥ The washing machine _____ still _____ _____.

세탁기는 아직 보증 기간이 끝나지 않았습니다.

⑦ They should _____ that _____ their English.

그들은 실수가 자신들의 영어를 향상시킨다는 것을 깨달아야 한다.

⑧ Most _____ continue to _____ him as the greatest American _____.

대부분의 역사학자들은 계속해서 그를 가장 위대한 미국 대통령으로 간주해.

TEST 02

MY SCORE

········· / 15

01 대화를 듣고, 그림에서 남자가 설명하고 있는 사람을 고르시오.

02 대화를 듣고, 두 사람이 대화하는 장소로 가장 적절한 곳을 고르시오.

① 식당　　　　　② 수영장
③ 스키장　　　　④ 놀이터
⑤ 헬스클럽

03 다음을 듣고, 여자의 직업으로 가장 적절한 것을 고르시오.

① 약사　　　　　② 의사
③ 무용수　　　　④ 정치인
⑤ 경찰관

04 대화를 듣고, 두 사람의 관계로 가장 적절한 것을 고르시오.

① 남편 - 아내
② 사장 - 비서
③ 의사 - 환자
④ 약사 - 손님
⑤ 식당 종업원 - 손님

05 대화를 듣고, 남자가 찾고 있는 안경의 위치로 가장 적절한 곳을 고르시오.

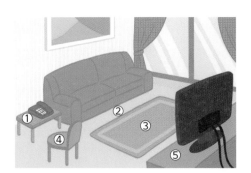

06 대화를 듣고, 무엇에 관한 내용인지 가장 적절한 것을 고르시오.

① 사과 가격
② 계산원의 불친절함
③ 슈퍼마켓을 이용하는 요일
④ 세일하는 물품과 그렇지 않은 물품
⑤ 계산대 앞에서 오래 기다려야 하는 이유

07 다음을 듣고, 비행에 관해 언급되지 않은 것을 고르시오.

① 도착지　　　　　② 도착지의 날씨
③ 기내 서비스　　　④ 비행 시간
⑤ 전자 기기 사용

08 대화를 듣고, 여자의 심정으로 가장 적절한 것을 고르시오.

① scared　　　　② curious
③ irritable　　　　④ worried
⑤ surprised

09 대화를 듣고, 남자가 구입할 코트로 가장 적절한 것을 고르시오.

① 18만 원짜리 양모 코트
② 18만 원짜리 양모와 폴리에스테르 혼방 코트
③ 49만 원짜리 양모 코트
④ 49만 원짜리 캐시미어 코트
⑤ 80만 원짜리 대만산 코트

10 대화를 듣고, 여자가 졸린 이유로 가장 적절한 것을 고르시오.

① 오늘 아침에 일찍 일어났기 때문에
② 윗집 소음으로 잠을 못 잤기 때문에
③ 매일 방과 후에 학원에 가기 때문에
④ TV 드라마를 보느라 밤을 새웠기 때문에
⑤ 시험을 보고 난 직후라 피곤하기 때문에

11 대화를 듣고, 남자가 여자에게 요청한 일로 가장 적절한 것을 고르시오.

① 택시 보내 주기
② 신문 구독 연장하기
③ 영화 예매 취소하기
④ 병원 진료 예약하기
⑤ 검진 결과지 발송해 주기

12 대화를 듣고, 대화 내용과 일치하지 <u>않는</u> 것을 고르시오.

① 여자는 지금 영화관에 가는 중이다.
② 남자는 여자가 보려고 하는 영화를 이미 보았다.
③ 여자는 Jennifer Conrad를 좋아한다.
④ 여자는 아직 영화표를 구입하지 않았다.
⑤ 남자는 여자에게 줄 영화표를 스마트폰으로 예매했다.

13 대화를 듣고, 남자의 마지막 말에 이어질 여자의 말로 가장 적절한 것을 고르시오.

① It's too bad their language is dying out.
② Cheer up. Everything will be great for you.
③ People should take steps to protect the ocean.
④ We should go to the zoo to see some gorillas and chimpanzees.
⑤ Exactly. They may disappear from the Earth due to humans.

14 대화를 듣고, 여자의 마지막 말에 이어질 남자의 말로 가장 적절한 것을 고르시오.

① That sounds easy. I'll give it a try.
② I guess you'll do better next time.
③ Great. I'll sign up for the service and use it.
④ You only get an allowance if you do your chores.
⑤ Sounds great. I'll start delivering newspapers tomorrow.

15 대화를 듣고, 남자의 마지막 말에 이어질 여자의 말로 가장 적절한 것을 고르시오.

① He is going to fix my car for me.
② He is supposed to come back here.
③ He shouldn't have stayed out so late.
④ He's going to take the driver's license test tomorrow.
⑤ His father ordered him not to leave the house for a week.

01 대화를 듣고, 그림에서 남자가 설명하고 있는 사람을 고르시오.

M Have you met the new guy yet? He
_____ _____ _____ today.

W No, I haven't. Is he here? Where is he?

M He's over there by the window.

W Which one is he? _____ _____
are over there.

M He's the one with the _____
_____ _____ _____.

W Oh, the one with the _____? He
looks smart.

M Right. That's him. Would you like to
go there and _____ _____
_____ him?

W Sure. Why not?

●●
several 몇몇의

02 대화를 듣고, 두 사람이 대화하는 장소로 가장 적절한
곳을 고르시오.

W George, jump right in. It's not too cold.
It's a nice day to _____ _____.

M I _____ _____ _____. I'll
get into the water in my own way.

W Don't get in too slowly. You're _____
_____ _____.

M Don't worry about me. Go do some laps
or something.

W Hey! _____ _____ _____!

M Are you afraid of a little water?

W Oh, boy, you asked for it! _____
_____!

M I give up. Sorry.

●●
block 막다 **do a lap** 한 바퀴 돌다 **splash** (물 등을) 튀기다[끼얹다]

03 다음을 듣고, 여자의 직업으로 가장 적절한 것을 고르
시오.

All right, Mr. Reed. I've finished the
_____. It looks like you're going to
_____ _____. Now don't worry; this
operation is very common. I have _____
_____ _____ doing surgery, and
there have never been any bad results. Your
_____ _____ should pay for most
of it, so you don't have to worry about the
cost either. As your condition is _____
_____, I'm going to schedule your
surgery for 10:30 a.m. tomorrow. Now, do
you have any questions?

●●
examination 검사, 진찰 **surgery** 수술 **operation** 수술
experience 경험; 경험하다 **medical insurance** 의료 보험

04 대화를 듣고, 두 사람의 관계로 가장 적절한 것을 고르
시오.

M How are you, Jackie?

W I'm fine. But _____ _____
_____ for my daughter. She is tired
these days.

M Oh. She'd better _____ _____
_____.

W Yes. Can I have some multivitamins with
calcium?

M All right. Do you want a _____
_____ _____ _____?

W Could I have two large ones, please? How much are they?

M The _____ _____ is _____ dollars. Here you are.

W Thank you very much. Have a nice day.

•• **total** 총, 전체의

---

05 대화를 듣고, 남자가 찾고 있는 안경의 위치로 가장 적절한 곳을 고르시오.

M Where are my glasses?

W You _____ them _____ _____ _____, so I moved them out of harm's way.

M Well, where are they? You know I'm blind without them.

W I'm trying to remember. They're _____ _____ _____ _____ _____.

M How about next to the TV? You always _____ _____ _____.

W No. Hmm... Let me sit down and think about this for a while.

M Where could they be?

W Oops! I'm _____ _____ your _____!

•• **out of harm's way** 안전한 곳으로 **remember** 기억하다 **stuff** 물건, 것

---

06 대화를 듣고, 무엇에 관한 내용인지 가장 적절한 것을 고르시오.

W Do you _____ if I _____ _____ _____ you? I only have one item.

M Not at all. Go ahead. I have a _____ _____ _____ _____ food.

W Thanks. Now all we have to do is to wait for the woman ahead of us.

M Yeah, she's been _____ _____ _____ about the price of apples. She insists that there's a sale, but the cashier disagrees.

W Really? _____ _____ we've been waiting so long.

M I guess so.

W I guess we _____ the _____ _____ to come to the supermarket.

M I've been telling that to myself for the past 20 minutes.

•• **whole** 전체의 **insist** 주장하다 **disagree** 이의를 제기하다, 동의하지 않다

---

07 다음을 듣고, 비행에 관해 언급되지 않은 것을 고르시오.

Good afternoon, passengers. This is your captain speaking. We will be _____ _____ Berlin, Germany, in a few minutes. The _____ in Berlin is cloudy with some _____ _____. We will have several in-flight movies _____ _____ _____ hot meals. We will be in the air _____ _____ _____ today, and we don't expect _____ _____ along the way. If there is anything we can do to make your experience more enjoyable, please _____ _____ _____ notify one of the flight crew. On behalf of the crew, I wish you a _____ _____.

•• **passenger** 승객 **depart** 출발하다 **in-flight** 기내의 **turbulence** 난기류 **hesitate** 주저하다 **notify** 알리다 **on behalf of** ~을 대표하여

08 대화를 듣고, 여자의 심정으로 가장 적절한 것을 고르시오.

M Are you ready to go out?

W I'm almost ready. I just want to _____ my _____ _____ first.

M You're wasting your money buying those tickets. It's _____.

W Ah... G... G... George. Can you come here?

M We can't afford to _____ _____ _____ _____ like this.

W G... G... George...

M What's wrong with you? Have you _____ your voice? You are _____ _____.

W The... the... numbers. WE ARE RICH!

M Did I say buying those tickets was _____ _____ _____ time and money? I _____ _____ _____ _____!

●●
hopeless 가망 없는 **pale** 창백한 **take back** (자기가 한 말을) 취소하다

09 대화를 듣고, 남자가 구입할 코트로 가장 적절한 것을 고르시오.

M Hello, ma'am. I would like to _____ _____ _____ _____ _____ for my wife.

W How about this one? It's _____ and costs only 490,000 won.

M Hmmm. That's a little expensive. Do you have _____ _____ ?

W This one here is _____ and goes for only 180,000 won.

M That looks nice. Can I have a closer look?

W Sure, go ahead.

M The tag on the inside of the coat says it's a mix of wool and polyester and was _____ _____ _____. It's not pure wool.

W Oh, I _____ _____ _____ you the wrong one. Here. This is the one I meant to give you.

M It looks nice. I'll buy this one.

●●
wool 양모, 양털 **tag** 태그, 꼬리표

10 대화를 듣고, 여자가 졸린 이유로 가장 적절한 것을 고르시오.

M Sora, what's wrong with you?

W I'm just so tired. I _____ _____ _____ _____ in class.

M Why are you so sleepy?

W Every day after school, I have to go to _____ and _____ _____.

M So what time do you finally get home?

W Around 10:30 p.m. Then, I eat and do my homework _____ _____ _____ _____.

M That's a tough schedule. _____ _____ _____ you're sleepy in class.

W I would do anything to sleep for an entire day.

M I know what you mean. Just _____ _____ _____ _____. I'll wake you right before class begins.

W Thanks.

●●
academy 학원 **tough** 힘든 **It's no wonder (that)** ~는 당연하다, 놀랄 일이 아니다 **take a nap** 잠깐 자다

11 대화를 듣고, 남자가 여자에게 요청한 일로 가장 적절한 것을 고르시오.

W Happy Taxi Service. May I help you?

M Hi. I need someone to come _____
_____ _____ _____ here.

W Where are you, sir?

M I'm at the Main Street Theater.

W And when do you want the taxi?

M _____ _____ _____
_____, so please tell the driver to
hurry.

W Yes, sir. I'll _____ _____ right
over soon.

M Thank you. I'll be _____ _____
_____ _____ in front of the
theater.

W We will be there in five minutes. Thanks
for _____ our company.

••
in a rush 급한, 바쁜 **choose** 선택하다

12 대화를 듣고, 대화 내용과 일치하지 <u>않는</u> 것을 고르시오.

M Where are you going in such a hurry?

W I'm just going to the movie theater
to _____ _____ _____
Jennifer Conrad _____.

M Oh, I've seen it. It's really good.

W I've heard it is. I am _____ _____
_____ _____ hers. I'm so
excited about seeing her movie.

M Have you _____ _____
_____?

W No, I'm going to buy one at the box office.

M You can save yourself a lot of time by
_____ one _____ _____
_____.

W I'm _____ _____ _____
using a smartphone to buy a ticket.
Please show me how to do that.

••
box office 매표소 **be familiar with** ~에 익숙하다

13 대화를 듣고, 남자의 마지막 말에 이어질 여자의 말로 가장 적절한 것을 고르시오.

W Have you read this _____ about the
_____ _____ in central Africa?

M No, I haven't had a chance to read the
paper yet.

W Well, it seems that their numbers are
declining quickly. A couple of _____
are in danger of _____ _____.

M I knew that gorillas and chimpanzees
were _____ _____, but I didn't
know it was that bad.

W It is. One of the _____ _____ is
the increase in the human population in
the areas where the great apes live.

M So humans are gradually _____ their
_____ _____.

W <u>Exactly. They may disappear from the
Earth due to humans.</u>

••
article 기사 **great ape** 유인원 **decline** 감소하다
species (생물의) 종(種) **threat** 위협 **population** 인구
gradually 점차, 서서히 **destroy** 파괴하다 **habitat** 서식지
disappear 사라지다

14 대화를 듣고, 여자의 마지막 말에 이어질 남자의 말로 가장 적절한 것을 고르시오.

M I want to buy a new smartphone, but I only _____ _____ _____ _____ of 10 dollars. I need to save more money.

W I see.

M Do you have any ideas about how I could _____ a little _____ _____?

W You could deliver newspapers.

M No, thank you. That _____ _____ _____ very early in the morning. I'm not a morning person.

W What about _____? That's what I do.

M What do you have to do?

W Well, I have to _____ my _____ _____ the baby and play with him.

M That sounds easy. I'll give it a try.

••
weekly 매주의 **allowance** 용돈 **earn** (돈을) 벌다
deliver 배달하다 **babysitting** 아기 돌보기 **attention** 주의

15 대화를 듣고, 남자의 마지막 말에 이어질 여자의 말로 가장 적절한 것을 고르시오.

M Daniel is really _____ _____ _____ his father.

W Yes, his sister told me. I think it's _____ _____ _____.

M I'll say. He used his father's new car without permission last night.

W And then he _____ it into the _____ _____.

M No wonder his father is really angry.

W It's understandable; the repairs are going to _____ _____ _____ _____.

M Anyway, why did he use the car?

W He just got his driver's license. So he wanted to _____ _____ in front of his friends.

M What a childish boy! So _____ is his father _____ _____ _____ with him?

W His father ordered him not to leave the house for a week.

••
fault 잘못 **permission** 허락 **crash** 부딪치다
understandable 이해할 수 있는 **show off** ~을 자랑하다
childish 유치한

A 다음을 듣고, 어휘와 우리말 뜻을 쓰시오.

① _____ _____

② _____ _____

③ _____ _____

④ _____ _____

⑤ _____ _____

⑥ _____ _____

⑦ _____ _____

⑧ _____ _____

⑨ _____ _____

⑩ _____ _____

⑪ _____ _____

⑫ _____ _____

B 우리말을 참고하여 빈칸에 알맞은 단어를 쓰시오.

① I _____ it all _____!

그 말 다 취소야!

② The _____ _____ is 75 dollars.

총 가격은 75달러입니다.

③ I have hundreds of _____ doing _____.

제게는 수백 번의 수술 경험이 있어요.

④ You're _____ _____ _____.

네가 길을 막고 있어.

⑤ _____ _____ _____ you're sleepy in class.

네가 수업 시간에 졸린 것도 당연하네.

⑥ Humans are _____ _____ their natural _____.

인류가 점차 그들의 자연 서식지를 파괴하고 있지.

⑦ Please don't _____ _____ _____ one of the flight crew.

주저하지 말고 승무원들 중 한 명에게 알려 주십시오.

⑧ I'm _____ _____ _____ using a smartphone to buy a ticket.

난 스마트폰을 사용해서 표를 사는 것에 익숙하지 않아.

MY SCORE

-------- / 15

01 다음을 듣고, 그림의 상황에 알맞은 대화를 고르시오.

①   ②   ③   ④   ⑤

02 대화를 듣고, 남자가 가려고 하는 장소로 가장 적절한 곳을 고르시오.

① 백화점   ② 영화관
③ 친구네 집   ④ 버스 정류장
⑤ 자동차 정비소

03 다음을 듣고, 여자의 직업으로 가장 적절한 것을 고르시오.

① 가수   ② 의사
③ 교사   ④ 영화감독
⑤ 엔지니어

04 대화를 듣고, 두 사람의 관계로 가장 적절한 것을 고르시오.

① 교수 - 학생
② 매표원 - 손님
③ 지휘자 - 연주자
④ 택시 기사 - 승객
⑤ 여행사 직원 - 고객

05 다음을 듣고, 내일 오후의 날씨로 가장 적절한 것을 고르시오.

①    ②

③    ④

⑤

06 대화를 듣고, 남자가 대화 직후에 할 일로 가장 적절한 것을 고르시오.

① 요금 지불하기
② 미용실 예약하기
③ 여자에게 차 대접하기
④ 여자의 머리 잘라 주기
⑤ 여자의 머리 감겨 주기

07 대화를 듣고, 여자의 심정으로 가장 적절한 것을 고르시오.

① proud   ② jealous
③ amazed   ④ nervous
⑤ annoyed

08 대화를 듣고, 남자가 구입할 비행기 표의 가격을 고르시오.

① 15만 원   ② 19만 원
③ 50만 원   ④ 75만 원
⑤ 90만 원

09 대화를 듣고, 여자가 커피를 마시려 하지 <u>않는</u> 이유로 가장 적절한 것을 고르시오.

① 커피를 좋아하지 않아서
② 오전에 이미 커피를 마셔서
③ 오후 2시에 다른 약속이 있어서
④ 커피를 마시면 두드러기가 생겨서
⑤ 지금 커피를 마시면 밤에 잠을 자지 못해서

10 대화를 듣고, 두 사람이 오늘 저녁에 할 일로 가장 적절한 것을 고르시오.

① 공원에서 운동하기
② 친구들과 집안 청소하기
③ 친구들과 밀린 숙제 하기
④ 공항에 부모님 마중 나가기
⑤ 친구들과 튤립 축제에 참가하기

11 대화를 듣고, 여자가 전화를 건 목적으로 가장 적절한 것을 고르시오.

① 제작이 완료되었는지 확인하려고
② 물건의 배송 소요 기간을 알아보려고
③ 수선 맡긴 물건의 견적을 알아보려고
④ 새로 나온 가방의 가격을 알아보려고
⑤ 분실 신고된 여행 가방이 있는지 확인하려고

12 대화를 듣고, 대화 내용과 일치하지 <u>않는</u> 것을 고르시오.

① 여자는 남자에게 무선 이어폰을 빌려주었다.
② 여자는 무선 이어폰을 오늘 밤에 사용하기를 원한다.
③ 남자의 개가 여자의 무선 이어폰을 물어뜯었다.
④ 여자는 무선 이어폰을 새로 구입할 것이다.
⑤ 남자는 오늘 저녁에 여자의 집에 갈 것이다.

13 대화를 듣고, 남자의 마지막 말에 이어질 여자의 말로 가장 적절한 것을 고르시오.

① You should finish your paper quickly.
② I don't want to think about it. It's painful.
③ Looks like it's going to get worse every day.
④ Well, if it could rain even a drop, things would be much better.
⑤ Whenever a huge hurricane strikes, there's always a large loss of life.

14 대화를 듣고, 여자의 마지막 말에 이어질 남자의 말로 가장 적절한 것을 고르시오.

① You've got it totally wrong.
② The color doesn't appeal to me.
③ Okay. I won't buy him one of those.
④ This sounds like a joke, but it's true.
⑤ Okay. There's something I've got to tell you.

15 다음 상황 설명을 듣고, Sally가 Sam에게 할 말로 가장 적절한 것을 고르시오.

① Don't mention it.
② Can you recommend someone?
③ I was worried you wouldn't like it.
④ I had a summer internship in the field.
⑤ Thanks for your advice. I'll keep that in mind.

01 다음을 듣고, 그림의 상황에 알맞은 대화를 고르시오.

① M Can you help me _____ _____ _____?

W All right. Please follow me.

② M Ma'am? You can _____ _____ _____.

W Thank you, young man.

③ M Did you _____ _____ _____?

W Yeah, and they're good seats, too.

④ M Hi. I'd like to return this, please.

W Sure. Can I _____ _____ _____?

⑤ M What a beautiful baby!

W Thank you. Her name's Heather.

●●
follow 따라오다 **receipt** 영수증

02 대화를 듣고, 남자가 가려고 하는 장소로 가장 적절한 곳을 고르시오.

W Bob, hi! What a surprise to see you on this train.

M Hi. _____ _____, _____ _____.

W Are you going to Seattle?

M Yeah. I don't like _____ _____, but my car is in the garage, so…

W Right. I remember you always _____ _____.

M Well, I _____ _____ _____ _____. I have to go to my friend's house for dinner.

W You're going to _____ _____ _____? Sounds like a good time.

●●
public transportation 대중교통 **garage** 정비소

03 다음을 듣고, 여자의 직업으로 가장 적절한 것을 고르시오.

Hi. My name is Olga Strauss. I _____ _____ Lincoln _____. For years, I had first-grade students, but _____ _____ _____, they moved me up to the fifth grade. I loved the little ones, but I'm excited to move on to _____- _____ _____. There's so much you can do with the _____ _____. I've got to finish _____ _____ _____, so I don't have a lot of time to talk right now. You're welcome to _____ _____ _____ sometime though.

●●
material 교재, 자료 **though** 하지만, 그렇지만

04 대화를 듣고, 두 사람의 관계로 가장 적절한 것을 고르시오.

M Hello. I-link. How may I help you?

W Hi. Do you have _____ _____ _____ for tomorrow night's concert?

M Let me check. We _____ S class and C class _____ _____.

W How much are the S class seats?

M They're 150 dollars a seat.

W Oh, that's _____ _____. How about the C class seats?

M They're 50 dollars.

W I think I'll _____ _____

_____ _____ the C class seats.

M All right. How many would you like?

W Three, please.

05 다음을 듣고, 내일 오후의 날씨로 가장 적절한 것을
고르시오.

Tomorrow is _____ to be a beautiful
day. The _____ _____ will be a
refreshing 19 degrees, and there will be
some _____ _____. The fog will
lift, however, as we head toward noon.
In the _____ _____ _____

_____, temperatures are expected
to rise all the way to 29 degrees. The
_____ will be _____, and there will
be a slight breeze from the west.

●●
low 최저치 **refreshing** 상쾌하게 하는
head toward ~를 향해서 가다 **temperature** 온도, 기온
rise 오르다, 상승하다 **slight** 약간의 **breeze** 미풍, 산들바람

06 대화를 듣고, 남자가 대화 직후에 할 일로 가장 적절한
것을 고르시오.

W Hello, Jack. Can you do my hair today?

M I don't know. I'm _____ _____
today. What would you like done this
time?

W Just _____ _____ _____ _____
this time.

M You should have called _____
_____ _____ to make an
appointment.

W I know, but it just _____ _____
_____. Can you fit me in?

M Well, all right, as long as it doesn't take
longer than 30 minutes. As you know, I
have other clients waiting. You're lucky
you're _____ _____ _____
_____.

W You have no idea how much I appreciate
this.

M Okay. _____ _____ the chair
before I change my mind.

W Thanks, Jack.

●●
booked 예약된 **trim** (머리를) 다듬기 **ahead of time** 미리
slip one's mind 깜빡하다, 잊어버리다 **loyal** 충성도 높은

07 대화를 듣고, 여자의 심정으로 가장 적절한 것을 고르
시오.

M Where are you going today, Anne?

W I'm going to _____ _____
_____. She just finished medical
school.

M That's fantastic. You must be very happy
for her today.

W Both her father and I are so pleased.
She decided to _____ _____
_____ _____, and she finally did
it.

M Are you going to take any pictures there?

W Yes, I brought my camera. After the
ceremony, we are _____ _____
_____ _____.

M I hope you have a great afternoon.
Please _____ my _____ to your
daughter.

W I will, thanks.

●●
graduation 졸업식 **pleased** 기쁜
extend congratulations to ~에게 축하 인사를 하다

08 대화를 듣고, 남자가 구입할 비행기 표의 가격을 고르시오.

W World Wide Travel. May I help you?

M Yes, I'd like a _____-_____ _____ to New York, please. I'm looking for the cheapest ticket.

W Well, if you _____ _____ Vancouver, the price will be _____ won.

M Is that the cheapest ticket you have?

W If you stop in Tokyo, Vancouver, and Chicago before going on to New York City, then the price _____ _____ _____ won.

M That sounds better. That's a lot of stops though.

W It is. But if you want _____ _____ _____, that's what you have to do.

M Okay. I'll take it. I don't _____ _____ _____ if I can save a little money.

W Very good. Will that be cash or credit card?

round-trip 왕복 여행의 **stop in** ~를 경유하다, ~에 잠시 머무르다

09 대화를 듣고, 여자가 커피를 마시려 하지 <u>않는</u> 이유로 가장 적절한 것을 고르시오.

M How about some coffee?

W I'd love some, but it's already 2 p.m. If I have some now, I'll _____ _____ _____ _____.

M No kidding. Caffeine really _____ you that way?

W Yes, I'm very _____ _____ _____. What about you?

M I can drink coffee just before going to bed, and I'm fine.

W It's funny how people _____ _____ to certain substances.

M What about some _____ _____ then?

W Yes, I can have that.

affect 영향을 미치다 **sensitive** 민감한 **substance** 물질 **herbal** 허브의

10 대화를 듣고, 두 사람이 오늘 저녁에 할 일로 가장 적절한 것을 고르시오.

M Hey, Betty. Do you want to go to a _____ _____ with us this weekend?

W I'm sorry, but I can't. I have to _____ my _____ _____ this weekend because my parents are coming next week.

M Oh, that's too bad. I have an idea! _____ _____ our friends _____ _____ this evening and cleaned your apartment? Then, you _____ _____ _____ for the weekend.

W I can't ask you to do that. It's a very nice idea though.

M It's no problem at all. We really want you _____ _____ _____ _____ this weekend.

W Okay, then. Can you come at 6 p.m.?

M We'll be there.

messy 지저분한

11 대화를 듣고, 여자가 전화를 건 목적으로 가장 적절한 것을 고르시오.

M Exquisite Store. How may I help you?

W Hello. I visited your store to _____ my _____ _____ last week.

M Oh, is that the one with the _____ _____?

W Yes, I would also like to know _____ _____ it will _____.

M We think that it will cost 35,000 won _____ _____. Will that be okay with you?

W It's a little more expensive _____ _____ _____ _____. But I need it soon. How long will it take to _____ _____ _____?

M It will take 10 days. Then, you can pick it up.

W All right. _____ _____ _____ you fix it, please let me know.

●●
at most 최대한으로 잡아서, 기껏해야 **as soon as** ~하는 대로, ~하자마자

12 대화를 듣고, 대화 내용과 일치하지 <u>않는</u> 것을 고르시오.

W Peter, can you give me back the _____ _____ that I _____ you?

M I thought you didn't need to use them until this weekend.

W Yes, but I want to listen to music tonight after doing my homework.

M Well... I _____ _____ _____ right now.

W You can't return them? Why? Did you lose them?

M No, actually, my dog _____ _____ _____.

W What? Your dog broke my wireless earphones?

M Yes. I was _____ _____ _____ you. I'm really sorry.

W But I wanted to use them today! And I don't have enough money to _____ _____ _____ _____.

M I will buy you some new ones. And I'll _____ _____ to your home this evening.

●●
wireless 무선의 **chew up** ~를 물어뜯다

13 대화를 듣고, 남자의 마지막 말에 이어질 여자의 말로 가장 적절한 것을 고르시오.

W I've been writing a _____ _____ about _____ for my geology class.

M Really? I wrote a paper about them, too.

W I've been reading a report on the very bad earthquake in Iran in 2003.

M Is that the one that _____ _____ _____ called Bam?

W Yes, that's the one. It killed around 40,000 people.

M _____ _____ _____!

W The earthquake struck very early in the morning.

M So I _____ most people were still _____ in bed.

W Many people didn't know what hit them.

M I wonder if another big one will

_____ _____ _____

_____ .

W I don't want to think about it. It's painful.

● ●

earthquake 지진 **geology** 지질학 **disaster** 재앙
suppose 추측하다, 생각하다 **wonder** 궁금하다

14 대화를 듣고, 여자의 마지막 말에 이어질 남자의 말로
가장 적절한 것을 고르시오.

W I hope you're not busy on Friday night.

M I don't have _____ _____

_____ . Why?

W We're having a birthday party.

M _____ _____ is it?

W It's John's. We're going to surprise him. I
hope you can go to it.

M Sure, I'll go. Is there _____ I can

_____ _____ ?

W No. We already have everything we need.
Thanks though.

M I _____ _____ I should get him

for his birthday.

W I don't know, but don't get him a necktie.

_____ _____ _____

_____ him.

M Okay. I won't buy him one of those.

15 다음 상황 설명을 듣고, Sally가 Sam에게 할 말로
가장 적절한 것을 고르시오.

Sally's just graduated from her university.
She's been _____ _____ to many
companies. She got a phone call from one
of those companies, so she is _____
to have a _____ _____ tomorrow.
Since she doesn't have any _____

_____ , she's very _____ . Her
friend Sam tells her that the company
wants someone who _____ _____
_____ people, so she has to show them
how _____ and personable she is. In
this situation, what would Sally most likely
say to Sam?

Sally: Thanks for your advice. I'll keep that in
mind.

● ●

graduate 졸업하다 **résumé** 이력서 **job interview** 구직 면접
outgoing 사교적인, 외향적인 **personable** 매력적인

A 다음을 듣고, 어휘와 우리말 뜻을 쓰시오.

① _____   ⑦ _____

② _____   ⑧ _____

③ _____   ⑨ _____

④ _____   ⑩ _____

⑤ _____   ⑪ _____

⑥ _____   ⑫ _____

B 우리말을 참고하여 빈칸에 알맞은 단어를 쓰시오.

① Can I _____ your _____?

당신의 영수증을 볼 수 있을까요?

② I'd like a(n) _____-_____ ticket to New York.

저는 뉴욕으로 가는 왕복표를 사고 싶습니다.

③ My dog _____ _____ your wireless earphones.

우리 개가 네 무선 이어폰을 물어뜯었어.

④ _____ are expected to _____ all the way to 29 degrees.

온도가 29도까지 오를 것으로 예상됩니다.

⑤ She is scheduled to have a(n) _____ _____ tomorrow.

그녀는 내일 구직 면접을 볼 예정이다.

⑥ It just _____ _____.

나는 그만 그것을 깜빡했다.

⑦ _____ _____ _____ you fix it, please let me know.

그것을 수선하시는 대로 제게 알려 주세요.

⑧ You should have called _____ _____ _____ to make an appointment.

당신은 예약하기 위해 미리 전화하셨어야 합니다.

MY SCORE
_____ / 15

01 다음을 듣고, 그림의 상황에 알맞은 대화를 고르시오.

① ② ③ ④ ⑤

02 대화를 듣고, 두 사람이 대화하는 장소로 가장 적절한 곳을 고르시오.

① 집
② 공원
③ 택시 승강장
④ 버스 정류장
⑤ 안내 데스크

03 대화를 듣고, 여자가 미래에 갖고자 하는 직업으로 가장 적절한 것을 고르시오.

① 교수
② 배우
③ 승무원
④ 바리스타
⑤ 아나운서

04 대화를 듣고, 두 사람의 관계로 가장 적절한 것을 고르시오.

① 의사 - 간호사
② 수리 기사 - 고객
③ 식당 종업원 - 손님
④ 병원 접수원 - 환자
⑤ 호텔 접수원 - 투숙객

05 다음 표를 보면서 대화를 듣고, 두 사람이 관람할 영화와 상영 시각을 고르시오.

Movie Time			
Godfather V	House of Horrors	June	Dusty
2:00 p.m.	10:45 a.m.	9:50 a.m.	10:00 a.m.
2:30 p.m.	1:00 p.m.	12:50 p.m.	1:00 p.m.
3:40 p.m.	3:00 p.m.	4:00 p.m.	4:00 p.m.
	6:35 p.m.	7:00 p.m.	9:00 p.m.

① June, 7:00 p.m.
② Dusty, 9:00 p.m.
③ Dusty, 4:00 p.m.
④ Godfather V, 3:40 p.m.
⑤ House of Horrors, 6:35 p.m.

06 대화를 듣고, 남자가 전화를 건 목적으로 가장 적절한 것을 고르시오.

① 약속을 취소하려고
② 교통 정보를 제공하려고
③ 서점의 위치를 물어보려고
④ 약속 시간에 늦을 것을 알리려고
⑤ 슈퍼마켓 앞으로 나와 달라고 부탁하려고

07 다음을 듣고, 여자의 말의 목적으로 가장 적절한 것을 고르시오.

① 친구의 편지에 답하려고
② 온라인 회원 가입을 권유하려고
③ 홈페이지 개편 소식을 공지하려고
④ 회원을 위한 할인 행사를 안내하려고
⑤ 온라인 회원 가입에 대한 감사를 전하려고

08 대화를 듣고, 남자의 심정으로 가장 적절한 것을 고르시오.

① envious   ② shocked

③ pleasant   ④ relieved

⑤ frustrated

09 대화를 듣고, 여자가 탑승할 버스의 출발 시각과 행선지를 고르시오.

① 9시 15분 – 서울   ② 9시 15분 – 인천

③ 9시 30분 – 서울   ④ 9시 30분 – 인천

⑤ 9시 45분 – 인천

10 대화를 듣고, 여자가 학교 도서관에서 공부하려는 이유로 가장 적절한 것을 고르시오.

① 집안이 너무 시끄러워서

② 방 안의 조명이 밝지 않아서

③ 도서관에 참고 서적이 많이 있어서

④ 집에서는 동생이 공부하는 것을 방해해서

⑤ 도서관에서 친구들과 같이 공부하기 위해서

11 대화를 듣고, 남자가 오늘 할 일로 가장 적절한 것을 고르시오.

① 영어 공부하기

② Magi 교수님 만나기

③ Doris 교수님 만나기

④ 여자와 영화 보러 가기

⑤ 여자와 저녁 식사 하기

12 대화를 듣고, 대화 내용과 일치하지 <u>않는</u> 것을 고르시오.

① 여자는 필기 시험을 보기로 되어 있다.

② 여자는 대학에서 2년간 공부했다.

③ 여자는 1년 전에 대학 공부를 수료했다.

④ 여자는 프랑스어와 영양학을 공부한 적이 있다.

⑤ 여자는 아시아 요리 과목에 가장 큰 흥미를 느꼈다.

13 대화를 듣고, 남자의 마지막 말에 이어질 여자의 말로 가장 적절한 것을 고르시오.

① It's easier than I thought. Thanks a lot.

② You're good at playing computer games.

③ Well, I didn't want to think about it again.

④ It's pretty simple. I'll show you how to do this tomorrow.

⑤ You should teach me how to deal with this stressful situation.

14 대화를 듣고, 여자의 마지막 말에 이어질 남자의 말로 가장 적절한 것을 고르시오.

① Let's start a campaign right away.

② I've decided to become a vegetarian.

③ Just look at the state of the world these days.

④ Well, I'm going to do something about it myself.

⑤ That's what we call an environmentally friendly battery.

15 다음 상황 설명을 듣고, Jennifer에게 조언할 말로 가장 적절한 것을 고르시오.

① If I don't pass it, I'll take it again another time.

② I'm glad that you did so well on your exam.

③ Don't worry! You did your best on the chemistry exam.

④ Why don't you go to graduate school after finishing college?

⑤ The next time, you had better study harder to improve your grade.

01 다음을 듣고, 그림의 상황에 알맞은 대화를 고르시오.

① M Could I have some change for a dollar?

W Sure. Here are three _____ and five _____.

② W Will you _____ me _____ _____?

M Sure. How much?

③ M You look upset. What's wrong?

W Someone took my purse _____ _____ _____ _____.

④ M Here is your allowance. _____ _____ you don't spend too much money _____ _____.

W No problem. I won't.

⑤ W Could you _____ _____ _____ how to use this ATM?

M No problem. What are you going to do with that?

•• **quarter** 25센트짜리 동전 **nickel** 5센트짜리 동전

02 대화를 듣고, 두 사람이 대화하는 장소로 가장 적절한 곳을 고르시오.

M May I help you?

W Yeah, thanks. I'm staying at the Cosmopolitan Plaza in town. What's the _____ _____ to _____ _____? I'd like to have a tour map, too.

M Here you are. You can take a cab, bus, limo, or hotel shuttle.

W _____ do you _____?

M That depends. A cab is faster but more expensive.

W The bus is cheaper but a little slow.

M It would probably be a good idea to _____ _____ _____ _____.

W All right. Where do I catch it?

M Just go through those doors, and look for the shuttle sign. When it comes by, _____, and the driver will _____ _____ _____.

W Thank you for your help.

•• **cab** 택시 **limo** 리무진 버스

03 대화를 듣고, 여자가 미래에 갖고자 하는 직업으로 가장 적절한 것을 고르시오.

M How are your _____ _____ going?

W Great! But I'm a bit _____ _____ these days.

M Why?

W Well, I'm making coffee.

M You're a barista?

W You got it.

M So you're taking classes _____ _____ _____ and working at night?

W Yes. I have to do that. I need the money to _____ _____.

M Well, one day, you'll get paid back when you become a _____ _____. Keep going. Remember, "No _____, no _____."

W Thanks a lot.

worn out 지친 **support oneself** 스스로 부양하다
actress 여자 배우 **gain** 얻는 것, 이익

04 대화를 듣고, 두 사람의 관계로 가장 적절한 것을 고르시오.

W Hello. This is Miracle Clinic. How may I help you?

M Hi. I'd like to _____ _____ _____ with the doctor on Wednesday.

W Can you make it on Wednesday at 2:30?

M No, I'm sorry, but I can't. Could you _____ _____ _____?

W Yes. How about Wednesday at 10:00? Can I _____ _____ _____?

M Fine. My name is David Stevenson.

W And your phone number?

M It's 526-0012.

W 526-0012?

M Yes.

W I'll see you on Wednesday at 10:00 then.

M Okay. _____ _____ _____.

05 다음 표를 보면서 대화를 듣고, 두 사람이 관람할 영화와 상영 시각을 고르시오.

W So what should we see?

M I heard *Dusty* _____ _____ _____.

W The only time that's left is the 9 o'clock show, and that's too late.

M Well, we could catch *House of Horrors* at 6:35.

W We could do that, but I'm _____ _____ _____ about horror movies.

M Come on. It's not that scary. I'm going to buy tickets for the _____ _____ of *House of Horrors*. Okay?

W I guess I _____ _____ _____.

review 평론, 비평 **showing** (영화) 상영

06 대화를 듣고, 남자가 전화를 건 목적으로 가장 적절한 것을 고르시오.

W Hello. Samson residence.

M Hi, Nancy. It's me, Jim.

W Jim, where are you? We've _____ _____ for you.

M Actually, I _____ _____ _____ _____. I'll be a little late.

W Okay. Where are you now?

M I'm in front of the Five Star Supermarket next to the bookstore.

W I know where you are. _____ _____ on King Road, and then _____ _____ onto Spring Lane.

M Oh, okay. Now I know where I am. Thanks. See you soon.

W You are about _____ _____ _____. Take your time. We'll be waiting for you.

residence 거주지, 주택 **lane** 도로, 길

07 다음을 듣고, 여자의 말의 목적으로 가장 적절한 것을 고르시오.

Thank you for _____ _____ Korea1post.com. You now have _____ _____ _____ to all of the reporting from *Korea1post*. You'll find a lot more than that on our website. Korea1post.com _____ _____ _____, videos and graphics, e-mail newsletters, and other services to _____ _____ _____ your life and more.

••
register 가입하다, 등록하다   **have access to** ~을 이용할 수 있다
provide 제공하다

08 대화를 듣고, 남자의 심정으로 가장 적절한 것을 고르시오.

W You look so sad. What's up?

M It's the manager. I asked her _____ _____ if I could _____ this coming Saturday _____.

W So did she change the schedule?

M No, she didn't. But my parents are _____ _____ _____, and I have to work at this restaurant.

W Why don't you talk to her about _____ _____ _____ _____ to you?

M I already did. She _____ _____ _____ the schedule. Maybe I should quit this job.

W Relax. There must be another way. Let's _____ _____ _____ together.

••
in advance 미리   **have ~ off** ~에는 쉬다   **refuse** 거부하다
put heads together 머리를 맞대고 의논하다

09 대화를 듣고, 여자가 탑승할 버스의 출발 시각과 행선지를 고르시오.

M Ticket, please.

W Here you go, sir.

M You're _____ _____ _____ _____, ma'am.

W The wrong bus? What do you mean?

M This is the bus to Seoul. You're looking for the _____ _____ bus to _____. The one you're supposed to be on has just left.

W I can't believe it. I _____ _____ _____ _____ by two o'clock today for a job interview.

M Don't worry. The bus to Incheon leaves _____ _____ _____. You can take the next bus.

W Thanks, sir.

••
be supposed to ~해야 하다, ~하기로 되어 있다

10 대화를 듣고, 여자가 학교 도서관에서 공부하려는 이유로 가장 적절한 것을 고르시오.

W Isn't there any way to _____ _____ _____ in this room _____?

M No, that's impossible. Why do you ask?

W I've been getting headaches lately.

M You may have to _____ your _____ _____.

W Do you really think so? I hope my eyes aren't getting worse.

M Well, it's hard to say unless you _____ your _____ _____.

W I'll make an appointment with the eye doctor next week.

M Until then, you should read in a well-lit room.

W Then _____ _____ _____ in the school library.

●● **prescription** 처방

11 대화를 듣고, 남자가 오늘 할 일로 가장 적절한 것을 고르시오.

W Good morning, Peter.

M Hi, Jane. How are you feeling today?

W Fine. _____ _____ _____ to go to the Italian restaurant today?

M I intended to do so, but Professor Magi told me to _____ _____ Doris _____.

W Why? Is there a special reason?

M Perhaps Professor Doris expects me to help him with his research.

W Oh, I see. Then I _____ _____ to go with me.

M I'm sorry, but I can't. By the way, you've improved your English a lot.

W Thanks for your praise. You really encourage me to study hard. But I still _____ _____ _____ words properly.

M You're _____ _____.

●● **intend to** ~하려고 생각하다 **professor** 교수
perhaps 아마도 **force** 억지로 ~하게 하다 **praise** 칭찬
encourage 용기를 북돋우다 **properly** 적절히, 제대로

12 대화를 듣고, 대화 내용과 일치하지 <u>않는</u> 것을 고르시오.

M Good afternoon, Ms. Fields. Sit down, please.

W Good afternoon, sir.

M Before you _____ the _____ _____, I'd like to ask you several questions, Ms. Fields. Where did you learn cooking and serving?

W I took a two-year _____ _____ at the University of Paris.

M When did you finish it?

W A year ago, sir.

M What other subjects did you take?

W _____, _____, and some others.

M Which subject interested you the most?

W _____ _____, sir.

●● **subject** 과목, 학과 **nutrition** 영양학 **cuisine** 요리(법)

13 대화를 듣고, 남자의 마지막 말에 이어질 여자의 말로 가장 적절한 것을 고르시오.

M Why are you _____ _____ _____? What's the matter?

W I don't think you can help me.

M _____ your computer _____?

W No, I'm trying to _____ _____ _____ on the screen _____.

M Oh, that's not difficult.

W I thought you didn't know anything about computers.

M Didn't I tell you I'm _____ computer science?

W No, you didn't. Well, I've been trying to do it without any success _____ _____ _____ _____.

M I'll show you. Look. You open this menu, click here, click on the percentage you want, say 200%, and you're _____ _____. There it is — _____ _____ _____.

W It's easier than I thought. Thanks a lot.

••
bite one's nails 손톱을 물어뜯다 **crash** (컴퓨터가) 갑자기 고장 나다 **major in** ~을 전공하다

14 대화를 듣고, 여자의 마지막 말에 이어질 남자의 말로 가장 적절한 것을 고르시오.

W I heard that you're interested in _____ _____ _____.

M Yes, I've been using those products to conserve the environment. Why do you ask?

W I saw a really interesting documentary on new _____ _____ _____ last night.

M Oh, I'm sorry I missed that.

W The one that really made me surprised was the _____ _____ _____ _____.

M Spinach! That's a vegetable. I can't believe it.

W It's true. Spinach batteries can convert light _____ _____ to power something like a laptop computer.

M That's what we call an environmentally friendly battery.

••
environmentally friendly 환경 친화적인 **product** 제품 **conserve** 보존하다 **technology** 기술 **spinach** 시금치 **convert** 전환시키다 **electricity** 전기

15 다음 상황 설명을 듣고, Jennifer에게 조언할 말로 가장 적절한 것을 고르시오.

Jennifer _____ _____ very much at the party last night. She _____ _____ about her chemistry _____. This morning, she took her chemistry examination. Unfortunately, she didn't do well. If she _____ _____ hard, she _____ _____ _____ much better. Now she is worrying about her _____ _____ and _____ that she didn't take the time to study hard. In this situation, what would you most likely advise Jennifer to do?

You: The next time, you had better study harder to improve your grade.

••
completely 완전히 **chemistry** 화학 **unfortunately** 불행하게도 **regret** 후회하다

정답 및 해석 p. 33

A 다음을 듣고, 어휘와 우리말 뜻을 쓰시오.

① _____ ⑦ _____

② _____ ⑧ _____

③ _____ ⑨ _____

④ _____ ⑩ _____

⑤ _____ ⑪ _____

⑥ _____ ⑫ _____

B 우리말을 참고하여 빈칸에 알맞은 단어를 쓰시오.

① _____ batteries can convert light into _____.
시금치 건전지는 빛을 전기로 전환시킬 수 있다.

② She _____ forgot about her _____ examination.
그녀는 화학 시험에 대해 완전히 잊어버렸다.

③ Why are you _____ _____ _____ ?
너는 왜 손톱을 물어뜯고 있어?

④ I _____ _____ _____ to go with me.
내가 너를 억지로 데려갈 수는 없겠구나.

⑤ Didn't I tell you _____ _____ _____ computer science?
내가 컴퓨터 공학을 전공하고 있다고 네게 말하지 않았던가?

⑥ You now _____ free online _____ _____ all of the
reporting from us. 당신은 이제 우리가 제공하는 모든 보도를 온라인으로 무료 이용할 수 있습니다.

⑦ Let's _____ _____ _____ _____ .
우리 함께 머리를 맞대고 의논해 보자.

⑧ I asked her _____ _____ if I could _____ this coming
Saturday _____ . 나는 그녀에게 내가 이번 주 토요일에 쉴 수 있을지 미리 물어봤어.

MY SCORE

.... / 15

01 다음을 듣고, 그림의 상황에 알맞은 대화를 고르시오.

①   ②   ③   ④   ⑤

02 대화를 듣고, 두 사람이 대화하는 장소로 가장 적절한 곳을 고르시오.

① 공항   ② 우체국
③ 도서관   ④ 기차역
⑤ 여행사

03 다음을 듣고, 여자의 직업으로 가장 적절한 것을 고르시오.

① 요리사   ② 과학자
③ 은행원   ④ 승무원
⑤ 식당 종업원

04 대화를 듣고, 두 사람의 관계로 가장 적절한 것을 고르시오.

① 딸 - 아빠
② 화가 - 기자
③ 교사 - 학생
④ 경찰 - 시민
⑤ 사진사 - 손님

05 다음을 듣고, 남자가 이용할 교통 수단으로 언급되지 않은 것을 고르시오.

①    ②

③ 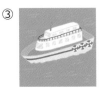   ④

⑤

06 대화를 듣고, 여자가 주장하는 것으로 가장 적절한 것을 고르시오.

① 역사를 공부할 필요가 있다.
② 같은 실수를 반복해서는 안 된다.
③ 만화책을 읽으면서 스트레스를 풀 수 있다.
④ 글쓰기를 통해 자기 자신을 이해할 수 있다.
⑤ 사극 드라마를 보면 역사 공부에 도움이 된다.

07 대화를 듣고, 두 사람의 심정으로 가장 적절한 것을 고르시오.

① sad   ② relieved
③ frightened   ④ discouraged
⑤ disappointed

08 대화를 듣고, 여자가 첫 달에 남자에게 내야 하는 금액을 고르시오.

① $250   ② $500
③ $550   ④ $750
⑤ $800

09 대화를 듣고, 남자가 늦은 이유로 가장 적절한 것을 고르시오.

① 교통사고를 당했기 때문에
② 사고 현장을 구경했기 때문에
③ 교통사고로 도로가 막혔기 때문에
④ 사고 현장을 목격하고 신고했기 때문에
⑤ 부상 당한 사람을 병원에 데려다 줬기 때문에

10 대화를 듣고, 여자가 대화 직후에 할 일로 가장 적절한 것을 고르시오.

① 화장실 가기
② 과일 구매하기
③ 후식 주문하기
④ 식사비 지불하기
⑤ 케이크 예약하기

11 대화를 듣고, 남자가 여자에게 요청한 일로 가장 적절한 것을 고르시오.

① 보고서 타이핑하기
② 약속 시간 변경하기
③ 보고서의 오탈자 수정하기
④ Anne을 사무실로 불러오기
⑤ Anne에게 보고서 가져다 주기

12 대화를 듣고, 대화 내용과 일치하지 <u>않는</u> 것을 고르시오.

① 남자는 수업을 들으러 가는 중이다.
② 남자가 들으려 하는 수업은 10시에 시작한다.
③ 지금 시각은 9시 15분이다.
④ 남자의 시계는 항상 빠르게 간다.
⑤ 남자는 아래층에 있는 수리점에 시계를 맡기지 않을 것이다.

13 대화를 듣고, 여자의 마지막 말에 이어질 남자의 말로 가장 적절한 것을 고르시오.

① They know what they're doing.
② You should quit worrying about them.
③ They bought a new car without telling me.
④ They don't want to get divorced because of their children.
⑤ They should have bought the apartment when they were financially ready.

14 대화를 듣고, 남자의 마지막 말에 이어질 여자의 말로 가장 적절한 것을 고르시오.

① Fried foods don't agree with me.
② That sounds nice. I've eaten it here before.
③ That'd be great. I really recommend the oyster soup.
④ That sounds good. Then I'll have the beefsteak tonight.
⑤ Are you done with that beefsteak? Mind if I finish it off for you?

15 다음 상황 설명을 듣고, Paul이 경찰관에게 할 말로 가장 적절한 것을 고르시오.

① I was trying to feed the cat on my way home.
② The cat caused the accident. It wasn't my fault.
③ Send an ambulance here, please. It seems very serious.
④ I missed your call because my phone was switched to vibration mode.
⑤ The accident occurred right across from here. It was the bus driver's fault.

01 다음을 듣고, 그림의 상황에 알맞은 대화를 고르시오.

① W Mr. Horn, may I _____ _____ _____?

　　M Of course. What's your name?

② M How do you like this blouse?

　　W I am not sure... Do you have it _____ _____ _____?

③ W Yes! I win!

　　M Good game. I'll _____ _____ the next time though.

④ W _____ this _____ _____?

　　M It's one hundred percent stainless steel.

⑤ W Mmm... What's that smell?

　　M _____ _____ chocolate cake. Do you want some?

autograph (유명인의) 사인, 서명 **beat** 이기다

02 대화를 듣고, 두 사람이 대화하는 장소로 가장 적절한 곳을 고르시오.

M Good afternoon. May I see your _____ and _____, please?

W Yes, here it is, and here's my visa.

M Thank you. You have a tourist visa _____ _____ _____.

W Yes, that's right. I _____ _____ some in the U.S.

M Where are you going?

W I'm going to spend some time in Atlanta. After that, I'm going to Washington, Chicago, and California.

M Where is your Form I-94? I _____ _____ it.

W Oh, here it is.

M All right. _____ _____ _____! You can go ahead.

W Thank you very much.

passport 여권 **Form I-94** 출입국 허가서

03 다음을 듣고, 여자의 직업으로 가장 적절한 것을 고르시오.

The funny thing is that I _____ really _____ _____ at home. My husband usually takes care of that, and, luckily, he's quite a good cook. There is one _____ to that _____ though. If I'm _____ a _____ _____, I try it out at home first. My teenage daughter is _____ _____ than most restaurant critics, so I always _____ her opinion _____ when I create new dishes for the restaurant.

exception 예외 **recipe** 요리법 **critic** 비평가, 평론가
take ~ into account ~을 고려하다 **opinion** 의견
create 만들다

04 대화를 듣고, 두 사람의 관계로 가장 적절한 것을 고르시오.

W Look! I have something to show you.

M What's that, Jane?

W This! I _____ _____ _____ _____ today.

M Wow! What a wonderful picture!

W Do you like it?

M Do I like it? I love it, sweetheart! But who is this lady?

W This is your mother _____

_____ _____.

M What? Is this your grandmother? But you never met your grandmother, did you?

W You're right, but I found an old photo on your desk, and I thought the lady in the photo must be _____ _____

_____.

M You are so smart! Yes, you're right. This lady in your picture looks just like my mother _____ _____

_____.

• •
late 돌아가신, 고인이 된

05 다음을 듣고, 남자가 이용할 교통 수단으로 언급되지 <u>않은</u> 것을 고르시오.

We are taking an _____ _____

_____ to Incheon International Airport. Later, we are going to _____ _____ London. Then, we will travel around London for about 4 days. We will take a _____ -_____ bus on a city tour. After that, we are going to take the EuroStar to Paris. It's a _____ -_____ train that travels from London to Brussels and Paris and _____ _____ the Channel Tunnel. In Paris, I'd also like to go to the Louvre Museum. This is our _____ _____ _____ Europe, so we are really excited.

• •
international 국제적인 **double-decker bus** 2층 버스

06 대화를 듣고, 여자가 주장하는 것으로 가장 적절한 것을 고르시오.

M Hey there, Martha. What are you reading?

W It's a history book.

M _____ _____ _____ _____ of reading about things that have already happened?

W Someone once said that _____ who _____ _____ _____ are doomed to repeat it.

M It is pretty _____ for me to read a history book though. _____ _____ read comic books or something.

W I understand, but the past is not _____ _____ _____ _____. We can only know ourselves by studying history.

M Well, I guess you _____ _____ _____. Can you recommend any fun history books?

• •
be doomed to ~하게 마련이다 **would rather** 차라리 ~하겠다
separate 따로 떨어진 **have a point** 일리가 있다

07 대화를 듣고, 두 사람의 심정으로 가장 적절한 것을 고르시오.

M Well, what do you think?

W That was the _____ movie _____ _____ _____.

M Yeah, it was bad, wasn't it?

W There was _____ _____, and the dialogue just went on and on and on.

M Don't you think we should ask for our money back?

W Forget the money. I want those two hours of my life back. I feel so _____ _____.

M Anyway, the next time, we'll _____ _____ _____ _____.

W I hope so. I don't want to experience that again.

●●
plot 줄거리 **dialogue** (책·연극·영화에 나오는) 대화
ripped off 사기 당한, 바가지 쓴

08 대화를 듣고, 여자가 첫 달에 남자에게 내야 하는 금액을 고르시오.

W Excuse me. Are you the _____?

M Yes, I am. Are you the person _____ _____ the apartment who called yesterday?

W That's right. How much is the _____ here?

M It's _____ _____ a month plus a _____-dollar security deposit.

W A security deposit? What's that?

M You pay the deposit only once, and you _____ _____ _____ when you move out. You have to pay it the first month.

W I see. And the other bills?

M The _____ _____ is about 30 dollars a month, and the telephone is another 20 dollars. You pay them _____ _____ _____ _____ the month after you receive the bills.

W The place looks great. When can I move in?

M You can move in at the _____ _____ _____ _____ if you want.

●●
landlord 집주인 **rent** 임차료, 집세
security deposit 임대 보증금 **electricity bill** 전기세
receive 받다

09 대화를 듣고, 남자가 늦은 이유로 가장 적절한 것을 고르시오.

W Mr. Jones, I believe you are late again.

M I'm sorry. You see...

W I don't want to _____ _____ _____. This is the second time this month, isn't it?

M That's right, but I have a good reason.

W You know, you need to feel _____ _____ your _____.

M There was a car accident!

W What did you say?

M On my way to work, I saw a car accident, so I stopped to help. I _____ _____ _____ _____ to the hospital to get medical attention. I may have even saved her life.

W Oh... In that case, Mr. Jones, I _____ _____ _____ I said. You did the right thing.

M Thank you.

●●
excuse 변명, 핑계 **responsible** 책임이 있는 **injured** 부상을 입은
attention 치료, 보살핌

10 대화를 듣고, 여자가 대화 직후에 할 일로 가장 적절한 것을 고르시오.

W Let's order some more food!

M I don't think so. I don't think I can

   _____ _____ _____.

W Okay. That was a great meal, wasn't it?

M _____ _____ _____.

W I can't remember when I ate so much. We have to eat dessert.

M Dessert? _____ _____

   _____ if I eat another bite.

W Why don't you have something like some sliced fruit?

M No, thank you. You really _____

   _____, don't you?

W Yeah, it's my weakness. I'll _____ something _____ _____ then.

•• **bite** 음식: 한 입 **explode** 터지다, 폭발하다 **weakness** 약점

11 대화를 듣고, 남자가 여자에게 요청한 일로 가장 적절한 것을 고르시오.

M Oh, Ms. Green, can you _____

   _____ _____ for me? Anne is busy now.

W Certainly, sir. I would be glad to.

M I must have _____ _____

   _____ this _____ by 4 o'clock.

W Let's see. There are ten pages. It should take me _____ _____

   _____. That will be 4:10.

M Can you finish it before that?

W I can try.

M Good. It's very important. You _____

   _____ _____ right to my office.

W Yes, sir.

M And, Ms. Green, it must be _____

   _____. There mustn't be any mistakes in it at all.

W I don't usually _____ _____ when I'm typing.

•• **Certainly**. 물론이죠. **copy** 복사(본) **absolutely** 굉장히 **correct** 정확한

12 대화를 듣고, 대화 내용과 일치하지 <u>않는</u> 것을 고르시오.

W Where are you going?

M I'm going to class.

W You're too early. It _____ _____

   _____ 10 o'clock.

M What time is it now?

W It's only _____ _____

   _____ _____.

M Oh, my watch is wrong. It doesn't work very well. Sometimes it runs too fast, and sometimes it runs too slow.

W There's a watch _____ _____

   _____.

M I don't want to take my watch there.

W Why not?

M He _____ _____ _____. Do you know another place?

W No, I don't.

•• **downstairs** 아래층에

13 대화를 듣고, 여자의 마지막 말에 이어질 남자의 말로 가장 적절한 것을 고르시오.

M I'm a bit worried about our son and

   _____-_____-_____.

W Is their marriage going badly?

M No, not at all. But they just bought a new apartment next to the park.

W It must be very expensive. _____
_____ _____ _____ a new
apartment?

M They've both got to be working to afford
the _____ _____ on their
mortgage.

W I think they can _____ _____.
Why are you worried?

M What I'm worried about is what would
happen if _____ of them _____
_____ _____.

W If that happened, they would have to try
to keep up the monthly payments.

M <u>They should have bought the apartment</u>
<u>when they were financially ready.</u>

daughter-in-law 며느리 **mortgage** (담보) 대출(금)
financially 재정적으로

14 대화를 듣고, 남자의 마지막 말에 이어질 여자의 말로
가장 적절한 것을 고르시오.

M Let's _____ _____ _____ in
the corner over there, shall we?

W Okay. Let's take that one.

M I _____ _____ _____ to
this restaurant when I was in college. It
wasn't very expensive, and it served very
good food.

W Did you? _____ _____
_____ here before. Did you eat
dinner here very often?

M Yes, I ate here often.

W Then you're very _____ _____
this restaurant, aren't you?

M Yes, I am.

W _____ is this restaurant _____
for?

M Well, the beefsteak is excellent. It was
very _____ _____ _____ in
my time.

W <u>That sounds good. Then I'll have the</u>
<u>beefsteak tonight.</u>

college 대학

15 다음 상황 설명을 듣고, Paul이 경찰관에게 할 말로
가장 적절한 것을 고르시오.

A few months ago, Paul had an accident. He
was _____ _____ _____ when
a cat ran in front of his car. He _____
_____ and missed the cat. But his
car _____ _____ _____. A
policeman was standing on the corner
when the accident happened. He _____
_____ _____ immediately. The
_____ _____ and took Paul to the
hospital with the policeman. While they
were going to the hospital, Paul wanted
to talk to the policeman about _____
the accident _____ _____. In
this situation, what would Paul say to the
policeman?

Paul: <u>The cat caused the accident. It wasn't</u>
<u>my fault.</u>

sharply 재빨리 **immediately** 즉시 **take place** (일·문제 등이)
일어나다

A 다음을 듣고, 어휘와 우리말 뜻을 쓰시오.

① _____ ⑦ _____

② _____ ⑧ _____

③ _____ ⑨ _____

④ _____ ⑩ _____

⑤ _____ ⑪ _____

⑥ _____ ⑫ _____

B 우리말을 참고하여 빈칸에 알맞은 단어를 쓰시오.

① I feel so _____ _____.

나는 정말로 사기 당한 기분이야.

② _____ _____ read comic books or something.

나는 차라리 만화책 같은 걸 읽겠어.

③ May I _____ _____ _____?

제가 당신의 사인을 받을 수 있을까요?

④ I guess you _____ _____ _____.

네 말에도 일리가 있는 것 같네.

⑤ I don't want to _____ _____ _____.

저는 어떠한 변명도 듣고 싶지 않습니다.

⑥ I always _____ her opinion _____ _____.

나는 항상 그녀의 의견을 고려해.

⑦ The past _____ _____ _____ from the present.

과거는 현재와 따로 떨어져 있는 것이 아니야.

⑧ _____ _____ _____ to that rule though.

그래도 그 규칙에는 한 가지 예외가 있어.

MY SCORE

.... / 15

01 다음을 듣고, 그림의 상황에 알맞은 대화를 고르시오.

①   ②   ③   ④   ⑤

02 대화를 듣고, 두 사람이 대화하는 장소로 가장 적절한 곳을 고르시오.

① 호텔   ② 세탁소
③ 문구점   ④ 헬스클럽
⑤ 스포츠 용품 가게

03 다음을 듣고, 남자의 직업으로 가장 적절한 것을 고르시오.

① 기자   ② 군인
③ 경찰   ④ 판매원
⑤ 회사 부서장

04 대화를 듣고, 두 사람의 관계로 가장 적절한 것을 고르시오.

① 경찰 - 시민
② 승무원 - 승객
③ 호텔 직원 - 투숙객
④ 관광 가이드 - 여행객
⑤ 출입국 관리원 - 입국 승객

05 대화를 듣고, 여자가 찾고 있는 동물을 고르시오.

①    ②

③ 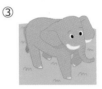   ④

⑤

06 대화를 듣고, 무엇에 관한 내용인지 가장 적절한 것을 고르시오.

① 지진   ② 쓰나미
③ 화산 폭발   ④ 건물 붕괴
⑤ 환경 오염

07 대화를 듣고, 마지막 말에서 느껴지는 남자의 태도로 가장 적절한 것을 고르시오.

① selfish   ② critical
③ positive   ④ cautious
⑤ indifferent

08 대화를 듣고, 여자가 지불한 핸드백 가격을 고르시오.

① $20   ② $40
③ $60   ④ $80
⑤ $100

정답 및 해석 p. 42

09 대화를 듣고, 여자가 선물을 사는 이유로 가장 적절한 것을 고르시오.

① 친구의 생일을 축하하기 위해서
② 남편의 승진을 축하하기 위해서
③ 동생의 대학 입학을 축하하기 위해서
④ 친구에게 감사의 마음을 전하기 위해서
⑤ 부모님의 결혼 기념일을 축하하기 위해서

10 대화를 듣고, 남자가 여자에게 조언한 것으로 가장 적절한 것을 고르시오.

① 평소에 자기계발을 꾸준히 해야 한다.
② 대학에 진학하는 것은 선택의 문제이다.
③ 자신의 마음이 가는 대로 행동해야 한다.
④ 다른 사람의 말에 항상 귀를 기울여야 한다.
⑤ 경영학 학위를 취득하면 취업에 도움이 된다.

11 대화를 듣고, 여자가 점검한 것으로 언급되지 <u>않은</u> 것을 고르시오.

① 메모장   ② 펜
③ 모니터   ④ 의자
⑤ 쓰레기통

12 대화를 듣고, 대화 내용과 일치하지 <u>않는</u> 것을 고르시오.

① 남자는 침실이 1개인 아파트를 찾고 있다.
② 여자는 남자에게 역 근처의 아파트를 권해 주었다.
③ 여자가 권해 준 아파트의 집세에는 전기세가 포함되어 있다.
④ 여자가 권해 준 아파트의 계약 기간은 2년이다.
⑤ 여자는 남자에게 집을 보러 갈 것을 제안했다.

13 대화를 듣고, 남자의 마지막 말에 이어질 여자의 말로 가장 적절한 것을 고르시오.

① He ought to get a job at a zoo.
② He'll give you a warning this time.
③ I think we have a misunderstanding.
④ I couldn't believe how hard the test was.
⑤ That's fantastic. What a great feeling that must be!

14 대화를 듣고, 여자의 마지막 말에 이어질 남자의 말로 가장 적절한 것을 고르시오.

① Yes, that's why I'm so upset.
② I know this must be a shock to you.
③ Let me know if there is anything I can do for you.
④ That's great! I've got some good news to share with you.
⑤ No, she wasn't. I would never have imagined that to be true.

15 다음 상황 설명을 듣고, Daniel이 지선이의 친구에게 할 말로 가장 적절한 것을 고르시오.

① She is planting flowers.
② She is looking for her mother.
③ She is helping her mother now.
④ She is painting "Welcome" on a sign.
⑤ She is cleaning the room to put up decorations.

01 다음을 듣고, 그림의 상황에 알맞은 대화를 고르시오.

① W _____ are _____ _____ you promised me?

M I'll finish them by tomorrow. I promise.

② W Do you have any _____ _____ _____?

M Yes, I'd like to check this suitcase.

③ W Where are you going?

M I'm just _____ _____ the store.

④ W Let's play basketball.

M No, not today. I'm too tired.

⑤ W Hi. I'm Carrie White.

M It's a pleasure to meet you. _____ _____ so much about you.

●●
promise 약속하다 **baggage** 수하물

02 대화를 듣고, 두 사람이 대화하는 장소로 가장 적절한 곳을 고르시오.

W Hi. Can I help you find anything?

M Yes, actually, I'm looking for _____ _____ _____ _____ _____.

W Do you have any _____ _____ in mind?

M Something not too tight looking, I guess.

W All right. _____ _____ do you wear?

M A medium.

W How about this in navy blue? It would be perfect for you.

M That looks pretty good. I like it. Where can I _____ _____ _____?

W The _____ _____ are right over there by the counter.

●●
particular 특별한 **medium** 중간; 중간의

03 다음을 듣고, 남자의 직업으로 가장 적절한 것을 고르시오.

I'm _____ _____ _____ the Marketing Department. There are 20 people in the department _____ myself, so I can be fairly busy at times. The _____ _____ _____ _____ all work forty hours a week, but I almost always work over fifty hours a week. Still, I like it. I like _____ _____ _____, and I like being in a position where I can _____ _____ _____ _____ the direction the company takes.

●●
be in charge of ~을 책임지고[담당하고] 있다 **department** 부서 **fairly** 아주, 완전히 **be in control** 관리[통제]하다 **influence** 영향 **direction** 방향

04 대화를 듣고, 두 사람의 관계로 가장 적절한 것을 고르시오.

M Good afternoon.

W May I _____ _____ _____, please?

M Yes, here it is, and here's my visa.

W Thank you. _____ _____?

M Pleasure.

정답 및 해석 p. 42

W All right. You have a _____ _____ good for three months.

M Yes, that's correct. I _____ _____ _____ some in Canada.

W Where are you going?

M I'm going to spend some time in Quebec. After that, I'm going to Ottawa and Ontario.

W All right. Enjoy your stay!

M Thank you. Have a nice day.

05 대화를 듣고, 여자가 찾고 있는 동물을 고르시오.

M We finally _____ _____ _____ the zoo, Hanna.

W Yeah, Daddy. I am looking around here for an animal that I need to _____ _____ _____ about in class.

M Is this the animal that you are looking for?

W No, it's not. That one is too fat. It looks like a _____ .

M What about that animal over there?

W No, its neck is too long. That looks like a _____ .

M Exactly what kind of animal do you want to find?

W I am looking for an animal with _____ , _____ _____ and two _____ growing from its nose. It looks like an elephant, but the elephant has _____ _____ _____ . However, this animal does not.

M Look over there. Is that the animal you are looking for?

W Yes, that's right. That's the one. It's a rhinoceros. Let's _____ and _____ _____ at it.

●●
presentation 발표 **hippo** 하마 **giraffe** 기린 **horn** (소·양 등의) 뿔 **rhinoceros** 코뿔소

06 대화를 듣고, 무엇에 관한 내용인지 가장 적절한 것을 고르시오.

W Did you _____ _____ the _____ ?

M What earthquake? What are you talking about? I didn't feel anything shaking.

W Well, it _____ in Japan, and some _____ in Busan even _____ . A lot of people were very frightened.

M I had no idea. I guess we are kind of safe in Seoul. Was anyone _____ _____ ?

W I don't think so although there was a lot of property damage.

M I'm not sure how I would _____ if an earthquake _____ Seoul.

W You would probably act just like everyone else and _____ _____ _____ your _____ .

●●
originate 시작되다, 일어나다 **collapse** 무너지다, 붕괴되다 **frightened** 깜짝 놀란, 겁이 난 **seriously** 심하게 **property** 재산, 소유물 **hide** 숨다

07 대화를 듣고, 마지막 말에서 느껴지는 남자의 태도로 가장 적절한 것을 고르시오.

M What are you doing?

W I'm _____ the Internet for a _____ - _____ _____ .

M What kind of job are you looking for?

W Anything.

M I _____ _____ _____ newspapers in the morning, but it was hard to get up early.

W I _____ _____ in the mornings. I can never get up before nine o'clock.

M Maybe you could be a tutor.

W I have _____ _____ _____.

M Waitress?

W I _____ do _____ _____.

M Do you really want to find a part-time job? No job is easy.

●●
search 살펴보다, 찾아보다 **part-time job** 아르바이트, 시간제 일
tutor 가정 교사

08 대화를 듣고, 여자가 지불한 핸드백 가격을 고르시오.

W Oh, my god! Where did you get that handbag?

M I _____ _____ _____ yesterday. I bought it for my wife. Why do you ask?

W I have the _____ _____ _____.

M Isn't it adorable? And what a price!

W How much did you pay for it?

M It was _____ _____ for _____ dollars. Stephanie, what's wrong? Are you okay?

W I'm not okay. I _____ _____ _____ _____ last week.

M Oh, I'm sorry to hear that. Bad luck.

●●
downtown 시내에서 **exact** 바로 그 ~
adorable 사랑스러운, 반할 만한 **double** 두 배의

09 대화를 듣고, 여자가 선물을 사는 이유로 가장 적절한 것을 고르시오.

M Hi, Sally. What are you doing in this department store?

W I'm looking for a _____ _____ _____ _____.

M Is it your friend's birthday?

W No.

M Then _____ is the _____?

W She helped me a lot when we were university students, so I want to let her know I _____ _____ _____. What about you?

M I am looking for a gift for my parents for their _____ _____. Do you have any ideas for a gift?

W How about a bottle of wine? I'm going to _____ _____ now. Let's go together.

M Good idea. Why didn't I think of that?

●●
occasion (특정한) 일, 경우 **effort** 노력 **anniversary** 기념일
section 코너, 구역

10 대화를 듣고, 남자가 여자에게 조언한 것으로 가장 적절한 것을 고르시오.

M What are you thinking about, Melissa?

W _____ _____ going back to university to get a _____ _____ _____.

M Why is that?

W Well, I don't like my job very much, so I want to _____ _____ _____.

M What would you study?

52

W I think I would get an MBA. What do you think?

M I think you should _____ _____ _____. If you think you should do it, then do it.

W That's really _____ _____. Thank you.

M Not at all.

••
consider 생각하다, 고려하다 **advanced** 고급의 **degree** 학위
upgrade (등급·품질 등을) 향상시키다, 높이다

11 대화를 듣고, 여자가 점검한 것으로 언급되지 않은 것을 고르시오.

M Did you set the _____ _____ up for the meeting today?

W Yes, I did. There's a _____ _____ on each seat.

M What about pens?

W _____ _____ _____ next to the pads.

M And monitors?

W I _____ _____ the _____, and there is no problem.

M Did you _____ _____ _____ _____ in the room? There are going to be 12 men at the meeting.

W There are 15 chairs in the room.

M What about water?

W There is _____ _____ _____ _____ and some glasses on the table in the corner.

M That sounds good.

••
conference room 회의실 **extra** 여분의, 추가의
pitcher 병, 주전자

12 대화를 듣고, 대화 내용과 일치하지 <u>않는</u> 것을 고르시오.

M I'm looking for an _____ one-bedroom apartment.

W Here's something you might like: a one-bedroom apartment near the station.

M That's a _____ _____. What's the rent?

W 200 dollars a month plus one month's deposit.

M Does that _____ _____?

W It includes everything _____ _____.

M How long is the _____?

W 2 years.

M When is it available?

W At the end of the month. Let's go over and _____ _____ at it now.

••
inexpensive 비싸지 않은 **location** 위치 **include** 포함하다
utilities 공과금, 공공 요금 **lease** 임대차 기간

13 대화를 듣고, 남자의 마지막 말에 이어질 여자의 말로 가장 적절한 것을 고르시오.

M I'm always a bit _____ _____ _____ Peter.

W Why's that? He's such a nice guy.

M He is, but he's _____ _____ _____ for exotic pets.

W I didn't know that. What does he have?

M Well, last week when I was there, he had a baby iguana _____ _____ the place.

W A lizard? Ugh! That would _____ _____ _____.

M I hate that kind of pet. But that's not the only thing he's got.

W He has more pets?

M Yeah... He's _____ _____ _____ for quite a while.

W He ought to get a job at a zoo.

●●
exotic 색다른, 별난 **give ~ the creeps** ~를 섬뜩하게 하다
zoo 동물원

14 대화를 듣고, 여자의 마지막 말에 이어질 남자의 말로 가장 적절한 것을 고르시오.

W What's the matter? You _____ _____ _____ you've been _____.

M I have. I've just come from the vet.

W What happened?

M We had to have our cat _____ _____ _____.

W What do you mean?

M She was painlessly _____ _____ _____ _____. She had a tumor which was incurable.

W Oh, dear! I'm really sorry to hear that. _____ _____ was she?

M She was 15, which is quite old for a cat.

W Your cat was like a member of the family, wasn't she?

M Yes, that's why I'm so upset.

●●
as if 마치 ~인 것처럼 **vet** 동물 병원; 수의사 **painlessly** 고통 없이
tumor 종양 **incurable** 치료할 수 없는

15 다음 상황 설명을 듣고, Daniel이 지선이의 친구에게 할 말로 가장 적절한 것을 고르시오.

Last Saturday, Daniel's family was very busy at home. They _____ about twenty people to Daniel's birthday party. Everybody had a _____ _____ _____ _____. Daniel's wife was _____ _____ in the kitchen. His daughter Ji-sun was helping her mother. His son Su-ho was cleaning the room to _____ _____ _____. While Daniel was _____ "Welcome" on a _____, the telephone rang. It was from one of Ji-sun's friends. She asked him _____ Ji-sun _____ _____. In this situation, what would Daniel most likely say to her?

Daniel: She is helping her mother now.

●●
prepare 준비하다 **decoration** 장식

A 다음을 듣고, 어휘와 우리말 뜻을 쓰시오.

1. _____
2. _____
3. _____
4. _____
5. _____
6. _____
7. _____
8. _____
9. _____
10. _____
11. _____
12. _____

B 우리말을 참고하여 빈칸에 알맞은 단어를 쓰시오.

1. Does that _____ _____?
   거기에는 공과금이 포함되나요?

2. Daniel's wife was _____ _____ in the kitchen.
   Daniel의 아내는 부엌에서 음식을 준비하고 있었다.

3. I am looking for a gift for my parents for their _____ _____.
   나는 부모님의 결혼 기념일을 위한 선물을 찾고 있어.

4. Did you set the _____ _____ up for the meeting today?
   오늘 회의를 위해 회의실을 준비했나요?

5. I _____ _____ that _____ last week.
   저는 지난주에 그 가격의 두 배를 지불했거든요.

6. I'm _____ the Internet for a(n) _____-_____ job.
   나는 아르바이트를 구하려고 인터넷을 살펴보는 중이야.

7. You _____ _____ _____ you've been crying.
   너 울고 있는 것처럼 보여.

8. _____ _____ _____ _____ the Marketing
   Department. 저는 마케팅 부서를 책임지고 있습니다.

MY SCORE

.... / 15

01 다음을 듣고, 그림의 상황에 알맞은 대화를 고르시오.

① ② ③ ④ ⑤

02 대화를 듣고, 두 사람이 대화하는 장소로 가장 적절한 곳을 고르시오.

① 은행 ② 동물원
③ 미술관 ④ 옷 가게
⑤ 분실물 보관소

03 대화를 듣고, 두 사람의 관계로 가장 적절한 것을 고르시오.

① 요리사 - 손님
② 제빵사 - 수강생
③ 배달 기사 - 고객
④ 슈퍼마켓 점원 - 손님
⑤ 호텔 지배인 - 종업원

04 대화를 듣고, 남자의 직업으로 가장 적절한 것을 고르시오.

① 목수 ② 경찰관
③ 수리 기사 ④ 아파트 관리인
⑤ 이삿짐센터 직원

05 다음을 듣고, 오늘의 기상도와 일기 예보가 일치하지 <u>않는</u> 도시를 고르시오.

① 서울 ② 강원
③ 경기
④ 광주
⑤ 제주도

06 대화를 듣고, 무엇에 관한 내용인지 가장 적절한 것을 고르시오.

① 교통사고 후유증
② 자전거에 치였던 일
③ 다리에 난 상처 치료 방법
④ 교통사고로 인한 금전적 손해
⑤ 여자에게 어렸을 때 발생한 사고

07 다음을 듣고, 남자가 여행 중에 느낀 점으로 가장 적절한 것을 고르시오.

① 볼거리는 별로 없었다.
② 기대가 커서 실망도 컸다.
③ 교통이 불편해서 피곤했다.
④ 기대한 만큼 만족스러웠다.
⑤ 혼자 여행을 해서 조금 외로웠다.

08 대화를 듣고, 여자의 심정으로 가장 적절한 것을 고르시오.

① nervous ② hopeful
③ delighted ④ concerned
⑤ disappointed

09 대화를 듣고, 남자의 시간당 수입이 얼마나 늘었는지 고르시오.

① $1.25 ② $1.50
③ $1.75 ④ $2.00
⑤ $8.25

10 대화를 듣고, 여자가 다이어트를 하려는 이유로 가장 적절한 것을 고르시오.

① 원하는 옷을 입기 위해서
② 관절 건강을 지키기 위해서
③ 좋은 몸매를 유지하기 위해서
④ 건강에 좋은 음식을 먹기 위해서
⑤ 보디빌딩 대회에 참가하기 위해서

11 대화를 듣고, 여자가 대화 직후에 할 일로 가장 적절한 것을 고르시오.

① 전화를 건다.
② Bill에게 간다.
③ 옷을 사러 간다.
④ 돈을 인출하러 간다.
⑤ 사무실까지 걸어간다.

12 대화를 듣고, 대화 내용과 일치하지 않는 것을 고르시오.

① 여자의 오빠는 사업에 성공한 사람이다.
② 여자의 오빠가 선거에 출마하는 것은 이번이 두 번째이다.
③ 여자의 오빠는 시장 선거에 출마할 것이다.
④ 여자의 오빠는 가족 친화적인 정책을 공약으로 내세울 것이다.
⑤ 여자의 오빠가 제시할 공약에 남자는 호의적이다.

13 대화를 듣고, 남자의 마지막 말에 이어질 여자의 말로 가장 적절한 것을 고르시오.

① I'd say she was impossible to please.
② I was put in such an awkward position.
③ Who's going to take responsibility?
④ That was the most embarrassing situation I've ever been in.
⑤ That would be great, but if she's asking too much, let me know.

14 대화를 듣고, 여자의 마지막 말에 이어질 남자의 말로 가장 적절한 것을 고르시오.

① I'm disappointed with your attitude.
② Are you sure you can get all your money back?
③ I'm sending this back to you, and I expect a full refund.
④ Don't forget to take the coupons with you to the store!
⑤ There's a 16-percent interest charge if you pay for this with monthly payments.

15 대화를 듣고, 남자의 마지막 말에 이어질 여자의 말로 가장 적절한 것을 고르시오.

① You have a gift for playing the drums.
② I'm looking forward to playing the violin.
③ I've been playing the drums since I was 13.
④ I wish I could go to your graduation concert.
⑤ Do you know anyone who can give me lessons?

01 다음을 듣고, 그림의 상황에 알맞은 대화를 고르시오.

① M I'm so glad you could come.

　 W I _____ _____ _____
　　　 this party for the world.

② M Could you _____ _____
　　　 _____ _____? You're making
　　　 me nervous.

　 W Sorry. I'll slow down.

③ M Come on in. The water is fine.

　 W No, thanks. I'll _____ _____
　　　 _____ later.

④ M Happy birthday!

　 W Wow! I can't believe you _____
　　　 _____ _____ _____ for
　　　 my birthday!

⑤ M That'll be 29 dollars and 90 cents,
　　　 please.

　 W Here's a 50.

nervous 불안한 perfume 향수

02 대화를 듣고, 두 사람이 대화하는 장소로 가장 적절한 곳을 고르시오.

　 W Hi. Can I help you find anything?

　 M Yes, I'm looking for some _____ and
　　　 _____.

　 W Do you have any _____ _____
　　　 _____ _____?

　 M Something not too wild looking, I guess.

　 W How about these gray ones?

　 M They look pretty good. Can I _____
　　　 _____ _____?

　 W Of course. The fitting room is _____
　　　 _____ _____. Please follow me.

　 M Thank you.

shorts 반바지 fitting room 탈의실

03 대화를 듣고, 두 사람의 관계로 가장 적절한 것을 고르시오.

　 M Here you go — one large cheese pizza
　　　 with _____ _____ toppings.

　 W Wait. I _____ _____ I _____
　　　 _____. I ordered a pepperoni pizza.

　 M You did? Oh, just a second. I think it's in
　　　 the delivery box on the bike. I _____
　　　 _____.

　 W Oh, good. I'm glad you have it. _____
　　　 _____.

　 M Sorry about that. Here's your pepperoni
　　　 pizza.

　 W Thanks. Here's 20 dollars. _____
　　　 _____ _____.

　 M Thanks. Have a good day.

　 W You, too.

confused 헷갈리는, 혼란스러운 starving 배가 아주 고픈
change 잔돈, 거스름돈

04 대화를 듣고, 남자의 직업으로 가장 적절한 것을 고르시오.

　 M Good afternoon, Ms. Smith! You called
　　　 us this morning for some _____
　　　 _____ _____? How
　　　 may I help you?

W Yes, I _____ _____ the windows
_____. Please help me with the dirty
windows in my house.

M Well, they get that way, but many people
don't know how to clean them.

W It seems like such a _____ and
_____ _____. That's why I need
your help.

M That's good. I just happen to have all the
cleaning tools that I need.

W Can I _____ _____ _____
_____?

M Leave them to me, ma'am. I'll take care of
them.

W How kind of you. It's dangerous. You
_____ _____ _____.

M Don't worry. I'll give them the best of
care.

dangerous 위험한 **tool** 도구

05 다음을 듣고, 오늘의 기상도와 일기 예보가 일치하지
않는 도시를 고르시오.

Good morning. Here is today's weather for
some _____ _____ Korea. Today
is going to be sunny in Seoul _____
_____ _____ _____ 28
degrees Celsius. It's going to be cloudy
in Kangwon Province with a high of 19
degrees. There's going to be _____
with _____ and _____ _____
in Gwangju. On Jeju Island, it will be mostly
_____, and there will be _____
_____ from the south. Gyeonggi
Province will enjoy sunny skies and
_____ _____ with a high of 24
degrees.

Celsius 섭씨 **province** (행정 단위인) 도(道), 주(州) **thunder** 천둥
lighting 번개 **mild** 온화한

06 대화를 듣고, 무엇에 관한 내용인지 가장 적절한 것을
고르시오.

M Where did you _____
_____ _____ on your leg?

W When I was six, I was hit by a car, so I had
to _____ _____ _____.

M Were you seriously hurt?

W My leg was broken, but there was
no serious _____-_____
_____.

M Getting hurt when you're a kid is a
_____ thing, isn't it?

W It sure is. Even my mother was crying.
But pretty soon, life was fine again.
_____ anything bad ever _____
_____ _____?

M Not like that. I fell off my bike once or
twice, but that was it.

W Well, you should _____ _____
_____.

huge 큰, 거대한 **scar** 상처 **operation** 수술
long-term 장기적인 **scary** 무서운 **happen** (일이) 생기다, 발생하다

07 다음을 듣고, 남자가 여행 중에 느낀 점으로 가장 적절한
것을 고르시오.

My whole life, I dreamed of visiting England
and seeing all its _____ _____.
On my first day, I saw Big Ben, the
_____ _____ in the middle of
London, as well as the River Thames. I also
had a chance to visit Buckingham Palace,
where the queen lives. I also _____

_____ _____ _____ visit some English pubs and meet some interesting people. Probably _____ _____ _____ _____ of my trip was seeing the double-decker buses. I _____ _____, but I was never lonely. My trip to England was something that I _____ _____.

●●
sight 명소, 관광지 **palace** 궁전, 왕실 **pub** 선술집

08 대화를 듣고, 여자의 심정으로 가장 적절한 것을 고르시오.

W Oh, a box of white chocolates. How sweet! _____ _____ _____ _____?

M No particular reason. I was just thinking about you. That's all.

W What a kind gesture. You are _____ _____. Thank you.

M It was nothing. I hope you like them.

W I get it now. Today is March 14. It's White Day. I _____ _____ _____ _____.

M I never forget it. You mean the world to me, so I always remember special occasions.

W I think I'm _____ _____ _____ in the world.

●●
gesture 태도; 몸짓 **considerate** 사려 깊은

09 대화를 듣고, 남자의 시간당 수입이 얼마나 늘었는지 고르시오.

W Hi, Mike. What's up?

M I just _____ _____ _____.

W Really? Do you like it better than your old one?

M The _____ is _____ _____. At my old job, I was making _____ dollars and _____ cents an hour. Now I'm making _____ dollars an hour. Plus, I get benefits like medical and dental insurance.

W Good for you. You _____ _____ _____ some good luck.

M Thanks. I've been searching for a better job for a while.

W I wonder _____ _____ _____ _____ looking for a better job, too.

M Maybe you should. There are jobs out there. You just have to find them.

●●
pay 보수, 급료 **benefit** 혜택, 이득 **dental** 치과의, 치아의
deserve ~할 만하다, ~할 가치가 있다

10 대화를 듣고, 여자가 다이어트를 하려는 이유로 가장 적절한 것을 고르시오.

W Guess what? Today, I'm starting a diet.

M Really? Why do you need to _____ _____ _____ _____? You already seem very thin. Do you intend to be a _____ in a bodybuilding _____ or something?

W It's not that I need to lose weight. I just need to _____ _____ _____.

M Oh, I see what you mean.

W No more doughnuts, cakes, ice cream, and potato chips.

M It takes a lot of _____ _____
   to _____ _____ the things you
   like.

W It does, but I know I can do it.

••
intend to ~할 작정이다 **contestant** 참가자 **competition** 대회
will power 의지력 **give up** ~을 포기하다

11 대화를 듣고, 여자가 대화 직후에 할 일로 가장 적절한
    것을 고르시오.

M Good morning. You're _____
   _____ _____.

W Yes, I know. I walked to the office.

M Is it _____ _____ _____?

W It's about a mile. And I stopped, too. I
   looked in all the store windows.

M Did you _____ _____ at
   _____?

W Yes, I looked at coats.

M Did you like _____ _____
   _____?

W I liked a blue coat, but it was too
   expensive for me.

M That's always the way it is. By the way,
   Bill called a few minutes ago. He wanted
   you to _____ _____ _____.

W Thanks. I'm going to call him right away.

••
sweat 땀을 흘리다

12 대화를 듣고, 대화 내용과 일치하지 않는 것을 고르
    시오.

W My brother has decided to _____
   _____ _____.

M Really? Why is that? He's such _____
   _____ _____.

W Well, he's gone as far as he wants to
   go in business and is looking for a new
   challenge.

M What is he aiming for?

W City Hall. He's going to _____
   _____ _____ during the next
   mayoral election.

M What's he going to promise?

W He's going to promise to _____ many
   more _____-_____
   if he is elected.

M That's the most important thing for
   me. I hope he _____ _____
   _____.

••
politics 정치 **challenge** 도전 **aim for** ~을 목표로 하다
run for ~에 입후보하다 **mayor** 시장 **election** 선거
introduce 도입하다 **policy** 정책

13 대화를 듣고, 남자의 마지막 말에 이어질 여자의 말로
    가장 적절한 것을 고르시오.

M I've just had a terrible hour and a half.

W I can see. You _____ _____.
   What happened?

M Well, I had a _____ _____ who
   wanted to buy a pair of shoes _____
   _____. And you know we've got
   quite a good selection.

W We certainly do.

M She asked me to _____ her
   _____ _____ _____ we had
   in the shop.

W That's not a nice thing to do. Was she
   satisfied with them?

M Not at all. She _____ _____
   every single one.

W Did she buy a pair?

M No, after complaining about the shoes and the service, she _____ _____.

W I'd say she was impossible to please.

exhausted 지친, 기진맥진한 **selection** 선택 가능한 것들
satisfied 만족하는 **complain** 불평하다

14 대화를 듣고, 여자의 마지막 말에 이어질 남자의 말로 가장 적절한 것을 고르시오.

M Why are you talking to your computer? Is it lonely?

W No, don't be silly. I'm trying out some new _____ _____ _____.

M How does it work?

W Well, I just say what I want to _____ _____ the microphone, and my words _____ _____ the screen.

M It's like magic. It must be very expensive.

W It's not cheap. But if I'm not satisfied with it, I can _____ it _____ _____ _____ within 30 days.

M Are you sure you can get all your money back?

recognition 인식 **microphone** 마이크 **appear** 나타나다
free of charge 무료로

15 대화를 듣고, 남자의 마지막 말에 이어질 여자의 말로 가장 적절한 것을 고르시오.

M Thank you for coming to my graduation concert.

W It was a great concert. _____ _____ _____ _____ _____ the violin like you.

M I'm sure you could if you tried. You should take some lessons.

W I took some when I was younger, but I _____ _____.

M Why was that?

W I found that I was tone-deaf, which really _____ _____ _____.

M In that case, why don't you _____ _____ _____ _____ _____?

W That's a good idea. I'll try.

M Then being tone-deaf _____ _____.

W Do you know anyone who can give me lessons?

hopeless 가망 없는 **tone-deaf** 음감이 없는, 음치의
impossible 불가능한

● 정답 및 해석 p. 57

A 다음을 듣고, 어휘와 우리말 뜻을 쓰시오.

① _____ _____   ⑦ _____ _____

② _____ _____   ⑧ _____ _____

③ _____ _____   ⑨ _____ _____

④ _____ _____   ⑩ _____ _____

⑤ _____ _____   ⑪ _____ _____

⑥ _____ _____   ⑫ _____ _____

B 우리말을 참고하여 빈칸에 알맞은 단어를 쓰시오.

① You're _____ me _____.
당신은 저를 불안하게 만들고 있어요.

② She _____ _____ every single shoe.
그녀는 모든 신발에 대해 불평했어.

③ I get _____ like medical and _____ insurance.
나는 의료 보험과 치과 보험 같은 혜택을 받아.

④ Where did you get that _____ _____ on your leg?
네 다리에 난 그 큰 상처는 어디에서 입은 거니?

⑤ You're _____ _____ _____.
너는 땀을 많이 흘리고 있구나.

⑥ I can return it _____ _____ _____ within 30 days.
나는 30일 안에 그것을 무료로 반품할 수 있어.

⑦ He's going to _____ _____ _____ during the next
election. 그는 다음번 선거에서 시장으로 입후보할 거야.

⑧ It takes a lot of _____ _____ to _____ _____
the things you like. 네가 좋아하는 것들을 포기하려면 많은 의지력이 필요해.

01 다음을 듣고, 그림의 상황에 알맞은 대화를 고르시오.

①   ②   ③   ④   ⑤

02 대화를 듣고, 두 사람이 대화하는 장소로 가장 적절한 곳을 고르시오.

① 교실   ② 상점
③ 사무실   ④ 도서관
⑤ 수리점

03 다음을 듣고, 남자의 직업으로 가장 적절한 것을 고르시오.

① 농부   ② 정원사
③ 과학자   ④ 요리사
⑤ 엔지니어

04 대화를 듣고, 두 사람의 관계로 가장 적절한 것을 고르시오.

① 의사 – 환자
② 경찰 – 운전자
③ 구급대원 – 학생
④ 수리 기사 – 고객
⑤ 택시 기사 – 승객

05 대화를 듣고, 여자가 설명하고 있는 사람을 고르시오.

①   ②

③   ④

⑤

06 다음을 듣고, 고객 페이지를 통해서 할 수 있는 일로 언급되지 <u>않은</u> 것을 고르시오.

① 물품의 취소   ② 물품의 반송
③ 물품의 재고 확인   ④ 예상 배송일 확인
⑤ 물품의 배송 상태 추적

07 대화를 듣고, 남자의 심정으로 가장 적절한 것을 고르시오.

① proud   ② fearful
③ lonely   ④ grateful
⑤ disappointed

08 대화를 듣고, 여자가 구입할 비행기 표의 가격을 고르시오.

① 16만 원   ② 17만 원
③ 60만 원   ④ 70만 원
⑤ 80만 원

09 대화를 듣고, 남자가 도시로 이사하려는 이유로 가장 적절한 것을 고르시오.

① 자신의 꿈을 이루기 위해서
② 공개 댄스 오디션에 참가하기 위해서
③ 유명한 댄스 학교에 합격했기 때문에
④ 도시에 살고 있는 친구의 권유 때문에
⑤ 도시에 살아보는 것이 어릴 적 꿈이었기 때문에

10 대화를 듣고, 여자의 의견으로 가장 적절한 것을 고르시오.

① 소수의 잘못 때문에 다수가 피해를 본다.
② 안전한 환경을 만들기 위해 소수만 노력한다.
③ 소수의 의견이라는 이유로 배척되어서는 안 된다.
④ 법이 모든 사람에게 공평하게 적용되는 것은 아니다.
⑤ 도서관 열람실 내에서의 휴대폰 사용은 금지되어야 한다.

11 대화를 듣고, 남자가 주말에 할 일로 가장 적절한 것을 고르시오.

① 속초에 간다.
② 늦잠을 잔다.
③ 공원에 간다.
④ 집안 청소를 한다.
⑤ 휴가 계획을 세운다.

12 대화를 듣고, 대화 내용과 일치하지 <u>않는</u> 것을 고르시오.

① Laura는 두 사람과 함께 가기로 했다.
② 여자는 남자의 얼굴이 빨개졌다고 생각한다.
③ 남자는 Laura를 좋아한다.
④ Laura는 남자의 데이트 신청을 거절했다.
⑤ 남자는 여자의 격려에 고마워하고 있다.

13 대화를 듣고, 남자의 마지막 말에 이어질 여자의 말로 가장 적절한 것을 고르시오.

① Thank you very much.
② Come this way, please.
③ I feel so lucky to meet you.
④ What do you want me to do?
⑤ I'm sure they won't have a problem.

14 대화를 듣고, 여자의 마지막 말에 이어질 남자의 말로 가장 적절한 것을 고르시오.

① She just seems to have a gift.
② She'll be by your side until the end.
③ I know these must be difficult times for you.
④ I don't know. I think I have an upset stomach.
⑤ I think she feels sorry about what she said to you.

15 대화를 듣고, 여자의 마지막 말에 이어질 남자의 말로 가장 적절한 것을 고르시오.

① I wouldn't go in there right now.
② Why are you worried about going there?
③ Okay. I'm looking forward to meeting him.
④ Of course. There's nothing you can do about it.
⑤ Yes. You'd better do it now, or you'll be sorry later.

01 다음을 듣고, 그림의 상황에 알맞은 대화를 고르시오.

① W Do you want to eat some?

　M Yes, _____ _____.

② W I'd like a T-bone steak.

　M _____ would you like _____ _____?

③ W This looks delicious, doesn't it?

　M Yes, let's _____ _____ _____.

④ W Is it _____ _____ or _____ _____?

　M For here, please.

⑤ W _____ _____ will it _____?

　M It will only take about five minutes.

••
serving (음식의) 1인분

02 대화를 듣고, 두 사람이 대화하는 장소로 가장 적절한 곳을 고르시오.

M Could you tell me the good things and the bad things about this computer?

W Sure. _____ _____ _____, I can say that there aren't _____ _____ _____ about this model.

M Hmm, are you sure?

W Yes. This is the best computer _____ _____ _____.

M Sounds interesting. Tell me more.

W This model is almost _____ _____ _____ _____ as our other models.

M Three times?

W Uh-huh, and with this computer, you can _____ _____ _____.

M Sounds good.

W That's right. Would you like to buy this one?

••
interesting 흥미로운　**almost** 거의　**complex** 복잡한　**task** 업무

03 다음을 듣고, 남자의 직업으로 가장 적절한 것을 고르시오.

My family has been _____ _____ _____ _____ for five generations. We're really proud of that fact. Agricultural technology has changed a lot though, especially during my lifetime. These days, there are environmentally friendly _____ _____, and some of our fields _____ _____ completely _____. We also have new types of _____ and use high-tech _____ _____. This means that the vegetables and the grains we produce today are _____ _____ _____ and cheaper than those produced in my parents' day.

••
generation 세대　**agricultural** 농업의　**chemical** 화학 물질
organic 유기농의　**seed** 씨앗, 종자　**high-tech** 첨단 기술의
method 방법　**grain** 곡물　**produce** 생산하다　**quality** 품질

04 대화를 듣고, 두 사람의 관계로 가장 적절한 것을 고르시오.

M Are you hurt?

W Luckily, I am fine. But my husband _____ _____ _____.

M Okay. It's on the way now. May I see your driver's license, please?

W Yes. Here you are.

M _____ _____ _____ ?

W Well, a car went through the red light. I slammed on the breaks, and my car _____ _____ the road and _____ _____ .

M Did the other driver stop?

W No, he didn't. He _____ even _____ .

M All right. Could you come to the police station after you and your husband get better? I have to _____ _____ _____ _____ .

W Yes, I will.

●●
slam (브레이크 등을) 세게 밟다   get better 호전되다, 좋아지다
fill out ~를 작성하다

05 대화를 듣고, 여자가 설명하고 있는 사람을 고르시오.

W This guy is so handsome! He's _____ _____ fashion models.

M Where? Who's handsome?

W This guy in the magazine. I like _____ _____ .

M Let me see. I don't see any handsome men here.

W The one with the _____ _____ . He has a _____ . He looks really sharp in this suit, doesn't he?

M There are a few guys wearing a suit.

W The one who's wearing the _____ and the _____ _____ .

M Frankly speaking, I think I look much better than any of those guys.

●●
m(o)ustache 콧수염   vest 조끼
frankly speaking 솔직히 말해서

06 다음을 듣고, 고객 페이지를 통해서 할 수 있는 일로 언급되지 않은 것을 고르시오.

We'd like to let you know we _____ _____ _____ today. You can _____ the _____ of your _____ online by visiting the Your Account page at our website. There, you can track the order and shipment status, review estimated _____ _____ , _____ unshipped items, and _____ items. Thanks for shopping at pamon.com, and we _____ _____ _____ _____ again soon!

●●
ship 보내다, 수송하다   track 추적하다   status 상태, 사정
estimated 예상[추측]의   cancel 취소하다

07 대화를 듣고, 남자의 심정으로 가장 적절한 것을 고르시오.

M You spent your entire day helping me _____ _____ _____ . Thank you.

W Don't mention it. I _____ _____ _____ today anyway.

M I really _____ your help. I don't know any other people who give their time like you.

W No, really, it's my pleasure to _____ _____ .

M You have to let me know when I can

_____ _____ _____.

W Certainly.

●●
weed 잡초를 뽑다 **lend a hand** 도움을 주다
favor 은혜, 친절한 행위

08 대화를 듣고, 여자가 구입할 비행기 표의 가격을 고르시오.

M Fly Away Travel Agency. May I help you?

W I would like to take a vacation to
Hong Kong for _____ _____
_____ _____. How much will it
cost?

M That depends. _____ are you
_____ _____ _____?

W On the 28th of the month.

M If you leave on the 28th of the month,
the airline ticket will be 800,000 won.

W _____ _____ I leave on the
30th? Is it any cheaper?

M Let me have a look on the computer. Yes.
In fact, the price _____ _____
_____ won if you leave on that date.

W It's still steep for me.

M Well, if you leave on the 25th, it's only
600,000 won.

W But I can't leave that early because of
my job. I guess I will _____ on the
_____. Can you book a ticket for
me?

M Yes, I'll _____ _____ _____
on the 30th.

●●
travel agency 여행사 **What if ~?** ~라면 어떻게 되는가?
in fact 사실은 **steep** 너무 비싼

09 대화를 듣고, 남자가 도시로 이사하려는 이유로 가장 적절한 것을 고르시오.

M I've decided to leave this town and
_____ _____ _____
_____.

W What is the reason?

M There's nothing for me in this town.
I want to _____ _____
_____ in the city.

W What will you do there? Will you continue
with your _____ _____?

M Yes, I want to _____ _____ a
dance school there.

W So you've absolutely decided to leave?

M I've totally decided. I _____
_____ _____ _____.

W I wish you luck even though I will miss
you.

●●
decide 결심하다, 결정하다 **career** 직업, 경력
enroll in ~에 등록하다 **totally** 완전히

10 대화를 듣고, 여자의 의견으로 가장 적절한 것을 고르시오.

W Did you hear that we're not permitted to
_____ cell phones _____ the
_____ _____?

M That's good. I heard that someone was
taking pictures in there.

W But why should everyone _____
_____ for the actions of a few?

M To _____ a _____ _____.
That's why.

W You're right, but there must be a better
way to _____ _____
_____.

M I agree with you.

••
be not permitted to ~하는 것이 허용되지 않다
public bath 공중 목욕탕   **punish** 처벌하다
ensure 보장하다; 지키다, 보호하다   **deal with** (문제 등을) 처리하다

11 대화를 듣고, 남자가 주말에 할 일로 가장 적절한 것을 고르시오.

M What are you going to _____ _____ _____ _____, Sora?

W Oh, I really want to rest, _____ _____, stay home, and read the Sunday paper. What are you going to do?

M My family and I are planning to _____ _____ _____ _____ to Bukhansan National Park. It may be hot in the city, but it's always cool there.

W That's a good idea. By the way, when are you going to _____ _____ _____?

M Next month.

W That's August. It's still going to be warm then.

M That's right. So my family and I will have a great time in Sokcho.

W Oh, you are a _____ _____.

12 대화를 듣고, 대화 내용과 일치하지 <u>않는</u> 것을 고르시오.

M Hey, Rachel, is Laura going with us?

W Yes. Why?

M No reason. I'm just asking.

W Just asking? But why is your face _____ _____? Aha. Someone _____ _____ _____ _____ Laura, doesn't he?

M Who has a crush?

W Come on, Sam. If you like her, you've got to tell her. Maybe she likes you.

M But I am afraid to _____ _____ _____.

W What are you so afraid of?

M I'd totally die if she _____ _____ _____.

W But that's better than _____ _____ _____ _____. You've got to let her know.

M I don't know... Well, maybe you're right. Thanks for _____ me.

••
have a crush on ~에게 홀딱 반하다
ask out ~에게 데이트를 신청하다   **turn down** ~을 거절하다
keep to oneself 마음 속에 담아두다

13 대화를 듣고, 남자의 마지막 말에 이어질 여자의 말로 가장 적절한 것을 고르시오.

M Excuse me, ma'am. I would like to go to the Sejong Center. How can I _____ _____ _____ _____?

W I think the place is on line 5. Now we are on line 3. You need to _____ _____ _____ _____.

M At which station do I need to change?

W You have to _____ _____ at the next station. You should take the subway on line 5 _____ _____ Bangwha.

M I really appreciate your help.

W Why don't you get off here with me? I'm getting off, too.

M Oh, really? I'm glad that we're _____ in the _____ _____.

W Come this way, please.

••
transfer to ~로 갈아타다

---

14 대화를 듣고, 여자의 마지막 말에 이어질 남자의 말로 가장 적절한 것을 고르시오.

W Did you go to Linda's _____ _____?

M Yes, the house is fabulous, and the food was so good. She _____ everything _____ _____.

W I'm so envious of Linda. She _____ _____ _____ for cooking.

M I know. Everything she makes tastes perfect.

W I tried some of her recipes myself, but they just didn't seem to _____ _____ _____.

M You're not the only one. My sister _____ _____ _____ her chocolate cake the other day. It tasted all right but was not half as good as Linda's.

W _____ _____ _____ she does it.

M She just seems to have a gift.

••
housewarming party 집들이 **fabulous** 멋진, 굉장한
envious 부러운 **talent** 재능 **the other day** 며칠 전에

---

15 대화를 듣고, 여자의 마지막 말에 이어질 남자의 말로 가장 적절한 것을 고르시오.

M I heard that you are planning to _____ _____ _____ this weekend.

W No, that _____ _____ _____.

M Why?

W My brother and his family will be coming to town this weekend.

M Is he the one who _____ _____ for The *New York Times*?

W Right. Why don't you come over this Saturday and meet him?

M I'd love to, but I can't. Can I _____ _____ _____ _____?

W Sure. They'll be here for a week. So just _____ _____ _____ _____ you can come.

M Okay. I'm looking forward to meeting him.

••
take a rain check 다음을 기약하다

○ 정답 및 해석 p. 65

A 다음을 듣고, 어휘와 우리말 뜻을 쓰시오.

① _____   ⑦ _____

② _____   ⑧ _____

③ _____   ⑨ _____

④ _____   ⑩ _____

⑤ _____   ⑪ _____

⑥ _____   ⑫ _____

B 우리말을 참고하여 빈칸에 알맞은 단어를 쓰시오.

① You need to _____ _____ line 5.

당신은 5호선으로 갈아타셔야 해요.

② I have to _____ _____ a report.

저는 보고서를 작성해야 해요.

③ I want to _____ _____ a dance school there.

나는 거기에서 댄스 학교에 등록하고 싶어.

④ You can _____ the _____ of your order online.

당신은 주문 물품의 상태를 온라인으로 추적할 수 있습니다.

⑤ You can handle _____ _____ with this computer.

당신은 이 컴퓨터로 복잡한 업무들을 처리할 수 있어요.

⑥ There must be a better way to _____ _____ the problem.

그 문제를 처리하기 위한 더 나은 방법이 분명히 있을 거야.

⑦ Someone _____ _____ _____ _____ Laura.

누군가가 Laura에게 홀딱 반했구나.

⑧ We _____ _____ _____ _____ bring cell phones

into the public bath.

우리는 공중 목욕탕에 휴대폰을 갖고 들어가는 것이 허용되지 않는다.

MY SCORE
-------- / 15

01 다음을 듣고, 그림의 상황에 알맞은 대화를 고르시오.

①   ②   ③   ④   ⑤

02 대화를 듣고, 두 사람이 대화하는 장소로 가장 적절한 곳을 고르시오.

① 식당   ② 서점
③ 공항   ④ 은행
⑤ 버스 터미널

03 대화를 듣고, 남자의 직업으로 가장 적절한 것을 고르시오.

① 기자   ② 의사
③ 변호사   ④ 구급대원
⑤ 식당 지배인

04 대화를 듣고, 두 사람의 관계로 가장 적절한 것을 고르시오.

① 교수 - 학생
② 면접관 - 지원자
③ 회사 상사 - 직원
④ 수리 기사 - 고객
⑤ 관광 가이드 - 여행객

05 대화를 듣고, 여자가 전화를 건 목적으로 가장 적절한 것을 고르시오.

① 길을 물어보려고
② 파티에 초대하려고
③ 음식을 주문하려고
④ 만남을 제안하려고
⑤ 일자리에 지원하려고

06 대화를 듣고, 그림에서 Bobby가 누구인지 고르시오.

07 다음을 듣고, 누가 누구에게 쓴 편지인지 고르시오.

① 아들이 엄마에게
② 남편이 아내에게
③ 남자가 여자 친구에게
④ 남자가 회사 동료에게
⑤ 남자가 자신의 팬들에게

08 대화를 듣고, 남자의 태도로 가장 적절한 것을 고르시오.

① 친절하다   ② 이기적이다
③ 부주의하다   ④ 고집스럽다
⑤ 무관심하다

09 대화를 듣고, 여자가 비행기를 타려고 하는 날짜를 고르시오.

① April 10
② May 10
③ June 22
④ June 28
⑤ July 22

10 대화를 듣고, 두 사람이 차를 세운 이유로 가장 적절한 것을 고르시오.

① 타이어에 문제가 생겼기 때문에
② 사고 현장을 신고해야 했기 때문에
③ 아버지에게 전화를 드려야 했기 때문에
④ 차가 고장이 나서 견인을 해야 했기 때문에
⑤ 이모네 집으로 가는 길을 잃어버렸기 때문에

11 대화를 듣고, 무엇에 관한 내용인지 가장 적절한 것을 고르시오.

① 꿈
② 취미
③ 날씨
④ 낚시
⑤ 물고기

12 대화를 듣고, 대화 내용과 일치하지 <u>않는</u> 것을 고르시오.

① 비행기 출발 시각이 날씨 때문에 미뤄졌다.
② 비행기는 오전 10시 30분에 출발할 예정이다.
③ 두 사람은 비행을 취소할 것이다.
④ 두 사람은 자판기 옆 좌석에서 휴식을 취할 것이다.
⑤ 여자는 간식을 사러 갈 것이다.

13 대화를 듣고, 여자의 마지막 말에 이어질 남자의 말로 가장 적절한 것을 고르시오.

① It usually doesn't take long.
② I just sold it two months ago.
③ Let me arrange for you to meet him.
④ Do you want to buy another camera?
⑤ If it didn't work, you'd better call a technician.

14 대화를 듣고, 남자의 마지막 말에 이어질 여자의 말로 가장 적절한 것을 고르시오.

① I wish I had one.
② You look better than I thought you would.
③ Oh, how thoughtful of you. You're the best.
④ We can pick up some flowers on the way over there.
⑤ I talked to the doctor, and she said everything was going to be okay.

15 다음 상황 설명을 듣고, 박 선생님이 George와 Julia 에게 할 말로 가장 적절한 것을 고르시오.

① You don't have much choice.
② You have to focus on class.
③ You are invited to the party tonight.
④ You'd better study early in the morning.
⑤ You should write the answers on the blackboard.

01 다음을 듣고, 그림의 상황에 알맞은 대화를 고르시오.

① M How's this?

　W No good. You need to kick it harder if you want to _____ _____ _____.

② M How does this feel?

　W The drill feels okay.

③ M I can't wear these; they're too small.

　W Sorry, but we're _____ _____ _____ the larger sizes.

④ M Can't you give me some more time?

　W No, the report _____ _____ _____ by tomorrow.

⑤ M I'm afraid you _____ _____ _____.

　W Oh, no! Are you sure?

● ●
score a goal 골을 넣다, 득점하다 **be out of** ~이 소진되다[바닥나다]
cavity 충치

02 대화를 듣고, 두 사람이 대화하는 장소로 가장 적절한 곳을 고르시오.

W Welcome. _____ _____ of you are there?

M Two. Can we sit by a window?

W I'll see what we have available.

M Thank you. If there are no window seats, maybe something in a _____ _____ will do.

W Sir, all of the window seats are taken. Actually, we only have one table available right now.

M Where is it _____?

W I'm afraid it's near the kitchen. It's not exactly the best seat in the house.

M I see. _____ _____ do you think it will be until another table _____ _____?

W Another table will be ready in _____ _____.

M That sounds great. Then we'll wait for that table.

● ●
available 이용할 수 있는 **private** 조용히 있을 수 있는
actually 사실은, 실제로 **located** ~에 위치한
exactly 엄밀하게는, 정확하게

03 대화를 듣고, 남자의 직업으로 가장 적절한 것을 고르시오.

W Thanks for seeing me today. I _____ _____ _____ in the grocery store. I might need to _____ _____ _____ _____.

M Thanks for coming in. Can you tell me what happened?

W Well, I was _____ _____ _____ _____ in the store. I suddenly slipped and fell and _____ _____ _____ _____.

M That sounds terrible. Did the store do anything after that?

W The store manager just called an ambulance for me. I want to know if I can _____ _____ _____ _____ for what happened to me.

● ●
land (땅에) 부딪치다, 떨어지다 **sue** 고소하다

04 대화를 듣고, 두 사람의 관계로 가장 적절한 것을 고르시오.

M _____ _____ , please, Ms. Kim.

W Thank you very much.

M So you're looking for a job at our company. Are you interested in working _____ _____ or _____ _____?

W I would like to work full time.

M And _____ _____ do you go to?

W The University of New York.

M Oh, yes. I see that on your application. When will you graduate?

W Next January. I only have _____ _____ _____.

M Do you have any _____ or _____ _____?

W Well, I can use design software, and I know how to speak Japanese.

●●
full time 전일제의 **semester** 학기

05 대화를 듣고, 여자가 전화를 건 목적으로 가장 적절한 것을 고르시오.

M Hello? This is Ken.

W Hello, Ken. This is Nancy.

M Hi, Nancy. _____ are you _____ _____?

W Listen. I was wondering… If you _____ _____ _____ _____ on Saturday night, would you like to go out with me? We could have dinner or go to the movies.

M Oh, Saturday… It's my mother's birthday, so the whole family is _____ _____ on Saturday.

W Oh, I see.

M But I'm free on Friday night.

W Great. _____ _____ _____ Friday then.

M Okay. What time?

W Can I _____ _____ _____ around 6 o'clock?

M Okay. That sounds good to me.

06 대화를 듣고, 그림에서 Bobby가 누구인지 고르시오.

W Where's Bobby? I can't find him anywhere.

M He's down there _____ _____ with the others.

W I still can't see him.

M He's right _____ _____ _____ the _____, and he's _____ _____ the _____.

W Oh, that one?

M Yes. I can only see the back of his head, but it looks like him.

W I'm surprised he's _____ _____ his _____ as usual.

M Me, too.

●●
goalpost 골대 **as usual** 평상시처럼

07 다음을 듣고, 누가 누구에게 쓴 편지인지 고르시오.

There are many things that are difficult for me to understand sometimes. One of them is when I happen to _____

_____ _____ _____ on my left hand. Images and feelings _____ _____ _____. Then comes the still unbelievable realization: _____ _____ _____. If I close my eyes, I can see your smile. I still find it hard to believe that _____ _____ _____ _____. I feel so fortunate. I believe no one could love me _____ _____ _____ _____.

●●
happen to 우연히 ~하다 **rush** (갑자기) 몰려들다, 돌진하다
unbelievable 믿기 어려운 **realization** 깨달음, 인식
fortunate 운 좋은

08 대화를 듣고, 남자의 태도로 가장 적절한 것을 고르시오.

W So what do you want to do today?

M I _____ _____ _____. Do you have any ideas?

W We could go to the music concert. Do you like _____ _____?

M It's okay.

W Or how about a roller coaster ride? _____ that _____ _____?

M Sure. That sounds fine. It _____ _____ to me what we do.

W You must _____ _____ _____. Don't you like one idea over the other?

M Not at all. To be honest with you, I'm _____ _____ _____ _____ now.

●●
preference 더 좋아하는 것, 선호

09 대화를 듣고, 여자가 비행기를 타려고 하는 날짜를 고르시오.

M Hi, Susan. Did you _____ a ticket to come here?

W Yes, I did. I just called a travel agency to _____ _____ from June 28 to _____ _____.

M I can't wait to see you again. Was there a seat available?

W No, I am _____ _____ _____ _____.

M What if you can't get a ticket? It must be a _____ _____ _____ _____. Do you still have the June 28 ticket confirmed?

W No, that wasn't a confirmed seat. Besides, you told me to arrive there _____ _____ _____ _____.

M I know, but I thought the ticket you booked earlier _____ _____.

W No, it wasn't. But don't worry too much. It's only May 10 now. I still have a lot of time. There will be a seat for me.

M I hope so.

●●
confirmed 확정된, 확인된

10 대화를 듣고, 두 사람이 차를 세운 이유로 가장 적절한 것을 고르시오.

M I think we have to _____ _____. There's a problem with the tire.

W I guess we'll be late for my aunt's dinner.

M We have no choice. I'd better _____ _____.

W Look. All we have to do is _____

_____ _____.

M Do you know how to do that?

W Oh, yes. I've done it _____

_____. Dad taught me how to do it.

M Go ahead. Here's the tire iron.

W There we go. Finished in five minutes.

M I have to say I'm _____ _____.

W It was really nothing. Let's go. We're late.

●●
pull over 길 한쪽에 차를 대다 **mechanic** 정비사
tire iron 타이어를 떼어내는 지렛대

11 대화를 듣고, 무엇에 관한 내용인지 가장 적절한 것을
고르시오.

M Have you ever _____ _____?

W I can't say that I have. What do you like
about it?

M I _____ _____

_____, and the silence is beautiful.
It's just the fish and me. It's a wonderful
sport.

W It's one of those things I've always

_____ _____ _____.

M You should try fishing sometime.

W Sure. I'll _____

_____ _____.

M How about this weekend? I hear the
weather will be _____.

W All right. Let's go fishing.

●●
silence 침묵 **gorgeous** 아주 좋은[멋진]

12 대화를 듣고, 대화 내용과 일치하지 <u>않는</u> 것을 고르
시오.

M When is the _____ _____?

W They've just announced that our flight
will be _____ for 4 hours due to

_____ _____ _____.

M What? Oh, no! That means it won't be
leaving until 10:30 in the morning.

W I'm afraid so. What shall we do _____

_____ _____?

M Let's find some seats so that we can

_____ _____ and take a nap.

W Sounds like a good idea. We've had a
busy day, and I'm pretty tired.

M Me, too. Look. There are some seats

_____ _____ the _____

_____. Let's go before somebody
else gets to them.

W _____ _____ _____ for me,
and I will buy some snacks.

●●
boarding time 탑승 시간 **announce** 방송으로 알리다, 발표하다
delay 지연시키다 **in the meantime** 그동안에
vending machine 자판기

13 대화를 듣고, 여자의 마지막 말에 이어질 남자의 말로
가장 적절한 것을 고르시오.

W Why has the _____ _____?

M Oh, it probably stopped because the
paper has jammed.

W What should I do? I have to _____
these two _____.

M You'll have to open the door and look
inside the machine to check.

W Oh, yes. I can see where a sheet of paper

_____ _____ _____.

M You need to _____ _____

_____ printed inside the door to
remove it and then restart the machine.

W I will try as you said.

M Did you do it?

W I did, but I _____ _____

_____ the jammed paper at all.

M If it didn't work, you'd better call a

technician.

• •

photocopier 복사기 **jam** (기계에) 걸리다, 끼이다
document 서류, 문서 **instruction** 지시, 설명 **remove** 제거하다

14 대화를 듣고, 남자의 마지막 말에 이어질 여자의 말로
가장 적절한 것을 고르시오.

M How's your leg?

W Much better, but I'm so _____

_____ _____ _____ in the

house all day.

M Well, you can't expect to be up and

around so soon after _____ your

_____.

W I suppose not, but it is very frustrating.

M When are you going to _____

_____ _____ _____?

W Next week. I can't wait to get it off.

M I know. I've brought something to

_____ _____ _____.

W What is it? I can't wait to see it.

M It's a bottle of the very _____

_____ _____.

W Oh, how thoughtful of you. You're the

best.

• •

be stuck in ~에 갇혀 있다 **be up and around** (회복해서) 걸어
다닐 수 있게 되다 **frustrating** 좌절감을 주는 **cast** 깁스

15 다음 상황 설명을 듣고, 박 선생님이 George와 Julia
에게 할 말로 가장 적절한 것을 고르시오.

This is the English classroom. The students

are studying English and _____

_____ _____ Mrs. Park, the English

teacher. She is now teaching the present

continuous tense and is _____ on the

_____. _____ _____ George

and Julia is listening carefully and answering

her. George is reading a detective story.

Julia is _____

_____ _____ and seems to be

thinking about the party tonight. Mrs.

Park wants them to _____ _____

_____ _____. In this situation,

what would Mrs. Park most likely say to

them?

Mrs. Park: You have to focus on class.

• •

detective story 탐정 소설 **concentrate on** ~에 집중하다

정답 및 해석 p. 73

A 다음을 듣고, 어휘와 우리말 뜻을 쓰시오.

① _____   ⑦ _____

② _____   ⑧ _____

③ _____   ⑨ _____

④ _____   ⑩ _____

⑤ _____   ⑪ _____

⑥ _____   ⑫ _____

B 우리말을 참고하여 빈칸에 알맞은 단어를 쓰시오.

① _____ is the table _____?

그 테이블은 어디에 위치해 있습니까?

② When is the _____ _____?

탑승 시간이 언제니?

③ You need to _____ the _____.

너는 지시 사항들을 따라야 해.

④ I think we have to _____ _____.

우리가 길 한쪽으로 차를 대야 할 것 같아.

⑤ There are some seats next to the _____ _____.

저기 자판기 옆에 자리가 좀 있어.

⑥ I'm afraid you _____.

유감스럽게도 당신은 충치가 있으시네요.

⑦ What shall we do _____?

우리 그동안에 뭘 할까?

⑧ You need to kick it harder if you want to _____ _____

_____.

당신이 골을 넣고 싶다면 그것을 더 세게 차야 해요.

MY SCORE
.... / 15

01 다음을 듣고, 그림의 상황에 알맞은 대화를 고르시오.

①   ②   ③   ④   ⑤

05 대화를 듣고, 남자가 전화를 건 목적으로 가장 적절한 것을 고르시오.

① 물품을 주문하려고
② 물품 주문을 취소하려고
③ 물품의 재고를 확인하려고
④ 물품의 배송일을 문의하려고
⑤ 물품의 배송 지연 사실을 알려 주려고

02 대화를 듣고, 두 사람이 대화하는 장소로 가장 적절한 곳을 고르시오.

① 공원   ② 호텔
③ 집안   ④ 식당
⑤ 영화관

06 대화를 듣고, 여자가 찾고 있는 지갑의 위치로 가장 적절한 곳을 고르시오.

03 대화를 듣고, 여자의 장래 희망으로 가장 적절한 것을 고르시오.

① 판사   ② 경찰관
③ 수의사   ④ 해양 생물학자
⑤ 동물원 사육사

07 다음을 듣고, 남자의 상황으로 가장 적절한 것을 고르시오.

① 지금 서울에 있다.
② 미나에게서 이메일을 받았다.
③ 미나의 생일 파티에 참석할 것이다.
④ 수업 시간에 적극적인 편이다.
⑤ 토론토에서 오랫동안 공부하고 있다.

04 대화를 듣고, 두 사람의 관계로 가장 적절한 것을 고르시오.

① 의사 - 환자
② 교수 - 학생
③ 약사 - 손님
④ 교사 - 학부모
⑤ 카페 주인 - 손님

08 대화를 듣고, 여자의 심정으로 가장 적절한 것을 고르시오.

① bored   ② jealous
③ amazed   ④ pleased
⑤ concerned

09 대화를 듣고, 남자가 학교에 도착하는 시각을 고르시오.

① 7:15 a.m.　　② 7:30 a.m.
③ 8:15 a.m.　　④ 8:30 a.m.
⑤ 9:15 a.m.

10 대화를 듣고, 두 사람이 Steve를 걱정하는 이유로 가장 적절한 것을 고르시오.

① 부모에게 반항해서
② 성적이 너무 저조해서
③ 선생님께 항상 야단을 맞아서
④ 친구들과 잘 어울리지 못해서
⑤ 남들 앞에서 말하는 것을 부끄러워해서

11 대화를 듣고, 무엇에 관한 내용인지 가장 적절한 것을 고르시오.

① 택시 잡기의 어려움
② 도로 위 차량의 속도 위반
③ 자동차 경적의 지나친 사용
④ 차량 운전자들의 신경질적인 태도
⑤ 자동차 배기가스로 인한 대기 오염

12 대화를 듣고, 대화 내용과 일치하지 않는 것을 고르시오.

① 교황의 장례식이 언론에 보도되었다.
② 남자는 로마에 가서 직접 교황의 장례식을 봤다.
③ 백만 이상의 사람들이 오늘 로마에 모였다.
④ 수많은 가톨릭 신자들이 교회 미사에 참석하고 있다.
⑤ 교황은 St. Peter의 묘실에 묻힐 것이다.

13 대화를 듣고, 남자의 마지막 말에 이어질 여자의 말로 가장 적절한 것을 고르시오.

① Don't give away the ending!
② There's absolutely no smoking in the theater!
③ It's much better to watch it on the big screen.
④ Don't get the first row. My neck will hurt if I sit there.
⑤ The next movie I go to see will be a romantic comedy.

14 대화를 듣고, 여자의 마지막 말에 이어질 남자의 말로 가장 적절한 것을 고르시오.

① I'm sure you'll get the job.
② I feel like the world is coming to an end.
③ I think there'll be a position opening up soon.
④ Thank you for applying, but you're not the right fit.
⑤ They said you weren't exactly the man they were looking for.

15 다음 상황 설명을 듣고, Bill이 부동산 중개인에게 할 말로 가장 적절한 것을 고르시오.

① I'm pretty sure it's going to work out.
② Do you want to take a look at the house?
③ I was lucky to buy the house very cheaply.
④ I'd like to see the one on Broadway Avenue.
⑤ Let's go back to my office and take care of the paperwork.

01 다음을 듣고, 그림의 상황에 알맞은 대화를 고르시오.

① M How did you enjoy everything?

　W It was just fine. Thanks. Can we ＿＿＿＿＿ ＿＿＿＿＿ ＿＿＿＿＿, please?

② M There's a 10-year ＿＿＿＿＿ on this.

　W Really? I'll take it.

③ M Would you like to ＿＿＿＿＿ ＿＿＿＿＿ ＿＿＿＿＿?

　W No, thanks.

④ M May I help you?

　W Yes, I ＿＿＿＿＿ ＿＿＿＿＿ ＿＿＿＿＿ under the name of Karen Jackson.

⑤ M I ＿＿＿＿＿ ＿＿＿＿＿ ＿＿＿＿＿ ＿＿＿＿＿.

　W Me neither. We should check out another place.

●●
bill 계산서　**warranty** (품질 등의) 보증, 보증서

02 대화를 듣고, 두 사람이 대화하는 장소로 가장 적절한 곳을 고르시오.

M You ＿＿＿＿＿ ＿＿＿＿＿ ＿＿＿＿＿ before, have you?

W No, this is my first time. I'm ＿＿＿＿＿ ＿＿＿＿＿.

M Well, this is the living room, and over there is the kitchen.

W ＿＿＿＿＿ ＿＿＿＿＿? I would like to see it.

M Of course you would. I'll show you. Okay, here are the two bedrooms, and there's the bathroom.

W ＿＿＿＿＿ ＿＿＿＿＿ ＿＿＿＿＿ ＿＿＿＿＿ you have! I envy you.

M Thanks. I ＿＿＿＿＿ ＿＿＿＿＿ ＿＿＿＿＿.

●●
envy 부러워하다　**decorate** 꾸미다, 장식하다

03 대화를 듣고, 여자의 장래 희망으로 가장 적절한 것을 고르시오.

M ＿＿＿＿＿ do you ＿＿＿＿＿ ＿＿＿＿＿ ＿＿＿＿＿ in the future?

W I am interested in rule, justice, and fairness. So I would like to ＿＿＿＿＿ people ＿＿＿＿＿ ＿＿＿＿＿.

M Wow, that's an interesting ＿＿＿＿＿. By the way, are there many women ＿＿＿＿＿ ＿＿＿＿＿ ＿＿＿＿＿?

W Yes, there are a lot these days. How about you, Sean?

M I like science and love the ocean a lot. I've also studied whales, fish, and all the things in the sea. Thus, I want to be a ＿＿＿＿＿ ＿＿＿＿＿.

W You must go to the ocean a lot.

M That's right. It must be wonderful to ＿＿＿＿＿ ＿＿＿＿＿ ＿＿＿＿＿.

W I hope you become a good scientist.

●●
justice 정의　**fairness** 공정　**court** 법정　**occupation** 직업
whale 고래

04 대화를 듣고, 두 사람의 관계로 가장 적절한 것을 고르시오.

M Hi. How are you?

W Fine. Thank you. Er, I'm _____ _____ _____ _____ something.

M Okay. Would you like some coffee? There's a coffee vending machine over there.

W No, thanks. I already _____ _____ _____ of coffee.

M So what's up?

W _____ Fleming, I may be _____ _____ _____ something.

M Do you have a cold?

W I think so. I have a terrible headache and need time to get some rest. Er, Professor, can I _____ _____ for a big _____?

M I know what you have in mind. You _____ _____ your paper yet, have you?

W No, I haven't. Could you give me _____ _____ _____ _____ to finish it?

●● come down with (병에) 걸리다

05 대화를 듣고, 남자가 전화를 건 목적으로 가장 적절한 것을 고르시오.

W Hello?

M Is this Mary Patrick?

W Yes, this is she.

M Hi, Ms. Patrick. This is G Shopping.

W Oh, hi. Has the _____ _____ I ordered _____ _____?

M That's why I'm calling. We've just received a message from the manufacturer. There _____ _____ _____ _____ on your order. It's _____ _____.

W Oh, no. I need it for a party I'm going to have this Friday.

M I'm afraid it will be _____ _____ before it's _____.

W One week? That's not good.

M What would you like us to do? Do you want us to _____ _____ _____?

W Well, I really want the rice cooker, so I'll wait for it.

●● rice cooker 밥솥   manufacturer 제조자 out of stock 재고가 없는

06 대화를 듣고, 여자가 찾고 있는 지갑의 위치로 가장 적절한 곳을 고르시오.

W Jim, have you _____ _____ _____? It's got to be somewhere in this room.

M I saw it next to the computer monitor this morning.

W No, it's not there. I just _____ _____ _____.

M _____ _____ _____ under the desk?

W Yes, I did, but it wasn't there _____.

M Oh, sorry. I forgot. I moved it somewhere, but I _____ _____.

W Try to think of where you put it. I have to go to work now.

M I got it! I put it _____ _____

_____ _____ _____ so that

the baby wouldn't get it.

W Oh, now I see it. Thanks.

●●
bookcase 책장

07 다음을 듣고, 남자의 상황으로 가장 적절한 것을 고르시오.

Hi, Mina! It's your friend, Jinsu. I'm in

Toronto. I just _____ your email.

Thanks. I am sorry I _____ _____

_____ _____ make it to your

birthday party. Things are fine here. I

just had my first class on Monday. After

my first class, I wished I could _____

_____ _____ the class. But I know

I will _____ _____ somehow, so

don't worry about me too much. I hope you

enjoy your birthday with our other friends.

I already _____ _____ _____

with you guys in Seoul.

●●
participate in ～에 참여하다 **survive** 살아남다, 생존하다

08 대화를 듣고, 여자의 심정으로 가장 적절한 것을 고르시오.

W Where were you today, Martin?

M I just _____ _____ at the

shopping mall.

W Really? Someone told me _____

_____ _____ with another

woman. Is that true?

M Well, yes and no.

W So it is true. I can't believe you were

spending time _____ _____

_____.

M No, it's not like that. You see...

W What? You'd better have a _____

_____.

M It was my _____ that _____

_____ _____. She was in town

for the day, so we had coffee.

●●
hang out 많은 시간을 보내다

09 대화를 듣고, 남자가 학교에 도착하는 시각을 고르시오.

W You are a very _____ student, aren't

you, Billy? You always arrive at school

early.

M That's right, Ms. Johnson.

W Well, _____ _____ _____

_____ for your 9:15 class every

day gives you _____ _____

_____ _____. You are a model

student.

M Thanks, Ms. Johnson.

W Do your parents encourage you to

study _____ _____ _____

_____?

M Yes, they're always telling me I can do

_____ _____ _____ as long

as I study hard.

W They are right. If you study hard, you will

_____ _____ _____ in your

life.

M Thanks for the encouragement.

●●
diligent 성실한, 부지런한 **model student** 모범생

10 대화를 듣고, 두 사람이 Steve를 걱정하는 이유로 가장 적절한 것을 고르시오.

W This is the second time Steve's teacher _____ _____ this year.

M What happened?

W The teacher said he didn't seem to _____ _____ _____ the other kids. I don't know what to do.

M You and I work all day long, and he always plays by himself after class. Maybe he _____ _____.

W I know, but what can we do for him? _____ _____ _____ to talk with him, he doesn't say very much.

M We need to do something about him. This weekend, I will take him to the mountain we _____ _____ _____ together. He really liked that.

W That's a good idea. I will talk to my boss about _____ _____ _____ _____ to stay with him at home next week.

●●
get along with ~와 잘 지내다 **by oneself** 혼자서
take ~ off ~ 동안 쉬다

11 대화를 듣고, 무엇에 관한 내용인지 가장 적절한 것을 고르시오.

M I think drivers _____ _____ _____ in Seoul.

W You're telling me.

M In most of Europe's large cities, the use of the _____ _____ is strictly _____.

W Oh, really?

M Yes. Motorists who use their horns in situations _____ _____ _____ get fined.

W Is that right? I think that's a very good _____.

M It sure is. Honking not only _____ _____ street noise but also makes people _____.

W That's right. I hope the Korean authorities do something about this _____ _____ of car horns.

M So do I.

●●
honk (자동차 경적을) 울리다 **strictly** 엄격하게 **restricted** 제한된
motorist 운전자 **emergency** 비상 사태 **fine** 벌금을 물리다
authorities 당국 **excessive** 지나친, 과도한

12 대화를 듣고, 대화 내용과 일치하지 <u>않는</u> 것을 고르시오.

M The papers, TV, and radio are all _____ _____ _____ about the pope's _____ today.

W Did you see the funeral mass in Rome for Pope John Paul?

M Yes, I _____ _____ _____ on TV. It was a very solemn occasion.

W I know. _____ _____ _____ that more than a million people are in Rome today to mourn the pope's death.

M And it's not just in Rome. All over the world, millions of Catholics are mourning the _____ _____.

W Yes, many of them are _____ _____ _____ for the pope.

M Where will the pope _____ _____?

W He will be buried in a crypt in St. Peter's. _____ _____ many of his predecessors were buried before him.

pope 교황 funeral 장례식 mass 군중 solemn 엄숙한, 근엄한
mourn 애도하다 service 미사, 예배 bury 묻다, 매장하다
crypt 묘실 predecessor 전임자

13 대화를 듣고, 남자의 마지막 말에 이어질 여자의 말로 가장 적절한 것을 고르시오.

M How was the movie?

W It was a really _____ _____.

M It certainly was. There seemed to be one killing about _____ _____ _____.

W I know. I began to _____ _____ _____ it long before the end.

M Why are so many movies full of violence?

W I suppose the reason is that violent movies _____ _____ _____ _____ _____.

M You must be right.

W <u>The next movie I go to see will be a romantic comedy.</u>

violent 폭력적인

14 대화를 듣고, 여자의 마지막 말에 이어질 남자의 말로 가장 적절한 것을 고르시오.

M You _____ _____. What have you been doing?

W I just _____ _____ _____ for a reporter's job.

M I didn't know you were moving to another company.

W I told you I had a problem with my boss. That's why I've _____ _____ _____.

M Anyway, how did the interview go? Did they _____ _____ _____ your résumé _____ _____?

W Yes, they did, especially since I'm working for their main competitor.

M What's your overall feeling about _____ _____ _____?

W I think I made a good impression. But I'm _____ _____ if I _____ _____ the interview.

M <u>I'm sure you'll get the job.</u>

relieved 안도한 go through ~를 살펴보다 competitor 경쟁자
overall 전체적인 impression 인상, 감명

15 다음 상황 설명을 듣고, Bill이 부동산 중개인에게 할 말로 가장 적절한 것을 고르시오.

Bill is _____ _____ a new apartment. He has to move to a new city in order to _____ _____ _____ at a university. He wants to live somewhere near the university or _____ _____ on a bus line. And he needs to move in by the first of next month. He is at a _____ _____ _____ in the new city. The agent is _____ _____ _____ of the apartments they have _____ and which fit his preferences. He just _____ _____ _____ _____. In this situation, what would Bill most likely say to the agent?

Bill: <u>I'd like to see the one on Broadway Avenue.</u>

real estate agency 부동산 중개소

정답 및 해석 p. 81

A 다음을 듣고, 어휘와 우리말 뜻을 쓰시오.

① _____   ⑦ _____

② _____   ⑧ _____

③ _____   ⑨ _____

④ _____   ⑩ _____

⑤ _____   ⑪ _____

⑥ _____   ⑫ _____

B 우리말을 참고하여 빈칸에 알맞은 단어를 쓰시오.

① It was a really _____ _____.

그건 매우 폭력적인 영화였어.

② I think I made a(n) _____ _____.

내가 좋은 인상을 준 것 같아.

③ I actively _____ _____ the class.

나는 수업에 적극적으로 참여했어.

④ I am interested in rule, _____, and _____.

나는 규칙, 정의, 공정에 관심이 있어.

⑤ I put your purse on _____ of the _____.

나는 당신의 지갑을 책장 위에 놓아두었어요.

⑥ It's _____.

그것은 재고가 없습니다.

⑦ He is at a(n) _____ in the new city.

그는 새 도시의 부동산 중개소에 있다.

⑧ He didn't seem to _____ _____ _____ the other kids.

그는 다른 아이들이랑 잘 지내지 못하는 것 같았어.

MY SCORE
.... / 15

01 다음을 듣고, 그림의 상황에 알맞은 대화를 고르시오.

① ② ③ ④ ⑤

02 대화를 듣고, 두 사람이 대화하는 장소로 가장 적절한 곳을 고르시오.

① 공항　　　　② 식당
③ 호텔　　　　④ 슈퍼마켓
⑤ 극장 매표소

03 대화를 듣고, 여자의 직업으로 가장 적절한 것을 고르시오.

① 의사　　　　② 변호사
③ 패션 디자이너　　④ 부동산 중개인
⑤ 컴퓨터 프로그래머

04 대화를 듣고, 두 사람의 관계로 가장 적절한 것을 고르시오.

① 판매원 - 고객
② 은행원 - 고객
③ 버스 기사 - 승객
④ 호텔 직원 - 투숙객
⑤ 식당 종업원 - 손님

05 대화를 듣고, 남자가 전화를 건 목적으로 가장 적절한 것을 고르시오.

① 택배를 배달하려고
② 인터뷰를 요청하려고
③ 신문 구독을 신청하려고
④ 과외 일자를 조정하려고
⑤ 에어컨 수리를 의뢰하려고

06 대화를 듣고, 남자가 이번 주말에 할 일로 가장 적절한 것을 고르시오.

①　　②

③　　④

⑤

07 대화를 듣고, 여자의 고민으로 가장 적절한 것을 고르시오.

① 이웃에게 한 거짓말이 탄로 났다.
② 이웃과의 점심 식사를 원하지 않는다.
③ 친구 때문에 이웃에게 선의의 거짓말을 했다.
④ 친구에게 한 거짓말 때문에 죄책감을 느낀다.
⑤ 병원 진료 때문에 이웃과의 점심 식사를 못하게 되었다.

정답 및 해석 p. 82

08 Melissa의 가족에 관한 다음 내용을 듣고, 일치하는 것을 고르시오.

① 엄마는 하루 종일 청소를 하신다.
② 아빠가 매일 아침 아이들을 깨우신다.
③ 엄마는 요리사이다.
④ 아빠는 회사에서 늦게까지 일하신다.
⑤ 아이들이 집으로 돌아오면 엄마가 요리를 하고 계신다.

09 대화를 듣고, 남자가 돈을 갚는 데 걸리는 기간을 고르시오.

① 1개월　　　　② 3개월
③ 5개월　　　　④ 7개월
⑤ 9개월

10 대화를 듣고, 여자의 기분이 좋지 않은 이유로 가장 적절한 것을 고르시오.

① 체중이 늘어서
② 독감에 걸려서
③ 엄마에게 야단을 맞아서
④ 주문한 요리가 맛이 없어서
⑤ 남자가 비꼬면서 이야기해서

11 다음을 듣고, 무엇에 관한 안내 방송인지 고르시오.

① 분실물　　　　② 할인 판매
③ 인테리어 강좌　　④ 도로 통행 제한
⑤ 마트 연장 영업

12 대화를 듣고, 대화 내용과 일치하지 <u>않는</u> 것을 고르시오.

① 남자는 유럽으로 여행을 갔었다.
② 남자는 런던에서 자신의 짐이 없어졌음을 알았다.
③ 누군가가 남자의 짐을 실수로 가져갔다.
④ 남자의 짐은 파리로 보내졌다.
⑤ 남자가 자신의 짐을 되찾는 데 이틀이 걸렸다.

13 대화를 듣고, 남자의 마지막 말에 이어질 여자의 말로 가장 적절한 것을 고르시오.

① You really ought to have a talk with him.
② You have to wash his clothes the next time.
③ You can express your appreciation to Paul.
④ You'd better put the dishes away right after a meal.
⑤ You should go to the supermarket to get some more towels.

14 대화를 듣고, 여자의 마지막 말에 이어질 남자의 말로 가장 적절한 것을 고르시오.

① How do I know where I am?
② I don't want to think about it.
③ Umm, I see the Watson Discount Mall.
④ I would like to let you know where I am.
⑤ You should ask someone who can help you right now.

15 다음 상황 설명을 듣고, Addy가 아버지에게 할 말로 가장 적절한 것을 고르시오.

① I'd like to try it sometime.
② Did you have a good trip?
③ How was your trip to France?
④ I really appreciate your coming over.
⑤ I'm expecting you to have lots of gifts for me.

01 다음을 듣고, 그림의 상황에 알맞은 대화를 고르시오.

① W Is it okay now?

    M Will you _____ _____ a little more, please?

② W I would like to take a picture.

    M Why not? I _____ _____ _____.

③ W I'm thirsty. Can I have something to drink?

    M Sure. Here you go. Why don't we _____ _____ _____ _____?

④ W Can you _____ _____ _____ a bit?

    M I have to sell it according to what's on the _____ _____.

⑤ W How much is this drink?

    M It's only two dollars.

••
thirsty 목마른 **lower** 내리다. 낮추다 **according to** ~에 따라서 **price tag** 가격표

02 대화를 듣고, 두 사람이 대화하는 장소로 가장 적절한 곳을 고르시오.

M Hi. Two tickets for *Love Me Tender*, please.

W I'm afraid we're _____ _____ for the 7:30 show.

M Oh, no. I _____ _____ _____ earlier.

W We still have seats for the 9:35 show though.

M No, that's okay. What else is playing right now?

W Well, *Moon War* still _____ _____ _____.

M Give me two tickets to that then.

W Here you are, sir. That'll be 20 dollars.

03 대화를 듣고, 여자의 직업으로 가장 적절한 것을 고르시오.

M Hi, June. It's been a long time. How do you like your new office?

W Actually, I don't like it. So I've _____ to look for _____ _____.

M What's the matter with your office now?

W It's a little far from my home, and it's _____ _____ for me _____ _____ on my work. I have to create a software program by this month.

M Oh, really? Then why don't you move near my place? The _____ are _____. And there is a big parking lot in the area.

W That sounds nice.

M Do you want to go and _____ _____ _____?

W Sure. I hope I can find a good place.

••
focus on ~에 집중하다 **neighbor** 이웃 사람

04 대화를 듣고, 두 사람의 관계로 가장 적절한 것을 고르시오.

M How may I help you?

W I'd like to make an international call, please.

M You can dial _____ _____ _____ _____ if you like.

W I'm sorry. I don't understand what to do.

M Just pick up. Then dial 011, your

_____ and _____ _____,

and your number.

W Okay. Thanks for your help.

M You're welcome. Would you like us to

_____ _____ _____ to your

room?

W Yes, please.

M All right. I'll take care of it for you.

W Thank you.

●●
international 국제의, 국제적인 **dial** 전화를 걸다
charge (요금·값을) 청구하다

05 대화를 듣고, 남자가 전화를 건 목적으로 가장 적절한
것을 고르시오.

W Hello. This is Kristin speaking.

M Hello, Kristin Gray. My name is Bob White.
I'm a _____ from the *Times*.

W I see. What are you calling about?

M I have read your post that your five-year-
old boy can speak English _____.
_____ _____ _____ and
_____ to you about how your son
has learned English?

W Yes. It _____ would make an
interesting story! Can you come this
Friday at 2 p.m.?

M Sounds great. May I _____
_____ _____?

W Sure. It's 1580 Robinson Street,
Apartment #1202.

M I got it. Thank you very much.

W You're welcome. I'll see you then.

●●
reporter 기자 **post** 게시글 **fluently** 유창하게

06 대화를 듣고, 남자가 이번 주말에 할 일로 가장 적절한
것을 고르시오.

W Hi, James. Hey, are you okay? You don't
_____ _____ _____.

M Oh, hi, Laura. I'm okay. I just feel heavy
and sluggish.

W You know... You'd feel better if you
exercised. _____ _____
_____ try swimming? Or maybe we
could play some tennis.

M No, I just want to _____ _____
_____ this weekend.

W Well, okay, if that's what you want.
However, you _____ _____
_____ eat well and get some rest.

M Thank you for your advice.

W Sure. If you feel better in _____
_____ _____ _____, give
me a call. We can play some tennis or go
swimming.

M Okay. I'll do that.

●●
sluggish 나른한, 둔한

07 대화를 듣고, 여자의 고민으로 가장 적절한 것을 고르
시오.

W Hey, Jacob. Can you _____ me
_____ _____ _____?

M Sure. What is it?

W My neighbor _____ _____
_____ we could eat lunch together
today.

M So what's wrong with that?

W Well, I told her I would, but I _____
_____.

M Just tell her a _____ _____. Tell her you have a doctor's appointment or something.

W But I would _____ _____ about that.

M Look. A white lie is not a big deal.

W White or not, it is still lying. I'll have to _____ _____ _____ _____.

●●
guilty 죄책감을 느끼는 **big deal** 큰 문제, 대단한 것

08 Melissa의 가족에 관한 다음 내용을 듣고, 일치하는 것을 고르시오.

My name is Melissa. Every morning, my father _____ my brother and me _____ and makes breakfast. Then, my mother goes to work, and my father _____ _____. He cooks and cleans all day. He is an _____ _____ and makes wonderful pizza and cakes. Whenever we _____ _____ _____ _____, we can smell food cooking in the kitchen. I know a lot of families _____ the mother stays home and the father works. But our family is _____, and I think it's _____ _____.

●●
stay 계속 있다, 머무르다 **amazing** 굉장한, 놀라운 **quite** 아주, 정말

09 대화를 듣고, 남자가 돈을 갚는 데 걸리는 기간을 고르시오.

M Let's go to the computer store.

W What for?

M I've _____ _____ _____ _____ a laptop computer there. It's on sale for only _____ dollars. The regular price is 1,200 dollars.

W Have you saved any money?

M So far I've _____ _____ dollars, and my father _____ me _____ _____ of the money that I need.

W You borrowed money from your father? How will you _____ _____ _____?

M Well, I am making 200 dollars every month at my part-time job. If I am really thrifty, then I can pay him back _____ dollars _____ _____.

W Are you confident about that?

M Oh, yeah. I will keep my promise to my father.

W Wow, you are a good son.

●●
have one's eye on ~을 눈여겨보다 **regular price** 정가
so far 지금까지 **thrifty** 절약하는 **confident** 자신이 있는

10 대화를 듣고, 여자의 기분이 좋지 않은 이유로 가장 적절한 것을 고르시오.

M What's wrong, Kate?

W I hate _____ _____. I've gained weight.

M When I met you a month ago, you said you had _____ _____.

W Well, I had had a bad cold for a month, so I lost almost three kilos.

M Losing three kilograms is quite a lot, don't you think?

W Yeah, but I soon _____ _____ _____.

M I can't tell. You still look good.

W Anyway, this is my mother's _____.

M What are you talking about?

W My mom cooks tasty food every evening. My mom's food is really good, so I _____ _____ _____ _____ _____ eat a lot.

M Ha-ha. I think your mother _____ _____ _____ if she heard what you said.

fault 책임, 잘못 have no choice but to ~할 수밖에 없다
offended 기분이 상한

11 다음을 듣고, 무엇에 관한 안내 방송인지 고르시오.

Attention, Buymart shoppers! Let me _____ your _____ _____ the sale going on in aisle nine. This is your chance to _____ _____ _____ famous name brands. All fitted sheets are 20% off. Towels and _____ _____ are 30% off, and _____ are 50% off. Ralph Laurel, Pierre Cardini, Lori Ashley, and _____ _____ other top brands are available. Be sure to _____ _____ aisle nine and _____ _____ these _____ before they're all gone!

direct (주의 등을) 돌리다, 향하게 하다 aisle 통로
sheet 시트, 얇은 천 be sure to 꼭 ~을 하다
stop by ~에 (잠깐) 들르다 bargain 특가품, 싼 물건

12 대화를 듣고, 대화 내용과 일치하지 않는 것을 고르시오.

W How was your trip?

M I _____ _____ _____ _____ on my trip to Europe.

W Why? What happened? Did you have an accident?

M No, my _____ _____ _____. When I arrived in London and went to collect my bag from the baggage carousel, it never arrived.

W Somebody must have _____ _____ _____ _____, right?

M No, it had been _____ _____ _____ by mistake.

W Did you get it back?

M Yes, I did, but it _____ _____ _____ _____. I was so upset.

W I'm sorry to hear that.

carousel 회전식 원형 컨베이어

13 대화를 듣고, 남자의 마지막 말에 이어질 여자의 말로 가장 적절한 것을 고르시오.

W Do you _____ _____ _____ your new roommate?

M Well, to be honest with you, I need some advice about how to _____ _____ _____ with your brother, my new roommate.

W What's the problem?

M Paul is a good roommate overall, but he does some things that _____ _____ _____.

W Can you be more specific?

M Well, he's kind of lazy. He _____ his _____ _____ everywhere, and he never _____ _____ the kitchen counter after he uses it.

W That sounds like Paul.

M What do you mean?

W　He really is a good guy, but he is not

_____ _____ _____

anything for himself.

M　Hmm, then what should I do?

W　You really ought to have a talk with him.

●●

advice 조언, 충고　**overall** 전반적으로　**drive** ~하게 만들다
specific 구체적인　**for oneself** 혼자서

14 대화를 듣고, 여자의 마지막 말에 이어질 남자의 말로
가장 적절한 것을 고르시오.

W　Hello. This is the _____ operator.

M　Help. Please help me!

W　Yes, sir. Please calm down and _____

exactly what _____ _____.

M　Okay. My car _____ _____ on

the road. I have a lady passenger, and

she's going into labor.

W　Now _____ _____ _____,

sir. Explain exactly where you are.

M　I'm... I'm in the _____ _____ of

the Lincoln _____ about 15 miles

from City Hall, and this lady isn't going to

wait.

W　Okay, now what's the _____

_____ to your location?

M　Umm, I see the Watson Discount Mall.

●●

passenger 승객　**go into labor** 출산이 임박하다　**lane** 차선
expressway 고속도로　**landmark** 주요 지형지물

15 다음 상황 설명을 듣고, Addy가 아버지에게 할 말로
가장 적절한 것을 고르시오.

Addy's father went to the _____

_____ a month ago. He came back

yesterday afternoon. Her _____

_____ went to the international

airport to meet him. Her younger brother

_____ _____ _____ and said,

"Daddy is over there." They all looked at

him. He looked fine. He had a big suitcase

in _____ _____ _____

_____. Addy thought he must have

_____ _____ _____ gifts

for them. She wanted to ask him, but she

didn't. Instead, she _____ _____

_____ _____ him about how his

trip was. In this situation, what would Addy

most likely say to him?

Addy: Did you have a good trip?

●●

spot 발견하다, 알아채다　**plenty of** 많은　**instead** 대신에
be about to 막 ~하려는 참이다

정답 및 해석 p. 89

A 다음을 듣고, 어휘와 우리말 뜻을 쓰시오.

① _____ ⑦ _____

② _____ ⑧ _____

③ _____ ⑨ _____

④ _____ ⑩ _____

⑤ _____ ⑪ _____

⑥ _____ ⑫ _____

B 우리말을 참고하여 빈칸에 알맞은 단어를 쓰시오.

① The _____ _____ is 1,200 dollars.
정가는 1,200달러야.

② It's too noisy for me to _____ _____ my work.
너무 시끄러워서 내 일에 집중할 수가 없어.

③ Do you _____ _____ _____ your new roommate?
네 새로운 룸메이트와 잘 지내고 있니?

④ I _____ _____ _____ about how to handle the problem.
나는 그 문제를 어떻게 다루어야 할지에 관해서 조언이 좀 필요해.

⑤ Be sure to _____ _____ _____ nine and check out these bargains. 9번 통로에 꼭 들러서 이 특가품들을 확인해 보세요.

⑥ I _____ _____ _____ _____ to eat a lot.
나는 음식을 많이 먹을 수밖에 없어.

⑦ I'd like to _____ _____ _____ _____, please.
저는 국제 전화를 걸고 싶은데요.

⑧ _____, she _____ _____ _____ ask him about his trip. 대신에, 그녀는 그에게 그의 여행에 대해서 막 물어보려는 참이다.

TEST 12

MY SCORE

_____ / 15

01 대화를 듣고, 남자가 찾고 있는 메모지의 위치로 가장 적절한 곳을 고르시오.

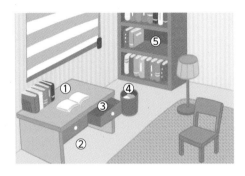

02 대화를 듣고, 두 사람이 대화하는 장소로 가장 적절한 곳을 고르시오.

① 식당   ② 서점
③ 박물관   ④ 유치원
⑤ 교수실

03 다음을 듣고, 여자의 직업으로 가장 적절한 것을 고르시오.

① 교수   ② 정치인
③ 건축가   ④ 뉴스 진행자
⑤ 영화 제작자

04 대화를 듣고, 두 사람의 관계로 가장 적절한 것을 고르시오.

① 간호사 – 환자
② 판매원 – 고객
③ 호텔 접수원 – 투숙객
④ 식당 지배인 – 종업원
⑤ 관광 가이드 – 여행객

05 대화를 듣고, 남자가 전화를 건 목적으로 가장 적절한 것을 고르시오.

① 진료 예약을 하려고
② 취업 상담을 신청하려고
③ 선생님에게 문병을 가려고
④ 수강 신청 일자를 문의하려고
⑤ 아들의 결석 사실을 알리려고

06 대화를 듣고, 그림에서 여자의 딸이 누구인지 고르시오.

07 대화를 듣고, 무엇에 관한 내용인지 가장 적절한 것을 고르시오.

① 다양한 운동 방법
② 하루의 적정 운동량
③ 스트레스를 받는 이유
④ 스트레스로 유발되는 병
⑤ 스트레스를 해소하는 방법

08 다음을 듣고, 다음 주의 날씨로 가장 적절한 것을 고르시오.

① strong winds
② sunny and hot
③ cloudy and rainy
④ cloudy and warm
⑤ rain showers and thunderstorms

09 대화를 듣고, 여자가 지불한 금액을 고르시오.

① $5   ② $25
③ $30   ④ $35
⑤ $40

10 대화를 듣고, 남자가 벌금을 급히 내러 가는 이유로 가장 적절한 것을 고르시오.

① 양심적인 운전자가 되기로 결심해서
② 여자가 서둘러 내야 한다고 독촉해서
③ 다음에 내러 갈 시간이 없을 것 같아서
④ 벌금을 내지 않아 면허가 정지된 적이 있어서
⑤ 기한 내에 내지 못하면 벌금이 두 배가 되어서

11 대화를 듣고, 여자가 파티에 갖고 가야 할 것으로 가장 적절한 것을 고르시오.

① 없음   ② 풍선
③ 피자   ④ 양초
⑤ 음료

12 대화를 듣고, 대화 내용과 일치하지 <u>않는</u> 것을 고르시오.

① 남자의 어머니가 아버지에게 화를 내셨다.
② 남자의 어머니는 요리를 잘하신다.
③ 남자의 아버지는 어제 집에 늦게 들어오셨다.
④ 남자의 아버지가 TV 채널을 계속 돌리셨다.
⑤ 여자는 남자의 어머니에게 공감하고 있다.

13 대화를 듣고, 여자의 마지막 말에 이어질 남자의 말로 가장 적절한 것을 고르시오.

① I can't follow you.
② That's very kind of him.
③ I promise it won't happen again.
④ Just around the corner on your left.
⑤ I would appreciate it if you did that.

14 대화를 듣고, 남자의 마지막 말에 이어질 여자의 말로 가장 적절한 것을 고르시오.

① Why are you so upset?
② Mind your own business.
③ You shouldn't give up so easily.
④ Relax. It could be worse, you know.
⑤ You must feel on top of the world now.

15 대화를 듣고, 남자의 마지막 말에 이어질 여자의 말로 가장 적절한 것을 고르시오.

① It was an earthquake under the sea, wasn't it?
② That's amazing. He was one of the few lucky ones.
③ I've never heard of an earthquake of that magnitude.
④ He was the bravest and strongest man I have ever known.
⑤ You don't have to look too far back in history to realize that.

01 대화를 듣고, 남자가 찾고 있는 메모지의 위치로 가장 적절한 곳을 고르시오.

M Ms. Jones, where is that memo from Mr. Horner?

W I left it _____ _____ _____ your desk this morning, sir.

M Hmm… I can't find it. Where is it?

W Did you _____ _____ _____?

M Yes, but it's not there either.

W Could it have dropped on the floor?

M Do you mean _____ _____ _____? Oh, here it is.

W Where is it?

M It _____ in the _____ _____.

●●
drawer 서랍 **underneath** ~의 밑에 **trash bin** 쓰레기통

02 대화를 듣고, 두 사람이 대화하는 장소로 가장 적절한 곳을 고르시오.

W Good morning. May I _____ _____?

M Sure, please. Have a seat here.

W You're the _____ _____, right?

M Yes, my name is Daniel, but you can call me Dan.

W Nice to meet you, Dan. I'm Nancy.

M _____ _____ _____ to meet you.

W I've heard many great things about you.

M That's a relief.

W Professor Kim _____ _____ _____ _____ you. He says you're great at doing research.

M Thank you. I'm new here, so you'll have to _____ _____ _____.

W I'll be more than happy to help you. Just let me know when.

M Thanks.

●●
relief 안심, 안도 **speak highly of** ~를 극찬하다

03 다음을 듣고, 여자의 직업으로 가장 적절한 것을 고르시오.

There are _____ _____ about the cost of living, housing, and rising inflation. Let me _____ _____ _____ _____ focusing on the economy. I _____ _____ _____, reform the welfare system, and restore moral leadership to this country. The people of this country _____ _____! They want a leader they can _____ _____, and that's what this campaign is all about: leadership. I _____ _____ _____ my beliefs, and I stand by my convictions.

●●
concern 우려 **tax** 세금 **reform** 개혁하다
welfare system 복지 제도 **restore** 복원하다 **moral** 도덕적인
conviction 신념, 확신

04 대화를 듣고, 두 사람의 관계로 가장 적절한 것을 고르시오.

W Welcome to the Happy Plaza. Do you _____ _____ _____?

M Yes, I do. I'll be _____ _____ three nights.

W What is your name?

M Andrew Smith.

W _____ _____ _____ _____ have a room with a view of the ocean?

M I would love to _____ _____ _____ _____.

W Here is your key for room 212. To get to your room, _____ _____ _____ on the right up to the second floor.

M Great. Thanks.

W If you have any questions or requests, please _____ _____ _____ _____ _____. There is also wi-fi available 24 hours a day.

M Thanks.

●●
request 요청, 부탁

05 대화를 듣고, 남자가 전화를 건 목적으로 가장 적절한 것을 고르시오.

W Saint Andrew Elementary School. How can I help you?

M Hi. Is this the _____ _____?

W Yes, it is. What can I do for you?

M I'm Gino Arlington, and my boy Louis is sick. He _____ be able to _____ _____ _____ today. He is in the third grade in Mrs. Smith's class.

W Aw, that's too bad. Has he _____ _____ _____?

M No, I'm afraid it's an ear infection.

W Poor Louis. _____ me who his teacher is.

M Becky Smith. Please let her know _____ _____ _____.

●●
secretary 비서 **ear infection** 귓병 **remind** 다시 한 번 알려 주다 **absent** 결석한

06 대화를 듣고, 그림에서 여자의 딸이 누구인지 고르시오.

W That's my daughter over there. Her name is Candy.

M Where is she? She must be beautiful like you.

W She is _____ _____ _____ with the other kids.

M Which one is she?

W She's _____ _____ _____ _____. Can you see her?

M Do you mean the one playing with the blocks?

W No, the one _____ _____.

M Oh, I see her now. What a cute hairstyle!

W I _____ _____ _____ like that every morning.

●●
wave 손을 흔들다 **braid** (머리 등을) 땋다

07 대화를 듣고, 무엇에 관한 내용인지 가장 적절한 것을 고르시오.

W What do you do to _____ your _____?

M Well, I don't do anything. That's the problem. What do you do?

W I have a _____ _____

_____, so that relieves a lot of my

stress.

M That's a really smart idea. Sometimes

I _____ _____ _____

_____.

W You need to do something about that.

Why don't you _____ _____

_____ _____ with me

tomorrow?

M All right. What time do you go there?

W 6 a.m. Do you still want to go?

M I think _____ _____ _____.

●●
relieve (고통 등을) 없애 주다, 완화하다 **routine** (매일 하는) 일과
gym 체육관

08 다음을 듣고, 다음 주의 날씨로 가장 적절한 것을 고르
시오.

The weather forecast is next on *Channel Six
News*. It looks as though the forecast for

the next week will be _____.
The clouds and rain over the last few

days _____ _____ in the next 24

hours. _____ _____ _____

_____ promise to be gloriously

_____ with temperatures in the early

to mid-thirties. Make sure to _____

_____ _____ _____ if you're

going to the beach this week. Enjoy it

while you have it because this great

weather _____ _____ _____

again _____ rain showers and

thunderstorms.

●●
as though ~인 것처럼 **outstanding** 매우 좋은, 뛰어난
disappear 사라지다 **gloriously** 기분 좋게, 멋지게
make sure to 반드시 ~하다 **sunscreen** 자외선 차단제
thunderstorm 뇌우(천둥과 번개를 동반한 비)

09 대화를 듣고, 여자가 지불한 금액을 고르시오.

M Please put your suitcase _____

_____ _____.

W Okay. Is it too heavy?

M _____ _____ for each bag is

_____ kilograms.

W How heavy is mine?

M It is 32 kilograms. You have to pay

_____ _____ _____ _____

_____ _____ over the limit.

W That seems a little excessive.

M I'm sorry, but _____ _____

_____.

W Well, then here's the cash.

M Thank you. Enjoy your flight.

●●
scale 저울 **limit** 제한, 한도

10 대화를 듣고, 남자가 벌금을 급히 내러 가는 이유로
가장 적절한 것을 고르시오.

W Where are you going in such a hurry,

Jake?

M I have to _____ this _____

_____ within two days, or the

_____ _____.

W Really? I've never heard of something like

that.

M It's true. The ticket is 25 dollars, but

if I _____ _____ _____

_____, it will be 50 dollars.

W I suppose that's a good way to get people

to pay on time.

M You're probably right about that. It just

never feels good _____ _____

_____.

W I don't drive that often, so it's not a big problem for me.

M I drive everywhere, so I have to be _____ _____ _____ _____.

11 대화를 듣고, 여자가 파티에 갖고 가야 할 것으로 가장 적절한 것을 고르시오.

W Hello, Paul. It's Cindy. I just _____ _____ _____ to your party.

M Can you make it?

W Well, let me see. It's next Saturday evening at 7:00 _____ _____ _____, right?

M That's right. I hope you can come.

W It would be my pleasure. Can I _____ _____?

M _____ _____.

W Okay. I'll be glad to go. I'm looking forward to it.

M _____ _____ _____ _____ seeing you then.

W See you then.

12 대화를 듣고, 대화 내용과 일치하지 <u>않는</u> 것을 고르시오.

M My mother _____ _____ _____ with my father yesterday evening.

W Why? Did he complain about her cooking?

M Oh, no. She's _____ _____ _____.

W Did he come home late?

M No. It was when they were watching television.

W While watching TV? What made her _____ _____?

M My father _____ _____ _____ _____ with the remote control.

W That can be _____. My younger brother does it all the time.

13 대화를 듣고, 여자의 마지막 말에 이어질 남자의 말로 가장 적절한 것을 고르시오.

W Mike, the light in the basement has _____ _____.

M I'll _____ _____ _____ in a minute.

W No, no. I already tried that, but it still doesn't work.

M Maybe there's a short. Did you try the fuse box?

W Yes, and that _____ _____ _____.

M Then we should call an electrician, shouldn't we?

W Do you _____ _____ _____?

M It's on the bulletin board.

W I'll _____ _____ _____ right away.

M <u>I would appreciate it if you did that.</u>

DICTATION 12

••
basement 지하실 **replace** 갈다, 교체하다 **bulb** 전구
fuse box 두꺼비집 **electrician** 전기 기사
bulletin board 게시판

14 대화를 듣고, 남자의 마지막 말에 이어질 여자의 말로
가장 적절한 것을 고르시오.

W What's the matter? You look really

_____.

M I just got my _____ _____. I
failed.

W You flunked? How could that be? You

_____ _____ _____

_____ for months.

M Apparently, that wasn't enough.

W I'm really _____ _____

_____ _____.

M So am I.

W You can try again next year. Cheer up.

M I don't know. Maybe I _____

_____ _____ be a lawyer.

W You shouldn't give up so easily.

••
depressed 의기소침한, 우울한 **flunk** (시험에) 떨어지다
apparently 분명히

15 대화를 듣고, 남자의 마지막 말에 이어질 여자의 말로
가장 적절한 것을 고르시오.

M Have you _____ _____

_____ on TV from the countries
affected by the tsunami _____?

W Yes, I've been really depressed by all the
sad stories.

M Me, too. Many of the people who live

there have _____ _____

_____ _____, and the survivors
seem to be stunned by the disaster.

W I know. If that had happened to me, I
don't know what I _____ _____

_____.

M On the other hand, there have been

some _____ _____ _____.

W I haven't heard any of those.

M There was one man who managed to

_____ _____ _____ the top
of a tree after the tsunami carried him
inland.

W That's amazing. He was one of the few
lucky ones.

••
stunned 망연자실한 **on the other hand** 반면에
manage to 간신히 ~하다 **hang on to** ~을 꽉 붙잡다
inland 오지로, 내륙으로

A 다음을 듣고, 어휘와 우리말 뜻을 쓰시오.

1. _____ _____
2. _____ _____
3. _____ _____
4. _____ _____
5. _____ _____
6. _____ _____
7. _____ _____
8. _____ _____
9. _____ _____
10. _____ _____
11. _____ _____
12. _____ _____

B 우리말을 참고하여 빈칸에 알맞은 단어를 쓰시오.

1. What do you do to _____ your _____?
   스트레스를 해소하기 위해서 넌 무얼 하니?

2. My father kept changing the channels with the _____ _____.
   우리 아버지는 리모컨으로 채널을 계속 돌리셨어.

3. I have a(n) _____ _____ _____.
   나는 규칙적인 운동 일과를 갖고 있다.

4. I'll _____ _____ _____ in a minute.
   내가 금방 전구를 갈게요.

5. Please let her know _____ _____ _____.
   그가 결석할 거라고 그녀에게 알려 주세요.

6. I _____ _____ _____ like that every morning.
   내가 매일 아침 그녀의 머리카락을 그렇게 땋아 준다구.

7. Professor Kim _____ you.
   김 교수님께서는 당신을 아주 극찬하세요.

8. _____ _____ _____, there have been some incredible stories.
   반면에 몇 개의 놀라운 소식들이 있었지.

01 대화를 듣고, 두 사람이 만나기로 한 시각을 고르시오.

①

②

③

④

⑤

02 대화를 듣고, 두 사람이 대화하는 장소로 가장 적절한 곳을 고르시오.

① 학교　　　　② 병원
③ 사무실　　　④ 기차역
⑤ 슈퍼마켓

03 다음을 듣고, 남자가 설명하고 있는 운동 종목으로 가장 적절한 것을 고르시오.

① 축구, 야구　　　② 배구, 축구
③ 배구, 농구　　　④ 농구, 테니스
⑤ 테니스, 배구

04 대화를 듣고, 두 사람의 관계로 가장 적절한 것을 고르시오.

① 승무원 - 승객
② 교통경찰 - 시민
③ 변호사 - 의뢰인
④ 자동차 판매원 - 고객
⑤ 렌터카 회사 직원 - 고객

05 대화를 듣고, 남자가 전화를 건 목적으로 가장 적절한 것을 고르시오.

① 자신의 아들을 찾으려고
② 여자의 출장 일자를 확인하려고
③ John이 집에 있는지 알아보려고
④ John의 휴대폰 번호를 물어보려고
⑤ 축구 경기를 보러 갈 것을 제안하려고

06 대화를 듣고, 머그잔의 위치로 가장 적절한 곳을 고르시오.

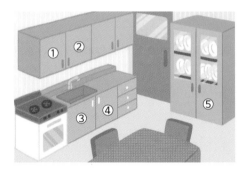

07 대화를 듣고, 무엇에 관한 내용인지 가장 적절한 것을 고르시오.

① 방과 후 활동
② 동물원 방문 계획
③ 토끼와 개의 다른 점
④ 반려동물 키우기의 어려움
⑤ 어린 시절 키우던 반려동물

08 대화를 듣고, 여자의 심정으로 가장 적절한 것을 고르시오.

① upset　　　　② hopeful
③ relieved　　　④ ashamed
⑤ depressed

09 대화를 듣고, 남자와 아들의 나이 차이로 가장 적절한 것을 고르시오.

① 15살   ② 19살
③ 20살   ④ 30살
⑤ 35살

10 대화를 듣고, 여자가 남자에게 충고한 것으로 가장 적절한 것을 고르시오.

① 부모님의 입장에서 생각해 보아야 한다.
② 부모로서 자녀에게 모범을 보여야 한다.
③ 항상 다음 기회가 있음을 기억해야 한다.
④ 자신을 위해서는 조금 이기적일 필요가 있다.
⑤ 목표를 이루려면 시간을 효율적으로 사용해야 한다.

11 대화를 듣고, 여자가 응급 전화를 건 이유로 가장 적절한 것을 고르시오.

① 여자가 아파서
② 여자의 여동생이 아파서
③ 여자가 교통사고를 목격해서
④ 여자의 집이 홍수로 침수되어서
⑤ 여자의 집에 야생 동물이 들어와서

12 대화를 듣고, 대화 내용과 일치하지 <u>않는</u> 것을 고르시오.

① Mary는 사람들과 대화하는 중이다.
② Mary는 예전에는 모든 사람들에게 친절했었다.
③ Mary는 협회 부회장으로 선출되었다.
④ 여자는 Mary의 행동이 바람직하다고 생각한다.
⑤ 남자는 Mary가 행동 방식을 바꿔야 한다고 생각한다.

13 대화를 듣고, 남자의 마지막 말에 이어질 여자의 말로 가장 적절한 것을 고르시오.

① You must be happy.
② They all know what to do.
③ I'll do my best to save you.
④ We should be very careful all the time.
⑤ I could have helped you if I had been there.

14 대화를 듣고, 여자의 마지막 말에 이어질 남자의 말로 가장 적절한 것을 고르시오.

① Of course I do. There is a jazz dance club.
② No, I don't. Could you fill out this application?
③ The speech club will give you a lot of opportunities.
④ You don't have to worry about making a lot of speeches.
⑤ Yes, I do. There are two clubs that teach you foreign languages.

15 다음 상황 설명을 듣고, Ben이 Paul에게 할 말로 가장 적절한 것을 고르시오.

① It makes me so mad when I do that!
② I'm really displeased with his behavior.
③ Let's go to the Customer Service Department to complain.
④ I can't sleep. There's something that is really bothering me.
⑤ Stop thinking about work and take it easy as much as possible.

01 대화를 듣고, 두 사람이 만나기로 한 시각을 고르시오.

W Hello.

M Hi, Jill. It's me again.

W Oh, hi. Did you _____ _____?

M Yeah. Are we meeting at seven or eight?

W We're going to _____ _____

_____.

M Ah, now I remember. Okay, see you

tomorrow night.

W No, wait. It's _____ _____

_____ _____, not eight at night!

M It is? Wow! I am all _____ _____,

aren't I?

•• **be mixed up** 헷갈려 하다, 혼동하다

02 대화를 듣고, 두 사람이 대화하는 장소로 가장 적절한
곳을 고르시오.

M Good morning, Kate!

W Oh, hi. How are you doing?

M Pretty good. And you?

W I'm just a little tired. Anyway, I _____

_____ _____ _____ lately.

M Well, I was away for a week. I had

_____ _____ _____ in Asia

last week.

W Oh, how did they go?

M Great! I made some _____

_____ on that trip.

W Good for you. But you must be

exhausted.

M Yes, I still have jet lag, so I'm going to

_____ only _____ _____

_____ today. By the way, are we

going to have a sales meeting at 10:30?

W That's right. We _____ _____

_____ a look at this sales document

_____ _____ _____ _____.

•• **deal** 거래 **jet lag** 시차로 인한 피로

03 다음을 듣고, 남자가 설명하고 있는 운동 종목으로
가장 적절한 것을 고르시오.

I'm going to _____ _____

_____. Men, women, and children like

sports. Some like tennis or _____.

Others like soccer or baseball. I'm going to

tell you first about two sports. One uses a

ball and a high net. Six players _____

the ball _____ _____ _____

with their hands. The other team _____

_____ _____. The other sport

uses a ball and two baskets. Five players

on each team use their hands to _____

and _____ the ball. Each team tries

to throw the ball _____ _____

_____ _____.

•• **volleyball** 배구

04 대화를 듣고, 두 사람의 관계로 가장 적절한 것을 고르
시오.

M I'd like to _____ _____

_____ for several weeks.

W Do you have a reservation?

M No, I don't.

W All right. I'll see _____ _____

_____ _____. Would you like

a subcompact, compact, mid-size, or

luxury car?

M I don't need much room, just good

fuel economy and safety. _____

_____ _____ _____?

W I have a minivan ready. Would that be all

right with you?

M Fine. How much _____ _____

_____?

W Well, if you rent it for a week or more, I

would recommend the unlimited mileage

plan.

M How does it work?

W You pay a flat rate for a week, and

then you can _____ _____

_____ _____ you want.

M Okay. I'll take it.

●●
subcompact car 경차 **mid-size car** 중형차
luxury car 고급 대형 승용차 **fuel economy** (자동차) 연비
safety 안전 **recommend** 추천하다 **unlimited** 무제한의
flat rate 고정 요금

05 대화를 듣고, 남자가 전화를 건 목적으로 가장 적절한
것을 고르시오.

M Hello? Is this John's home?

W Yes, it is. May I _____ _____

_____? My son isn't home right now.

M Hello, Mrs. Mester. I'm Scott Myers'

father.

W Oh, hello, Mr. Myers. How is your wife

doing?

M She's out of town on a business trip. I

am just _____ if Scott is _____

_____ _____.

W Yes, he was. But he and John _____

_____ to play soccer.

M Oh, I see. I just came home and found

that Scott _____ _____

_____.

W When they come back, I'll tell him

_____ _____ _____ _____.

M Thank you.

W Sure. I'll see you around.

●●
business trip 출장

06 대화를 듣고, 머그잔의 위치로 가장 적절한 곳을 고르
시오.

M Where do you _____ _____

_____? I need a cup of coffee.

W They're _____ _____ _____

over there.

M Which cabinet? Your kitchen is full of

cabinets.

W You're right. Sorry. It's the cabinet

_____ _____ _____.

M You have to be more specific than that.

W It's the _____ one _____

_____ _____, and it's directly

over the sink.

M Aha. Now I've found it.

●●
cabinet 수납장

07 대화를 듣고, 무엇에 관한 내용인지 가장 적절한 것을
고르시오.

M Look at those rabbits over there! Aren't

they cute? The kids seem very excited.

W Did you ever _____ _____

_____ when _____?

M Yeah, I had a pet rabbit called Mary.
I _____ _____ _____
_____ home after class every day
because I was always thinking about my
rabbit.

W What happened to her?

M Well, she lived _____ _____
_____ _____, and then she
died. She was really cute.

W That's too bad. I _____ _____
_____ a dog when I was _____.

M Did you have fun with him?

W Oh, yeah. I had the greatest time playing
with him.

M Pets seem to really _____
_____ _____ _____.

●●
childhood 어린 시절

08 대화를 듣고, 여자의 심정으로 가장 적절한 것을 고르
시오.

W Where were you yesterday? We
_____ _____ _____
_____ for lunch.

M I know, but something came up.

W Something came up? You _____
_____ at least _____ to tell me.

M There was no telephone around.

W What about your cell phone?

M Sorry. The _____ _____
_____.

W It seems you _____ _____
_____ for everything. I don't even
want to have you as a friend.

09 대화를 듣고, 남자와 아들의 나이 차이로 가장 적절한
것을 고르시오.

W Can I look at your high school _____,
honey?

M Sure. Why not?

W _____ _____ _____ _____
_____ in this picture? You look really
young here.

M I was 19 years old. That was such a crazy
time in my life.

W High school was fun, wasn't it? But now
we're _____ _____ _____.
Time really flies.

M _____ _____ me that I am
already _____.

W They say that the older you get, the
_____ _____ _____ _____
_____. Now our son is _____
years old.

M This is depressing. Let's change the
subject.

●●
yearbook 졸업 앨범

10 대화를 듣고, 여자가 남자에게 충고한 것으로 가장
적절한 것을 고르시오.

W How was your _____ _____?

M Well, I guess it was just okay.

W What do you mean by "just okay"?
_____ _____ _____ your
parents. They must have been very
proud of you.

M But I _____ actually _____
_____ _____ my ceremony.

W Why is that?

M　As you know, I _____ _____

　　_____ _____ next week. If I

　　fail it this time, then I have to spend the

　　entire year studying again.

W　_____ about it from your parents'

　　_____ _____ _____. Your

　　graduation ceremony must be very

　　important to them.

M　I know, but I _____ three _____

　　_____ flying there and back.

W　Come on. I'm sure you will get a good

　　result on the exam.

attend 참석하다　**point of view** 입장, 관점

11　대화를 듣고, 여자가 응급 전화를 건 이유로 가장 적절한
　　　것을 고르시오.

M　911. Where's the _____?

W　35 Oakhurst Lane.

M　What's your name?

W　Jenny Tyler. Please hurry. It's my little

　　sister. She _____ _____

　　_____ _____ by mistake, and

　　now she's very sick. I don't know what to

　　do!

M　Just calm down. A _____ _____

　　is on the way.

W　_____ the team _____

　　_____, please!

cleaner 세제　**rescue** 구조, 구출

12　대화를 듣고, 대화 내용과 일치하지 <u>않는</u> 것을 고르
　　　시오.

W　Do you see Mary over there?

M　Yeah. She's been _____ _____

　　these days.

W　Look at her! She only seems to be

　　interested in talking to the important

　　people here.

M　I know, but she wasn't always like that.

　　She used to be _____ _____

　　_____.

W　What made her change?

M　This started after she was _____

　　_____ _____ of the association.

　　It seems that she wants to _____

　　_____ _____ important people.

W　That's not the best way to behave if you

　　need everybody's cooperation.

M　That's true. She should realize what

　　she's doing and _____ _____

　　_____ she _____.

W　That's what I'm saying.

weird 별난, 이상한　**vice president** 부회장　**association** 협회
communicate 의사소통하다　**behave** 행동하다
cooperation 협력

13　대화를 듣고, 남자의 마지막 말에 이어질 여자의 말로
　　　가장 적절한 것을 고르시오.

W　I saw a _____ _____ on my way

　　to school.

M　How did it happen?

W　A truck driver was driving too fast

　　and _____ _____ _____

　　_____.

M　I wonder what happened to the people.

W　I heard that one person died and that the

　　truck driver was _____ _____

　　and _____ _____ a nearby

　　hospital.

M The other day, I failed to use my turn signal, and I almost _____ _____ _____ _____ _____. I was really lucky.

W <u>We should be very careful all the time.</u>

●●
oncoming 다가오는   **injured** 부상을 입은
turn signal 방향 지시등

14 대화를 듣고, 여자의 마지막 말에 이어질 남자의 말로 가장 적절한 것을 고르시오.

M Have you decided _____ _____ you're going to _____ ?

W No. Because I'm a _____, I don't know what clubs are on campus.

M Well, why don't you join the speech club?

W What's that for? Do you get to _____ a lot of _____ ?

M That's right. It helps you _____ _____ in public speaking.

W But I'm afraid of talking in front of many people. I think it's a bit _____.

M Then how about the yoga club? That will help you relax.

W _____ _____. Do you know any club that teaches you how to dance?

M <u>Of course I do. There is a jazz dance club.</u>

●●
freshman (대학의) 신입생, 1학년생   **public** 대중의
challenging 힘든   **boring** 지루한

15 다음 상황 설명을 듣고, Ben이 Paul에게 할 말로 가장 적절한 것을 고르시오.

Paul has been _____ _____ _____ all night. He can't sleep because he's _____ _____ _____. There was a new guy last week. The boss assigned the guy to help Paul on the _____ _____ that he's been _____ _____. The guy is supposed to be Paul's assistant. But he _____ _____ all of Paul's work and making a whole bunch of suggestions. Paul's so _____ that he _____ _____. His old friend Ben wants to advise him to _____ _____ _____ his _____ and to take things easy. In this situation, what would Ben most likely say to Paul?

Ben: <u>Stop thinking about work and take it easy as much as possible.</u>

●●
toss and turn 잠이 안 와서 몸을 뒤척이다   **assign** 선임하다, 맡기다
assistant 보조원, 조수   **criticize** 비판하다   **suggestion** 제안
take things easy 마음을 편히 하다

정답 및 해석 p. 105

A 다음을 듣고, 어휘와 우리말 뜻을 쓰시오.

① _____

② _____

③ _____

④ _____

⑤ _____

⑥ _____

⑦ _____

⑧ _____

⑨ _____

⑩ _____

⑪ _____

⑫ _____

B 우리말을 참고하여 빈칸에 알맞은 단어를 쓰시오.

① I still have _____ _____.

제게는 아직 시차로 인한 피로감이 있어요.

② A(n) _____ _____ is on the way.

구조 팀이 가고 있어요.

③ She's out of town on a(n) _____ _____.

그녀는 도시를 떠나 출장을 갔어요.

④ I made some _____ _____ on that trip.

저는 그 여행에서 몇 개의 큰 거래를 성사시켰어요.

⑤ Ben wants to advise him to _____ things _____.

Ben은 그에게 마음을 편히 하라고 조언하기를 원한다.

⑥ She's been elected _____ _____ of the association.

그녀는 협회의 부회장으로 선출되었어요.

⑦ Can I look at your _____ _____ _____?

제가 당신의 고등학교 졸업 앨범을 봐도 돼요?

⑧ Think about it from your parents' _____ _____ _____.

네 부모님의 입장에서 그것에 대해 생각해 봐.

MY SCORE

········· / 15

01 대화를 듣고, 남자가 예약한 시각을 고르시오.

①   ②

③   ④

⑤

02 대화를 듣고, 두 사람이 대화하는 장소로 가장 적절한 곳을 고르시오.

① 버스 안　　　② 거리 위
③ 전철 안　　　④ 비행기 안
⑤ 엘리베이터 안

03 다음을 듣고, 여자의 직업으로 가장 적절한 것을 고르시오.

① 군인　　　② 교사
③ 언어학자　　　④ 택시 기사
⑤ 기계 설계 기사

04 대화를 듣고, 두 사람의 관계로 가장 적절한 것을 고르시오.

① 은행원 – 고객
② 세입자 – 집주인
③ 택시 기사 – 승객
④ 이삿짐 센터 직원 – 고객
⑤ 부동산 중개업자 – 고객

05 대화를 듣고, 여자가 전화를 건 목적으로 가장 적절한 것을 고르시오.

① 쇼핑을 같이 가려고
② 운동을 같이 하려고
③ 불만을 이야기하려고
④ 점심 식사에 초대하려고
⑤ 일요일에 교회에 같이 가려고

06 다음 표를 보면서 대화를 듣고, Olivia가 탑승한 비행기로 가장 적절한 것을 고르시오.

	Flight Number	Arrival Time	From	Status
①	053	8:00	San Francisco	Delayed
②	694	8:20	Salt Lake City	On Time
③	705	8:35	Portland	On Time
④	950	9:00	Phoenix	Arrived
⑤	821	9:20	Los Angeles	Arrived

07 대화를 듣고, 무엇에 관한 내용인지 가장 적절한 것을 고르시오.

① 영화　　　② 음악
③ 잡지　　　④ 철학
⑤ 화가

08 다음을 듣고, 남자의 의견으로 가장 적절한 것을 고르시오.

① 스트레스는 만병의 근원이다.
② 휴식은 현대인들에게 필수이다.
③ 운동으로 삶의 질을 높일 수 있다.
④ 규칙적인 생활은 건강에 유익하다.
⑤ 현대인들은 운동할 시간이 없을 만큼 바쁘다.

09 대화를 듣고, 여자가 생각하는 남자는 어떤 사람인지 고르시오.

① 게으른 사람
② 안전을 중시하는 사람
③ 자기 안전만 생각하는 사람
④ 자기보다 남을 먼저 생각하는 사람
⑤ 쓸데없는 일에 시간을 낭비하는 사람

10 대화를 듣고, 남자가 표 값으로 지불한 총 금액을 고르시오.

① $30   ② $70
③ $90   ④ $120
⑤ $150

11 대화를 듣고, 남자가 여자에게 소리를 줄여 달라고 말한 이유로 가장 적절한 것을 고르시오.

① 에세이를 써야 해서
② 다른 음악을 듣고 있어서
③ 랩 음악을 좋아하지 않아서
④ 엄마가 소리를 줄이라고 해서
⑤ 옆집에서 시끄럽다고 연락이 와서

12 대화를 듣고, 대화 내용과 일치하지 <u>않는</u> 것을 고르시오.

① 여자는 차가 없어서 불편함을 느낀다.
② 남자는 작년에 차를 구입했다.
③ 여자는 새 차를 보러 갈 예정이다.
④ 남자는 여자가 차를 살펴보는 데 도움을 줄 것이다.
⑤ 두 사람은 오후 6시에 만나기로 했다.

13 대화를 듣고, 남자의 마지막 말에 이어질 여자의 말로 가장 적절한 것을 고르시오.

① I'd like to learn yoga from him.
② Why don't you come over here?
③ Yeah, I started about two months ago.
④ How do you know about my yoga teacher?
⑤ He has never learned yoga before, hasn't he?

14 대화를 듣고, 여자의 마지막 말에 이어질 남자의 말로 가장 적절한 것을 고르시오.

① It's too expensive.
② Well, they're a little tight.
③ I feel great this afternoon.
④ I want something cheaper.
⑤ You always sell good shoes.

15 다음 상황 설명을 듣고, Emma가 Jamie에게 할 말로 가장 적절한 것을 고르시오.

① You have to have medical examinations regularly.
② Keep your hospital gown on until after the surgery.
③ I don't think you'll be able to get through the night.
④ You're tough. You'll get back on your feet in no time.
⑤ Better than I thought I would. Thank you for coming by.

01 대화를 듣고, 남자가 예약한 시각을 고르시오.

W Endicott Beauty Salon. How may I help you?

M Hi. I _____ _____ _____ _____ go there without making an appointment.

W No, sorry. We work strictly by appointment.

M Well, when is _____ _____ I could make an appointment?

W You could come in tomorrow at 2:30, 4:30, or 6:00.

M _____ _____ _____ there in the morning? Say, 8:00 or so?

W I'm sorry, but that time _____ _____ _____.

M Then I'd like to _____ _____ _____ for 2:30 p.m.

W Okay. I'll see you tomorrow at 2:30.

•• **appointment** (병원·미용실 등의) 예약

02 대화를 듣고, 두 사람이 대화하는 장소로 가장 적절한 곳을 고르시오.

W Could you tell me _____ _____ _____ _____ Jongno?

M Are you going to drive?

W I am going to _____ _____ _____.

M Well, you had better take the subway. First, you _____ _____ _____ a bus at the bus stop _____ _____ .

W Which number should I take?

M Number 160. And _____ _____ at Sindorim Station.

W Get off at Sindorim Station?

M Yes, and then take the subway there.

W The green line?

M No, the blue line. Oh, you should be careful. Don't _____ _____ _____ _____ Incheon or Suwon.

•• **ought to** ~해야 하다

03 다음을 듣고, 여자의 직업으로 가장 적절한 것을 고르시오.

I could have done a lot of different things, but I _____ _____ _____ _____ for Tectonics. It's a challenging job. You see, my company manufactures industrial-use _____ _____ . It's too technical for most people, so I won't bore you with the details. Basically, I _____ _____ _____ and redesign them every time a new model _____ _____ . There are a lot of _____ in this _____ .

•• **manufacture** 제조하다 **industrial-use** 공업용의 **mechanical** 기계의 **equipment** 장치 **technical** 기술적인 **bore** 지루하게 하다 **basically** 기본적으로 **redesign** 다시 디자인하다 **expert** 전문가

04 대화를 듣고, 두 사람의 관계로 가장 적절한 것을 고르시오.

W Hello?

M Hello, Mrs. Andrews? This is Tommy from ABC _____ _____ .

W Hi. Have you found an apartment for me yet?

M Yes, I have a _____ _____ _____ _____ _____ on Park Avenue. It's 150,000 dollars.

W Oh, that's too expensive for me.

M Well, I have another one on Cook Street. It's only 95,000 dollars. But it _____ _____ _____ _____ .

W Oh, that's not big enough.

M Well, how about getting a mortgage?

W I think _____ _____ _____ _____ .

●●
avenue (도시의) ~가(街), 대로

05 대화를 듣고, 여자가 전화를 건 목적으로 가장 적절한 것을 고르시오.

M Hello?

W Oh, hello, Ken. How are you doing?

M Just fine. Thanks. How about you, Cathy?

W Can't complain. Well, Tony and I were wondering... Are you and Rosa _____ _____ _____ ?

M Sunday? Oh... We were _____ _____ _____ shopping on Sunday. Why? What's going on?

W Oh, we just thought it would be nice to _____ you _____ _____ _____ _____ .

M Well, let me talk about it with Rosa. I'll let you know for sure tonight. Is that all right?

W Okay. I'll be _____ _____ _____ .

M Sure. Talk to you later.

●●
for sure 확실히

06 다음 표를 보면서 대화를 듣고, Olivia가 탑승한 비행기로 가장 적절한 것을 고르시오.

M _____ _____ _____ is Olivia coming in on?

W I can't remember. It's _____ _____ ... something.

M Anyway, she's coming in from Phoenix, right?

W No, actually, her flight _____ _____ L.A.

M I thought she lived in Phoenix.

W She does, but she _____ _____ in L.A. to visit a friend on the way.

M Oh! Hey, is that her flight?

W You're right. _____ _____ _____ _____ . Let's hurry and meet her.

●●
stop off 잠시 들르다

07 대화를 듣고, 무엇에 관한 내용인지 가장 적절한 것을 고르시오.

W Do you like Mozart?

M Yes, Mozart is _____ _____ _____ , especially his *Marriage of Figaro*.

W It's very moving, isn't it? What about _____ _____ _____ _____ , for example, jazz?

M I also really like jazz. Miles Davis and Charlie Parker are the best.

W I didn't know you _____ _____ _____ _____ .

M I think everyone loves music. It's part of being human, I think.

W And a philosopher, too. You seem to be a
   very _____ _____.

M I don't think so, but thanks for the
   _____.

●●
especially 특히 **moving** 감동적인 **for example** 예를 들면
philosopher 철학자 **compliment** 칭찬

08 다음을 듣고, 남자의 의견으로 가장 적절한 것을 고르시오.

Fifteen to _____ _____ _____
_____ three days a week could perhaps
_____ _____ _____. Yet many
of us don't get any exercise at all. We work
or go to school, come home, eat, watch
television, and go to bed. The next day,
we _____ _____ _____.
Exercise makes us _____ _____.
We sleep better. We have more energy.
We are happier in general. Once we finally
decide to _____ _____ _____
_____ ourselves, our lives can
_____ for the better _____.

●●
relaxed 편안한, 긴장을 푼 **in general** 일반적으로
for the better 더 나은 쪽으로

09 대화를 듣고, 여자가 생각하는 남자는 어떤 사람인지 고르시오.

W What is that noise?

M It's the new _____ _____ I
   _____. It will tell us if there's a fire in
   the house.

W That's a great idea. Everyone should
   have one.

M It's _____ to _____ it once a
   month to make sure it works.

W You really _____ _____
   _____ about _____, don't you?

M Safety is so important. We can avoid a
   lot of unnecessary pain if we are smart.

W I _____ _____.

M I also check our door locks once a
   week to make sure they're functional.
   _____ _____ _____
   _____.

●●
install 설치하다 **important** 중요한 **make sure** ~임을 확인하다
unnecessary 불필요한 **functional** 가동되는

10 대화를 듣고, 남자가 표 값으로 지불한 총 금액을 고르시오.

M Guess _____ _____ _____
   today.

W Give me a hint!

M It's something you have always
   _____ _____ _____.

W I don't know. I give up. Just tell me.

M I _____ _____ for
   The Phantom of the Opera tomorrow
   night. The tickets were only _____
   _____ _____.

W Wow! Are you going to take me with you?

M Of course! Why do you think I bought
   many tickets?

W Thanks. Can I ask you who _____
   _____ _____ _____ for?

M It's for your sister. You once said she was
   crazy about that musical, too.

W _____ _____ of you! Thanks.
   Really, thanks.

●●
phantom 유령 **each** 각각 **be crazy about** ~에 푹 빠져 있다
thoughtful 사려 깊은

11 대화를 듣고, 남자가 여자에게 소리를 줄여 달라고 말한 이유로 가장 적절한 것을 고르시오.

M Julia!

W What?

M _____ _____ _____ _____, please.

W What's the problem? Don't you like rap music?

M Yes, I do, but I _____ _____ _____ _____ and listen to music at the same time.

W Are you saying you can't do two things _____ _____ _____ _____?

M Don't be sarcastic. Just turn it down, or I will call Mom.

W Okay, okay. Relax.

M Thank you. I'll _____ my essay _____ _____ _____, so you can turn up your music then. Okay?

W All right.

••
at the same time 동시에 **sarcastic** 빈정대는, 비꼬는

12 대화를 듣고, 대화 내용과 일치하지 <u>않는</u> 것을 고르시오.

W It's inconvenient _____ _____ _____ _____ _____. I always have to ask around for a ride.

M I know what you mean. _____ _____ I bought a car last year.

W So I'm going to look at a _____ _____ this evening.

M That's great. You're going to have a car.

W But you know I don't know anything about cars.

M Hmm... Do you want me to go with you and _____ _____ _____?

W Yes, it would be great if _____ _____ _____ _____ there's nothing wrong with it.

M No problem. What time shall we meet?

W At 6 p.m. Are you okay with that?

M Sure. See you then.

••
inconvenient 불편한 **That's why ~** 그것이 ~한 이유이다 **secondhand** 중고의

13 대화를 듣고, 남자의 마지막 말에 이어질 여자의 말로 가장 적절한 것을 고르시오.

W Hi, Tom. I'm glad that you made it. Come on in.

M Wow! _____ _____ _____ the party is in full swing.

W Yeah. Everybody is having fun. Oh, I'd _____ _____ _____ my sister, Jennifer.

M _____ _____ is she?

W She's sitting on the sofa over there.

M Do you mean the woman wearing the red blouse with the _____ _____ _____?

W That's right.

M Uh, and who's the man sitting next to her? The man with the _____ _____?

W Oh, that's Bob, my yoga teacher.

M Yoga teacher! I never knew _____ _____ _____ _____.

W <u>Yeah, I started about two months ago.</u>

••
in full swing 한창 진행 중인 **leather** 가죽 **be into** ~에 관심이 있다

14 대화를 듣고, 여자의 마지막 말에 이어질 남자의 말로 가장 적절한 것을 고르시오.

W What kind of shoes would you like, sir? We have _____ _____ _____ shoes.

M Well, I'm looking for some walking shoes. Would suede shoes be good for that?

W Yes, they would, but perhaps calfskin shoes _____ _____ _____ _____.

M Okay. Could you show me _____ _____ _____ each kind?

W Certainly, sir. What's your size, please?

M _____ _____ _____ _____.

W Here's a pair in your size. They are very good for the price.

M Could I try them on?

W Certainly. _____ _____ _____ _____?

M <u>Well, they're a little tight.</u>

●●
various 다양한 **casual** 캐주얼의, 평상복의 **perhaps** 아마, 어쩌면
calfskin 송아지 가죽

15 다음 상황 설명을 듣고, Emma가 Jamie에게 할 말로 가장 적절한 것을 고르시오.

Jamie was _____ _____ _____, and the news that she might only live up to six months was a _____ _____ to her, her family, and her friends. However, she was determined to look into all _____ _____ that might cure her or extend her life because she didn't want to leave her husband and lovely little daughter. She decided to look up _____ _____ _____ for hope of preserving her life. And Emma _____ _____ _____ her friend Jamie. In this situation, what would Emma most likely say to Jamie?

Emma: <u>You're tough. You'll get back on your feet in no time.</u>

●●
be diagnosed with ~로 진단받다 **cancer** 암
be determined to ~하기로 결심하다 **treatment** 치료(법)
cure 치료하다 **extend** (기간을) 연장하다, 늘이다
preserve 보전하다, 지키다

정답 및 해석 p. 113

A 다음을 듣고, 어휘와 우리말 뜻을 쓰시오.

① _____ _____

② _____ _____

③ _____ _____

④ _____ _____

⑤ _____ _____

⑥ _____ _____

⑦ _____ _____

⑧ _____ _____

⑨ _____ _____

⑩ _____ _____

⑪ _____ _____

⑫ _____ _____

B 우리말을 참고하여 빈칸에 알맞은 단어를 쓰시오.

① We have _____ _____ of shoes.

우리는 다양한 종류의 신발을 가지고 있답니다.

② _____ _____ I bought a car last year.

그것이 내가 작년에 차를 샀던 이유야.

③ I test it once a month to _____ ___ _____ it works.

나는 그것이 작동함을 확인하기 위해 한 달에 한 번 그것을 점검한다.

④ My company manufactures industrial-use _____ _____.

우리 회사는 공업용 기계 장치를 제조합니다.

⑤ She _____ _____ _____ that musical.

그녀는 그 뮤지컬에 푹 빠져 있다.

⑥ We can _____ a lot of _____ _____ if we are smart.

우리가 현명하면 불필요한 고통을 많이 피할 수 있다.

⑦ Our lives can change _____ _____ immediately.

우리의 삶은 즉시 더 나은 쪽으로 바뀔 수 있습니다.

⑧ I can't do two things _____.

나는 두 가지 일을 동시에 할 수 없다.

MY SCORE
.... / 15

01 대화를 듣고, 여자의 현재 몸무게를 고르시오.

① 95 pounds ② 110 pounds

③ 115 pounds ④ 156 pounds

⑤ 168 pounds

02 대화를 듣고, 두 사람이 대화하는 장소로 가장 적절한 곳을 고르시오.

① 식당 ② 병원
③ 시장 ④ 체육관
⑤ 영화관

03 다음을 듣고, 남자의 직업으로 가장 적절한 것을 고르시오.

① 가수 ② 군인
③ 교수 ④ 경호원
⑤ 비행기 조종사

04 대화를 듣고, 두 사람의 관계로 가장 적절한 것을 고르시오.

① 비서 - 사장 ② 기자 - 매니저
③ 면접관 - 지원자 ④ 의사 - 운동선수
⑤ 배우 - 영화감독

05 대화를 듣고, 여자가 전화를 건 목적으로 가장 적절한 것을 고르시오.

① 길을 물어보려고
② 소음에 항의하려고
③ 피자를 주문하려고
④ 부엌 리모델링을 의뢰하려고
⑤ 누수로 인해 도움을 요청하려고

06 다음을 듣고, 오늘의 날씨로 가장 적절한 것을 고르시오.

①  ②

③  ④

⑤

07 대화를 듣고, 남자가 생각하는 가장 중요한 자질로 적절한 것을 고르시오.

① 관용 ② 친절
③ 공감 ④ 도덕성
⑤ 호기심

08 대화를 듣고, 대화의 마지막에 남자가 느꼈을 심정으로 가장 적절한 것을 고르시오.

① furious ② jealous
③ worried ④ relieved
⑤ embarrassed

09 대화를 듣고, 두 사람이 이번 학기에 책 값으로 지불한 총 금액을 고르시오.

① $200   ② $300
③ $500   ④ $600
⑤ $900

13 대화를 듣고, 남자의 마지막 말에 이어질 여자의 말로 가장 적절한 것을 고르시오.

① I wish I could do that.
② I can't believe you did this to me.
③ Try not to think about what she said.
④ I'm really uncomfortable about her behavior.
⑤ I'm sorry. I'll be more considerate in the future.

10 대화를 듣고, 여자가 강아지를 싫어하는 이유로 가장 적절한 것을 고르시오.

① 대소변을 잘 가리지 못해서
② 강아지 털 알레르기가 있어서
③ 가끔 공격적인 행동을 보여서
④ 강아지에게서 특유의 냄새가 나서
⑤ 어렸을 때 개에게 물린 적이 있어서

14 대화를 듣고, 여자의 마지막 말에 이어질 남자의 말로 가장 적절한 것을 고르시오.

① Do you need anything else?
② I am sorry. I am not a pharmacist.
③ Why don't you go to a drugstore?
④ Oh, yeah. Why not? Show me your ID.
⑤ No, I can't give you any medicine without a prescription.

11 대화를 듣고, 남자가 해야 할 일로 언급되지 <u>않은</u> 것을 고르시오.

① 욕실 청소   ② 책상 정리
③ 부엌 청소   ④ 잠자리 정돈
⑤ 장난감 정리

15 다음 상황 설명을 듣고, Bob이 Laura에게 할 말로 가장 적절한 것을 고르시오.

① It's better if you don't get it wet for a couple of days.
② You have to know how to handle this kind of situation.
③ You should check who's out there before opening the door.
④ I think you should be more careful when you drive in the dark.
⑤ I don't appreciate your attitude. I'm so angry that I'm speechless.

12 대화를 듣고, 대화 내용과 일치하지 <u>않는</u> 것을 고르시오.

① 두 사람은 오랜만에 만났다.
② 여자는 요즘 피곤함을 느낀다.
③ 여자는 오늘 고객들을 만나기로 되어 있다.
④ 남자는 여자에게 할 일을 기록해 보라고 조언했다.
⑤ 남자는 여자가 일정을 기록하는 것을 도와주었다.

01 대화를 듣고, 여자의 현재 몸무게를 고르시오.

W My goal is to get down to 110 pounds by my twenty-fifth birthday.

M Isn't that _____ for someone _____ _____ _____?

W I'm only five feet six and a half inches.

M Wait. How tall is that _____ _____?

W It's about 168 cm.

M Really? Then you definitely _____ _____ _____ _____ pounds.

W But that's how much _____ _____ right now!

M Exactly. And you look very good!

••
goal 목표 **height** 키, 신장 **definitely** 확실히, 분명히

02 대화를 듣고, 두 사람이 대화하는 장소로 가장 적절한 곳을 고르시오.

M How's that pasta _____ _____?

W It's delicious. How's your dish?

M Not bad. But it's not as good as _____ _____.

W Do you _____ _____ _____ of my pasta?

M Sure.

W Do you love pasta?

M Who doesn't like pasta?

W Well, it's _____ _____ _____ favorite _____ of food.

M It's not my favorite, but I like it. My favorite food is steak.

W Steak? I _____ _____ _____ meat. I _____ _____ to meat.

M No seafood for me. It makes me sick.

W That's too bad.

••
expect 기대하다 **care for** ~을 좋아하다 **seafood** 해산물

03 다음을 듣고, 남자의 직업으로 가장 적절한 것을 고르시오.

To be honest, I _____ _____ _____ just to earn money for college. I wasn't even interested in _____ _____. Strangely enough though, after _____ my two-year _____, I didn't want to leave. Of course, I was lucky to have really _____ _____ who taught me a lot. I _____ all about _____, and I even got special training as a communications expert. You can't learn _____ _____ _____ _____ anywhere else. That's for sure.

••
to be honest 솔직히 말하자면 **national defense** 국방 **commitment** 복무, 책무 **weapon** 무기

04 대화를 듣고, 두 사람의 관계로 가장 적절한 것을 고르시오.

M Hello?

W Hello? Is this Mia's phone?

M Yes. But I am her manager. She is _____ _____. What can I do for you?

W My name is Sandra. I'm with *News Magazine*. My magazine has decided to do a story about her new album and _____ with her. If it's possible, can I see her today?

M Well, she just _____ _____ at 3 p.m., so if you don't mind, she can see you for half an hour. Is this enough?

W Yes. That's perfect.

M Then _____ _____ _____ meet in her office in Gangnam?

W Great! I'm _____ _____ _____ _____ you and Mia there.

at the moment 지금, 현재

05 대화를 듣고, 여자가 전화를 건 목적으로 가장 적절한 것을 고르시오.

M Hello? _____ _____. How may I help you?

W Hello, Mr. Smith? This is Ms. Cook.

M Uh, Ms. Cook... in apartment 1306?

W No, not 1306. 1308.

M Oh, right. What can I do for you? Is it the kitchen sink again?

W No, it's not the sink. The _____ in the bedroom _____ _____.

M All right. I'll be up sometime in the afternoon.

W _____ _____ _____ if you could come up right now. There's water all over the floor.

M That's a bad leak. _____ _____ _____ soon.

W Thanks a lot.

ceiling 천장 **leak** (물·가스 등이) 새다; 누출

06 다음을 듣고, 오늘의 날씨로 가장 적절한 것을 고르시오.

Good morning. This is Lucy Scott with today's weather. It's a _____ 49°F out there right now, but that will change soon. Highs today are expected to reach all the way _____ _____ _____ - _____ before going back down again as _____ _____ _____. Visibility will not be good today. The fog we're currently experiencing will _____ _____ _____, and the hazy weather will continue until tomorrow.

chilly 쌀쌀한, 추운 **reach** 이르다, 도달하다 **set in** 시작되다 **visibility** 가시도, 시야 **currently** 현재 **hazy** 안개 낀, 흐린

07 대화를 듣고, 남자가 생각하는 가장 중요한 자질로 적절한 것을 고르시오.

M My wife and I are going to have a baby.

W Congratulations! That's incredible.

M Thanks. I'm sure it's _____ to be a _____. We have to teach children the important things about life.

W I think generosity is _____ _____ _____. What do you think?

M That's important.

W Kindness is another thing. Teaching _____ _____ is good, too.

M You're right again. But I think the most important thing is _____.

W Why do you say that?

M A child should also learn to _____

_____ _____ _____.

W That's a good point.

••
generosity 관용, 너그러움   **share** 나누다, 공유하다   **empathy** 공감

08 대화를 듣고, 대화의 마지막에 남자가 느꼈을 심정으로 가장 적절한 것을 고르시오.

W Hi. How are you?

M Where have you been? I _____

_____ _____ in a month.

W I was in the hospital. I had to _____

_____ _____.

M An operation? What kind of operation?

W I had to _____ a large lump

_____ from my breast.

M Lump? Oh, my god. I can't believe it. Was it serious?

W No, the doctor said it _____

_____ and everything would be fine.

M _____ _____ it wasn't serious.

W Yes, I feel fine now. No need to worry.

M _____ _____ _____

_____ you're fine.

••
operation 수술   **lump** 혹   **remove** 제거하다   **breast** 가슴, 유방

09 대화를 듣고, 두 사람이 이번 학기에 책 값으로 지불한 총 금액을 고르시오.

W I _____ _____ _____

_____ university books are.

M What do you mean?

W One of my books _____ 100 dollars.

M I know. They are expensive. This semester, I spent _____ on books.

W It seems they're getting far too expensive. I had to pay _____

_____ this semester.

M But you got a scholarship, didn't you?

W School still costs too much. I have

_____ _____, too.

M Like what?

W You live at home, but I live _____

_____ _____. I have to pay 600 dollars every month.

M I guess I see your point.

••
scholarship 장학금   **expense** 돈이 드는 일   **dormitory** 기숙사

10 대화를 듣고, 여자가 강아지를 싫어하는 이유로 가장 적절한 것을 고르시오.

W What is that, Eric?

M It's my new puppy.

W _____ _____ _____ from me, please!

M Relax. He is _____ _____

_____ dog.

W I really don't care how gentle you think he is.

M _____ are you _____ like that?

W When I was a little girl, a dog _____

me _____ _____.

M Oh, _____ _____ you are so

_____ of dogs. Don't worry. He won't bite you. I've trained him well.

••
gentle 순한, 온화한   **bite** 물다

11 대화를 듣고, 남자가 해야 할 일로 언급되지 <u>않은</u> 것을 고르시오.

M Mom, can I go outside to play?

W Well, did you get your _____

_____ _____ done?

M Oh, Mom. Do I have to?

W You know the rules. No playing until your

_____ _____ _____.

M So what is my work?

W Well, first, you have to _____

_____ _____, including the

toilet. And don't forget to scrub the

bathtub.

M Is there anything else?

W Don't forget to wipe the walls. After

that, sweep and _____ _____

_____ _____, and be sure to

polish the table in the living room.

M Okay, I will.

W And then _____ _____

_____, pick up all your toys, and

_____ _____ _____.

••
chore (정기적으로 하는) 일, 가사 scrub 문질러 씻다
sweep (빗자루로) 쓸다 mop 대걸레로 닦다
polish (윤이 나도록) 닦다 make one's bed 잠자리를 정돈하다

12 대화를 듣고, 대화 내용과 일치하지 <u>않는</u> 것을 고르
시오.

W Richard, I'm so lucky to see you!

M _____ _____ _____

_____ since I saw you. How are you

doing?

W I'm not doing very well. I'm so _____

_____ _____.

M What's the matter?

W I have so many things to do. I don't know

_____ _____ _____.

M Tell me what you have to do today.

W I have to make a reservation call. And I

have to _____ _____ _____.

I also have to write a report to submit to

my company.

M First, _____ _____ what you

have to do _____ _____. You

will know what to do first.

W You mean recording today's schedule,

right?

M Yes, that's right. That way, you can

_____ your _____ _____.

W Thank you for your advice.

••
client 고객, 의뢰인 submit 제출하다 record 기록하다
manage 관리하다

13 대화를 듣고, 남자의 마지막 말에 이어질 여자의 말로
가장 적절한 것을 고르시오.

W I have a real problem.

M I'm shocked you said that. You're the one

who _____ _____ _____

_____ any problems.

W Thank you for saying that but...

M What's the matter with you?

W I work so hard during the week that

I'm _____ _____ _____

_____ anything on the weekend.

M So _____ _____ do you

_____ _____ during the week?

W I work until 10 p.m.

M If I _____ _____ _____

_____, I think I'd go home a little

earlier and then _____ _____

_____.

W <u>I wish I could do that.</u>

••
be in one's shoes ~의 입장에 처하다

14 대화를 듣고, 여자의 마지막 말에 이어질 남자의 말로 가장 적절한 것을 고르시오.

W Can I get some medicine here?

M Do you _____ _____ _____ from a doctor?

W Yes, I do.

M Let's see. I'll _____ the prescription for you. Here you are.

W How should I take the medicine?

M You should take it three times a day _____ _____ _____ _____.

W By the way, I have a terrible sore throat.

M How _____ have you _____ _____?

W For three days I used a throat spray. But it didn't help me. Can you _____ me _____ _____?

M No, I can't give you any medicine without a prescription.

●●
prescription 처방전, 처방 **sore throat** 인후통

15 다음 상황 설명을 듣고, Bob이 Laura에게 할 말로 가장 적절한 것을 고르시오.

Laura _____ _____ on the third floor of an apartment building. The front door has a peephole, a tiny piece of glass through which Laura can look out her door to _____ _____ _____ _____ on her door or ringing her doorbell. The peephole is a security device, but Laura _____ _____ _____. When someone knocks, she just opens the door. She thinks that she lives in a _____ _____, so security is not really a problem. But her friend Bob saw the news about _____ _____ _____ apartments where women live alone. He's _____ _____ _____. In this situation, what would Bob most likely say to Laura?

Bob: You should check who's out there before opening the door.

●●
peephole (문 등에 나 있는) 작은 구멍 **tiny** 아주 작은
security 안전, 보안 **device** 장치 **burglar** 강도, 절도범
break into ~에 침입하다

A 다음을 듣고, 어휘와 우리말 뜻을 쓰시오.

① _____ _____   ⑦ _____ _____

② _____ _____   ⑧ _____ _____

③ _____ _____   ⑨ _____ _____

④ _____ _____   ⑩ _____ _____

⑤ _____ _____   ⑪ _____ _____

⑥ _____ _____   ⑫ _____ _____

B 우리말을 참고하여 빈칸에 알맞은 단어를 쓰시오.

① Don't forget to _____ the _____ .

욕조를 문질러 씻는 것을 잊지 말아라.

② The _____ in the bedroom is _____ .

침실의 천장에서 물이 새고 있어요.

③ By the way, I have a terrible _____ _____ .

그런데, 저는 목이 몹시 아픕니다.

④ She is busy _____ _____ _____ .

그녀는 지금 바쁩니다.

⑤ _____ _____ _____ and put all your toys away.

네 잠자리를 정돈하고 네 장난감을 모두 치워 두거라.

⑥ _____ _____ _____ , I joined the military to earn money.

솔직히 말하자면, 저는 돈을 벌기 위해 군대에 갔어요.

⑦ That way, you can _____ _____ _____ .

그런 방식으로 당신은 바쁜 일정을 관리할 수 있어요.

⑧ I have to write a report to _____ _____ _____

_____ . 저는 회사에 제출할 보고서를 써야 해요.

01 대화를 듣고, 여자가 남자에게 <u>하지 말라고</u> 충고한 것으로 가장 적절한 것을 고르시오.

①   ②

③  ④

⑤

02 대화를 듣고, 두 사람이 대화하는 장소로 가장 적절한 곳을 고르시오.

① 병원 ② 방송국
③ 백화점 ④ 자동차 정비소
⑤ 중고차 판매장

03 대화를 듣고, 남자의 직업으로 가장 적절한 것을 고르시오.

① 형사 ② 사진사
③ 과학자 ④ 요리사
⑤ 연극배우

04 대화를 듣고, 두 사람의 관계로 가장 적절한 것을 고르시오.

① 약사 - 손님 ② 의사 - 환자
③ 코치 - 운동선수 ④ 면접관 - 지원자
⑤ 헬스 트레이너 - 고객

05 대화를 듣고, 남자가 예약한 요일과 시각을 고르시오.

① Thursday at 7:00
② Friday at 5:30
③ Friday at 6:00
④ Friday at 7:00
⑤ Saturday at 7:00

06 대화를 듣고, 여자 화장실의 위치로 가장 적절한 곳을 고르시오.

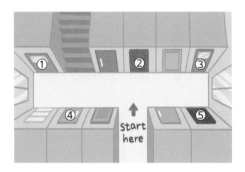

07 다음을 듣고, 약을 복용하지 말아야 할 경우로 가장 적절한 것을 고르시오.

① 휴식 중에 ② 식사 전에
③ 귀가 후에 ④ 취침 전에
⑤ 근무 중에

08 대화를 듣고, Kevin에 대한 여자의 심정으로 가장 적절한 것을 고르시오.

① angry ② proud
③ envious ④ worried
⑤ grateful

09 대화를 듣고, 남자의 가방에 들어 있던 귀중품의 대략적인 가치가 얼마인지 고르시오.

① $350　　　　② $500
③ $600　　　　④ $700
⑤ $800

10 대화를 듣고, 여자가 퍼즐 맞추기를 좋아하는 이유로 가장 적절한 것을 고르시오.

① 생각하게 만들므로
② 공부에 도움이 되므로
③ 자신의 무지함을 깨닫게 하므로
④ 시간을 때우기에 가장 좋으므로
⑤ 다른 사람과 함께 맞춰 나가면서 친해지므로

11 대화를 듣고, 남자의 마지막 말에 이어질 내용으로 가장 적절한 것을 고르시오.

① 맨해튼의 쇼핑 명소
② 우울증을 극복하는 방법
③ 뉴욕이 대도시가 된 이유
④ 고소공포증을 치료하는 방법
⑤ 미국에 고층 건물이 세워진 이유

12 대화를 듣고, 대화 내용과 일치하지 <u>않는</u> 것을 고르시오.

① 여자는 영어 수업 시간에 대화문을 암기한다.
② 여자는 암기가 영어 회화에 도움이 된다고 생각한다.
③ 남자는 암기하는 것에 어려움을 느낀다.
④ 여자의 암기 비결은 손으로 여러 번 쓰는 것이다.
⑤ 남자는 여자가 영어 회화를 잘한다고 생각한다.

13 대화를 듣고, 여자의 마지막 말에 이어질 남자의 말로 가장 적절한 것을 고르시오.

① Thanks a lot for your help.
② Please accept my apologies.
③ Okay, Mom. I'll be right down.
④ You're welcome. See you then.
⑤ Okay, let's cool down and think about this for a minute.

14 대화를 듣고, 남자의 마지막 말에 이어질 여자의 말로 가장 적절한 것을 고르시오.

① I had a little trouble catching a cab.
② I'll just give you a warning this time.
③ Yeah. Then we could get to work faster.
④ Why don't you ask somebody for directions?
⑤ My car broke down on the way to work this morning.

15 대화를 듣고, 여자의 마지막 말에 이어질 남자의 말로 가장 적절한 것을 고르시오.

① What are friends for?
② I hope to do even better next year.
③ Get on with your work while I'm away.
④ It was my pleasure to care for your parents.
⑤ Good. I was worried you wouldn't like this picture.

01 대화를 듣고, 여자가 남자에게 <u>하지 말라고</u> 충고한 것으로 가장 적절한 것을 고르시오.

W It looks like you _____ _____ _____.

M It's not that bad, is it?

W Well, you _____ _____ very _____.

M I know I can't jog.

W Mr. Johnson, I think it'll be _____ even to _____ on your leg.

M Oh, dear. How am I going to drive?

W Well, you should _____ _____ any _____ _____. It might put too much strain on your ankle.

M Yes, I understand.

●●
sprain 삐다, 접질리다 **avoid** 피하다 **object** 물건, 물체
strain 무리, 부담

02 대화를 듣고, 두 사람이 대화하는 장소로 가장 적절한 곳을 고르시오.

W Hi. I have a problem with my car. I _____ _____ _____ on the radio, and I thought that maybe you _____ _____ _____.

M What's the matter with it?

W It's the transmission. It's making _____ _____.

M Let's take a look at it. Is it _____ _____?

W Yes. It's over there.

M Wow! What kind of car is that?

W It's a 1949 Peugeot.

M No kidding. Where did you get it?

W I _____ _____ _____ a movie studio in Hollywood.

M Really? I've never seen one before. Anyway, let me _____ _____ _____ with the transmission.

●●
ad 광고(= **advertisement**) **transmission** (자동차의) 변속기

03 대화를 듣고, 남자의 직업으로 가장 적절한 것을 고르시오.

M Mrs. Rose, you _____ the convenience store _____, didn't you?

W Yes, I did. I _____ _____ _____ when he went into the store and when he came out.

M Now, look at these pictures. Do you see that man?

W Yes, he's the one! He's the man I saw!

M He _____ _____ when he went into the store, was he?

W No, he wasn't. He _____ _____ _____ _____.

M Now, do you see the woman in these pictures?

W No... Sorry, but I _____ _____ _____. The only thing that I can remember is that she was wearing a hat and sunglasses.

●●
witness 목격하다 **convenience store** 편의점
robbery 강도, 도둑질

04 대화를 듣고, 두 사람의 관계로 가장 적절한 것을 고르시오.

M Does this hurt?

W No.

M Or does this hurt?

W Yes. It's my leg — my left leg. I keep _____ _____ _____ in it.

M Could you describe this pain to me?

W It's like... like feeling pins and needles all over my left leg. I _____ _____ _____ well at all.

M Do you mean the pain has been keeping you awake?

W Yes. It's been _____ _____ _____ almost every night.

M Now, tell me... How long have you had this problem?

W The pain? _____ _____ _____ _____ now.

M I'd like you to rest for a few days and take this medicine. You _____ _____ _____ for a long time or exercise for a couple of weeks.

●●
describe 설명하다, 말하다 **pins and needles** 찌릿하는[저리는] 느낌 **awake** 자지 않는, 깨어 있는 **a couple of** 몇 개의, 두서너 개의

05 대화를 듣고, 남자가 예약한 요일과 시각을 고르시오.

W Carlson's Ritzy Restaurant. How can I help you?

M Hi. I'd like to _____ a table for four _____ _____ _____ _____.

W We already have quite a few reservations for Friday evening. What time do you want?

M I _____ _____ _____ sometime around 7:00.

W I'm so sorry, sir. We're _____ _____ for 7:00. Would 5:30 or 6:00 be all right?

M Yes, I suppose _____ would be _____.

W Wonderful. May I have your name, please?

M Sure. Please reserve it _____ _____ _____ _____ Noah.

W We'll see you then. Thank you for calling.

●●
reserve 예약하다 **acceptable** 그런대로 괜찮은

06 대화를 듣고, 여자 화장실의 위치로 가장 적절한 곳을 고르시오.

W Excuse me, but where's the _____ _____?

M Actually, we don't have any bathrooms in this office.

W _____ _____ _____ a bathroom somewhere in this building.

M You'll have to go out, turn left, and _____ _____ _____ _____ of the hall.

W The end of the hall. Okay.

M It's right _____ _____ _____.

W All right. I know where that is.

●●
ladies' room 여자 화장실 **hall** (건물 안의) 복도 **stairwell** 계단통

TEST 16   131

07 다음을 듣고, 약을 복용하지 말아야 할 경우로 가장 적절한 것을 고르시오.

Please _____ _____ _____

_____ take this medicine if you are

required to be alert. This product can make

you _____. Do not take this medicine

if you intend to do _____ _____

_____. It's better to take this medicine

while you are resting or just before bed. You

may _____ other _____ _____

from taking this medicine such as nausea,

dizziness, and headaches.

be required to ~해야 하다, ~하도록 요구되다
alert 정신을 차리고 있는, 기민한 **drowsy** 졸리는
side effect 부작용 **nausea** 메스꺼움 **dizziness** 현기증

08 대화를 듣고, Kevin에 대한 여자의 심정으로 가장 적절한 것을 고르시오.

W I can't believe Kevin got a better mark
  than me on the exam. I _____
  _____ _____ with his friends.

M That's just the kind of guy he is. He
  doesn't care how many people he steps
  on.

W Once, I also saw him pick on a girl
  because she _____ _____.

M Yeah, that sounds like him.

W I really _____ _____ _____.
  We should do something about him.

M You're not the only one.

W He _____ selfishness and
  indifference toward everyone else.

M You've got that right. Most people in our
  class _____ _____ _____
  _____.

cheat (시험에서) 커닝하다, 부정 행위를 하다 **pick on** ~을 괴롭히다
represent (~의) 표본이 되다 **selfishness** 이기심
indifference 무관심

09 대화를 듣고, 남자의 가방에 들어 있던 귀중품의 대략적인 가치가 얼마인지 고르시오.

W Can I help you, sir?

M Yes, my suitcase _____ _____
  _____ _____.

W What does it look like?

M It's big and black with a silver handle.

W Did you have any _____ _____
  _____?

M Yes, I did. I had my clothes, worth around
  _____ dollars, some books worth
  around _____ dollars, and a gold
  necklace worth around _____
  dollars.

W Did you buy _____ for your baggage?

M Yes, but the insurance is only for a loss
  of 500 dollars.

W Please _____ _____ _____
  _____. We will look for your suitcase
  and will call you as soon as we find it.

M Thank you very much.

valuables 귀중품

10 대화를 듣고, 여자가 퍼즐 맞추기를 좋아하는 이유로 가장 적절한 것을 고르시오.

W What is a three-letter word for a
  poisonous snake?

M Are you doing crossword puzzles again?
  Don't you ever _____ _____
  _____ them?

W _____ _____ _____, I love them. Come on. Help me out.

M Cobra? No, that can't be it. Oh, boa! No, that's not poisonous.

W Do you see? Puzzles _____ _____ _____.

M They _____ me too much. They remind me how much I don't know.

W Oh, well. I _____ _____ finding the answer.

M Oh, now I have it: asp. What do I win?

W You win my admiration.

●●
letter 글자, 문자 poisonous 독이 있는
on the contrary 그와 반대로 frustrate 좌절감을 주다
admiration 찬사, 감탄

11 대화를 듣고, 남자의 마지막 말에 이어질 내용으로 가장 적절한 것을 고르시오.

M Did you just get back from New York?

W Yes, at nine this morning.

M Tell me. _____ did you _____ _____ the skyscrapers there?

W Do you mean those _____ _____ buildings? As far as I could judge, they were _____.

M Why?

W They are too high. The sunlight _____ _____ the streets below. This makes shopping in Manhattan like walking down one long, dark corridor after another.

M Do you know _____ Americans _____ _____?

W To make me unhappy?

M No, silly. Let me tell you about it now.

●●
skyscraper 고층 건물 extremely 몹시, 극도로
as far as ~하는 한 judge 판단하다 corridor 복도, 회랑

12 대화를 듣고, 대화 내용과 일치하지 않는 것을 고르시오.

M What do you do in your English class?

W We memorize _____.

M Do you mean you _____ them _____ _____?

W Yes. Lots of them.

M What good does that do?

W When you memorize something, you can _____ _____ _____. I think it really helps me speak English.

M I _____ _____ _____ _____ memorizing things. How do you do that?

W I usually write dialogues on a piece of paper, and I _____ _____ _____ _____ all the time. Whenever I'm free, I always try to memorize them.

M That's why you are _____ _____ speaking English.

●●
memorize 암기하다 dialogue (책 등에 나오는) 대화
learn ~ by heart ~을 외우다

13 대화를 듣고, 여자의 마지막 말에 이어질 남자의 말로 가장 적절한 것을 고르시오.

W Peter, I'm going to the grocery store. Can you _____ _____ and _____ your little brother?

M Mom, I'm _____ my _____ now. Can you go there later?

W No, I have to get some meat and vegetables for dinner.

M Can't Dad watch him?

W He just went to the _____ to _____ _____. I'll be gone for 30 minutes.

M But what about my paper?

W You can _____ _____ _____ after dinner.

M Then can you buy me some ice cream?

W I will. I've got to go. _____ _____ now.

M Okay, Mom. I'll be right down.

●●
term paper 학기말 리포트

14 대화를 듣고, 남자의 마지막 말에 이어질 여자의 말로 가장 적절한 것을 고르시오.

W There is a lot of traffic at this time of day.

M It's always like this _____ _____ _____.

W This is the _____ _____ I've ever seen on this road.

M I'll say! We've been sitting in traffic for over an hour.

W If you look around, you'll see that in most cars, there's _____ _____ _____, the driver.

M You're right. That makes me mad. I think people should _____ _____ _____ like us.

W You're telling me. If everyone carpooled or took other _____ _____ _____, we could reduce traffic problems.

M We should start _____ _____ _____ to work tomorrow.

W Yeah. Then we could get to work faster.

●●
rush hour 출퇴근 시간대 **occupant** 타고 있는 사람
carpool 카풀(승용차 함께 타기)을 하다
means of transportation 교통수단

15 대화를 듣고, 여자의 마지막 말에 이어질 남자의 말로 가장 적절한 것을 고르시오.

W Hello, Steve. Long time, no see. I _____ _____ yesterday.

M Hi. Welcome back! Did you _____ _____ _____ _____, Sandy?

W Yes. It was wonderful. Fresh air, clear skies, and sunshine every day.

M Come in, and tell me more about your trip.

W I'd love to, but I have to go to the office now. I've _____ _____ _____ _____ _____ to do.

M Oh, Sandy.

W I just came here to _____ _____ _____. This is for you.

M Oh, thanks. It's such a beautiful picture. You shouldn't have done this.

W I really _____ you _____ _____ my kitty while I was away.

M What are friends for?

●●
look after ~을 돌보다

A 다음을 듣고, 어휘와 우리말 뜻을 쓰시오.

① _____ _____ ⑦ _____ _____

② _____ _____ ⑧ _____ _____

③ _____ _____ ⑨ _____ _____

④ _____ _____ ⑩ _____ _____

⑤ _____ _____ ⑪ _____ _____

⑥ _____ _____ ⑫ _____ _____

B 우리말을 참고하여 빈칸에 알맞은 단어를 쓰시오.

① I _____ him _____ with his friends.
나는 그가 친구들과 커닝하는 걸 봤어.

② Did you _____ any _____ in your bag?
당신의 가방 안에 귀중품이 들어 있었습니까?

③ There is a lot of traffic during _____ _____.
출퇴근 시간대에는 교통량이 많아.

④ You may experience other _____ _____ from taking this
medicine. 당신은 이 약의 복용으로 다른 부작용을 경험하실 수도 있습니다.

⑤ It looks like you _____ _____ _____.
당신은 발목을 삔 것 같군요.

⑥ You should _____ lifting any _____.
당신은 무거운 물건을 드는 걸 피하셔야 해요.

⑦ I'd like to _____ _____ _____ for four for Friday night.
저는 금요일 밤에 네 명이 앉을 테이블을 예약하고 싶어요.

⑧ If everyone took other _____ _____ _____, we could
reduce traffic problems. 만일 모든 사람들이 다른 교통수단을 탄다면, 우리는 교통 문제를 줄일 수 있어.

TEST 17

MY SCORE
········ / 15

01 대화를 듣고, 남자가 설명하고 있는 동작을 고르시오.

02 대화를 듣고, 두 사람이 대화하는 장소로 가장 적절한 곳을 고르시오.

① 공원　　　　② 마트
③ 세탁소　　　④ 미술관
⑤ 주유소

03 다음을 듣고, 남자의 직업으로 가장 적절한 것을 고르시오.

① 작가　　　　② 의사
③ 교수　　　　④ 판매원
⑤ 컴퓨터 프로그래머

04 대화를 듣고, 두 사람의 관계로 가장 적절한 것을 고르시오.

① 의사 - 환자　　　② 경찰 - 운전자
③ 변호사 - 목격자　④ 수리 기사 - 고객
⑤ 구급대원 - 운전자

05 대화를 듣고, 여자가 전화를 건 목적으로 가장 적절한 것을 고르시오.

① 피아노 가격을 물어보려고
② 피아노 레슨을 취소하려고
③ 피아노 레슨에 관해 문의하려고
④ 피아노 교사 자리를 알아보려고
⑤ 피아노 레슨 시간의 변경을 알리려고

06 대화를 듣고, 그림에서 여자가 누구인지 고르시오.

07 다음을 듣고, Papero의 기능으로 언급되지 <u>않은</u> 것을 고르시오.

① 얼굴 인식
② 목소리 인식
③ 숙제 돕기
④ 잘못된 행동 교정해 주기
⑤ 아이들과 놀아 주기

08 대화를 듣고, 남자의 심정으로 가장 적절한 것을 고르시오.

① excited　　　② gloomy
③ nervous　　　④ delighted
⑤ frightened

09 대화를 듣고, 두 사람이 다리를 건너기 위해 지불해야 할 왕복 요금과 이용 수단을 고르시오.

① $20 – 페리
② $20 – 자가용
③ $40 – 페리
④ $40 – 자가용
⑤ $80 – 자가용

10 대화를 듣고, 남자가 여자의 말을 믿지 <u>못했던</u> 이유로 가장 적절한 것을 고르시오.

① 자신의 가게에서는 빵을 매일 굽기 때문에
② 빵의 유통기한이 충분히 남았기 때문에
③ 여자가 전에도 여러 번 같은 이유로 불평했기 때문에
④ 남자가 아무도 믿지 못하는 성격이기 때문에
⑤ 여자가 갖고 온 빵은 남자가 판매한 빵이 아니기 때문에

11 대화를 듣고, 상황에 대한 설명으로 가장 적절한 것을 고르시오.

① 여자는 응급차를 운전하던 중이었다.
② 여자가 과속으로 경찰관에게 걸렸다.
③ 여자가 음주 운전으로 경찰관에게 걸렸다.
④ 여자가 경찰관의 운전면허증 제시를 거부했다.
⑤ 여자가 차선 위반으로 무인 감시 카메라에 찍혔다.

12 대화를 듣고, 대화 내용과 일치하지 <u>않는</u> 것을 고르시오.

① 남자가 사용하는 욕조의 수도꼭지에 문제가 있다.
② 여자는 남자의 집에 배관공을 보내줄 것이다.
③ 남자의 집에 있는 스토브의 버너가 고장 났다.
④ 남자의 전화기에서 발신음이 나지 않는다.
⑤ 여자는 전화 회사에 직접 전화할 것이다.

13 대화를 듣고, 남자의 마지막 말에 이어질 여자의 말로 가장 적절한 것을 고르시오.

① Right! I've got a stomachache all the time.
② Okay. It looks like we'll have to run some tests.
③ All right, but I need to take your blood pressure.
④ Yes. I had it checked during my last physical examination.
⑤ Yes. The nurse already told me some of your symptoms.

14 대화를 듣고, 남자의 마지막 말에 이어질 여자의 말로 가장 적절한 것을 고르시오.

① Perhaps you are right.
② What makes you so sure?
③ She's probably not going to come.
④ Can you give me some more time?
⑤ I think you should stay away from her.

15 대화를 듣고, 여자의 마지막 말에 이어질 남자의 말로 가장 적절한 것을 고르시오.

① I went to the wrong place.
② Are you being straight with me?
③ Then let's have lunch delivered here.
④ Really? Let's go somewhere else then.
⑤ You got it the last time. Let me get it this time.

DICTATION 17

01 대화를 듣고, 남자가 설명하고 있는 동작을 고르시오.

W Hic! Hic!

M Uh-oh. It sounds like you _____ _____ _____.

W Help me. Hic! How do I get rid of them?

M First, hold your breath, and _____ _____ your _____.

W Mm-hmm.

M Good. Now, with one hand, lightly _____ _____ _____ of your _____.

W Like this? Hic!

M Don't talk! Keep _____ _____ _____, or drink a glass of water.

hiccup 딸꾹질 **get rid of** ~을 끝내다, 제거하다 **breath** 숨, 호흡 **puff out** (공기를 채워) ~을 부풀리다

02 대화를 듣고, 두 사람이 대화하는 장소로 가장 적절한 곳을 고르시오.

M This is our newest piece. The _____ is incredibly _____.

W It's fabulous!

M Isn't it? Of course, all his oil paintings are _____ _____.

W Do you have any of his other pieces _____ _____?

M Certainly. In fact, the one behind you is his.

W Your showroom is _____ _____ beautiful _____!

M That's what we're here for: to _____ them all.

piece 작품 **talented** 재능이 있는 **fabulous** 굉장한, 멋진 **expressive** 표현이 풍부한 **for sale** 판매용의 **showroom** 전시실 **display** 전시하다

03 다음을 듣고, 남자의 직업으로 가장 적절한 것을 고르시오.

There are good parts and bad parts to this job. The pay is the best part. I was making 50,000 dollars a year straight _____ _____ _____ if you can believe that. I also feel like I'm on the cutting edge of _____ _____. On the other hand, it is boring. All I do is _____ line after line of _____. In addition, my eyes are getting bad from _____ _____ _____ all day.

cutting edge 최첨단 **stare at** ~을 바라보다, 응시하다

04 대화를 듣고, 두 사람의 관계로 가장 적절한 것을 고르시오.

W Mr. Rivers, would you please _____ _____ _____ what you were doing when the accident happened and _____ _____ _____?

M Yes, I was driving to work. It was about seven thirty in the morning, and there was a silver SUV in front of me. We were _____ _____ _____ Bread Street when a white car suddenly shot out from a side street. The silver SUV _____ _____ _____, but it was impossible. It _____ the white car.

W I see. Now, how fast was the car in front of you going when the _____ _____?

M The silver car? I guess 80 kilometers an hour.

W And the white car suddenly appeared _____ any _____ or _____?

M Yes, that's right.

W Thank you, Mr. Rivers.

••
shoot out 불쑥 나타나다 **run into** ~와 충돌하다 **warning signal** 경고 신호

05 대화를 듣고, 여자가 전화를 건 목적으로 가장 적절한 것을 고르시오.

M Hello.

W Hi. I'd like to speak to Cindy, please.

M I'm sorry. She hasn't gotten back yet. She is at lunch.

W Can I _____ _____ _____ then?

M Sure, just a minute. Let me get a pen. Okay. Go ahead.

W Can you tell her that her _____ _____ _____ _____ from 3:00 to 4:00? Tell her that if she has any questions, she should _____ _____ _____ call me.

M Sure. I'll tell her. Does she have your phone number?

W I guess so, but _____ _____ _____, I'll give it to you. It's 734-3100.

M Okay.

••
feel free to 마음 놓고 ~해도 괜찮다

06 대화를 듣고, 그림에서 여자가 누구인지 고르시오.

M Is this an old class photo of yours?

W Yeah. See if you can find me. I'm _____ _____ _____ _____ if that helps.

M Is this you with the short and curly hair?

W No, I _____ _____ _____ back then.

M Did you _____ _____ back then, too?

W Yes.

M Then this must be you. Wow! Look at all _____ _____.

W Yeah, I was the queen of big hair.

M You look better now.

••
middle 가운데, 중앙

07 다음을 듣고, Papero의 기능으로 언급되지 <u>않은</u> 것을 고르시오.

Papero is a childcare robot. Although it looks like a toy, Papero can _____ _____ and _____ and even respond to changing facial expressions. It can _____ kids _____ _____ _____ and even report misbehavior to parents via a built-in mobile phone and _____ _____. This robot could be a good substitute for a pet or a friend to _____ _____ _____.

••
recognize 인식하다 **misbehavior** 잘못된 행동 **via** ~을 통해 **built-in** (기계 등이) 내장된 **connection** 연결 **substitute** 대체물

08 대화를 듣고, 남자의 심정으로 가장 적절한 것을 고르시오.

W Hey!

M Aaaaahh! You _____ _____!

W I got you, didn't I?

M You shouldn't do that again. Do you want to give me a _____ _____?

W Sorry. I couldn't resist. You seemed _____ _____ _____.

M Now I forgot what I was thinking about.

W It was funny to see your _____.

M Yes, funny for you but _____ for me.

W Anyway, how are you?

M I'll be fine once I _____ _____.

●●
heart attack 심장마비 **resist** (하고 싶은 것을 하지 않고) 참다
thought 생각, 사고 **horrific** 끔찍한, 불쾌한

09 대화를 듣고, 두 사람이 다리를 건너기 위해 지불해야 할 왕복 요금과 이용 수단을 고르시오.

W Wow. We are going to Prince Edward Island, where the writer of *Anne of Green Gables* lived.

M We're _____ the toll bridge. Can you give me some money?

W How much does it _____ _____ _____?

M The cost to drive the car across the bridge is _____ _____.

W That's really expensive. Why is that?

M This is _____ _____ _____ in the world.

W Oh, really? I had no idea. How long is it?

M It's 16 kilometers long. Before the bridge was constructed, people _____ _____. The cost of a ferry then was 20 dollars.

W Do we _____ _____ _____ for the toll when we _____ _____ as well?

M No, we only have to pay when going to Prince Edward Island.

●●
approach 다가가다, 접근하다 **toll** 통행료 **bridge** 다리
construct 건설하다 **ferry** 페리, 나룻배

10 대화를 듣고, 남자가 여자의 말을 믿지 <u>못했던</u> 이유로 가장 적절한 것을 고르시오.

M May I help you?

W I bought _____ _____ _____ _____ in your store this morning. When I took the bread home, I noticed some _____ on it.

M That's impossible, ma'am. We _____ _____ _____ every day.

W Take a look for yourself. Do you see it?

M Well, I _____ _____ that you're right. There is mold on the bread. We are so sorry.

W Can I take another loaf?

M Sure. Please _____ _____ _____ do that.

W I'll take this one.

M Here's a coupon for a 25% discount on your _____ _____ here.

●●
loaf 덩어리 **notice** 알아채다 **mold** 곰팡이 **admit** 인정하다
purchase 구매

11 대화를 듣고, 상황에 대한 설명으로 가장 적절한 것을 고르시오.

M Can I see your _____ and _____, please?

W What seems to be the problem, officer?

M The _____ _____ here is 80km _____ _____. You were going 110km per hour.

W I didn't realize I was going so fast.

M The computer tells me you already have two prior speeding tickets. So I _____ _____ _____ _____ with a warning this time.

W I was _____ _____ _____ to go to the hospital to see my mother.

M Do you think that's an _____ for driving so fast? Please be mindful of the speed limit!

W Okay, officer. Here is my license.

●●
registration 등록증 **prior** 이전의 **let off** ~를 봐주다
be mindful of ~를 유념하다

12 대화를 듣고, 대화 내용과 일치하지 <u>않는</u> 것을 고르시오.

M Mrs. Kim, this is Sung-ho, your tenant in 302.

W Hi. What's up?

M There are a few problems with the apartment. First, the _____ in the _____ drips constantly.

W I'll ask the plumber to drop by and fix it tomorrow.

M In addition, one of the _____ on the stove _____ _____.

W What's the matter with it?

M I can't _____ the _____. I think you'll have to get an electrician.

W I'll see what I can do. Is that everything?

M Well, there's one more thing. I can't get a dial tone on the phone. It's dead.

W I'm sorry. There's _____ _____ _____ _____ about that. You'll have to call the phone company.

●●
tenant 세입자 **faucet** 수도꼭지 **bathtub** 욕조
drip (액체가) 똑똑 떨어지다 **constantly** 계속 **plumber** 배관공
control 조절하다 **dial tone** (전화) 발신음

13 대화를 듣고, 남자의 마지막 말에 이어질 여자의 말로 가장 적절한 것을 고르시오.

M Good morning, Jane. I haven't seen you for a long time. Please _____ _____, and tell me what seems to be the trouble.

W I'm not quite sure, sir. I feel generally weak, and I _____ _____ _____ out of bed this morning.

M Can you tell me anything more specific than that?

W I have had a _____ _____ and a headache since Saturday.

M Do you have a _____?

W I don't know as I have no thermometer, but my throat seems full of fire.

M Well, hold this thermometer in your mouth a minute while I _____ _____.

W Do I have a temperature?

M Less than a degree. But your _____ _____ seems very low to me. Have you ever _____ _____ before?

W <u>Yes. I had it checked during my last</u>
<u>physical examination.</u>

••
generally 대체로, 일반적으로 **stiff** 뻣뻣한 **thermometer** 체온계
pulse 맥박 **blood pressure** 혈압
physical examination 건강 검진

14 대화를 듣고, 남자의 마지막 말에 이어질 여자의 말로
가장 적절한 것을 고르시오.

M Are you _____ this Saturday?

W Yes, I think so.

M Do you _____ _____ _____
_____ with Julia and me?

W Well... I don't know.

M You just said that you don't have
anything special for this Saturday.

W To be honest, I always _____
_____ _____ Julia if I can.

M Why do you do that? I think she's fun.

W Perhaps, but she _____ _____
people's _____. She's nice to their
faces, but she criticizes them to other
people.

M I _____ _____ that.

W <u>I think you should stay away from her.</u>

••
stay away from ~를 가까이하지 않다

15 대화를 듣고, 여자의 마지막 말에 이어질 남자의 말로
가장 적절한 것을 고르시오.

M How about some coffee?

W That's a great idea. I _____ dead
_____.

M Where shall we go?

W Oh, we _____ _____ _____
_____ anywhere. There is a coffee
vending machine around that corner.

M Okay. Here is 1,000 won.

W Oh, no!

M What's the matter?

W This machine is _____ _____
_____. And I _____ _____
my money back.

M Forget it. Let's go to the coffee shop
across the street.

W The last time I was there, it was so
_____ that I had to _____
_____ _____.

M <u>Really? Let's go somewhere else then.</u>

••
out of order 고장 난 **crowded** (사람들이) 붐비는

● 정답 및 해석 p. 137

A 다음을 듣고, 어휘와 우리말 뜻을 쓰시오.

① _____   ⑦ _____

② _____   ⑧ _____

③ _____   ⑨ _____

④ _____   ⑩ _____

⑤ _____   ⑪ _____

⑥ _____   ⑫ _____

B 우리말을 참고하여 빈칸에 알맞은 단어를 쓰시오.

① We're _____ the toll _____.
우리는 통행료를 받는 다리로 다가가고 있어.

② Your _____ _____ seems very low.
당신의 혈압은 너무 낮은 것 같군요.

③ The van _____ _____ the white car.
그 승합차는 하얀색 차와 충돌했다.

④ The _____ in the _____ drips constantly.
욕조의 수도꼭지에서 물이 계속 떨어져요.

⑤ My eyes are getting bad from _____ _____ the monitor all day.
하루 종일 모니터를 보면서 내 눈은 나빠지고 있습니다.

⑥ _____ _____ _____ call me anytime.
마음 내킬 때 언제든지 내게 전화 줘.

⑦ This machine is _____ _____ _____.
이 기계가 고장 났어.

⑧ I bought _____ _____ _____ bread in your store this morning.
제가 오늘 아침에 당신의 가게에서 빵 한 덩이를 샀는데요.

MY SCORE

_____ / 15

01 대화를 듣고, 그림에서 여자의 동생이 누구인지 고르시오.

02 대화를 듣고, 두 사람이 대화하는 장소로 가장 적절한 곳을 고르시오.

① 해변 ② 숲속
③ 사막 ④ 박물관
⑤ 수족관

03 다음을 듣고, Nick의 직업으로 가장 적절한 것을 고르시오.

① 군인 ② 경찰관
③ 트럭 운전사 ④ 자동차 판매원
⑤ 비행기 조종사

04 대화를 듣고, 두 사람의 관계로 가장 적절한 것을 고르시오.

① 사장 - 비서 ② 의사 - 환자
③ 교사 - 학생 ④ 점원 - 고객
⑤ 운전사 - 승객

05 다음을 듣고, 여자가 전화를 건 목적으로 가장 적절한 것을 고르시오.

① 남편 생일 파티에 초대하려고
② 휴가 계획에 대해 물어보려고
③ 부모님의 병문안을 부탁하려고
④ 파티 장소가 변경되었음을 알려 주려고
⑤ 생일 선물을 보내 주어 고맙다는 인사를 하려고

06 다음을 듣고, 그림에서 남자의 가장 친한 친구가 누구인지 고르시오.

07 대화를 듣고, 여자가 구직 면접에서 가장 중요하다고 생각하는 것을 고르시오.

① showing off
② being likable
③ listening carefully
④ describing experience
⑤ appearing knowledgeable

08 대화를 듣고, 무엇에 관한 내용인지 가장 적절한 것을 고르시오.

① 남자의 당뇨병
② 남자의 식이요법
③ 여자의 체중 감량
④ 두 사람의 장래 희망
⑤ 여자의 건강 검진 결과

09 대화를 듣고, 남자가 환불받게 될 금액을 고르시오.

① $50 ② $350
③ $1,000 ④ $1,050
⑤ $1,400

10 대화를 듣고, 여자가 자신이 코미디언이 되기가 어렵다고 말한 이유로 가장 적절한 것을 고르시오.

① 말을 더듬어서
② 무대 공포증이 있어서
③ 유머 감각이 전혀 없어서
④ 코미디 공연을 실패한 경험이 많아서
⑤ 부모님이 코미디언이 되는 것을 반대해서

11 대화를 듣고, 두 사람이 동의한 점으로 가장 적절한 것을 고르시오.

① Einstein은 사실 천재가 아니다.
② 기술은 나쁜 용도로도 쓰일 수 있다.
③ Einstein은 음악가로서 더 소질이 있었다.
④ Einstein이 어떤 것도 발견하지 말았어야 했다.
⑤ Einstein의 발견 덕분에 많은 사람들이 치료받았다.

12 대화를 듣고, 대화 내용과 일치하지 <u>않는</u> 것을 고르시오.

① 남자는 전공을 변경했다.
② 남자의 원래 장래 희망은 회계사였다.
③ 남자는 회계학 수업을 좋아한다.
④ 남자는 음악가로서 생계를 유지하는 일이 어렵다고 생각한다.
⑤ 여자는 남자의 선택을 존중한다.

13 대화를 듣고, 남자의 마지막 말에 이어질 여자의 말로 가장 적절한 것을 고르시오.

① I don't know where exactly.
② We need to use sunscreen at the beach.
③ I'll never forget the time I spent with you.
④ Thank you for coming here to see me off.
⑤ As a matter of fact, I went to the beach every day.

14 대화를 듣고, 남자의 마지막 말에 이어질 여자의 말로 가장 적절한 것을 고르시오.

① See you next Monday.
② What dorm do you live in?
③ I think we should meet earlier than six.
④ We'll have to schedule these regularly.
⑤ I'm afraid I've taken up too much of your valuable time.

15 대화를 듣고, 여자의 마지막 말에 이어질 남자의 말로 가장 적절한 것을 고르시오.

① That sounds like a good idea.
② I wasn't expecting it to be so much.
③ I think you'd better tell your brother.
④ I didn't mean to get you in trouble. I'm sorry.
⑤ You'd better buy it some other time. It's too expensive.

01 대화를 듣고, 그림에서 여자의 동생이 누구인지 고르시오.

M What picture is that?

W Look. It's a picture of my friends. My sister is here.

M Your sister? Which one is she?

W _____ _____ _____.

M Is your sister wearing a miniskirt?

W No, she isn't. She's wearing the _____ _____ with a large _____ _____ _____.

M A ribbon? Then this lady must be your sister.

W Yes, that's right. She's a _____ _____ _____.

M Hmmm. You look like her.

W Yeah. Everybody says that.

••
waist 허리

02 대화를 듣고, 두 사람이 대화하는 장소로 가장 적절한 곳을 고르시오.

W It's so _____ out here. I love this place.

M Yeah, me, too. I love the smell of aromatic trees.

W There's nothing like a _____ _____ _____ _____ to put you in a good mood.

M Shhhh! Quiet! I think I _____ _____ _____ over there.

W Look! They are eating something. Wow! They are so cute.

M Oops! We _____ _____ _____.

W I'm hungry.

M I'm starving, too. Let's go to a rest area and have lunch.

W Good idea. Why don't we eat _____ _____ _____ back there?

••
aromatic 향기로운 **woods** 숲 **in a good mood** 기분이 좋은 **stream** 개울, 시내

03 다음을 듣고, Nick의 직업으로 가장 적절한 것을 고르시오.

Did you hear about Nick? He _____ _____ _____ _____ after he left the Air Force. He gets full benefits, including medical and dental coverage, plus he gets to _____ _____ _____ _____ _____. Even his family gets to travel for free. Of course, you know what _____ _____ are like: they give him a lot of _____ _____. He can handle it though. He still has one of the best safety records around.

••
Air Force 공군 **benefits** 복리 후생, 특전
including ~을 포함하여 **coverage** (보험의) 보장, 보상 범위
commercial 민간의 **airline** 항공사

04 대화를 듣고, 두 사람의 관계로 가장 적절한 것을 고르시오.

M Yes?

W Excuse me. There's a Mr. Smith

_____ _____ _____. He says he is your friend. Do you want to talk to him?

M No. _____ him _____ _____ later. I'll be in a meeting with Dr. Cook from now until 12 o'clock.

W I see, Mr. Johnson.

M By the way, do you think you could possibly _____ _____ this evening? I'm afraid there's some work I really have to finish, and I can't do it _____ _____ _____.

W Work late? I... I suppose so if it's _____.

M Thank you. You'll only have to work _____ _____ _____ of overtime.

●● **possibly** 혹시, 가능한 한 **necessary** 필요한, 필수의 **overtime** 초과 근무

05 다음을 듣고, 여자가 전화를 건 목적으로 가장 적절한 것을 고르시오.

M Please leave a message and your phone number _____ _____ _____.

W Hi, Max. This is Cathy. I hope you had a _____ _____. Thanks for your postcard. This Sunday is _____ _____ _____. We want you to be at the party. I told him you are my best friend. My family wants to see you, too. So I wonder if you can _____ _____ _____ _____ on Sunday afternoon. My friend really wants to see you, too. Can you call

me _____ _____ _____ _____ this message?

●● **beep** 삐 소리 **postcard** 엽서

06 다음을 듣고, 그림에서 남자의 가장 친한 친구가 누구인지 고르시오.

Today, I would like to introduce my friends. Look at the person on the _____ in the _____ _____, wearing a baseball cap and a T-shirt. That's me, Kyle. That is my friend, Susan wearing the polka-dotted dress and sitting right next to me. Another friend, David, is right behind me. He's wearing the _____ shirt and glasses. The next person is Mike, who is _____ _____. He is the one with shoulder-length hair. He is not wearing glasses, but he has _____ _____ _____ _____. Beside Mike, there's a girl with curly hair wearing glasses. Her name is Mickey.

●● **row** 줄, 열(列) **polka-dotted** 물방울무늬의 **checkered** 체크무늬의

07 대화를 듣고, 여자가 구직 면접에서 가장 중요하다고 생각하는 것을 고르시오.

W Wow, you are really _____ _____ today.

M Yeah, I have a _____ _____ today. Can you give me some advice?

W Sure. It's important to _____ knowledgeable, but don't look like a showoff.

M Got it.

W You should also talk about your related _____ _____ because most companies want to _____ _____ who already knows what they need.

M Okay. What else?

W _____ _____ _____ _____ is to be likable. If the boss likes you, that's half the battle.

M Thanks for the tip.

be dressed up 옷을 잘 차려 입다
knowledgeable 아는 것이 많은 **showoff** 자랑쟁이
related 관련된 **hire** 고용하다 **likable** 호감이 가는

08 대화를 듣고, 무엇에 관한 내용인지 가장 적절한 것을 고르시오.

W What are you doing there? Is that a _____?

M Yes, it is. I have to give myself an injection every day. I _____ _____.

W Do you have to do that every day?

M Yes, my body doesn't produce insulin, so I _____ _____ _____ what my body fails to produce.

W I've never known anyone with diabetes before. It's _____ to _____ _____ _____ every day, isn't it?

M After a while, you don't think about it. It becomes routine.

W Do you have to do that _____ _____ _____ _____ your life?

M Yes, I do. It's not such a big deal.

needle 바늘 **injection** 주사 **diabetes** 당뇨병
fail to ~하지 못하다 **get a shot** 주사를 맞다 **rest** 나머지

09 대화를 듣고, 남자가 환불받게 될 금액을 고르시오.

W ABC Airlines. How may I help you?

M I'd like to _____ _____ _____ for the return portion of my ticket.

W May I see your ticket?

M Sure. I _____ _____ _____ I can get.

W It's not much, sir. You paid 1,400 dollars for a _____-_____ ticket last year. We can only give you the money after we deduct the full price of a one-way ticket and the _____ _____.

M Then how much can I get?

W _____ dollars.

M Okay. _____ _____ _____, please.

refund 환불(금) **portion** 몫, 부분 **deduct** 빼다, 공제하다
one-way 편도의 **process** 처리하다 **request** 요청, 요구

10 대화를 듣고, 여자가 자신이 코미디언이 되기가 어렵다고 말한 이유로 가장 적절한 것을 고르시오.

M That joke was really funny. You really should think about _____ _____ _____.

W Do you really think so?

M Absolutely. I don't know anyone who has _____ _____ _____ like you.

W I just look at the world from a funny viewpoint. It's very natural to me.

M You really should go to a comedy club or something and _____ _____ people.

W I don't think I can. I have stage fright. I _____ _____ when doing something _____ _____ _____ people.

M You are truly unique. I hope you can overcome your _____ _____.

··
joke 농담 **viewpoint** 관점, 시각 **natural** 당연한
entertain 즐겁게 하다 **stage fright** 무대 공포증 **anxious** 불안한
unique 독특한 **overcome** 극복하다

11 대화를 듣고, 두 사람이 동의한 점으로 가장 적절한 것을 고르시오.

W What are you reading there?

M It's a book about Albert Einstein. He was truly a _____.

W I don't know much about him _____ _____ his famous Theory of Relativity.

M It says here in the book that after the atomic _____ _____ _____ during World War II, Einstein wished he'd never discovered anything.

W He must have _____ _____ _____ of what he had discovered.

M Yes. In fact, he was very depressed about it.

W I guess there are _____ _____ _____ _____ for any type of technology.

M That's true.

··
genius 천재 **Theory of Relativity** 상대성 이론
atomic bomb 원자 폭탄 **discover** 발견하다

12 대화를 듣고, 대화 내용과 일치하지 <u>않는</u> 것을 고르시오.

W Billy, I can't wait to hear all about your school life. Are your classes good?

M Well, yes, they are. But... I _____ _____ _____ to music.

W To music? But I thought you were going to be an _____.

M Yes, I know. I wanted to be an accountant until I took some accounting classes. I _____ _____.

W But if you get a degree in music, how will you support yourself?

M Well, I don't know. What I really want to do is music, but I know _____ _____ it is to _____ _____ _____ as a musician.

W Do you really want to do this?

M Yes. I want to be a musician.

W Well, if that's what you want to be, then that's _____ _____ _____ _____.

··
major 전공 **accountant** 회계사 **degree** 학위 **living** 생활비

13 대화를 듣고, 남자의 마지막 말에 이어질 여자의 말로 가장 적절한 것을 고르시오.

M Welcome back to San Francisco.

W Thank you for coming to the airport to meet me, Tony.

M My pleasure. Your parents and Sarah are now at home. They're _____ _____ your welcome-home party. Did you have a nice trip, Alice?

W Yes, I did. Everything was wonderful.

M That's good. _____ did you

_____ last night?

W I stayed at a hotel in Honolulu. I was in Hawaii for a week.

M I can guess how you spent that week in Hawaii. You're _____ _____.

W <u>As a matter of fact, I went to the beach every day.</u>

tanned 햇볕에 탄 **as a matter of fact** 사실은

---

14 대화를 듣고, 남자의 마지막 말에 이어질 여자의 말로 가장 적절한 것을 고르시오.

M Would you _____ _____ _____ _____ the campus concert with me tonight?

W I didn't know there was going to be a concert. Who's playing?

M A group _____ Zest will come.

W Oh, great! That group is my favorite.

M The concert starts at seven o'clock. Do you want to _____ _____ _____ _____ first?

W Sure, but I want to _____ the _____.

M I'd really appreciate that. My _____ are pretty _____ right now.

W Well, then I'll buy my own concert ticket, too.

M Fine with me. I'll _____ _____ to your dormitory at _____ o'clock.

W <u>I think we should meet earlier than six.</u>

expense 경비, 비용 **fund** (이용 가능한) 돈, 자금

---

15 대화를 듣고, 여자의 마지막 말에 이어질 남자의 말로 가장 적절한 것을 고르시오.

M You really look down. What's the matter?

W I'm _____ _____.

M What happened?

W I was going to dust the dresser. It turns out that my brother's camera was on the dresser, but I didn't see it. It _____ _____ _____ _____, and it looks like the lens broke.

M That's too bad. But don't be so _____ _____ _____. These things happen. You didn't do it intentionally.

W Yeah, but I could have _____ _____ _____.

M Well, your brother doesn't know it yet, does he?

W No. _____ do you think I _____ _____ _____ now?

M <u>I think you'd better tell your brother.</u>

dust 먼지를 털다 **dresser** 서랍장 **turn out** ~인 것으로 드러나다 [밝혀지다] **intentionally** 의도적으로, 일부러

○ 정답 및 해석 p. 145

A 다음을 듣고, 어휘와 우리말 뜻을 쓰시오.

① _____

② _____

③ _____

④ _____

⑤ _____

⑥ _____

⑦ _____

⑧ _____

⑨ _____

⑩ _____

⑪ _____

⑫ _____

B 우리말을 참고하여 빈칸에 알맞은 단어를 쓰시오.

① She is wearing the _____-dotted dress.

그녀는 물방울무늬의 드레스를 입고 있습니다.

② _____ my _____, please.

제 요청을 처리해 주십시오.

③ You are really _____ _____ today.

너 오늘 옷을 정말 잘 차려 입었구나.

④ Look at the person on the left in the _____ _____.

앞줄 왼쪽에 있는 사람을 보세요.

⑤ I was going to _____ __ _____ _____.

나는 서랍장의 먼지를 털려고 했어.

⑥ I'd like to _____ _____ _____ for my ticket.

표를 환불받고 싶은데요.

⑦ You should talk about your _____ _____ _____.

너는 관련된 업무 경험에 대해 이야기해야 해.

⑧ Walking in the woods puts you _____ _____

_____.

숲속을 걷는 것은 당신을 기분 좋게 한다.

MY SCORE

.... / 15

01 대화를 듣고, 두 사람이 대화 직후에 할 운동으로 가장 적절한 것을 고르시오.

① 　　②

③ 　　④

⑤

02 대화를 듣고, 두 사람이 대화하는 장소로 가장 적절한 곳을 고르시오.

① 버스 안　　② 택시 안
③ 배의 위　　④ 기차 안
⑤ 비행기 안

03 다음을 듣고, 여자의 직업으로 가장 적절한 것을 고르시오.

① 기자　　② 은행원
③ 만화가　　④ 운동선수
⑤ 실내 디자이너

04 대화를 듣고, 두 사람의 관계로 가장 적절한 것을 고르시오.

① 교사 - 학생
② 변호사 - 의뢰인
③ 경마 기수 - 기자
④ 카레이서 - 정비원
⑤ 마라톤 선수 - 코치

05 대화를 듣고, 남자가 전화를 건 목적으로 가장 적절한 것을 고르시오.

① 세미나 장소를 예약하려고
② Eliza와 오후에 만날 약속을 하려고
③ 행사 불참에 대한 양해를 구하려고
④ 발표 준비를 도와줄 것을 요청하려고
⑤ 세미나 시간이 변경되었음을 알려 주려고

06 대화를 듣고, 그림에서 통화 내용을 잘못 메모한 부분을 고르시오.

TICKETS FOR	① Baseball game
WHAT DAY	② Thursday
BE READY	③ By 5:30 p.m.
GAME STARTS	④ At 7:00 p.m.
WHERE	⑤ Main stadium

07 대화를 듣고, 여자가 할 일로 가장 적절한 것을 고르시오.

① 대학원 논문 쓰기
② 독서실에서 공부하기
③ 수학 가정 교사 구하기
④ 남자의 수학 공부 도와주기
⑤ 학교 수학 선생님에게 도움 요청하기

08 다음을 듣고, 남자의 심정으로 가장 적절한 것을 고르시오.

① lonely　　② pleased
③ satisfied　　④ regretful
⑤ disappointed

09 대화를 듣고, 여자의 성격으로 가장 적절한 것을 고르시오.

① 검소하다 ② 무례하다
③ 정직하다 ④ 사려 깊다
⑤ 욕심이 많다

10 대화를 듣고, 남자가 손해 본 총 금액을 고르시오.

① $10,000 ② $12,000
③ $14,000 ④ $17,000
⑤ $70,000

11 대화를 듣고, 여자가 걱정하는 이유로 가장 적절한 것을 고르시오.

① 아빠가 아끼는 꽃병을 깨뜨려서
② 친구가 빌려준 책을 잃어버려서
③ 부모님과의 약속을 못 지킬 것 같아서
④ 남자가 부모님께 자신의 실수를 말해버려서
⑤ 엄마께 사 드리기로 한 꽃병을 구하지 못해서

12 대화를 듣고, 대화 내용과 일치하지 <u>않는</u> 것을 고르시오.

① 남자의 아빠는 청혼할 때 엄마를 레스토랑에 데리고 갔다.
② 남자의 아빠는 청혼할 때 긴장한 것처럼 보였다.
③ 남자의 아빠는 청혼할 때 반지를 떨어뜨렸다.
④ 남자의 엄마는 청혼 반지를 찾지 못했다.
⑤ 남자가 엄마에게서 들은 이야기는 아빠의 이야기와 다르다.

13 대화를 듣고, 남자의 마지막 말에 이어질 여자의 말로 가장 적절한 것을 고르시오.

① Yes, it was a very interesting experience.
② Those kinds of situations put me in a bad mood.
③ Yes, I have three years of experience in this field.
④ Yes, I really hit the ceiling when I heard the news.
⑤ I think I would have a better opportunity at NS Soft.

14 대화를 듣고, 여자의 마지막 말에 이어질 남자의 말로 가장 적절한 것을 고르시오.

① Of course. Just take your time, and you'll do fine.
② Cheer up! You will get good grades next semester.
③ You're telling me. I'm sick and tired of your criticism.
④ Not really! Don't you have anything nice to say to me?
⑤ It's hard to understand. I need some time to think about it.

15 대화를 듣고, 여자의 마지막 말에 이어질 남자의 말로 가장 적절한 것을 고르시오.

① I'm sorry. I thought you were someone else.
② Sure, they respect each other as individuals.
③ You're right, but I think it's also kind of a generation gap.
④ My wife and I have our own separate hobbies and friends.
⑤ That's true! We should be more careful when raising our children.

DICTATION 19

01 대화를 듣고, 두 사람이 대화 직후에 할 운동으로 가장 적절한 것을 고르시오.

W So what should we play?

M Let's play volleyball.

W _____ _____ _____ play volleyball with only two people?

M Oh, I didn't think of that. Well, we can play tennis.

W That's not a bad idea, but I don't have a tennis racket. Do you _____ _____ _____ _____?

M No, I only have one. But I do have two _____ _____ _____.

W Okay. Now that sounds more like it. Follow me. My cousin _____ _____ _____ at her house.

M Sounds like fun.

02 대화를 듣고, 두 사람이 대화하는 장소로 가장 적절한 곳을 고르시오.

W Can you hold the rudder for a while? I need to go to the restroom.

M Sure, but could you _____ _____ _____ a little first?

W Why? You want to go slower?

M Yeah. This is my first time out _____ _____ after all.

W There's nothing to be scared of.

M I know. Hey, can you _____ _____ _____ _____?

W Here you go. You look a little pinkish.

M I burn so quickly with the sun _____ _____ the _____ like this.

••
rudder (배의) 키 **let out** ~을 풀어 주다 **sail** 돛
pinkish 분홍빛이 도는 **reflect** 반사하다

03 다음을 듣고, 여자의 직업으로 가장 적절한 것을 고르시오.

I was a troublemaker when I was a kid. I used to drive my mother crazy because I _____ silly faces _____ _____ _____ in my room. In high school, I caught a lucky break; the school newspaper _____ a comic strip of mine. Since then, I've done _____ _____ and even some print _____. I feel really lucky to be able to earn money doing exactly _____ _____ _____ _____.

••
troublemaker 말썽꾼 **silly** 우스꽝스러운 **wallpaper** 벽지
publish (신문 등에서) 싣다, 게재하다 **comic strip** 만화
advertising 광고

04 대화를 듣고, 두 사람의 관계로 가장 적절한 것을 고르시오.

M Sara, can I ask you a few questions?

W Why not? But I have to be at the _____ _____ in a few minutes.

M Okay. I'll make it fast. First of all, congratulations! It's the first time a woman has _____ this _____ _____. How do you feel right now?

W It's hard to express how happy I am in words.

M How long _____ _____

_____ here?

W For three years.

M But not with this horse!

W That's right. I've only been _____

_____ _____ since this year.

M You've done a great job in such a short

time.

W Thanks. I've got to go. If you have more

questions, please _____ _____

_____.

• •
contact 연락하다

05 대화를 듣고, 남자가 전화를 건 목적으로 가장 적절한
것을 고르시오.

W Hello. Eliza White's _____. How may I

help you?

M Hi. This is Stan Lincoln calling.

W Oh, hello, Mr. Lincoln. How have you

been?

M Just fine. I was hoping _____

_____ _____ with Eliza

sometime this afternoon.

W I don't know, Mr. Lincoln. Her schedule is

_____ _____ today.

M This is really important. I have to meet

her before tomorrow's _____.

W Well, how about if I ask her and then call

you back?

M That sounds great. I'm looking forward to

_____ _____ _____.

• •
presentation 발표, 설명

06 대화를 듣고, 그림에서 통화 내용을 잘못 메모한 부분을
고르시오.

M Hello.

W Hi, Bobby. It's me, Linda.

M Oh, hi, Linda. What's up?

W Bobby, did you get the _____ for the

_____ _____?

M Yeah, I'm going to pick them up this

afternoon.

W This is the first time _____ ever

_____ _____ a baseball game.

M It should be a lot of fun. They always are.

W I don't know a single thing about

watching baseball.

M Don't worry. _____ _____

_____ _____.

W Okay, and by what time should I be

ready?

M You should be ready by no later than

_____ _____ because the game

starts _____ _____ _____,

and we need to have dinner before we

go.

W No problem. We're going to the

_____ _____, right?

M That's right.

• •
no later than 늦어도 ~까지는 **main stadium** 주 경기장

07 대화를 듣고, 여자가 할 일로 가장 적절한 것을 고르
시오.

W Your teacher says you're _____

_____ in math.

M I know, Mom. I don't know what to do.

W What do you mean?

M I just don't get it _____ _____
_____ _____ a lot of hours
studying math in the library. I find math
so hard.

W If I had time, I would help you, but I
am also busy _____ a _____
_____ _____. Well, there's one
thing I can do.

M What is that?

W I have to _____ _____
_____ _____. You've fallen
behind, but you can catch up.

M Do you think it will work?

W Of course, it will. Sometimes a little help
can _____ _____ _____
_____.

M Thank you very much, Mom.

••
fall behind 뒤처지다, 낙오하다 **graduate school** 대학원
catch up ~을 따라잡다 **go a long way** 큰 도움이 되다

08 다음을 듣고, 남자의 심정으로 가장 적절한 것을 고르
시오.

My father is in the hospital now. He
_____ _____ eight months ago
due to high blood pressure. He has been
in _____ _____ since then. When
I got my mother's call last year, I couldn't
believe what I was hearing. I _____
_____ _____ lose my father, and
he was too healthy to suddenly be so ill. I
_____ _____ and eat for a while.
Now I talk to my father, but he _____
_____. There is one thing I _____:
I never told him how much I love him and
_____ _____ I am for him.

••
collapse 쓰러지다 **intensive care** 중환자실

09 대화를 듣고, 여자의 성격으로 가장 적절한 것을 고르
시오.

M Can I ask you something, honey?

W Sure. Go ahead.

M Why don't you _____ _____ a
new jacket?

W What's wrong with the one I have on?

M First of all, you've had it _____
_____.

W So what? It's still good.

M And second, it's worn out and _____
_____.

W You know I never buy anything
_____ I absolutely need it.

M I'm telling you that you need one. Why
don't you listen to me?

W I _____ _____ _____
_____ money. I'll buy a new jacket
when I think I need one.

••
first of all 우선 **worn out** 닳아 해진
fall apart 너덜거리다, 산산이 부서지다 **unless** ~하지 않는다면

10 대화를 듣고, 남자가 손해 본 총 금액을 고르시오.

M Do you remember when I said you should
_____ in the _____ _____?

W Yes. Why?

M Well, forget what I told you. The value of
stocks _____ _____ so much
over the last few months.

W How much did you lose?

M Around _____ dollars in the last two
months.

W That is a lot of money. My neighbor lost
17,000 dollars in two weeks.

M I may have to _____ _____

_____ if this trend continues.

W Maybe you should invest in something

else until the _____ _____

becomes stable.

M I've been thinking about that, too.

••
invest 투자하다 **stock** 주식 **value** 가치 **decline** 감소하다
economic 경제의

11 대화를 듣고, 여자가 걱정하는 이유로 가장 적절한 것을 고르시오.

M Why the _____ _____, Janet?

W If I tell you, do you promise not to tell my

parents?

M I promise. What's wrong?

W Today, I accidentally _____ my

father's _____ _____ in the

living room, and I'm afraid my parents

will be angry when they get home.

M I'm sure if you tell them honestly what

happened, they _____ _____

_____ _____.

W Are you sure?

M I think they will understand. We all

_____ _____.

W I hope you're right about that.

M Here comes your mother now. Just tell

her _____ _____.

W Okay. Wish me luck.

••
accidentally 뜻하지 않게, 우연히 **vase** 꽃병

12 대화를 듣고, 대화 내용과 일치하지 <u>않는</u> 것을 고르시오.

M Mom, can I ask you about something?

W Sure, what?

M What was it like when Dad _____

_____ _____?

W Well, let me see... Your father _____

me to a _____. We had a great

dinner.

M Was Dad nervous?

W Was he nervous? He _____

_____!

M And he gave you a ring, didn't he?

W Yes. That was the funny part. He got the

ring out, but he was _____ so much

that he _____ _____ under the

table. Anyhow, why are you so curious

about that?

M Well, our teacher told us to ask both our

parents about something and _____

_____ they said _____

_____ _____.

W And did we say the same thing?

M Uh, _____ _____.

••
curious 알고 싶어 하는

13 대화를 듣고, 남자의 마지막 말에 이어질 여자의 말로 가장 적절한 것을 고르시오.

M Where is your school _____?

W Oh, it's in Dongdaemun-gu.

M What's your major?

W I'm _____ _____ computer

engineering.

M Have you taken any business classes or

anything?

W Yes, I've taken accounting, programming,

_____ _____, and some others.

M Have you ever _____ _____ _____ _____ before?

W Yes, I had a _____ - _____ _____ at NS Soft for six months.

M Oh, really?

W <u>Yes, it was a very interesting experience.</u>

●●
computer engineering 컴퓨터 공학   **conversation** 회화, 대화

14 대화를 듣고, 여자의 마지막 말에 이어질 남자의 말로 가장 적절한 것을 고르시오.

M It looks like something is _____ _____.

W Well, I just feel like the sun will never shine again.

M Come on! What's up with you?

W My boss has just given me my first independent _____ _____ _____.

M That's great news. What's the problem?

W Well, I'm not sure I've got _____ _____ to do a _____ _____. I don't really think I'm good enough.

M Just relax, and everything will be all right. If he didn't think you were good enough, he _____ _____ _____ you the assignment.

W Do you really think so?

M <u>Of course. Just take your time, and you'll do fine.</u>

●●
bother 괴롭히다   **independent** 독립된   **proper** 제대로 된
assignment 임무, 과제

15 대화를 듣고, 여자의 마지막 말에 이어질 남자의 말로 가장 적절한 것을 고르시오.

W Do you feel _____ with people _____ _____ _____?

M Sure. I think I'm outgoing, so I have a lot of friends.

W How about older people?

M I can't pinpoint it, but there is something I _____ _____ about them.

W Have you ever _____ with your parents because of your _____ _____?

M Yes, I think they've put too many restrictions on me.

W Why do you think so?

M For example, they don't _____ me _____ _____ _____ after 10 o'clock at night. And they are strict about junk food, chores, and money.

W You seem to think that older people are _____ _____ toward you.

M <u>You're right, but I think it's also kind of a generation gap.</u>

●●
pinpoint 정확히 꼬집어 말하다   **private** 사적인
restriction 제약, 제한   **considerate** 이해심 있는

A 다음을 듣고, 어휘와 우리말 뜻을 쓰시오.

1. _____   _____
2. _____   _____
3. _____   _____
4. _____   _____
5. _____   _____
6. _____   _____

7. _____   _____
8. _____   _____
9. _____   _____
10. _____   _____
11. _____   _____
12. _____   _____

B 우리말을 참고하여 빈칸에 알맞은 단어를 쓰시오.

1. Please _____ me later.

   나중에 제게 연락해 주세요.

2. I have to meet her before tomorrow's _____.

   저는 그녀를 내일 발표 전에 만나야 합니다.

3. I never buy anything _____ I absolutely need it.

   나는 물건이 반드시 필요하지 않으면 그것을 결코 사지 않는다.

4. I am busy taking a(n) _____ _____ course.

   나는 대학원 과정을 밟느라 바쁘다.

5. I drew _____ faces on the _____ in my room.

   저는 제 방의 벽지에 우스꽝스러운 얼굴들을 그렸습니다.

6. Your teacher says you're _____ _____ in math.

   너희 선생님께서 네가 수학이 뒤처지고 있다고 말씀하시더라.

7. You should be ready by _____ _____ five thirty.

   너는 늦어도 5시 30분까지는 준비되어 있어야 해.

8. I've taken accounting, programming, English conversation, _____

   _____ _____ .

   저는 회계학, 프로그래밍, 영어 회화, 그리고 몇몇 다른 것들을 수강했습니다.

MY SCORE

_____ / 15

01 대화를 듣고, 여자가 할 일로 언급되지 <u>않은</u> 것을 고르시오.

①   ②

③   ④

⑤

02 대화를 듣고, 두 사람이 대화하는 장소로 가장 적절한 곳을 고르시오.

① 부엌　　　　　② 사무실
③ 미술관　　　　④ 커피숍
⑤ 버스 정류장

03 대화를 듣고, 남자의 직업으로 가장 적절한 것을 고르시오.

① 교수　　　　　② 기자
③ 작가　　　　　④ 편집자
⑤ 아나운서

04 대화를 듣고, 두 사람의 관계로 가장 적절한 것을 고르시오.

① 배우 – 매니저　　② 경호원 – 관객
③ 매표원 – 관람객　④ 수의사 – 애견 주인
⑤ 관광 가이드 – 여행객

05 대화를 듣고, 여자가 전화를 건 목적으로 가장 적절한 것을 고르시오.

① 꽃을 주문하려고
② 남자를 초대하려고
③ 스카프를 찾으려고
④ 승용차를 함께 타려고
⑤ 꽃집 위치를 물어보려고

06 대화를 듣고, 남자가 취하고 있는 동작을 고르시오.

①   ②

③   ④

⑤

07 다음을 듣고, 어떤 동물에 관한 설명인지 고르시오.

① 닭　　　　　　② 소
③ 개　　　　　　④ 판다
⑤ 고양이

08 대화를 듣고, 여자의 심정으로 가장 적절한 것을 고르시오.

① bored　　　　　② regretful
③ confused　　　　④ delighted
⑤ frightened

09 대화를 듣고, 현재의 영화 관람료가 20년 전에 비해 얼마나 많이 올랐는지 고르시오.

① 10배 ② 14배
③ 16배 ④ 18배
⑤ 20배

10 대화를 듣고, 여자가 극장에 가지 <u>못하는</u> 이유로 가장 적절한 것을 고르시오.

① 친척 집에 방문하기로 해서
② 친구들과 백화점에 가기로 해서
③ 엄마가 극장에 가지 말라고 해서
④ 사촌들을 마중하러 터미널에 가야 해서
⑤ 사촌과 시간을 보내기로 엄마와 약속해서

11 대화를 듣고, 남자가 오늘 오후에 할 일로 가장 적절한 것을 고르시오.

① 빵 굽기
② 집안 청소하기
③ 우유와 빵 사 오기
④ 텔레비전 주문하기
⑤ 저녁 식사 준비하기

12 대화를 듣고, 대화 내용과 일치하지 <u>않는</u> 것을 고르시오.

① 남자는 어젯밤에 잠을 거의 자지 못했다.
② 남자는 잠을 자기 위해 책에 나온 방법을 시도해 보았다.
③ 남자의 옆집 이웃은 밤새도록 소음을 낸다.
④ 여자는 남자에게 이사 갈 것을 조언하고 있다.
⑤ 남자는 집주인에게 문제를 알렸지만 소용없었다.

13 대화를 듣고, 여자의 마지막 말에 이어질 남자의 말로 가장 적절한 것을 고르시오.

① Can I take a rain check?
② That's exactly what I believe.
③ I have to meet up with a lot of people.
④ You got it. Have you thought of anything good yet?
⑤ I think I should change my attitude toward the people I work with.

14 대화를 듣고, 남자의 마지막 말에 이어질 여자의 말로 가장 적절한 것을 고르시오.

① It needs a bit more salt. How's your pasta?
② Skipping breakfast is really bad for your health.
③ I agree it's good, but I prefer non-greasy food.
④ Since I read those articles, I have decided to eat less meat.
⑤ I'm starving. This is the only thing I've eaten all day.

15 대화를 듣고, 여자의 마지막 말에 이어질 남자의 말로 가장 적절한 것을 고르시오.

① I always take trips during vacations.
② I just stay in and watch TV on the weekends.
③ I go to the movies about three times a month.
④ I often read the newspaper, but sometimes I sleep.
⑤ I usually do oil paintings, but sometimes I work with sculptures, too.

01 대화를 듣고, 여자가 할 일로 언급되지 않은 것을 고르시오.

M Could you buy me some cookies at the store?

W Oh, sorry, but I'm _____ _____ _____ today.

M You're not? Well, what are you doing today then?

W The whole house is a _____, so I plan on wiping the windows, _____ _____ _____, and cleaning out the fridge.

M As long as you're cleaning, could you _____ _____ _____, too? As you know, I'm busy with my work.

W All right. But you have to do it the next time!

M I _____ _____ this time.

W Don't mention it.

●●
mess 엉망인 상태 **vacuum** 진공청소기로 청소하다 **fridge** 냉장고 **owe** 신세를 지다

02 대화를 듣고, 두 사람이 대화하는 장소로 가장 적절한 곳을 고르시오.

M It's really busy in here today.

W You're right. This line is taking forever.

M Why don't you _____ _____ _____ while I wait here in line?

W Good thinking. Can you get me a mocha latte?

M Don't you _____ _____ _____? It's so hot today.

W You're right. I'll have a mocha milkshake, please.

M I'll _____ _____ _____ _____ because the mocha is too sweet for me.

W Meet me _____ _____ _____ _____.

M All right.

●●
grab 잡다, 거머쥐다

03 대화를 듣고, 남자의 직업으로 가장 적절한 것을 고르시오.

W Peter, your _____ _____ last week was very impressive.

M Thank you, Julia. At least the time that I spent researching for it _____ _____.

W Indeed! A lot of people like it too.

M Really? How did you know?

W Take a look at our website. You can _____ _____ _____ from our netizens.

M Were there any negative comments?

W I read a few, but most of them were _____.

M That's good to hear! I hope that my next one gets the same response.

W Well, you're a _____ _____. Anyway, I need you to submit your news item tomorrow.

M Oh, I _____ _____ about the _____!

●●
pay off 성과를 내다 **indeed** 정말, 아주 **comment** 의견, 논평

negative 부정적인 positive 긍정적인 journalist 기자
submit 제출하다 deadline 마감 시간

04 대화를 듣고, 두 사람의 관계로 가장 적절한 것을 고르시오.

M What do you _____? There are so many good shows that I'd like to watch.

W These days, a lot of people are trying to _____ _____ for the musical _Cats_. _Grease_ is pretty _____, too.

M _Grease_ sounds good. I'd like to see it.

W Let me check on the computer. We have _____ _____ _____ _____ in the middle of the first floor and in the second row of the balcony.

M How much are the first floor seats?

W They are 50 dollars each.

M When do the _____ _____ _____?

W At 8 o'clock.

M Okay. I'll take two seats on the first floor.

popular 인기 있는 balcony (2층의) 발코니석

05 대화를 듣고, 여자가 전화를 건 목적으로 가장 적절한 것을 고르시오.

M Hello.

W Hi. It's Emma calling. May I speak to Tom?

M This is he. Hey, Emma. What's up?

W You didn't happen to _____ _____ _____, did you?

M What does it look like?

W It is blue with _____ flowers.

M Don't worry. I think I have it.

W Where did you find it?

M I found it in my car. I was _____ _____ it got there.

W I _____ _____ _____ it there when you drove me home yesterday.

06 대화를 듣고, 남자가 취하고 있는 동작을 고르시오.

W All right. Now we're going to try the bridge stretch.

M The bridge stretch? How do you do that?

W Start with your feet, hands, and _____ _____ _____ _____.

M And my knees and shoulders in the air? I feel like a zigzag.

W Right. Now _____ _____ _____ up as high as you can.

M This is not very comfortable.

W Now walk your hands in _____ _____ _____.

M Oww! I must look like an upside-down U. It's hard to do.

W Don't worry. You'll _____ _____ _____ it.

bottom 엉덩이 comfortable 편안한 upside-down 거꾸로의
get used to ~에 익숙해지다

07 다음을 듣고, 어떤 동물에 관한 설명인지 고르시오.

This is my favorite animal. Not many people like it _____ _____ _____ _____. They say it's ugly and stupid. They use its name to mean the same as "_____." They don't _____ it at all. In fact, it is a very important animal. The females give us _____ meat and

_____, and the males are very useful as natural _____ _____. Plus, the babies are really cute. All in all, I think it _____ a lot more _____.

coward 겁쟁이 **female** 암컷 **male** 수컷 **useful** 유용한
deserve ~을 받을 만하다 **respect** 존중, 존경

08 대화를 듣고, 여자의 심정으로 가장 적절한 것을 고르시오.

M Happy Parents' Day, Mom!

W Thank you. What's this? A card?

M Yes, I _____ _____ _____. Do you like it?

W It's great. It says, "Thank you for being such a wonderful parent all these years."

M I even _____ a picture of our family _____ _____.

W I see that. You spent a lot of time on this, didn't you?

M A few hours. I wanted this day _____ _____ _____.

W Thank you for being my number-one son. I'm so glad.

M So, Mom... _____ _____ _____ _____ this evening after Dad comes home?

W Well, let's think about it.

paste 풀로 붙이다

09 대화를 듣고, 현재의 영화 관람료가 20년 전에 비해 얼마나 많이 올랐는지 고르시오.

M Aunt June, what is this?

W What? Oh, that? That is old money.

M I've never _____ _____ _____ before.

W That is a 500-won bill. When I was your age, it only _____ _____ _____ to go to the movies. That was almost _____ _____ _____ _____.

M I can't believe it.

W The _____ _____ was only 100 won, and the most popular _____ were 120 won.

M Why was everything so cheap?

W It was a different time then. Now, everything is so expensive. To go to the movies now costs _____ _____ _____ won.

M Times have really changed, haven't they?

bill 지폐 **fare** 요금, 운임 **noodle** 국수

10 대화를 듣고, 여자가 극장에 가지 <u>못하는</u> 이유로 가장 적절한 것을 고르시오.

M Hey, Sarah, are you going to the movie theater tonight?

W I would love to, but _____ _____ _____ _____ to Seoul, and I promised my mother to _____ them to the _____ _____ this evening.

M Really? That's too bad because all our friends are going to be there.

W I know, and I feel sorry about that. But I _____ _____ _____ _____, and they seem so excited.

M Well, a promise is a promise.

W That's true. Please tell everyone there that I'm sorry I _____ _____.

M I'm sure they'll understand. Besides, it's important to spend time with _____ _____, too.

W You're right. I don't see them often.

M Have a good time this evening, and I'll see you soon.

W You, too.

••
department store 백화점 **besides** 게다가 **relative** 친척

11 대화를 듣고, 남자가 오늘 오후에 할 일로 가장 적절한 것을 고르시오.

M Here you go, Mom. I made you breakfast.

W Wow, what a surprise! You _____ _____ _____ for me before.

M I know. But I see you've been working very hard these days, so I thought I would _____ _____ _____ _____. And today is Sunday.

W I really appreciate it. How about _____ _____ _____ for me every Sunday?

M If you would like that, it would be my pleasure. Is there _____ _____ I can do for you today?

W Would you please turn the television to channel four?

M No problem. Anything else?

W Not right now, but I _____ some _____ and _____ this afternoon.

M Okay. I'll do that.

••
break 휴식 (시간)

12 대화를 듣고, 대화 내용과 일치하지 <u>않는</u> 것을 고르시오.

W Are you tired? You look pale.

M Yeah, I'm exhausted. I _____ _____ a wink last night.

W Again? You've been having trouble sleeping since last month.

M You're telling me. I've _____ _____ in the book.

W Like what?

M Counting sheep, drinking warm milk, and even wearing earplugs. _____ _____ _____. I may just have to move.

W How would moving help?

M Well, the guy who _____ _____ _____ blasts music all night long.

W Why don't you complain to the landlord?

M I did. Nothing helps because my neighbor is the landlord's _____, and he thinks he can do _____ _____ _____.

W That's terrible.

••
pale 창백한 **count** (수를) 세다 **earplug** 귀마개
blast (큰 소리를) 내다 **landlord** 집주인 **nephew** 조카

13 대화를 듣고, 여자의 마지막 말에 이어질 남자의 말로 가장 적절한 것을 고르시오.

M Have you found a babysitter yet?

W No, I've decided not to work but to _____ _____ my baby _____.

M Why did you change your mind?

W I think babies usually _____ _____ from their parents.

M   I think so, too.

W   As you know, children are apt to learn

_____ _____ _____.

Therefore, they just imitate their parents'

_____.

M   That's true. Do you think they learn more

by seeing than doing?

W   Yes, children unconsciously _____

_____ _____ _____ around

them.

M   That's exactly what I believe.

●●
be apt to ~하는 경향이 있다, ~하기 쉽다
therefore 그래서, 그러므로   **imitate** 흉내 내다
unconsciously 무의식적으로

14   대화를 듣고, 남자의 마지막 말에 이어질 여자의 말로
가장 적절한 것을 고르시오.

W   Can you come to my house for dinner

tomorrow night?

M   Sure. By the way, what's the occasion?

W   There is _____ _____

_____. I just want to have dinner

with you.

M   Thanks for _____ _____. What's

for dinner?

W   Vegetarian food.

M   Vegetarian food? As far as I know, you

like meat, don't you?

W   Yes, but there were some _____

_____ _____ about cholesterol,

the harmful substance that can

_____ _____.

M   Really? I didn't know that.

W   Since I read those articles, I have decided

to eat less meat.

●●
harmful 해로운   **substance** 물질   **obesity** 비만

15   대화를 듣고, 여자의 마지막 말에 이어질 남자의 말로
가장 적절한 것을 고르시오.

W   Do you ever drive to work?

M   No, I never drive to my office. _____

is _____ _____ in the morning.

W   Do you ever travel on the bus?

M   No, I don't. I never take the bus. It

_____ _____ to get to work.

W   Well, _____ _____ do you

_____ in the morning?

M   I usually take the train that arrives at

Seoul Station at 8:45.

W   Can you _____ _____

_____ on the train in the morning?

M   Oh, yes, I can. I always find a seat.

W   So tell me… _____ _____

_____ _____ on the train in the

morning?

M   I often read the newspaper, but

sometimes I sleep.

A 다음을 듣고, 어휘와 우리말 뜻을 쓰시오.

① _____ ⑦ _____

② _____ ⑧ _____

③ _____ ⑨ _____

④ _____ ⑩ _____

⑤ _____ ⑪ _____

⑥ _____ ⑫ _____

B 우리말을 참고하여 빈칸에 알맞은 단어를 쓰시오.

① Cholesterol can _____ _____ .

콜레스테롤은 비만을 일으킬 수 있다.

② Were there any _____ _____ ?

부정적인 의견들이 있었나요?

③ I think it _____ a lot more _____ .

내 생각에 그것은 훨씬 더 많은 존중을 받을 만합니다.

④ The _____ _____ was only 100 won.

버스 요금은 단돈 100원이었다.

⑤ I'll take my cousins to the _____ _____ this evening.

나는 오늘 저녁에 사촌들을 백화점에 데리고 갈 것이다.

⑥ Children unconsciously _____ whatever they see _____ them.

아이들은 무의식적으로 주변에 보이는 것은 무엇이든 흉내 낸다.

⑦ You'll _____ _____ _____ it.

당신은 그것에 익숙해질 거예요.

⑧ Children _____ _____ _____ learn by watching others.

아이들은 다른 사람들을 관찰함으로써 배우는 경향이 있다.

NEW
EDITION

실력을 확실히 올려주는 리스닝 프로그램

영어듣기 모의고사

CooL

LISTENING

조금배 ㅣ 백영실 ㅣ 김정인

3

DARAKWON

영어듣기 모의고사

CooL
LISTENING

정답 및 해석

3

문제 및 정답	받아쓰기 및 녹음내용	해석

01

다음을 듣고, 그림의 상황에 알맞은 대화를 고르시오.

① ② ③ ④ ⑤

① M Have some more. It's delicious.
　W No, thanks. I'm full. I <u>had better</u> <u>not</u> eat any more.
② M I think <u>it's broken</u>.
　W Oh, no! I'm sorry to hear that.
③ M Be careful. They're very rare.
　W Don't worry. I know <u>how to handle</u> them.
④ M Is there any more cake?
　W Sorry. I <u>ate</u> <u>it</u> <u>all</u>.
⑤ M I love this music.
　W Me, too. Would you like to dance with me?

① 남 좀 더 드세요. 맛있어요.
　여 고맙지만 괜찮습니다. 배가 불러요. 더 이상은 먹지 않는 게 좋을 것 같네요.
② 남 그거 망가졌나 봐.
　여 오, 이런! 안됐구나.
③ 남 조심해. 그거 아주 희귀한 거야.
　여 걱정 마. 다루는 법을 알아.
④ 남 케이크 좀 더 있니?
　여 미안해. 내가 다 먹어버렸어.
⑤ 남 난 이 음악을 정말 좋아해.
　여 나도 그래. 나랑 춤 출래?

●●
had better ~하는 편이 낫다 **broken** 망가진, 고장 난 **rare** 희귀한, 진귀한 **handle** 다루다, 취급하다

02

대화를 듣고, 두 사람이 대화하는 장소로 가장 적절한 곳을 고르시오.

① 농장　　② 빵집
③ 공장　　④ 부엌
⑤ 식당

M May I <u>take your order</u>, ma'am?
W Yes, I'll have the home-style chili.
M Do you want cornbread or a <u>baked potato</u> with that?
W Cornbread, please.
M All right. <u>Anything to drink</u>?
W I'd like a cup of decaffeinated coffee, please.
M Okay. I'll be back with your order in a <u>few minutes</u>.

남 주문하시겠어요, 손님?
여 네, 가정식 칠리를 시킬게요.
남 그것과 함께 옥수수빵을 드릴까요, 아니면 구운 감자를 드릴까요?
여 옥수수빵으로 주세요.
남 좋습니다. 음료는 무엇으로 하시겠어요?
여 카페인이 없는 커피 한 잔 주세요.
남 알겠습니다. 주문하신 것을 곧 가져다드릴게요.

●●
decaffeinated 카페인을 제거한[줄인]

03

다음을 듣고, 여자의 직업으로 가장 적절한 것을 고르시오.

① 선장 　　② 승무원
③ 구조대원 　④ 택시 기사
⑤ 식당 종업원

Ladies and gentlemen! We're now approaching Seoul, where the local time is 9 a.m. At this stage, you should be in your seats with your seatbelts firmly fastened. Personal television screens, footrests, and seat tables must be stowed, and all hand luggage should be stored either in the overhead lockers or under the seat in front of you. Ensure all electronic devices, including laptop computers and computer games, are turned off.

신사 숙녀 여러분! 지금 우리는 서울에 접근하고 있으며, 현지 시각은 오전 9시입니다. 이제, 승객 여러분들은 좌석에 앉으시고, 안전벨트를 꽉 착용해 주세요. 개인용 텔레비전 스크린, 발판, 좌석 테이블을 반드시 원래 위치에 놓아 주시고, 모든 휴대 가능 수화물은 머리 위에 있는 수납 공간이나 앞쪽에 있는 좌석 아래에 보관해 주십시오. 노트북 컴퓨터와 컴퓨터 게임을 포함한 모든 전자 기기의 전원을 반드시 꺼 주십시오.

●●
approach 접근하다 **firmly** 꽉, 단단히 **fasten** 매다, 채우다 **footrest** 발판 **stow** (안전한 곳에) 집어넣다 **overhead** 머리 위에 **ensure** 반드시 ~하게 하다 **electronic device** 전자 기기

04

대화를 듣고, 두 사람의 관계로 가장 적절한 것을 고르시오.

① 서점 점원 - 손님
② 버스 기사 - 승객
③ 환경미화원 - 행인
④ 아파트 주민 - 이웃
⑤ 세탁소 주인 - 손님

W Are you new to the neighborhood?
M Yes, I am. I just moved into my apartment a few days ago.
W Welcome to the neighborhood.
M Thanks. I'm new to the city. I'm originally from the east coast.
W Oh, I see. I hope you like it here in L.A.
M I hope so, too. By the way, do you know where the washing machines are?
W Yeah, the laundry room is in the basement.
M And which floor do you live on?
W I live on the third floor.
M Well, I'm on the second floor.
W I guess I'll see you around.

여 이 근처에 새로 이사 오셨나요?
남 네, 그래요. 며칠 전에 막 이 아파트로 이사 왔어요.
여 이웃이 되신 걸 환영합니다.
남 감사합니다. 저는 도시는 처음이에요. 원래 동부 해안 지역 출신이거든요.
여 오, 그렇군요. 이곳 LA를 좋아하셨으면 좋겠네요.
남 저도 그러길 바라요. 그런데, 세탁기가 어디에 있는지 아세요?
여 네, 세탁실은 지하층에 있어요.
남 그리고 몇 층에 사시나요?
여 저는 3층에 살고 있어요.
남 음, 저는 2층에 살고 있어요.
여 자주 뵐 수 있겠네요.

●●
neighborhood 근처, 이웃 **originally** 원래 **coast** 해안 (지방) **by the way** 그런데 **laundry room** 세탁실 **basement** 지하층

05 대화를 듣고, 그림에서 Janet이 누구인지 고르시오.

W	Wow. This fitness center has great <u>facilities</u>.
M	Yes, it does. All the members love this place. I like it, too.
W	You're really well built. You must <u>work out regularly</u>.
M	Thanks. I exercise every other day with my friend Janet. That's her right over there.
W	Where is she now? Is she jogging <u>on the treadmill</u>?
M	No, she's on the stationary bike.
W	Which one is she? The one with the <u>sleeveless shirt</u>?
M	No, she's wearing a short-sleeved T-shirt.
W	Is she wearing a cap?
M	No, she <u>has headphones on</u> because she's listening to music.

여 와. 이 헬스 클럽은 시설이 훌륭하다.

남 응, 그래. 모든 회원들이 이곳을 정말로 좋아하고 있어. 나 역시 좋아해.

여 너는 체격이 무척 좋구나. 규칙적으로 운동하는 것이 분명해.

남 고마워. 난 친구인 Janet과 이틀에 한 번 운동해. 저쪽에 있는 사람이 바로 그녀야.

여 지금 어디에 있는데? 러닝머신에서 뛰고 있는 사람이니?

남 아니, 실내 자전거를 타고 있어.

여 어떤 사람이 그녀이니? 민소매 셔츠를 입은 사람이니?

남 아니, 그녀는 반팔 티셔츠를 입고 있어.

여 모자를 쓰고 있니?

남 아니, 음악을 듣느라 헤드폰을 끼고 있어.

●●

facility 시설, 설비 **well built** 체격이 좋은 **treadmill** 러닝머신 **stationary bike** 실내 자전거 **sleeveless** 민소매의

---

06 대화를 듣고, 남자가 부모님께 드린 선물로 가장 적절한 것을 고르시오.

① 꽃 ② 목걸이
③ 자서전 ④ 감사 카드
⑤ 상품권

W	I want to give my mother something for her birthday. Can you help me?
M	How about a <u>necklace</u> and a nice card?
W	Yeah, that sounds good.
M	Just get her a present to <u>express your thanks</u>.
W	Have you given a present like that to your parents?
M	Well, when I was a university student, I <u>couldn't afford to</u> buy anything for them. So I made a small book about myself.
W	An autobiography for your parents?
M	Kind of. I wrote about my childhood and expressed how much I <u>appreciated them</u> in the book.
W	Wow, that's really nice. What was your parents' reaction?
M	They really loved it and still <u>treasure</u> the book.

여 엄마 생신에 뭔가를 드리고 싶어. 도와줄 수 있어?

남 목걸이와 멋진 카드 어때?

여 그래, 그거 좋은 생각이다.

남 그냥 네 감사함을 표현할 수 있는 선물을 사 드려.

여 너는 너희 부모님한테 그런 선물을 드려 본 적 있니?

남 음, 대학생 때 부모님을 위해 뭔가를 사 드릴 수 있는 형편이 안 되었어. 그래서 나 자신에 관한 작은 책을 만들었어.

여 부모님을 위한 자서전?

남 일종의 그런 거지. 내 어린 시절에 대해 쓰고 그 책에다 내가 부모께 얼마나 많이 감사하고 있는지를 표현했지.

여 와, 정말 멋지다. 부모님 반응은 어땠니?

남 정말로 좋아하셨고 지금도 그 책을 소중히 하고 계셔.

●●

necklace 목걸이 **express** 표현하다 **afford** 형편[여유]이 되다 **autobiography** 자서전 **appreciate** 감사하다 **reaction** 반응 **treasure** 소중히 하다

07 대화를 듣고, 여자의 심정으로 가장 적절한 것을 고르시오.

① excited
② envious
③ ashamed
④ satisfied
⑤ disappointed

M Hey, Tina. Did you get <u>a text message</u> from a university?

W Let me check. I have one.

M Do you think it's good news?

W I hope so. Let me see.

M Well... What does it say?

W It says they've <u>rejected</u> <u>my application</u>. Now what am I going to do?

M I'm so sorry, Tina. I know you were really looking forward to a <u>positive response</u> from them.

W I was. Now I have to think about what I'm going to do with my life. I <u>need to spend</u> some time <u>alone</u> now.

남 안녕, Tina. 대학에서 문자 메시지를 받았니?

여 확인해 볼게. 하나 받았어.

남 그게 좋은 소식인 것 같으니?

여 그러길 바라. 한번 보도록 할게.

남 그래… 뭐라고 쓰여 있니?

여 지원을 거절하겠다고 쓰여 있네. 나 이제 어떻게 하지?

남 너무 유감이다, Tina. 난 네가 대학에서 긍정적인 응답을 얻기를 정말로 기대하고 있었다는 것을 아는데.

여 그랬지. 이제 내 인생에서 무엇을 해야 할지 생각해 봐야겠어. 난 이제 혼자서 시간을 좀 보내야겠어.

● ●

reject 거절하다 **application** 지원, 신청
response 응답, 대답

---

08 대화를 듣고, 남자가 Denver 공항에 도착할 시각을 고르시오.

① 오후 1시경   ② 오후 2시경
③ 오후 6시경   ④ 오후 8시경
⑤ 오후 9시경

M Hi, Martha. It's Mike. I am at the airport <u>waiting</u> <u>for</u> <u>my flight</u>.

W What time is your flight?

M It leaves at <u>two</u> o'clock in the afternoon.

W I see. You <u>must</u> <u>be</u> very <u>tired</u> from your long trip. Did you have fun?

M Oh, yeah. I am just a little hungry, but everything is fine with me. It was a wonderful trip. By the way, is Mom or Dad there?

W No, <u>they</u> <u>are</u> <u>out</u> now. But don't worry. They know you will be here today. We will be waiting for you at Denver Airport.

M What a relief! I thought they had forgotten about my return. Do they know <u>what time</u> <u>I</u> <u>arrive</u> there?

W I think so. It only <u>takes</u> <u>four hours</u> from there, right? Just in case, I will call them now.

M Thanks.

남 안녕, Martha. 나 Mike야. 나는 공항에서 비행편을 기다리고 있어.

여 비행기가 몇 시지?

남 오후 2시에 출발해.

여 그렇구나. 오랫동안 여행해서 정말 피곤하겠다. 재미는 있었어?

남 오, 그럼. 배가 조금 고플 뿐이지만 다 괜찮아. 정말 재미있는 여행이었어. 그런데 참, 아빠나 엄마 거기 계시니?

여 아니, 지금 두 분 다 나가셨는데. 그렇지만 걱정하지 마. 부모님도 오늘 오빠가 도착하는 거 아시니까. 우리가 Denver 공항에서 기다리고 있을게.

남 다행이다! 난 또 내가 돌아가는 것을 잊어버리신 줄 알았는데. 내가 몇 시에 거기 도착하는지 알고 계시니?

여 그런 것 같은데. 거기서 오면 4시간밖에 안 걸리는 것 맞지? 만약을 위해서 내가 부모님께 지금 전화해 놓을게.

남 고마워.

● ●

flight 비행편 **forget** 잊다 **just in case** 만약을 위해서

09

대화를 듣고, 남자가 사과하는 이유로 가장 적절한 것을 고르시오.

① 예민하게 굴어서
② 책상을 연필로 두드려서
③ 실내에서 담배를 피워서
④ 음악을 크게 틀어 놓아서
⑤ 금연하겠다는 약속을 어겨서

M Would you mind <u>not tapping</u> <u>your pencil</u> on the desk? It's irritating me.

W Sorry. I didn't realize I was doing that.

M And your <u>breathing</u> is very <u>loud</u>. The sound is quite annoying.

W I had no idea I was doing that either.

M Look. Let me apologize. In fact, I'm trying to <u>quit smoking</u>, and it has made me very <u>irritable</u>.

W I understand. It's hard to quit cigarettes.

M This is my <u>third attempt</u> at quitting. I'm determined to do it this time.

W You need a strong will to do it. Good luck.

남 책상에 대고 연필을 두드리지 않으면 안 되겠니? 짜증나거든.

여 미안해. 내가 그러고 있는지 몰랐어.

남 그리고 네 숨소리가 너무 커. 그 소리가 상당히 거슬려.

여 그러고 있는지도 역시 몰랐어.

남 이봐. 내가 사과할게. 사실은, 나 담배를 끊으려고 노력 중인데, 그것이 날 정말로 예민하게 해.

여 이해해. 담배를 끊는다는 건 힘든 일이지.

남 이번이 세 번째 금연 시도야. 이번에는 해 보려고 결심했어.

여 금연을 하려면 강한 의지가 필요하지. 행운을 빌어.

●●

tap (가볍게) 두드리다 **irritate** 짜증나게 하다 **realize** 깨닫다 **breathing** 호흡 **apologize** 사과하다 **quit** 그만두다 **attempt** 시도 **be determined to** ~하기로 결심하다 **will** 의지

10

대화를 듣고, 여자가 전화를 건 목적으로 가장 적절한 것을 고르시오.

① 사은품을 요청하려고
② 신제품에 대하여 문의하려고
③ 아르바이트 일자리를 구하려고
④ 백화점 세일 기간을 알아보려고
⑤ 세탁기의 무상 수리를 의뢰하려고

M GL Electronics Service Department. This is William Smith. How may I help you?

W Hi. I <u>bought a washing machine</u> from your company, but now it's broken.

M When did you buy the machine, ma'am?

W Just three months ago.

M In that case, it should still be <u>under warranty</u>.

W That's what I figured. You'll fix it <u>for free</u>, right?

M Yes, but you'll need to show <u>proof of purchase</u>.

W That's no problem.

M Then we'll send you a <u>repairman</u> soon.

W Thank you very much.

남 GL 전자 서비스 부서의 William Smith입니다. 무엇을 도와드릴까요?

여 안녕하세요. 전 이 회사에서 만든 세탁기를 구입했었는데요, 그런데 지금 고장이 났어요.

남 언제 세탁기를 구입하셨나요, 고객님?

여 겨우 석 달 전에요.

남 그런 경우라면, 아직 보증 기간이 끝나지 않았습니다.

여 저도 그렇게 알고 있습니다. 무료로 수리해 주시는 거지요, 그렇죠?

남 네, 하지만 구매 필증을 보여 주셔야 할 겁니다.

여 문제 없어요.

남 그러면 수리 기사를 곧 보내 드리겠습니다.

여 대단히 감사합니다.

●●

under warranty 보증 기간 중인 **figure** 이해하다 **proof of purchase** 구매 필증 **repairman** 수리 기사

11 대화를 듣고, 여자가 남자에게 조언한 것으로 가장 적절한 것을 고르시오.

① 돈을 써야 돈을 벌 수 있다.
② 여행 가기 전에 항공권을 먼저 구입해라.
③ 물건을 살 때마다 꼼꼼히 살펴보아야 한다.
④ 남에게 돈을 빌리기보다는 돈을 빌려주어라.
⑤ 미래를 위해 매일 조금씩 돈을 저축해야 한다.

M Hey, Gina, you look like you're going somewhere. What's the suitcase?
W I'm on my way to France for a vacation.
M Are you serious? How can you afford that?
W Well, I spend a lot of time thinking about how to save money and actually saved some.
M Enough for a trip to Europe?
W Yes.
M I can't believe it. How could you do that?
W It's important to save a little for the future each day.
M You are my inspiration.
W I have to go to the airport now. Goodbye.

남 야, 지나야, 너 어디 가는 것 같다. 그 여행 가방은 뭐니?
여 휴가차 프랑스에 가는 중이야.
남 정말이야? 어떻게 비용을 충당할 수 있는데?
여 음, 나는 오랜 시간을 어떻게 돈을 모을까에 대해 생각하며 보내고, 실제로 어느 정도는 모았어.
남 유럽 가기에 충분할 만큼?
여 응.
남 믿을 수가 없네. 어떻게 그렇게 할 수 있었니?
여 미래를 위해 매일 조금씩 돈을 저축하는 것이 중요해.
남 네가 나에게 영감을 주었어.
여 나 지금 공항에 가 봐야 해. 안녕.

●●
inspiration 영감

12 대화를 듣고, 대화 내용과 일치하지 않는 것을 고르시오.

① 남자는 목요일에 역사 수업을 듣지 않았다.
② 여자는 남자에게 필기 노트를 빌려줄 수 있다고 말했다.
③ 남자는 Roosevelt가 제2차 세계대전 때의 대통령임을 알고 있다.
④ 남자는 여자에게 Roosevelt 대통령의 업적을 설명해 주었다.
⑤ 여자는 Roosevelt 대통령이 역대 최고의 대통령이었다고 생각한다.

M I didn't go to history class on Thursday. Did you go?
W Yes, and I can lend you my notes if you want to look at them. We talked about the 32nd president of the USA, Franklin Delano Roosevelt.
M I know he was the president during World War II, right?
W That's correct. Amazingly, Roosevelt did a lot of things without the use of his legs.
M What do you mean?
W He was disabled by polio, which left his legs almost useless, and he spent most of his life in a wheelchair.
M I didn't know that. How do you think he compares to other presidents?
W I think he was the best president ever. And most historians continue to regard him as one of the three or four greatest American presidents of all time.

남 난 목요일 역사 수업에 가지 않았어. 너는 갔었니?
여 응, 그리고 네가 보고 싶다면 내 필기 노트를 빌려줄 수도 있어. 우리는 미국 32대 대통령인 Franklin Delano Roosevelt에 대해 이야기했어.
남 나는 그가 제2차 세계대전 중 대통령인 것으로 알고 있는데, 맞니?
여 맞아. 놀랍게도, Roosevelt는 다리를 사용하지 않고도 많은 일을 했었어.
남 무슨 의미니?
여 그는 소아마비로 불구가 돼서, 다리를 거의 사용할 수 없게 되었고, 휠체어에서 삶의 대부분을 보냈어.
남 난 그런 줄 몰랐어. 그가 다른 대통령들과 비교해서 어떻다고 생각하니?
여 난 그가 역대 최고의 대통령이었다고 생각해. 그리고 대부분의 역사학자들은 계속해서 그를 가장 위대한 3, 4인의 역대 미국 대통령들 중 한 명으로 간주해.

●●
president 대통령 disabled 불구가 된, 장애를 가진 polio 소아마비 useless 쓸모 없는 compare to ~와 비교가 되다 historian 역사가 regard 간주하다, 여기다

13 대화를 듣고, 여자의 마지막 말에 이어질 남자의 말로 가장 적절한 것을 고르시오.

① That's a smart idea.
② You can make your own greenhouse.
③ You're right. I'm worried about the future of our planet.
④ No, I usually buy only environmentally friendly products.
⑤ I think it's time to look for the right house to move into.

W I can't stand this hot weather.
M You're not the only one. I can't stand it either.
W Why is it so hot?
M My teacher told me that it has a lot to do with the greenhouse effect.
W I've heard about that. Doesn't that come from all the carbon gases from factories?
M It sure does. Besides all the factories, so many cars contribute to the greenhouse effect. Heat trapped in the atmosphere makes it hotter and hotter.
W I think that's scary.
M You're right. I'm worried about the future of our planet.

여 이런 더운 날씨는 참을 수 없어.
남 너만 그런 게 아니야. 나도 참을 수 없어.
여 왜 이렇게 덥지?
남 많은 부분이 온실 효과와 관련이 있다고 선생님께서 말씀하셨어.
여 나도 그 이야기는 들었어. 공장에서 나오는 모든 탄소 가스들 때문 아니겠니?
남 정말 그래. 모든 공장들 외에도, 너무 많은 차량들이 온실 효과에 일조하고 있지. 대기 중에 갇힌 열기가 더욱 더 덥게 만들어.
여 무서운 거 같아.
남 맞아. 난 지구의 미래가 걱정돼.

●●
greenhouse effect 온실 효과 **carbon gas** 탄소 가스 **factory** 공장 **contribute to** ∼에 일조하다 **trap** 가두다 **atmosphere** 대기

---

14 대화를 듣고, 남자의 마지막 말에 이어질 여자의 말로 가장 적절한 것을 고르시오.

① Everybody is telling me that!
② I've cut down on snacking between meals.
③ You should introduce the doctor to them.
④ That's a good idea! I should start working out more often.
⑤ Try doing aerobic exercise to build endurance and to lose weight.

W Have you seen Mark lately?
M No, I've been so busy.
W Do you know he has gained 10kg since he got married three months ago?
M Really? His wife must be a good cook.
W Yes, she is. But she's gained 15kg, too.
M What a pity!
W I think they should do something to lose weight.
M I think so, too. I know a doctor who has a good diet program at his clinic.
W You should introduce the doctor to them.

여 최근에 Mark를 봤니?
남 아니, 난 매우 바빴어.
여 그가 3개월 전에 결혼한 이후로 10kg이나 찐 거 아니?
남 정말? 아내가 요리를 잘하나 보다.
여 응, 맞아. 하지만 그녀도 15kg이나 늘었어.
남 참 안됐다!
여 그들은 체중을 감량하기 위해 무언가를 해야 한다고 생각해.
남 나도 그렇게 생각해. 나는 병원에 좋은 식이요법 프로그램을 갖추고 있는 의사를 알고 있어.
여 네가 그 의사를 그들에게 소개시켜 줘야겠다.

15 다음 상황 설명을 듣고, Tommy가 학생들에게 할 말로 가장 적절한 것을 고르시오.

① Don't be afraid of making mistakes. Just speak up!
② Learn common words and phrases to pass the course.
③ You have only three minutes to complete the exercise.
④ Open your book and read the conversation silently once.
⑤ Listen to native speakers talk about various topics for the midterm.

Tommy lives in Chicago and teaches an English course. There are 20 students in his class. They are all <u>foreign</u> <u>students</u>. Most of them <u>have</u> <u>a</u> <u>hard</u> <u>time</u> speaking English. They don't like to make mistakes when they speak English. They are shy and <u>afraid</u> <u>of</u> <u>mistakes</u>. Yet they should realize that mistakes improve their English. A shy student has <u>fewer</u> <u>opportunities</u> to practice English than a confident one. So Tommy wants to <u>advise</u> shy students to be <u>more</u> <u>active</u>. In this situation, what would Tommy most likely say to them?

Tommy: <u>Don't be afraid of making mistakes. Just speak up!</u>

Tommy는 시카고에 살며 영어 수업을 하고 있다. 그의 학급 학생은 20명이다. 그들은 모두 외국 학생들이다. 대부분의 학생들은 영어를 말하는 데 고생을 한다. 그들은 영어로 말할 때 실수를 하는 것을 좋아하지 않는다. 그들은 부끄러워하고 실수를 겁낸다. 그러나 그들은 실수가 자신들의 영어를 향상시킨다는 것을 깨달아야 한다. 부끄러워하는 학생은 자신감 있는 학생보다 영어를 연습할 기회를 덜 갖게 된다. 그래서 Tommy는 부끄러워하는 학생들에게 더 적극성을 가지라고 조언하기를 원한다. 이런 상황에서 Tommy는 그들에게 뭐라고 말하겠는가?

Tommy: <u>실수를 하는 것을 겁내지 마세요. 그냥 큰 소리로 말하세요!</u>

• •
mistake 실수 **improve** 향상시키다
opportunity 기회 **confident** 자신감 있는
active 적극적인, 활동적인

◖ REVIEW TEST p. 15

A ① rare, 희귀한, 진귀한 ② fasten, 매다, 채우다 ③ facility, 시설, 설비 ④ afford, 형편[여유]이 되다
⑤ approach, 접근하다 ⑥ apologize, 사과하다 ⑦ confident, 자신감 있는 ⑧ appreciate, 감사하다
⑨ opportunity, 기회 ⑩ neighborhood, 근처, 이웃 ⑪ by the way, 그런데 ⑫ just in case, 만약을 위해서

B ① originally, coast ② electronic devices ③ positive response
④ how to handle ⑤ laundry room, basement ⑥ is, under warranty
⑦ realize, mistakes improve ⑧ historians, regard, president

	문제 및 정답	받아쓰기 및 녹음내용	해석

01 대화를 듣고, 그림에서 남자가 설명하고 있는 사람을 고르시오.

M Have you met the new guy yet? He <u>joined</u> <u>our</u> <u>company</u> today.

W No, I haven't. Is he here? Where is he?

M He's over there by the window.

W Which one is he? <u>Several guys</u> are over there.

M He's the one with the <u>file</u> <u>in</u> <u>his</u> <u>hand</u>.

W Oh, the one with the <u>glasses</u>? He looks smart.

M Right. That's him. Would you like to go there and <u>say</u> <u>hello</u> <u>to</u> him?

W Sure. Why not?

남 새로 온 남자 만나 봤어? 그는 오늘 우리 회사에 입사했어.

여 아니, 못 만나 봤어. 그 사람 여기 있니? 어디에 있어?

남 저기 창가에 있네.

여 어떤 사람이야? 몇 명의 남자가 거기 있잖아.

남 손에 파일을 들고 있는 사람이야.

여 오, 저 안경 쓴 사람? 똑똑해 보이는데.

남 맞아. 저 사람이야. 저기 가서 그에게 인사라도 할래?

여 좋아. 안 할 이유가 없지.

●●
several 몇몇의

---

02 대화를 듣고, 두 사람이 대화하는 장소로 가장 적절한 곳을 고르시오.

① 식당   ② 수영장
③ 스키장   ④ 놀이터
⑤ 헬스클럽

W George, jump right in. It's not too cold. It's a nice day to <u>be</u> <u>outdoors</u>.

M I <u>hate</u> <u>diving</u> <u>in</u>. I'll get into the water in my own way.

W Don't get in too slowly. You're <u>blocking</u> <u>the</u> <u>way</u>.

M Don't worry about me. Go do some laps or something.

W Hey! <u>Don't</u> <u>splash</u> <u>me</u>!

M Are you afraid of a little water?

W Oh, boy, you asked for it! <u>Water</u> <u>fight</u>!

M I give up. Sorry.

여 George, 바로 뛰어들어. 그렇게 차갑지는 않아. 밖에 있기에 좋은 날씨야.

남 다이빙 하는 건 정말 싫어. 나는 내 방식대로 물에 들어갈 거야.

여 너무 천천히 들어가지 마. 네가 길을 막고 있어.

남 내 걱정 마. 가서 몇 바퀴 돌던지 무언가를 해.

여 이봐! 내게 물 튀기지 마!

남 물 조금 가지고 무서워하는 거야?

여 이봐, 한번 해 보자는 거군! 물싸움이다!

남 항복이야. 미안.

●●
block 막다 **do a lap** 한 바퀴 돌다 **splash** (물 등을) 튀기다[끼얹다]

03

다음을 듣고, 여자의 직업으로 가장 적절한 것을 고르시오.

① 약사　　　② 의사 ✓
③ 무용수　　④ 정치인
⑤ 경찰관

All right, Mr. Reed. I've finished the examination. It looks like you're going to need surgery. Now don't worry; this operation is very common. I have hundreds of experiences doing surgery, and there have never been any bad results. Your medical insurance should pay for most of it, so you don't have to worry about the cost either. As your condition is somewhat serious, I'm going to schedule your surgery for 10:30 a.m. tomorrow. Now, do you have any questions?

좋아요, Reed 씨. 검사가 끝났어요. 수술이 필요할 것 같군요. 자, 걱정하지 마세요. 이 수술은 아주 일반적이니까요. 제게는 수백 번의 수술 경험이 있고, 나쁜 결과는 한 번도 없었어요. 의료 보험에서 대부분의 비용이 지불될 테니, 비용 또한 걱정할 필요가 없어요. 상태가 약간 심각하니까 수술 시간을 내일 오전 10시 30분으로 잡을게요. 자, 질문 있나요?

●●

examination 검사, 진찰　surgery 수술
operation 수술　experience 경험; 경험하다
medical insurance 의료 보험

04

대화를 듣고, 두 사람의 관계로 가장 적절한 것을 고르시오.

① 남편 - 아내
② 사장 - 비서
③ 의사 - 환자
④ 약사 - 손님 ✓
⑤ 식당 종업원 - 손님

M How are you, Jackie?

W I'm fine. But I'd like something for my daughter. She is tired these days.

M Oh. She'd better take some vitamins.

W Yes. Can I have some multivitamins with calcium?

M All right. Do you want a large or small bottle?

W Could I have two large ones, please? How much are they?

M The total price is 75 dollars. Here you are.

W Thank you very much. Have a nice day.

남 어떻게 지내요, Jackie?

여 잘 지내요. 그런데 딸에게 뭘 좀 사 주려고요. 그 애가 요즘 피곤해해요.

남 오. 따님은 비타민을 좀 드시는 게 좋아요.

여 네. 칼슘이 들어 있는 종합 비타민제 좀 주시겠어요?

남 알겠습니다. 큰 병으로 드릴까요, 아니면 작은 병으로 드릴까요?

여 큰 병으로 두 개 살 수 있을까요? 얼마이지요?

남 총 가격은 75달러입니다. 여기 있습니다.

여 정말 감사합니다. 즐거운 하루 보내세요.

●●

total 총, 전체의

05

대화를 듣고, 남자가 찾고 있는 안경의 위치로 가장 적절한 곳을 고르시오.

M Where are my glasses?

W You <u>left</u> them <u>on the floor</u>, so I moved them out of harm's way.

M Well, where are they? You know I'm blind without them.

W I'm trying to remember. They're <u>not on the table</u>.

M How about next to the TV? You always <u>put stuff there</u>.

W No. Hmm… Let me sit down and think about this for a while.

M Where could they be?

W Oops! I'm <u>sitting on</u> your <u>glasses</u>!

남 내 안경이 어디에 있지?

여 네가 이것을 바닥에 뒀더라, 그래서 내가 안전한 곳으로 옮겨 두었어.

남 음, 어디에 있는데? 네가 알다시피 난 안경 없이는 잘 안 보여.

여 기억하려고 노력 중이야. 테이블 위에는 없는데.

남 TV 옆에는? 너는 항상 거기에 물건들을 올려 두잖아.

여 아니야. 음… 앉아서 잠시 동안 생각해 봐야겠다.

남 그것이 어디에 있을까?

여 아이고! 내가 네 안경 위에 앉아 있네!

●●
out of harm's way 안전한 곳으로
remember 기억하다 **stuff** 물건, 것

06

대화를 듣고, 무엇에 관한 내용인지 가장 적절한 것을 고르시오.

① 사과 가격
② 계산원의 불친절함
③ 슈퍼마켓을 이용하는 요일
④ 세일하는 물품과 그렇지 않은 물품
⑤ 계산대 앞에서 오래 기다려야 하는 이유

W Do you <u>mind</u> if I <u>go ahead of</u> you? I only have one item.

M Not at all. Go ahead. I have a <u>whole cart full of</u> food.

W Thanks. Now all we have to do is to wait for the woman ahead of us.

M Yeah, she's been <u>arguing with the cashier</u> about the price of apples. She insists that there's a sale, but the cashier disagrees.

W Really? <u>That's why</u> we've been waiting so long.

M I guess so.

W I guess we <u>picked</u> the <u>wrong day</u> to come to the supermarket.

M I've been telling that to myself for the past 20 minutes.

여 제가 먼저 계산해도 괜찮으시겠습니까? 저는 물품 하나밖에 없거든요.

남 그럼요. 그렇게 하세요. 저는 카트 전체가 음식으로 꽉 차 있어요.

여 고맙습니다. 이제 우리는 앞에 있는 여자분을 기다리기만 하면 되겠군요.

남 네, 사과 가격 때문에 계산원이랑 실랑이를 벌이고 있네요. 여자분은 세일이라고 주장하는데, 계산원은 아니라고 하네요.

여 그래요? 그래서 우리가 이렇게 오랫동안 기다리고 있는 거군요.

남 그런 것 같아요.

여 슈퍼마켓에 오는 날을 잘못 잡았나 봐요.

남 저도 한 20분 동안 속으로 그렇게 말하고 있던 중이에요.

●●
whole 전체의 **insist** 주장하다 **disagree** 이의를 제기하다, 동의하지 않다

07 다음을 듣고, 비행에 관해 언급되지 <u>않은</u> 것을 고르시오.

① 도착지   ② 도착지의 날씨
③ 기내 서비스   ④ 비행 시간
⑤ 전자 기기 사용

Good afternoon, passengers. This is your captain speaking. We will be <u>departing for</u> Berlin, Germany, in a few minutes. The <u>weather</u> in Berlin is cloudy with some <u>rain</u> <u>showers</u>. We will have several in-flight movies <u>as</u> <u>well</u> <u>as</u> hot meals. We will be in the air <u>for</u> <u>10</u> <u>hours</u> today, and we don't expect <u>any</u> turbulence along the way. If there is anything we can do to make your experience more enjoyable, please <u>don't</u> <u>hesitate</u> <u>to</u> notify one of the flight crew. On behalf of the crew, I wish you a <u>pleasant</u> <u>flight</u>.

안녕하세요, 승객 여러분. 저는 기장입니다. 저희는 잠시 후에 독일, 베를린으로 출발할 예정입니다. 베를린은 소나기를 동반한 구름이 낀 날씨입니다. 저희는 몇 편의 기내 영화와 따뜻한 식사를 준비하겠습니다. 오늘은 10시간의 비행이 될 것이며, 여행하는 동안 난기류는 없을 것으로 예상됩니다. 여러분들의 좀 더 즐거운 경험을 위해 저희가 할 수 있는 일이 있으면 주저하지 말고 승무원들 중 한 명에게 알려 주십시오. 승무원들을 대표해 여러분들의 즐거운 비행을 기원합니다.

● ●

passenger 승객   **depart** 출발하다
in-flight 기내의   **turbulence** 난기류
hesitate 주저하다   **notify** 알리다
on behalf of ~을 대표하여

---

08 대화를 듣고, 여자의 심정으로 가장 적절한 것을 고르시오.

① scared   ② curious
③ irritable   ④ worried
⑤ surprised

M Are you ready to go out?
W I'm almost ready. I just want to <u>check</u> my <u>lotto</u> <u>numbers</u> first.
M You're wasting your money buying those tickets. It's <u>hopeless</u>.
W Ah... G... G... George. Can you come here?
M We can't afford to <u>keep</u> <u>throwing</u> <u>money</u> <u>away</u> like this.
W G... G... George...
M What's wrong with you? Have you <u>lost</u> your voice? You are <u>so</u> <u>pale</u>.
W The... the... numbers. WE ARE RICH!
M Did I say buying those tickets was <u>a</u> <u>waste</u> <u>of</u> time and money? I <u>take</u> <u>it</u> <u>all</u> <u>back</u>!

남 외출할 준비됐니?
여 거의 다 됐어. 그냥 내 로또 번호를 먼저 확인해 보고 싶어.
남 그런 복권 사는 데 돈을 낭비하는구나. 가망이 없는 일이야.
여 아… G… G… George. 이리 좀 와 볼래?
남 우리는 이런 데 계속해서 돈을 허비할 여유가 없어.
여 G… G… George…
남 왜 그러는 거야? 목소리가 안 나와? 너 아주 창백해.
여 그… 그… 숫자들이 말이야. 우린 이제 부자야!
남 내가 그런 것 사는 게 시간과 돈 낭비라고 했었나? 그 말 다 취소야!

● ●

hopeless 가망 없는   **pale** 창백한
take back (자기가 한 말을) 취소하다

09 대화를 듣고, 남자가 구입할 코트로 가장 적절한 것을 고르시오.

① 18만 원짜리 양모 코트
② 18만 원짜리 양모와 폴리에스테르 혼방 코트
③ 49만 원짜리 양모 코트
④ 49만 원짜리 캐시미어 코트
⑤ 80만 원짜리 대만산 코트

M Hello, ma'am. I would like to <u>buy a long coat</u> for my wife.

W How about this one? It's <u>cashmere</u> and costs only 490,000 won.

M Hmmm. That's a little expensive. Do you have <u>another kind</u>?

W This one here is <u>wool</u> and goes for only 180,000 won.

M That looks nice. Can I have a closer look?

W Sure, go ahead.

M The tag on the inside of the coat says it's a mix of wool and polyester and was <u>made in Taiwan</u>. It's not pure wool.

W Oh, I <u>must have given</u> you the wrong one. Here. This is the one I meant to give you.

M It looks nice. I'll buy this one.

남 안녕하세요. 제 아내를 위해서 긴 코트를 사고 싶은데요.

여 이건 어떠세요? 캐시미어인데 49만 원밖에 안 해요.

남 음. 조금 비싼데요. 다른 종류 있나요?

여 여기 있는 이것은 양모이고 18만 원밖에 안 합니다.

남 좋아 보이는군요. 더 자세히 봐도 될까요?

여 그럼요, 그렇게 하세요.

남 코트 안쪽에 있는 태그에는 양모와 폴리에스테르 혼방이고 대만산이라고 되어 있어요. 순수한 양모가 아니네요.

여 오, 제가 다른 걸 드린 게 틀림없어요. 여기요. 이것이 제가 드리려던 것입니다.

남 좋아 보이는군요. 이것으로 사겠습니다.

••
wool 양모, 양털 **tag** 태그, 꼬리표

---

10 대화를 듣고, 여자가 졸린 이유로 가장 적절한 것을 고르시오.

① 오늘 아침에 일찍 일어났기 때문에
② 윗집 소음으로 잠을 못 잤기 때문에
③ 매일 방과 후에 학원에 가기 때문에
④ TV 드라마를 보느라 밤을 새웠기 때문에
⑤ 시험을 보고 난 직후라 피곤하기 때문에

M Sora, what's wrong with you?

W I'm just so tired. I <u>can't stop falling asleep</u> in class.

M Why are you so sleepy?

W Every day after school, I have to go to <u>math</u> and <u>English academies</u>.

M So what time do you finally get home?

W Around 10:30 p.m. Then, I eat and do my homework <u>for another two hours</u>.

M That's a tough schedule. <u>It's no wonder</u> you're sleepy in class.

W I would do anything to sleep for an entire day.

M I know what you mean. Just <u>take a nap</u>. I'll wake you right before class begins.

W Thanks.

남 소라야, 무슨 일 있니?

여 그냥 많이 피곤해서. 수업 시간에 자는 걸 막을 수가 없어.

남 왜 그렇게 졸린 건데?

여 매일 방과 후에 수학이랑 영어 학원을 가야 하거든.

남 그럼 결국 몇 시에 집에 들어가니?

여 오후 10시 30분쯤. 그러고 나서 밥 먹고 또 2시간 정도 숙제를 하거든.

남 힘든 일정이구나. 네가 수업 시간에 졸린 것도 당연하네.

여 하루 종일 잠잘 수 있다면 뭐든지 할 거야.

남 무슨 말인지 알겠다. 잠깐이라도 자. 수업이 시작하기 직전에 깨워 줄게.

여 고마워.

••
academy 학원 **tough** 힘든 **It's no wonder (that)** ~는 당연하다, 놀랄 일이 아니다 **take a nap** 잠깐 자다

11

대화를 듣고, 남자가 여자에게 요청한 일로 가장 적절한 것을 고르시오.

① 택시 보내 주기
② 신문 구독 연장하기
③ 영화 예매 취소하기
④ 병원 진료 예약하기
⑤ 검진 결과지 발송해 주기

W Happy Taxi Service. May I help you?

M Hi. I need someone to come <u>to</u> <u>pick</u> <u>me</u> <u>up</u> here.

W Where are you, sir?

M I'm at the Main Street Theater.

W And when do you want the taxi?

M <u>I'm</u> <u>in</u> <u>a</u> <u>rush</u>, so please tell the driver to hurry.

W Yes, sir. I'll <u>send</u> <u>someone</u> right over soon.

M Thank you. I'll be <u>waiting</u> <u>for</u> <u>a</u> <u>taxi</u> in front of the theater.

W We will be there in five minutes. Thanks for <u>choosing</u> our company.

여 Happy 택시 회사입니다. 무엇을 도와 드릴까요?

남 안녕하세요. 이곳으로 누군가가 데리러 왔으면 하는데요.

여 어디에 계시는데요, 고객님?

남 Main Street 극장에 있습니다.

여 그리고 언제 택시가 필요합니까?

남 좀 급한데, 운전 기사님께 서둘러 달라고 말해 주세요.

여 네, 고객님. 그곳으로 곧 보내 드리겠습니다.

남 감사합니다. 그럼 극장 앞에서 택시를 기다리겠습니다.

여 5분 후에 그곳에 도착할 것입니다. 저희 회사를 선택해 주셔서 감사합니다.

••

in a rush 급한, 바쁜   **choose** 선택하다

12

대화를 듣고, 대화 내용과 일치하지 <u>않는</u> 것을 고르시오.

① 여자는 지금 영화관에 가는 중이다.
② 남자는 여자가 보려고 하는 영화를 이미 보았다.
③ 여자는 Jennifer Conrad를 좋아한다.
④ 여자는 아직 영화표를 구입하지 않았다.
⑤ 남자는 여자에게 줄 영화표를 스마트폰으로 예매했다.

M Where are you going in such a hurry?

W I'm just going to the movie theater to <u>see</u> <u>the</u> <u>latest</u> Jennifer Conrad <u>movie</u>.

M Oh, I've seen it. It's really good.

W I've heard it is. I am <u>a</u> <u>big</u> <u>fan</u> <u>of</u> hers. I'm so excited about seeing her movie.

M Have you <u>got</u> <u>a</u> <u>ticket</u>?

W No, I'm going to buy one at the box office.

M You can save yourself a lot of time by <u>buying</u> one <u>with</u> <u>a</u> <u>smartphone</u>.

W I'm <u>not</u> <u>familiar</u> <u>with</u> using a smartphone to buy a ticket. Please show me how to do that.

남 어딜 그렇게 서둘러서 가니?

여 Jennifer Conrad의 최신 영화를 보려고 막 극장에 가는 중이야.

남 오, 난 그거 봤어. 정말 재미있더라.

여 나도 들었어. 난 그녀의 광적인 팬이거든. 난 그녀의 영화를 본다는 게 너무 흥분돼.

남 표는 구했니?

여 아니, 매표소에서 사려고 해.

남 스마트폰으로 표를 사면 많은 시간을 절약할 수 있을 텐데.

여 난 스마트폰을 사용해서 표를 사는 것에 익숙하지 않아. 나에게 어떻게 하는지 알려 줘.

••

box office 매표소   **be familiar with** ~에 익숙하다

13 대화를 듣고, 남자의 마지막 말에 이어질 여자의 말로 가장 적절한 것을 고르시오.

① It's too bad their language is dying out.
② Cheer up. Everything will be great for you.
③ People should take steps to protect the ocean.
④ We should go to the zoo to see some gorillas and chimpanzees.
⑤ Exactly. They may disappear from the Earth due to humans.

W Have you read this article about the great apes in central Africa?
M No, I haven't had a chance to read the paper yet.
W Well, it seems that their numbers are declining quickly. A couple of species are in danger of dying out.
M I knew that gorillas and chimpanzees were under threat, but I didn't know it was that bad.
W It is. One of the main problems is the increase in the human population in the areas where the great apes live.
M So humans are gradually destroying their natural habitat.
W Exactly. They may disappear from the Earth due to humans.

여 중앙 아프리카에 있는 유인원에 대한 이 기사 읽어 봤니?
남 아니, 난 아직 그 신문을 읽어 볼 기회가 없었어.
여 음, 그들의 숫자가 급격하게 감소하고 있는 것 같더라. 두서너 종이 멸종 위험에 처해 있어.
남 난 고릴라와 침팬지들이 위협 받고 있는 것은 알았지만, 상황이 그렇게 안 좋은 줄은 몰랐어.
여 안 좋은 상황이야. 중대한 문제 중 하나는 유인원들이 사는 지역에서의 인구 증가지.
남 그래서 인류가 점차 그들의 자연 서식지를 파괴하고 있지.
여 맞아. 그들은 인간 때문에 지구상에서 사라질 수도 있어.

●●
article 기사 **great ape** 유인원 **decline** 감소하다 **species** (생물의) 종(種) **threat** 위협 **population** 인구 **gradually** 점차, 서서히 **destroy** 파괴하다 **habitat** 서식지 **disappear** 사라지다

---

14 대화를 듣고, 여자의 마지막 말에 이어질 남자의 말로 가장 적절한 것을 고르시오.

① That sounds easy. I'll give it a try.
② I guess you'll do better next time.
③ Great. I'll sign up for the service and use it.
④ You only get an allowance if you do your chores.
⑤ Sounds great. I'll start delivering newspapers tomorrow.

M I want to buy a new smartphone, but I only get a weekly allowance of 10 dollars. I need to save more money.
W I see.
M Do you have any ideas about how I could earn a little pocket money?
W You could deliver newspapers.
M No, thank you. That means getting up very early in the morning. I'm not a morning person.
W What about babysitting? That's what I do.
M What do you have to do?
W Well, I have to keep my attention on the baby and play with him.
M That sounds easy. I'll give it a try.

남 난 새 스마트폰을 사고 싶은데, 매주 용돈을 겨우 10달러 받아. 난 돈을 더 모아야 해.
여 그렇겠구나.
남 어떻게 약간의 쌈짓돈을 벌 수 있을지에 대해 좋은 생각 있니?
여 신문을 배달할 수 있지.
남 고맙지만 사양이야. 그 이야기는 아침에 정말 일찍 일어나야 한다는 거잖아. 난 아침형 인간이 아니야.
여 아기 돌보기는 어때? 내가 하는 건데.
남 뭘 해야 하지?
여 음, 아기에게 주의를 기울이고 아기와 같이 놀아 주면 돼.
남 그거 정말 쉽구나. 한번 해 봐야겠다.

●●
weekly 매주의 **allowance** 용돈 **earn** (돈을) 벌다 **deliver** 배달하다 **babysitting** 아기 돌보기 **attention** 주의

15 대화를 듣고, 남자의 마지막 말에 이어질 여자의 말로 가장 적절한 것을 고르시오.

① He is going to fix my car for me.
② He is supposed to come back here.
③ He shouldn't have stayed out so late.
④ He's going to take the driver's license test tomorrow.
✓⑤ His father ordered him not to leave the house for a week.

M Daniel is really in trouble with his father.
W Yes, his sister told me. I think it's all his fault.
M I'll say. He used his father's new car without permission last night.
W And then he crashed it into the garage door.
M No wonder his father is really angry.
W It's understandable; the repairs are going to cost him a lot.
M Anyway, why did he use the car?
W He just got his driver's license. So he wanted to show off in front of his friends.
M What a childish boy! So what is his father going to do with him?
W His father ordered him not to leave the house for a week.

남 Daniel은 정말 아버지와 문제가 있어.
여 맞아, 그의 누나가 나에게 이야기해 줬어. 난 그게 전부 그의 잘못이라고 생각해.
남 내 말이. 그는 지난 밤에 허락 없이 아버지의 새 차를 썼어.
여 그러고 나서는 차를 차고 문에다 부딪쳤고.
남 그의 아버지께서 정말로 화나신 것도 당연해.
여 이해가 돼. 수리비가 엄청나게 들 테니.
남 어쨌든, 그가 왜 자동차를 썼니?
여 그는 막 운전면허증을 땄어. 그래서 그는 친구들 앞에서 자랑하고 싶었지.
남 유치하기도 하지! 그래서 그의 아버지는 그에게 어떻게 하신대?
여 그의 아버지는 그가 일주일간 집에서 못 나가게 하셨어.

fault 잘못 **permission** 허락 **crash** 부딪치다 **understandable** 이해할 수 있는 **show off** ~을 자랑하다 **childish** 유치한

REVIEW TEST p. 23

A ① pale, 창백한 ② whole, 전체의 ③ weekly, 매주의 ④ article, 기사 ⑤ several, 몇몇의 ⑥ attention, 주의 ⑦ passenger, 승객 ⑧ examination, 검사, 진찰 ⑨ depart, 출발하다 ⑩ take a nap, 잠깐 자다 ⑪ in a rush, 급한, 바쁜 ⑫ show off, ~을 자랑하다

B ① take, back ② total price ③ experiences, surgery ④ blocking the way ⑤ It's no wonder ⑥ gradually destroying, habitat ⑦ hesitate to notify ⑧ not familiar with

01 ② 02 ③ 03 ③ 04 ② 05 ④ 06 ④ 07 ① 08 ④
09 ⑤ 10 ② 11 ③ 12 ④ 13 ② 14 ③ 15 ⑤

문제 및 정답	받아쓰기 및 녹음내용	해석

01

다음을 듣고, 그림의 상황에 알맞은 대화를 고르시오.

① ② ③ ④ ⑤

① M Can you help me <u>find</u> <u>my</u> <u>seat</u>?
  W All right. Please follow me.
② M Ma'am? You can <u>sit</u> <u>over</u> <u>here</u>.
  W Thank you, young man.
③ M Did you <u>get</u> <u>the</u> <u>tickets</u>?
  W Yeah, and they're good seats, too.
④ M Hi. I'd like to return this, please.
  W Sure. Can I <u>see</u> <u>your</u> <u>receipt</u>?
⑤ M What a beautiful baby!
  W Thank you. Her name's Heather.

① 남 제 좌석을 찾는 것을 도와주시겠어요?
  여 좋습니다. 저를 따라오세요.
② 남 부인? 여기 앉으세요.
  여 고마워요, 젊은이.
③ 남 표를 받았나요?
  여 네, 그 표들도 좋은 좌석이에요.
④ 남 안녕하세요. 이것을 반품하고 싶은데요.
  여 물론이죠. 영수증을 볼 수 있을까요?
⑤ 남 아기가 참 예쁘다!
  여 고마워. 아기 이름은 Heather야.

●●
follow 따라오다 **receipt** 영수증

02

대화를 듣고, 남자가 가려고 하는 장소로 가장 적절한 곳을 고르시오.

① 백화점   ② 영화관
③ 친구네 집   ④ 버스 정류장
⑤ 자동차 정비소

W Bob, hi! What a surprise to see you on this train.
M Hi. <u>Long</u> <u>time</u>, <u>no</u> <u>see</u>.
W Are you going to Seattle?
M Yeah. I don't like <u>public</u> <u>transportation</u>, but my car is in the garage, so...
W Right. I remember you always <u>hated</u> <u>trains</u>.
M Well, I <u>didn't</u> <u>have</u> <u>any</u> <u>choice</u>. I have to go to my friend's house for dinner.
W You're going to <u>your</u> <u>friend's</u> <u>house</u>? Sounds like a good time.

여 Bob, 안녕! 이 기차에서 널 만나다니 정말 놀라운걸.
남 안녕. 오랜만이야.
여 시애틀에 가니?
남 응. 대중교통을 좋아하진 않지만, 내 차가 정비소에 있어서…
여 맞아. 네가 항상 기차를 싫어했던 게 기억나.
남 그래, 선택의 여지가 없었어. 저녁 먹으러 친구네 집에 가야 하거든.
여 친구네 집에 가는 거라고? 재미있겠다.

●●
public transportation 대중교통 **garage** 정비소

18

03 다음을 듣고, 여자의 직업으로 가장 적절한 것을 고르시오.

① 가수　　　② 의사
③ 교사　　　④ 영화감독
⑤ 엔지니어

Hi. My name is Olga Strauss. I work at Lincoln Elementary. For years, I had first-grade students, but starting this year, they moved me up to the fifth grade. I loved the little ones, but I'm excited to move on to higher-level material. There's so much you can do with the fifth graders. I've got to finish planning my lessons, so I don't have a lot of time to talk right now. You're welcome to visit my class sometime though.

안녕하세요. 제 이름은 Olga Strauss예요. Lincoln 초등학교에서 일해요. 수년간 1학년 학생들을 가르쳤지만, 올해부터는 5학년으로 발령이 났지요. 저는 어린아이들이 좋지만, 더 높은 단계의 교재로 옮기게 되어 흥분돼요. 5학년 아이들과 할 수 있는 일들이 아주 많아요. 저는 수업 계획을 끝마쳐야 해서 지금 당장은 이야기할 시간이 많지 않아요. 하지만 언젠가 저희 학급을 방문하는 건 환영합니다.

●●
material 교재, 자료　**though** 하지만, 그렇지만

---

04 대화를 듣고, 두 사람의 관계로 가장 적절한 것을 고르시오.

① 교수 - 학생
② 매표원 - 손님
③ 지휘자 - 연주자
④ 택시 기사 - 승객
⑤ 여행사 직원 - 고객

M Hello. I-link. How may I help you?
W Hi. Do you have any tickets available for tomorrow night's concert?
M Let me check. We have S class and C class seats left.
W How much are the S class seats?
M They're 150 dollars a seat.
W Oh, that's too expensive. How about the C class seats?
M They're 50 dollars.
W I think I'll have to go with the C class seats.
M All right. How many would you like?
W Three, please.

남 여보세요. I-link입니다. 무엇을 도와드릴까요?
여 안녕하세요. 내일 밤에 이용할 수 있는 콘서트 표가 있나요?
남 확인해 보죠. S석과 C석이 남아 있어요.
여 S석은 얼마예요?
남 좌석당 150달러입니다.
여 오, 너무 비싸네요. C석은요?
남 50달러입니다.
여 C석을 사야 할 것 같아요.
남 좋습니다. 몇 좌석을 원하세요?
여 세 좌석 부탁드립니다.

05 다음을 듣고, 내일 오후의 날씨로 가장 적절한 것을 고르시오.

① ②

③ ④

⑤

Tomorrow is <u>expected</u> to be a beautiful day. The <u>morning</u> <u>low</u> will be a refreshing 19 degrees, and there will be some <u>light</u> <u>fog</u>. The fog will lift, however, as we head toward noon. In the <u>middle</u> <u>of</u> <u>the</u> <u>day</u>, temperatures are expected to rise all the way to 29 degrees. The <u>skies</u> will be <u>clear</u>, and there will be a slight breeze from the west.

내일은 날씨가 좋을 것으로 예상됩니다. 아침 최저 기온은 상쾌한 19도이고, 약간의 옅은 안개가 있겠습니다. 그러나 안개는 정오가 되면서 갤 것입니다. 한낮에 온도는 29도까지 오를 것으로 예상됩니다. 하늘은 맑고, 약한 서풍이 불겠습니다.

●●
low 최저치 **refreshing** 상쾌하게 하는 **head toward** ~를 향해서 가다 **temperature** 온도, 기온 **rise** 오르다, 상승하다 **slight** 약간의 **breeze** 미풍, 산들바람

---

06 대화를 듣고, 남자가 대화 직후에 할 일로 가장 적절한 것을 고르시오.

① 요금 지불하기
② 미용실 예약하기
③ 여자에게 차 대접하기
④ 여자의 머리 잘라 주기
⑤ 여자의 머리 감겨 주기

W Hello, Jack. Can you do my hair today?
M I don't know. I'm <u>fully</u> <u>booked</u> today. What would you like done this time?
W Just <u>a</u> <u>quick</u> <u>trim</u> this time.
M You should have called <u>ahead</u> <u>of</u> <u>time</u> to make an appointment.
W I know, but it just <u>slipped</u> <u>my</u> <u>mind</u>. Can you fit me in?
M Well, all right, as long as it doesn't take longer than 30 minutes. As you know, I have other clients waiting. You're lucky you're <u>such</u> <u>a</u> <u>loyal</u> <u>client</u>.
W You have no idea how much I appreciate this.
M Okay. <u>Get</u> <u>in</u> the chair before I change my mind.
W Thanks, Jack.

여 안녕하세요, Jack. 오늘 머리 좀 할 수 있을까요?
남 모르겠어요. 오늘 예약이 꽉 차서요. 이번에는 무엇을 하고 싶으신데요?
여 이번에는 그냥 빠르게 다듬기만 할 거예요.
남 예약하기 위해 미리 전화하셨더라면 좋았을 텐데요.
여 알아요, 그런데 그만 깜빡했어요. 절 끼워 넣어 줄 수 있어요?
남 음, 좋아요, 30분 이상 걸리지 않을 정도라면요. 아시다시피 기다리고 있는 다른 고객분들이 있으니까요. 당신이 단골 고객이라 운이 좋은 거예요.
여 제가 얼마나 많이 고마워하고 있는지 모르실 거예요.
남 알겠어요. 제 마음이 바뀌기 전에 의자에 앉으세요.
여 고마워요, Jack.

●●
booked 예약된 **trim** (머리를) 다듬기 **ahead of time** 미리 **slip one's mind** 깜빡하다, 잊어버리다 **loyal** 충성도 높은

07 대화를 듣고, 여자의 심정으로 가장 적절한 것을 고르시오.

① proud ✓
② jealous
③ amazed
④ nervous
⑤ annoyed

M Where are you going today, Anne?

W I'm going to my daughter's graduation. She just finished medical school.

M That's fantastic. You must be very happy for her today.

W Both her father and I are so pleased. She decided to go to medical school, and she finally did it.

M Are you going to take any pictures there?

W Yes, I brought my camera. After the ceremony, we are going out to eat.

M I hope you have a great afternoon. Please extend my congratulations to your daughter.

W I will, thanks.

남 Anne, 오늘 어디 가는 거예요?

여 내 딸 졸업식에 가요. 딸이 의대 공부를 막 끝냈거든요.

남 대단하네요. 따님 때문에 오늘 아주 행복하시겠어요.

여 애 아빠랑 저 둘 다 너무 기뻐요. 의대 진학을 결심하더니 결국 해내더군요.

남 거기서 사진을 찍으실 거예요?

여 네, 카메라를 가져왔어요. 식이 끝난 후에 외식할 거예요.

남 좋은 오후 보내시기를 바라요. 축하한다고 따님께 전해 주세요.

여 그럴게요, 고마워요.

●●
graduation 졸업식 **pleased** 기쁜
extend congratulations to ~에게 축하 인사를 하다

---

08 대화를 듣고, 남자가 구입할 비행기 표의 가격을 고르시오.

① 15만 원
② 19만 원
③ 50만 원
④ 75만 원 ✓
⑤ 90만 원

W World Wide Travel. May I help you?

M Yes, I'd like a round-trip ticket to New York, please. I'm looking for the cheapest ticket.

W Well, if you stop in Vancouver, the price will be 900,000 won.

M Is that the cheapest ticket you have?

W If you stop in Tokyo, Vancouver, and Chicago before going on to New York City, then the price drops to 750,000 won.

M That sounds better. That's a lot of stops though.

W It is. But if you want the cheapest ticket, that's what you have to do.

M Okay. I'll take it. I don't mind changing planes if I can save a little money.

W Very good. Will that be cash or credit card?

여 World Wide 여행사입니다. 무엇을 도와 드릴까요?

남 네, 뉴욕으로 가는 왕복표를 부탁합니다. 가장 싼 표를 찾고 있습니다.

여 음, 밴쿠버를 경유하면, 가격이 90만 원입니다.

남 그게 보유하고 계신 가장 싼 표입니까?

여 만약 뉴욕에 가기 전에 도쿄, 밴쿠버, 그리고 시카고를 경유하면, 가격은 75만 원까지 떨어집니다.

남 그게 더 낫겠군요. 경유지가 많긴 하지만요.

여 그렇긴 합니다. 하지만 고객님께서 가장 싼 표를 원하신다면 그렇게 하셔야만 합니다.

남 좋습니다. 그것으로 하겠습니다. 돈을 조금이라도 절약할 수 있다면 비행기를 갈아타는 것은 상관없습니다.

여 좋습니다. 현금으로 하시겠습니까, 아니면 신용 카드로 하시겠습니까?

●●
round-trip 왕복 여행의 **stop in** ~를 경유하다. ~에 잠시 머무르다

09

대화를 듣고, 여자가 커피를 마시려 하지 <u>않는</u> 이유로 가장 적절한 것을 고르시오.

① 커피를 좋아하지 않아서
② 오전에 이미 커피를 마셔서
③ 오후 2시에 다른 약속이 있어서
④ 커피를 마시면 두드러기가 생겨서
⑤ 지금 커피를 마시면 밤에 잠을 자지 못 해서

M How about some coffee?

W I'd love some, but it's already 2 p.m. If I have some now, I'll <u>be awake</u> <u>all</u> <u>night</u>.

M No kidding. Caffeine really <u>affects</u> you that way?

W Yes, I'm very <u>sensitive to caffeine</u>. What about you?

M I can drink coffee just before going to bed, and I'm fine.

W It's funny how people <u>react</u> <u>differently</u> to certain substances.

M What about some <u>herbal</u> <u>tea</u> then?

W Yes, I can have that.

남 커피 어때요?

여 마시고 싶지만 벌써 오후 2시예요. 지금 마시면, 밤새도록 깨어 있을 거예요.

남 농담이죠? 카페인이 정말로 당신에게 그렇게 영향을 미치나요?

여 네, 전 카페인에 매우 민감하거든요. 당신은요?

남 잠자기 직전에 커피를 마셔도 전 괜찮아요.

여 사람들이 특정 물질에 대해 다르게 반응하는 방식이 재밌어요.

남 그럼 허브 차는 어때요?

여 네, 그건 마실 수 있어요.

● ●

affect 영향을 미치다   **sensitive** 민감한
substance 물질   **herbal** 허브의

10

대화를 듣고, 두 사람이 오늘 저녁에 할 일로 가장 적절한 것을 고르시오.

① 공원에서 운동하기
② 친구들과 집안 청소하기
③ 친구들과 밀린 숙제 하기
④ 공항에 부모님 마중 나가기
⑤ 친구들과 튤립 축제에 참가하기

M Hey, Betty. Do you want to go to a <u>tulip</u> <u>festival</u> with us this weekend?

W I'm sorry, but I can't. I have to <u>clean</u> my <u>messy</u> <u>apartment</u> this weekend because my parents are coming next week.

M Oh, that's too bad. I have an idea! <u>What</u> <u>if</u> our friends <u>came</u> <u>over</u> this evening and cleaned your apartment? Then, you <u>will</u> <u>be</u> <u>free</u> for the weekend.

W I can't ask you to do that. It's a very nice idea though.

M It's no problem at all. We really want you <u>to go</u> <u>with</u> <u>us</u> this weekend.

W Okay, then. Can you come at 6 p.m.?

M We'll be there.

남 안녕, Betty. 이번 주말에 우리와 튤립 축제에 가지 않을래?

여 미안하지만 안 돼. 다음 주에 부모님이 오실 거라서 이번 주말에 지저분한 아파트를 청소해야 해.

남 아, 그거 참 안됐다. 내게 좋은 생각이 있어! 친구들이 오늘 저녁에 너희 집에 가서 아파트 청소를 해 주면 어떨까? 그러면 넌 주말에 시간이 날 거야.

여 너희들한테 그렇게 하라고 부탁할 수는 없어. 아주 좋은 생각이긴 하지만.

남 전혀 문제 없어. 우리는 네가 정말로 이번 주말에 우리랑 함께 갔으면 좋겠어.

여 좋아, 그럼. 오후 6시에 와 줄 수 있니?

남 갈게.

● ●

messy 지저분한

11 대화를 듣고, 여자가 전화를 건 목적으로 가장 적절한 것을 고르시오.

① 제작이 완료되었는지 확인하려고
② 물건의 배송 소요 기간을 알아보려고
③ 수선 맡긴 물건의 견적을 알아보려고
④ 새로 나온 가방의 가격을 알아보려고
⑤ 분실 신고된 여행 가방이 있는지 확인하려고

M Exquisite Store. How may I help you?

W Hello. I visited your store to <u>have</u> my <u>suitcase</u> <u>fixed</u> last week.

M Oh, is that the one with the <u>broken</u> <u>handle</u>?

W Yes, I would also like to know <u>how</u> <u>much</u> it will <u>cost</u>.

M We think that it will cost 35,000 won <u>at</u> <u>most</u>. Will that be okay with you?

W It's a little more expensive <u>than</u> I <u>had</u> <u>expected</u>. But I need it soon. How long will it take to <u>have</u> <u>it</u> <u>repaired</u>?

M It will take 10 days. Then, you can pick it up.

W All right. <u>As</u> <u>soon</u> <u>as</u> you fix it, please let me know.

남 Exquisite 매장입니다. 무엇을 도와드릴까요?

여 안녕하세요. 제가 지난 주에 여행 가방 수선을 맡기기 위해 매장을 방문했었는데요.

남 아, 그 손잡이가 망가진 가방 말이죠?

여 네, 비용이 얼마나 들지도 알고 싶은데요.

남 저희 생각에는 최대한으로 잡으면 35,000원일 것 같은데요. 이 정도면 괜찮으시겠어요?

여 제가 예상했던 것보다 조금 더 비싸긴 하네요. 그렇지만 당장 써야 하는 것이라서. 수선 기간은 얼마나 되죠?

남 10일 걸릴 겁니다. 그때 찾아 가실 수 있어요.

여 좋습니다. 그것을 수선하시는 대로 제게 알려 주세요.

●●

at most 최대한으로 잡아서, 기껏해야 **as soon as** ~하는 대로, ~하자마자

---

12 대화를 듣고, 대화 내용과 일치하지 <u>않는</u> 것을 고르시오.

① 여자는 남자에게 무선 이어폰을 빌려주었다.
② 여자는 무선 이어폰을 오늘 밤에 사용하기를 원한다.
③ 남자의 개가 여자의 무선 이어폰을 물어뜯었다.
④ 여자는 무선 이어폰을 새로 구입할 것이다.
⑤ 남자는 오늘 저녁에 여자의 집에 갈 것이다.

W Peter, can you give me back the <u>wireless</u> <u>earphones</u> that I <u>lent</u> you?

M I thought you didn't need to use them until this weekend.

W Yes, but I want to listen to music tonight after doing my homework.

M Well... I <u>can't</u> <u>return</u> <u>them</u> right now.

W You can't return them? Why? Did you lose them?

M No, actually, my dog <u>chewed</u> <u>them</u> <u>up</u>.

W What? Your dog broke my wireless earphones?

M Yes. I was <u>afraid</u> <u>to</u> <u>tell</u> you. I'm really sorry.

W But I wanted to use them today! And I don't have enough money to <u>buy</u> <u>a</u> <u>new</u> <u>pair</u>.

M I will buy you some new ones. And I'll <u>bring</u> <u>them</u> to your home this evening.

여 Peter, 내가 너에게 빌려준 무선 이어폰 돌려 주겠니?

남 나는 네가 이번 주말까지 그걸 사용할 필요가 없다고 생각했었는데.

여 응, 하지만 오늘 밤에 숙제를 마친 후에 음악을 듣고 싶어서 말이야.

남 음… 지금 당장은 돌려 줄 수가 없어.

여 돌려 줄 수 없다고? 왜? 잃어버렸니?

남 아니, 사실, 우리 개가 그걸 물어뜯었거든.

여 뭐? 네 개가 내 무선 이어폰을 부쉈다고?

남 응. 네게 말하기가 두려웠어. 정말 미안해.

여 하지만 나는 그걸 오늘 쓰고 싶었단 말이야! 그리고 새것을 살 돈도 없고.

남 내가 새것을 사 줄게. 그리고 오늘 저녁에 너희 집으로 갖다 줄게.

●●

wireless 무선의 **chew up** ~를 물어뜯다

13 대화를 듣고, 남자의 마지막 말에 이어질 여자의 말로 가장 적절한 것을 고르시오.

① You should finish your paper quickly.

② I don't want to think about it. It's painful.

③ Looks like it's going to get worse every day.

④ Well, if it could rain even a drop, things would be much better.

⑤ Whenever a huge hurricane strikes, there's always a large loss of life.

W I've been writing a <u>research paper</u> about <u>earthquakes</u> for my geology class.

M Really? I wrote a paper about them, too.

W I've been reading a report on the very bad earthquake in Iran in 2003.

M Is that the one that <u>destroyed the city</u> called Bam?

W Yes, that's the one. It killed around 40,000 people.

M <u>What a disaster</u>!

W The earthquake struck very early in the morning.

M So I <u>suppose</u> most people were still <u>asleep</u> in bed.

W Many people didn't know what hit them.

M I wonder if another big one will <u>hit the same area</u>.

W <u>I don't want to think about it. It's painful.</u>

여 난 지질학 수업에 제출할 지진에 대한 탐구 보고서를 쓰고 있어.

남 정말? 나도 그것에 대해 보고서를 썼는데.

여 난 2003년에 이란에서 발생한 최악의 지진에 대한 보고서를 읽고 있어.

남 Bam이라는 도시를 파괴한 지진 말이지?

여 맞아, 그거야. 약 4만 명을 죽였지.

남 엄청난 재앙이야!

여 지진은 매우 이른 아침에 일어났었어.

남 그래서 대부분의 사람들이 아직 침대에 누워 잠들어 있었겠지.

여 많은 사람들이 자신들에게 무엇이 닥쳤는지도 몰랐어.

남 난 그 지역에 또 다른 큰 지진이 일어날 것인지 궁금해.

여 <u>난 그것에 대해 생각하기도 싫어. 가슴 아파.</u>

●●
earthquake 지진 **geology** 지질학
disaster 재앙 **suppose** 추측하다, 생각하다
wonder 궁금하다

---

14 대화를 듣고, 여자의 마지막 말에 이어질 남자의 말로 가장 적절한 것을 고르시오.

① You've got it totally wrong.

② The color doesn't appeal to me.

③ Okay. I won't buy him one of those.

④ This sounds like a joke, but it's true.

⑤ Okay. There's something I've got to tell you.

W I hope you're not busy on Friday night.

M I don't have <u>any plans yet</u>. Why?

W We're having a birthday party.

M <u>Whose birthday</u> is it?

W It's John's. We're going to surprise him. I hope you can go to it.

M Sure, I'll go. Is there <u>anything</u> I can <u>help with</u>?

W No. We already have everything we need. Thanks though.

M I <u>wonder what</u> I should get him for his birthday.

W I don't know, but don't get him a necktie. <u>That's what I got</u> him.

M <u>Okay. I won't buy him one of those.</u>

여 금요일 밤에 네가 바쁘지 않으면 좋겠는데.

남 아직 계획은 없어. 왜?

여 우린 생일 파티를 열 거거든.

남 누구의 생일인데?

여 John의 생일이야. 그를 깜짝 놀라게 해 주려고 해. 네가 와 주면 좋겠어.

남 그래, 갈게. 뭔가 도와줄 일 있니?

여 아니. 필요한 건 벌써 모두 준비했어. 어쨌든 고마워.

남 그의 생일에 무얼 사 줘야 할지 모르겠군.

여 글쎄, 하지만 넥타이는 사 주지 마. 그건 내가 그에게 사 준 거니까.

남 <u>알았어. 그건 사 주지 않을게.</u>

15 다음 상황 설명을 듣고, Sally가 Sam에게 할 말로 가장 적절한 것을 고르시오.

① Don't mention it.
② Can you recommend someone?
③ I was worried you wouldn't like it.
④ I had a summer internship in the field.
⑤ Thanks for your advice. I'll keep that in mind.

Sally's just graduated from her university. She's been sending résumés to many companies. She got a phone call from one of those companies, so she is scheduled to have a job interview tomorrow. Since she doesn't have any work experience, she's very nervous. Her friend Sam tells her that the company wants someone who works well with people, so she has to show them how outgoing and personable she is. In this situation, what would Sally most likely say to Sam?

Sally: <u>Thanks for your advice. I'll keep that in mind.</u>

Sally는 대학을 갓 졸업했다. 그녀는 여러 회사에 이력서를 보내고 있다. 그녀는 그 회사들 중 하나로부터 전화를 받아서, 내일 구직 면접을 볼 예정이다. 그녀는 직무 경험이 없기에 매우 초조하다. 그녀의 친구인 Sam은 그녀에게 회사는 사람들과 함께 잘 일하는 사람을 원하기 때문에 그들에게 그녀가 얼마나 사교적이고 매력적인지를 보여줘야 한다고 말한다. 이런 상황에서, Sally는 Sam에게 뭐라고 말하겠는가?

Sally: <u>조언 고마워. 그 말 명심할게.</u>

●●
graduate 졸업하다 **résumé** 이력서
job interview 구직 면접 **outgoing** 사교적인, 외향적인 **personable** 매력적인

▶ REVIEW TEST p. 31

A ① slight, 약간의 ② résumé, 이력서 ③ affect, 영향을 미치다 ④ follow, 따라오다 ⑤ pleased, 기쁜
⑥ sensitive, 민감한 ⑦ suppose, 추측하다, 생각하다 ⑧ outgoing, 사교적인, 외향적인 ⑨ messy, 지저분한
⑩ earthquake, 지진 ⑪ graduation, 졸업식 ⑫ public transportation, 대중 교통

B ① see, receipt ② round, trip ③ chewed up
④ Temperatures, rise ⑤ job interview ⑥ slipped my mind
⑦ As soon as ⑧ ahead of time

문제 및 정답	받아쓰기 및 녹음내용	해석

01

다음을 듣고, 그림의 상황에 알맞은 대화를 고르시오.

① ② ③ ④ ⑤

① M Could I have some change for a dollar?

W Sure. Here are three <u>quarters</u> and five <u>nickels</u>.

② W Will you <u>lend</u> me <u>some money</u>?

M Sure. How much?

③ M You look upset. What's wrong?

W Someone took my purse <u>while</u> I <u>was</u> <u>away</u>.

④ M Here is your allowance. <u>Make</u> <u>sure</u> you don't spend too much money <u>at</u> <u>once</u>.

W No problem. I won't.

⑤ W Could you <u>explain</u> <u>to</u> <u>me</u> how to use this ATM?

M No problem. What are you going to do with that?

① 남 1달러 지폐를 잔돈으로 좀 바꿔 주시겠어요?

여 그럼요. 25센트 동전 3개와 5센트 동전 5개요.

② 여 돈 좀 빌려줄래?

남 그래. 얼마나?

③ 남 너 기분이 안 좋아 보여. 무슨 일이니?

여 내가 자리를 비운 사이에 누군가가 내 지갑을 가져갔어.

④ 남 용돈 여기 있다. 한 번에 너무 많은 돈을 쓰지 않도록 해라.

여 그럼요. 그렇게 할게요.

⑤ 여 이 현금 자동 입출금기를 이용하는 법을 제게 설명해 주시겠어요?

남 물론이죠. 그걸로 무얼 하실 건가요?

◑◑ **quarter** 25센트짜리 동전 **nickel** 5센트짜리 동전

02

대화를 듣고, 두 사람이 대화하는 장소로 가장 적절한 곳을 고르시오.

① 집   ② 공원
③ 택시 승강장   ④ 버스 정류장
⑤ 안내 데스크

M May I help you?

W Yeah, thanks. I'm staying at the Cosmopolitan Plaza in town. What's the <u>best</u> <u>way</u> to <u>get</u> <u>there</u>? I'd like to have a tour map, too.

M Here you are. You can take a cab, bus, limo, or hotel shuttle.

W <u>What</u> do you <u>recommend</u>?

M That depends. A cab is faster but more expensive.

W The bus is cheaper but a little slow.

M It would probably be a good idea to <u>take</u> <u>your</u> <u>hotel</u> <u>shuttle</u>.

W All right. Where do I catch it?

M Just go through those doors, and look for the shuttle sign. When it comes by, <u>wave</u>, and the driver will <u>pick</u> <u>you</u> <u>up</u>.

W Thank you for your help.

남 도와드릴까요?

여 네, 감사합니다. 시내에 있는 Cosmopolitan Plaza에 묵을 건데요. 거기에 가는 가장 좋은 방법이 뭔가요? 관광 안내도도 받고 싶습니다.

남 여기 있습니다. 택시, 버스, 리무진 버스, 혹은 호텔 셔틀버스를 타실 수 있어요.

여 뭘 추천하시겠어요?

남 사정에 따라 다르죠. 택시는 빠르지만 비싸요.

여 버스는 싸지만 조금 느리죠.

남 아마 호텔 셔틀버스를 타는 게 좋을 것 같아요.

여 좋아요. 어디서 타면 되나요?

남 저 문으로 나가서 셔틀버스 표시판을 찾으세요. 버스가 올 때, 손을 흔들면, 운전사가 태워 줄 거예요.

여 도와주셔서 감사해요.

◑◑ **cab** 택시 **limo** 리무진 버스

03 대화를 듣고, 여자가 미래에 갖고자 하는 직업으로 가장 적절한 것을 고르시오.

① 교수　　②✓ 배우
③ 승무원　　④ 바리스타
⑤ 아나운서

M How are your <u>acting</u> <u>classes</u> going?

W Great! But I'm a bit <u>worn</u> <u>out</u> these days.

M Why?

W Well, I'm making coffee.

M You're a barista?

W You got it.

M So you're taking classes <u>during</u> <u>the</u> <u>day</u> and working at night?

W Yes. I have to do that. I need the money to <u>support</u> <u>myself</u>.

M Well, one day, you'll get paid back when you become a <u>famous</u> <u>actress</u>. Keep going. Remember, "No <u>pain</u>, no <u>gain</u>."

W Thanks a lot.

남 연기 수업은 어떻게 되어 가니?

여 좋아! 하지만 요즘 좀 지쳐.

남 왜?

여 음, 커피를 만들고 있거든.

남 바리스타 하는 거야?

여 맞아.

남 그래서 낮에는 수업을 듣고 밤에는 일하고 있어?

여 응. 그렇게 해야만 해. 스스로 부양하려면 돈이 필요해.

남 그래, 어느 날, 네가 유명한 배우가 되면 보상이 될 거야. 계속 열심히 해. 기억해, "고통이 없으면 얻는 것도 없다."

여 정말 고마워.

●●
worn out 지친　**support oneself** 스스로 부양하다　**actress** 여자 배우　**gain** 얻는 것, 이익

---

04 대화를 듣고, 두 사람의 관계로 가장 적절한 것을 고르시오.

① 의사 - 간호사
② 수리 기사 - 고객
③ 식당 종업원 - 손님
④✓ 병원 접수원 - 환자
⑤ 호텔 접수원 - 투숙객

W Hello. This is Miracle Clinic. How may I help you?

M Hi. I'd like to <u>make</u> <u>an</u> <u>appointment</u> with the doctor on Wednesday.

W Can you make it on Wednesday at 2:30?

M No, I'm sorry, but I can't. Could you <u>make</u> <u>it</u> <u>earlier</u>?

W Yes. How about Wednesday at 10:00? Can I <u>have</u> <u>your</u> <u>name</u>?

M Fine. My name is David Stevenson.

W And your phone number?

M It's 526-0012.

W 526-0012?

M Yes.

W I'll see you on Wednesday at 10:00 then.

M Okay. <u>I</u> <u>appreciate</u> <u>it</u>.

여 안녕하세요. Miracle Clinic입니다. 무엇을 도와드릴까요?

남 안녕하세요. 저는 수요일에 진료 예약을 하고 싶은데요.

여 수요일 2시 30분에 오실 수 있나요?

남 아뇨, 죄송하지만 안 되겠어요. 좀 더 일찍 해 주실 수 있으세요?

여 네. 수요일 10시는 어떠세요? 이름을 말씀해 주시겠어요?

남 좋아요. 제 이름은 David Stevenson이에요.

여 전화번호는요?

남 526-0012입니다.

여 526-0012요?

남 네.

여 그럼 수요일 10시에 뵐게요.

남 네. 고맙습니다.

다음 표를 보면서 대화를 듣고, 두 사람이 관람할 영화와 상영 시각을 고르시오.

Movie Time			
Godfather V	House of Horrors	June	Dusty
2:00 p.m.	10:45 a.m.	9:50 a.m.	10:00 a.m.
2:30 p.m.	1:00 p.m.	12:50 p.m.	1:00 p.m.
3:40 p.m.	3:00 p.m.	4:00 p.m.	4:00 p.m.
	6:35 p.m.	7:00 p.m.	9:00 p.m.

① June, 7:00 p.m.
② Dusty, 9:00 p.m.
③ Dusty, 4:00 p.m.
④ Godfather V, 3:40 p.m.
⑤ House of Horrors, 6:35 p.m.

W So what should we see?
M I heard *Dusty* got great reviews.
W The only time that's left is the 9 o'clock show, and that's too late.
M Well, we could catch *House of Horrors* at 6:35.
W We could do that, but I'm not too hot about horror movies.
M Come on. It's not that scary. I'm going to buy tickets for the last showing of *House of Horrors*. Okay?
W I guess I have no choice.

여 그럼 우리 무얼 볼까?
남 'Dusty'가 호평을 받았다고 들었어.
여 유일하게 남은 건 9시 영화인데, 그건 너무 늦어.
남 음, 6시 35분에 하는 'House of Horrors'를 볼 수 있어.
여 그렇게 할 수도 있지만, 나는 공포 영화는 별로 안 좋아해.
남 에이. 그렇게 무섭지는 않다구. 내가 'House of Horrors'의 마지막 회 표를 살게. 괜찮지?
여 선택의 여지가 없는 것 같네.

●●
review 평론, 비평 **showing** (영화) 상영

대화를 듣고, 남자가 전화를 건 목적으로 가장 적절한 것을 고르시오.

① 약속을 취소하려고
② 교통 정보를 제공하려고
③ 서점의 위치를 물어보려고
④ 약속 시간에 늦을 것을 알리려고
⑤ 슈퍼마켓 앞으로 나와 달라고 부탁하려고

W Hello. Samson residence.
M Hi, Nancy. It's me, Jim.
W Jim, where are you? We've been waiting for you.
M Actually, I seem to be lost. I'll be a little late.
W Okay. Where are you now?
M I'm in front of the Five Star Supermarket next to the bookstore.
W I know where you are. Go north on King Road, and then take a left onto Spring Lane.
M Oh, okay. Now I know where I am. Thanks. See you soon.
W You are about three blocks away. Take your time. We'll be waiting for you.

여 여보세요. Samson의 집입니다.
남 안녕, Nancy. 나야, Jim.
여 Jim, 어디에 있니? 우리는 너를 기다리고 있어.
남 사실은, 난 길을 잃은 것 같아. 조금 늦겠어.
여 알았어. 지금 어디인데?
남 서점 옆에 있는 Five Star 슈퍼마켓 앞에 있어.
여 어디에 있는지 알겠다. King Road에서 북쪽으로 가, 그리고 나서 Spring Lane 쪽으로 좌회전을 해.
남 아, 알았어. 이제 내가 어디에 있는지 알겠어. 고마워. 곧 보자.
여 세 블록 정도 떨어져 있어. 천천히 와. 기다리고 있을게.

●●
residence 거주지, 주택 **lane** 도로, 길

07 다음을 듣고, 여자의 말의 목적으로 가장 적절한 것을 고르시오.

① 친구의 편지에 답하려고
② 온라인 회원 가입을 권유하려고
③ 홈페이지 개편 소식을 공지하려고
④ 회원을 위한 할인 행사를 안내하려고
⑤ 온라인 회원 가입에 대한 감사를 전하려고

Thank you for registering with Korea1post.com. You now have free online access to all of the reporting from *Korea1post*. You'll find a lot more than that on our website. Korea1post.com provides live talks, videos and graphics, e-mail newsletters, and other services to help you live your life and more.

Korea1post.com에 가입해 주셔서 감사합니다. 당신은 이제 *Korea1post*로부터 제공되는 모든 보도를 온라인으로 무료 이용할 수 있습니다. 저희 웹사이트에서 그 이상으로 훨씬 더 많은 것을 찾게 될 겁니다. Korea1post.com은 생방송 토론, 비디오 및 그래픽, 이메일 뉴스레터, 당신의 인생을 사는 데 도움이 될 만한 다른 서비스, 그 밖의 많은 것을 제공합니다.

··
register 가입하다, 등록하다 **have access to** ~을 이용할 수 있다 **provide** 제공하다

---

08 대화를 듣고, 남자의 심정으로 가장 적절한 것을 고르시오.

① envious ② shocked
③ pleasant ④ relieved
⑤ frustrated

W You look so sad. What's up?
M It's the manager. I asked her in advance if I could have this coming Saturday off.
W So did she change the schedule?
M No, she didn't. But my parents are coming to town, and I have to work at this restaurant.
W Why don't you talk to her about how important this is to you?
M I already did. She refused to change the schedule. Maybe I should quit this job.
W Relax. There must be another way. Let's put our heads together.

여 너 아주 슬퍼 보이네. 무슨 일이야?
남 매니저 때문에. 내가 그녀에게 이번 주 토요일에 쉴 수 있을지 미리 물어봤거든.
여 그래서, 매니저가 스케줄을 바꿔 주었니?
남 아니, 해 주지 않았어. 하지만 부모님이 상경하시기로 했는데, 난 이 식당에서 일해야 해.
여 매니저한테 네게 이것이 얼마나 중요한지 얘기해 보지 그러니?
남 이미 해 봤어. 매니저가 스케줄을 안 바꿔 주더라. 나 이 일을 그만둘까 봐.
여 진정해. 다른 방법이 있을 거야. 우리 함께 머리를 맞대고 의논해 보자.

··
in advance 미리 **have ~ off** ~에는 쉬다 **refuse** 거부하다 **put heads together** 머리를 맞대고 의논하다

09 대화를 듣고, 여자가 탑승할 버스의 출발 시각과 행선지를 고르시오.

① 9시 15분 – 서울
② 9시 15분 – 인천
③ 9시 30분 – 서울
④ 9시 30분 – 인천
⑤ 9시 45분 – 인천 ✓

M Ticket, please.
W Here you go, sir.
M You're <u>on the wrong bus</u>, ma'am.
W The wrong bus? What do you mean?
M This is the bus to Seoul. You're looking for the <u>nine thirty</u> bus to <u>Incheon</u>. The one you're supposed to be on has just left.
W I can't believe it. I <u>have to be there</u> by two o'clock today for a job interview.
M Don't worry. The bus to Incheon leaves <u>every fifteen minutes</u>. You can take the next bus.
W Thanks, sir.

남 표 주세요.
여 여기 있습니다, 기사님.
남 버스를 잘못 타셨어요, 고객님.
여 잘못 타다니요? 무슨 뜻이죠?
남 이건 서울로 가는 버스입니다. 고객님은 인천행 9시 30분 버스를 찾고 계시네요. 고객님이 타려는 버스는 방금 떠났습니다.
여 믿을 수가 없군요. 구직 면접이 있어서 오늘 2시까지 거기에 가야만 해요.
남 걱정 마세요. 인천행 버스는 15분마다 출발합니다. 다음 버스를 타시면 됩니다.
여 고맙습니다, 기사님.

••
be supposed to ~해야 하다, ~하기로 되어 있다

---

10 대화를 듣고, 여자가 학교 도서관에서 공부하려는 이유로 가장 적절한 것을 고르시오.

① 집안이 너무 시끄러워서
② 방 안의 조명이 밝지 않아서 ✓
③ 도서관에 참고 서적이 많이 있어서
④ 집에서는 동생이 공부하는 것을 방해해서
⑤ 도서관에서 친구들과 같이 공부하기 위해서

W Isn't there any way to <u>make the light</u> in this room <u>brighter</u>?
M No, that's impossible. Why do you ask?
W I've been getting headaches lately.
M You may have to <u>change</u> your <u>eyeglasses prescription</u>.
W Do you really think so? I hope my eyes aren't getting worse.
M Well, it's hard to say unless you <u>get</u> your <u>eyes tested</u>.
W I'll make an appointment with the eye doctor next week.
M Until then, you should read in a well-lit room.
W Then <u>I'd better study</u> in the school library.

여 이 방의 불을 좀 더 밝게 할 방법은 없을까?
남 아니, 그건 불가능해. 왜 물어?
여 최근에 두통이 있어서.
남 너 아마도 안경 처방을 바꿔야겠다.
여 정말로 그렇게 생각하니? 난 내 눈이 더 나빠지지 않았으면 좋겠어.
남 음, 시력 검사를 받지 않고서는 뭐라 말하기 힘들어.
여 다음 주에 검안사와 진료 예약을 해야겠어.
남 그때까지는 조명이 밝은 방에서 책을 읽어야 해.
여 그러면 나는 학교 도서관에서 공부하는 게 낫겠어.

••
prescription 처방

11 대화를 듣고, 남자가 오늘 할 일로 가장 적절한 것을 고르시오.

① 영어 공부하기
② Magi 교수님 만나기
③ Doris 교수님 만나기
④ 여자와 영화 보러 가기
⑤ 여자와 저녁 식사 하기

W Good morning, Peter.
M Hi, Jane. How are you feeling today?
W Fine. Did you decide to go to the Italian restaurant today?
M I intended to do so, but Professor Magi told me to meet Professor Doris today.
W Why? Is there a special reason?
M Perhaps Professor Doris expects me to help him with his research.
W Oh, I see. Then I can't force you to go with me.
M I'm sorry, but I can't. By the way, you've improved your English a lot.
W Thanks for your praise. You really encourage me to study hard. But I still fail to use words properly.
M You're too modest.

여 안녕, Peter.
남 안녕, Jane. 오늘 기분이 어때?
여 좋아. 너 오늘 이탈리아 음식점에 가기로 했니?
남 그렇게 하려고 했는데, Magi 교수님이 오늘 Doris 교수님을 만나 보라고 말씀하셔서.
여 왜? 특별한 이유라도 있니?
남 아마도 Doris 교수님이 내가 그의 연구를 돕기를 기대하시나 봐.
여 아, 그래. 그럼 내가 너를 억지로 데려갈 수는 없겠구나.
남 미안하지만 못 가게 됐네. 그런데, 너 영어 실력 많이 늘었다.
여 칭찬 고마워. 너는 정말 내가 열심히 공부하도록 용기를 북돋아 줘. 하지만 난 아직 단어를 적절히 사용하지는 못해.
남 넌 너무 겸손해.

● ●

intend to ~하려고 생각하다 professor 교수 perhaps 아마도 force 억지로 ~하게 하다 praise 칭찬 encourage 용기를 북돋우다 properly 적절히, 제대로

12 대화를 듣고, 대화 내용과 일치하지 <u>않는</u> 것을 고르시오.

① 여자는 필기 시험을 보기로 되어 있다.
② 여자는 대학에서 2년간 공부했다.
③ 여자는 1년 전에 대학 공부를 수료했다.
④ 여자는 프랑스어와 영양학을 공부한 적이 있다.
⑤ 여자는 아시아 요리 과목에 가장 큰 흥미를 느꼈다.

M Good afternoon, Ms. Fields. Sit down, please.
W Good afternoon, sir.
M Before you take the written test, I'd like to ask you several questions, Ms. Fields. Where did you learn cooking and serving?
W I took a two-year cooking course at the University of Paris.
M When did you finish it?
W A year ago, sir.
M What other subjects did you take?
W French, nutrition, and some others.
M Which subject interested you the most?
W Western cuisine, sir.

남 안녕하세요, Fields 씨. 앉으시죠.
여 안녕하세요.
남 필기 시험을 보시기 전에 제가 몇 가지 질문을 하고 싶습니다, Fields 씨. 어디서 요리와 서빙을 배우셨나요?
여 파리대학에서 2년 동안의 요리 과정을 밟았습니다.
남 언제 수료하셨나요?
여 1년 전에요.
남 다른 과목도 수강하셨나요?
여 프랑스어와 영양학 등을 수강했습니다.
남 어떤 과목이 가장 흥미로웠나요?
여 서양 요리입니다.

● ●

subject 과목, 학과 nutrition 영양학 cuisine 요리(법)

13 대화를 듣고, 남자의 마지막 말에 이어질 여자의 말로 가장 적절한 것을 고르시오.

① It's easier than I thought. Thanks a lot.
② You're good at playing computer games.
③ Well, I didn't want to think about it again.
④ It's pretty simple. I'll show you how to do this tomorrow.
⑤ You should teach me how to deal with this stressful situation.

M Why are you biting your nails? What's the matter?
W I don't think you can help me.
M Has your computer crashed?
W No, I'm trying to make this photo on the screen bigger.
M Oh, that's not difficult.
W I thought you didn't know anything about computers.
M Didn't I tell you I'm majoring in computer science?
W No, you didn't. Well, I've been trying to do it without any success for half an hour.
M I'll show you. Look. You open this menu, click here, click on the percentage you want, say 200%, and you're all set. There it is — twice as large.
W It's easier than I thought. Thanks a lot.

남 너는 왜 손톱을 물어뜯고 있어? 무슨 일이니?
여 넌 나를 도울 수 없을 거야.
남 컴퓨터가 갑자기 고장 났니?
여 아니, 난 이 사진을 화면에서 좀 더 크게 만들려고 해.
남 아, 그건 어렵지 않아.
여 난 네가 컴퓨터에 대해 아무것도 모르는 줄 알았는데.
남 내가 컴퓨터 공학을 전공하고 있다고 네게 말하지 않았던가?
여 아니, 안 했어. 음, 난 30분 동안을 아무 성과 없이 그걸 하려고 끙끙대는 중이야.
남 내가 보여 줄게. 봐. 이 메뉴를 열어서, 여기를 누르고, 네가 원하는 비율을 누르고, 예를 들면 200%, 그러면 다 된 거야. 여기 있잖아. 두 배 크기로.
여 어떻게 하는지 아니까 쉽네. 정말 고마워.

• •
bite one's nails 손톱을 물어뜯다 **crash** (컴퓨터가) 갑자기 고장 나다 **major in** ~을 전공하다

---

14 대화를 듣고, 여자의 마지막 말에 이어질 남자의 말로 가장 적절한 것을 고르시오.

① Let's start a campaign right away.
② I've decided to become a vegetarian.
③ Just look at the state of the world these days.
④ Well, I'm going to do something about it myself.
⑤ That's what we call an environmentally friendly battery.

W I heard that you're interested in environmentally friendly products.
M Yes, I've been using those products to conserve the environment. Why do you ask?
W I saw a really interesting documentary on new developments in technology last night.
M Oh, I'm sorry I missed that.
W The one that really made me surprised was the battery made from spinach.
M Spinach! That's a vegetable. I can't believe it.
W It's true. Spinach batteries can convert light into electricity to power something like a laptop computer.
M That's what we call an environmentally friendly battery.

여 난 네가 환경 친화적 제품에 관심이 있다고 들었어.
남 맞아, 난 환경을 보존하기 위해 그런 제품을 사용해 왔어. 왜 물어보는 거니?
여 난 어젯밤에 새로운 기술 발전에 대한 정말 흥미로운 다큐멘터리를 봤어.
남 오, 내가 놓친 것이 아쉽다.
여 나를 정말 놀라게 한 것은 시금치로 만들어진 건전지였어.
남 시금치라고! 그건 채소잖아. 믿기지가 않아.
여 정말이야. 시금치 건전지는 노트북 컴퓨터 같은 것에 전력을 공급하기 위해 빛을 전기로 전환시킬 수 있어.
남 그것이 소위 말하는 환경 친화적 건전지구나.

• •
environmentally friendly 환경 친화적인 **product** 제품 **conserve** 보존하다 **technology** 기술 **spinach** 시금치 **convert** 전환시키다 **electricity** 전기

15 다음 상황 설명을 듣고, Jennifer에게 조언할 말로 가장 적절한 것을 고르시오.

① If I don't pass it, I'll take it again another time.

② I'm glad that you did so well on your exam.

③ Don't worry! You did your best on the chemistry exam.

④ Why don't you go to graduate school after finishing college?

⑤ The next time, you had better study harder to improve your grade.

Jennifer <u>enjoyed</u> <u>herself</u> very much at the party last night. She <u>completely</u> <u>forgot</u> about her chemistry <u>examination</u>. This morning, she took her chemistry examination. Unfortunately, she didn't do well. If she <u>had</u> <u>studied</u> hard, she <u>could</u> <u>have</u> <u>done</u> much better. Now she is worrying about her <u>poor</u> <u>grade</u> and <u>regretting</u> that she didn't take the time to study hard. In this situation, what would you most likely advise Jennifer to do?

You: <u>The next time, you had better study harder to improve your grade.</u>

Jennifer는 어젯밤 파티에서 아주 즐거운 시간을 보냈다. 그녀는 화학 시험에 대해 완전히 잊어버렸다. 오늘 아침에 그녀는 화학 시험을 치렀다. 불행하게도, 그녀는 잘하지 못했다. 그녀가 열심히 공부했더라면 그녀는 훨씬 더 잘 했을 수도 있을 것이다. 지금 그녀는 자신의 낮은 점수에 대해 걱정하고 있고 자신이 열심히 공부할 시간을 내지 않았던 것을 후회하고 있다. 이런 상황에서, 당신은 Jennifer에게 무얼 하라고 조언하겠는가?

You: <u>다음번에는 네 성적을 올리기 위해 더 열심히 공부하는 게 좋을 거야.</u>

●●

completely 완전히 **chemistry** 화학
unfortunately 불행하게도 **regret** 후회하다

▶ REVIEW TEST p. 39

A ① cab, 택시 ② lane, 도로, 길 ③ regret, 후회하다 ④ praise, 칭찬 ⑤ worn out, 지친 ⑥ product, 제품 ⑦ provide, 제공하다 ⑧ register, 가입하다, 등록하다 ⑨ properly, 적절히, 제대로 ⑩ encourage, 용기를 북돋우다 ⑪ technology, 기술 ⑫ unfortunately, 불행하게도

B ① Spinach, electricity ② completely, chemistry ③ biting your nails ④ can't force you ⑤ I'm majoring in ⑥ have, access to ⑦ put our heads together ⑧ in advance, have, off

문제 및 정답	받아쓰기 및 녹음내용	해석

01

다음을 듣고, 그림의 상황에 알맞은 대화를 고르시오.

① ② ③ ④ ⑤

① W Mr. Horn, may I <u>have your autograph</u>?

M Of course. What's your name?

② M How do you like this blouse?

W I am not sure... Do you have it <u>in any different colors</u>?

③ W Yes! I win!

M Good game. I'll <u>beat you</u> the next time though.

④ W <u>What's</u> this <u>made of</u>?

M It's one hundred percent stainless steel.

⑤ W Mmm... What's that smell?

M <u>Freshly baked</u> chocolate cake. Do you want some?

① 여 Horn 씨, 당신의 사인을 받을 수 있을까요?

남 물론이죠. 성함이 어떻게 되시나요?

② 남 이 블라우스는 어떤가요?

여 잘 모르겠습니다… 다른 색상으로 있나요?

③ 여 그래! 내가 이겼어!

남 재미있는 게임이었어. 그래도 다음번엔 내가 널 이길 거야.

④ 여 이건 무엇으로 만든 거야?

남 100퍼센트 스테인리스 강철이야.

⑤ 여 음… 무슨 냄새지?

남 갓 구워 낸 초콜릿 케이크 냄새지. 좀 먹고 싶니?

autograph (유명인의) 사인, 서명 **beat** 이기다

02

대화를 듣고, 두 사람이 대화하는 장소로 가장 적절한 곳을 고르시오.

① 공항　② 우체국
③ 도서관　④ 기차역
⑤ 여행사

M Good afternoon. May I see your <u>passport</u> and <u>visa</u>, please?

W Yes, here it is, and here's my visa.

M Thank you. You have a tourist visa <u>for three months</u>.

W Yes, that's right. I <u>plan to travel</u> some in the U.S.

M Where are you going?

W I'm going to spend some time in Atlanta. After that, I'm going to Washington, Chicago, and California.

M Where is your Form I-94? I <u>can't see</u> it.

W Oh, here it is.

M All right. <u>Enjoy your stay</u>! You can go ahead.

W Thank you very much.

남 안녕하세요. 여권과 비자를 보여 주시겠어요?

여 네, 여기 여권과 비자가 있습니다.

남 감사합니다. 석 달짜리 관광 비자가 있으시군요.

여 네, 맞습니다. 미국에서 몇 군데를 여행할 계획입니다.

남 어디를 갈 예정입니까?

여 애틀랜타에서 시간을 좀 보낼 거예요. 그 다음엔 워싱턴, 시카고, 그리고 캘리포니아에 갈 예정입니다.

남 출입국 허가서는 어디에 있지요? 찾을 수가 없군요.

여 아, 여기에 있습니다.

남 알겠습니다. 즐겁게 지내세요! 가셔도 좋습니다.

여 대단히 감사합니다.

passport 여권 **Form I-94** 출입국 허가서

03

다음을 듣고, 여자의 직업으로 가장 적절한 것을 고르시오.

① 요리사 ② 과학자
③ 은행원 ④ 승무원
⑤ 식당 종업원

The funny thing is that I don't really cook much at home. My husband usually takes care of that, and, luckily, he's quite a good cook. There is one exception to that rule though. If I'm testing a new recipe, I try it out at home first. My teenage daughter is harder to please than most restaurant critics, so I always take her opinion into account when I create new dishes for the restaurant.

재미있는 것은 내가 집에서는 요리를 정말로 많이 하지는 않는다는 거야. 남편이 보통 요리를 책임지고, 다행히 그는 음식을 꽤 잘해. 그래도 그 규칙에는 한 가지 예외가 있어. 만일 내가 새로운 요리법을 실험할 때는 집에서 먼저 해 봐. 대부분의 식당 비평가들보다 십 대인 내 딸을 만족시키기가 더 어려워서, 식당을 위한 새로운 요리를 만들 때 나는 항상 그 애의 의견을 고려해.

exception 예외 **recipe** 요리법 **critic** 비평가, 평론가 **take ~ into account** ~을 고려하다 **opinion** 의견 **create** 만들다

04

대화를 듣고, 두 사람의 관계로 가장 적절한 것을 고르시오.

① 딸 – 아빠
② 화가 – 기자
③ 교사 – 학생
④ 경찰 – 시민
⑤ 사진사 – 손님

W Look! I have something to show you.
M What's that, Jane?
W This! I drew it all day today.
M Wow! What a wonderful picture!
W Do you like it?
M Do I like it? I love it, sweetheart! But who is this lady?
W This is your mother at age 25.
M What? Is this your grandmother? But you never met your grandmother, did you?
W You're right, but I found an old photo on your desk, and I thought the lady in the photo must be your late mother.
M You are so smart! Yes, you're right. This lady in your picture looks just like my mother in her twenties.

여 이거 보세요! 보여드릴 것이 있어요.
남 그게 뭐니, Jane?
여 이거요! 오늘 하루 종일 그렸어요.
남 와! 정말 멋진 그림인데!
여 마음에 드세요?
남 마음에 드냐고? 마음에 쏙 드는구나, 얘야! 그런데 이 여자분은 누구시니?
여 이분은 할머니의 25살 때 모습이에요.
남 뭐라고? 이분이 네 할머니라고? 하지만 너는 할머니를 한 번도 뵌 적이 없잖니, 그렇지?
여 맞아요, 하지만 아빠 책상에서 옛날 사진을 발견했는데요, 사진 속의 여자분이 아빠의 돌아가신 어머니일 거라고 생각했어요.
남 정말 똑똑하구나! 그래, 네 말이 맞다. 네 그림 속의 이 여자분은 우리 어머니의 20대 시절과 모습이 아주 똑같구나.

late 돌아가신, 고인이 된

05 다음을 듣고, 남자가 이용할 교통 수단으로 언급되지 <u>않은</u> 것을 고르시오.

① 　②

③ 　④

⑤

We are taking an <u>airport limousine bus</u> to Incheon International Airport. Later, we are going to <u>fly to</u> London. Then, we will travel around London for about 4 days. We will take a <u>double-decker</u> bus on a city tour. After that, we are going to take the EuroStar to Paris. It's a <u>high-speed</u> train that travels from London to Brussels and Paris and <u>passes through</u> the Channel Tunnel. In Paris, I'd also like to go to the Louvre Museum. This is our <u>first trip to</u> Europe, so we are really excited.

우리는 공항 리무진 버스를 타고 인천 국제공항으로 갈 거예요. 그 후에 비행기로 런던에 갈 거고요. 그런 다음에 런던에서 약 4일 동안 여행을 할 거예요. 우리는 시 여행 중에 2층 버스를 탈 거예요. 그 다음에 우리는 유로스타를 타고 파리로 갈 거예요. 이것은 런던에서 브뤼셀, 파리로 이동하고 Channel 터널을 통과하는 고속 열차예요. 파리에서는 루브르 박물관에도 가고 싶어요. 우리는 처음으로 유럽을 여행하는 거라서 정말 들떠 있어요.

•• **international** 국제적인 **double-decker bus** 2층 버스

---

06 대화를 듣고, 여자가 주장하는 것으로 가장 적절한 것을 고르시오.

☑① 역사를 공부할 필요가 있다.
② 같은 실수를 반복해서는 안 된다.
③ 만화책을 읽으면서 스트레스를 풀 수 있다.
④ 글쓰기를 통해 자기 자신을 이해할 수 있다.
⑤ 사극 드라마를 보면 역사 공부에 도움이 된다.

M Hey there, Martha. What are you reading?

W It's a history book.

M <u>What is the use</u> of reading about things that have already happened?

W Someone once said that <u>those</u> who <u>don't know history</u> are doomed to repeat it.

M It is pretty <u>boring</u> for me to read a history book though. <u>I'd rather</u> read comic books or something.

W I understand, but the past is not <u>separate from the present</u>. We can only know ourselves by studying history.

M Well, I guess you <u>have a point</u>. Can you recommend any fun history books?

남 안녕, Martha. 뭘 읽고 있니?

여 역사책을 읽고 있어.

남 이미 일어난 것들에 관해 읽는 것이 무슨 도움이 되니?

여 누군가가 전에 이런 말을 하더군, 역사를 모르는 사람들은 그것을 반복하게 마련이라고.

남 그렇지만 역사책을 읽는 건 내겐 퍽 지루한 일이야. 나는 차라리 만화책 같은 걸 읽겠어.

여 이해해, 하지만 과거는 현재와 따로 떨어져 있는 것이 아니야. 우리는 오로지 역사를 공부함으로써 우리 자신을 알 수 있어.

남 음, 네 말에도 일리가 있는 것 같네. 재미있는 역사책을 추천해 줄래?

•• **be doomed to** ~하게 마련이다 **would rather** 차라리 ~하겠다 **separate** 따로 떨어진 **have a point** 일리가 있다

07 대화를 듣고, 두 사람의 심정으로 가장 적절한 것을 고르시오.

① sad ② relieved
③ frightened ④ discouraged
⑤ disappointed ✓

M Well, what do you think?

W That was the <u>worst</u> movie <u>I've ever seen</u>.

M Yeah, it was bad, wasn't it?

W There was <u>no plot</u>, and the dialogue just went on and on and on.

M Don't you think we should ask for our money back?

W Forget the money. I want those two hours of my life back. I feel so <u>ripped off</u>.

M Anyway, the next time, we'll <u>choose</u> <u>a better one</u>.

W I hope so. I don't want to experience that again.

남 음, 어떻게 생각해?

여 그건 내가 본 영화 중에 최악이었어.

남 그래, 형편없었어, 그렇지 않니?

여 줄거리가 없었고, 대화도 그저 계속 반복되고.

남 우리가 돈이라도 돌려 달라고 요청해야 한다고 생각하지 않니?

여 돈은 잊어. 난 내 인생의 두 시간을 돌려받고 싶어. 정말로 사기 당한 기분이야.

남 하여간, 다음번에는 더 나은 영화를 골라야겠어.

여 그랬으면 좋겠어. 또 다시 그런 경험을 하고 싶지는 않거든.

• •

plot 줄거리 **dialogue** (책·연극·영화에 나오는) 대화 **ripped off** 사기 당한, 바가지 쓴

08 대화를 듣고, 여자가 첫 달에 남자에게 내야 하는 금액을 고르시오.

① $250 ② $500
③ $550 ④ $750 ✓
⑤ $800

W Excuse me. Are you the <u>landlord</u>?

M Yes, I am. Are you the person <u>interested in</u> the apartment who called yesterday?

W That's right. How much is the <u>rent</u> here?

M It's <u>500 dollars</u> a month plus a <u>250</u>-dollar security deposit.

W A security deposit? What's that?

M You pay the deposit only once, and you <u>get it back</u> when you move out. You have to pay it the first month.

W I see. And the other bills?

M The <u>electricity bill</u> is about 30 dollars a month, and the telephone is another 20 dollars. You pay them <u>directly to the bank</u> the month after you receive the bills.

W The place looks great. When can I move in?

M You can move in at the <u>end of the month</u> if you want.

여 실례합니다. 집주인이신가요?

남 네. 당신이 어제 전화 주셨던 아파트에 관심이 있는 그분이신가요?

여 맞아요. 여기 월세가 얼마인가요?

남 한 달에 500달러이고, 250달러의 임대 보증금도 있어요.

여 임대 보증금이요? 그건 뭐죠?

남 보증금은 단 한 번만 내면 되고 이사 나갈 때 돌려받는 거예요. 보증금은 첫 달에 내셔야 해요.

여 그렇군요. 다른 공과금은요?

남 전기세는 한 달에 약 30달러고요, 전화세는 20달러입니다. 청구서를 받으신 후 그 달에 직접 은행에다 내는 겁니다.

여 집이 아주 좋아 보이네요. 언제 이사를 할 수 있는 거죠?

남 원하시면 이번 달 말에 이사 오실 수 있어요.

• •

landlord 집주인 **rent** 임차료, 집세 **security deposit** 임대 보증금 **electricity bill** 전기세 **receive** 받다

09 대화를 듣고, 남자가 늦은 이유로 가장 적절한 것을 고르시오.

① 교통사고를 당했기 때문에
② 사고 현장을 구경했기 때문에
③ 교통사고로 도로가 막혔기 때문에
④ 사고 현장을 목격하고 신고했기 때문에
⑤ 부상 당한 사람을 병원에 데려다 줬기 때문에

W Mr. Jones, I believe you are late again.
M I'm sorry. You see…
W I don't want to hear any excuses. This is the second time this month, isn't it?
M That's right, but I have a good reason.
W You know, you need to feel responsible for your actions.
M There was a car accident!
W What did you say?
M On my way to work, I saw a car accident, so I stopped to help. I drove an injured woman to the hospital to get medical attention. I may have even saved her life.
W Oh… In that case, Mr. Jones, I take back everything I said. You did the right thing.
M Thank you.

여 Jones 씨, 또 늦으신 것 같군요.
남 죄송합니다. 당신도 아시다시피…
여 어떠한 변명도 듣고 싶지 않습니다. 이번 달에만 두 번째예요, 그렇지 않나요?
남 맞습니다, 하지만 타당한 이유가 있어요.
여 아시다시피, 당신은 자신의 행동에 대해 책임을 느낄 필요가 있어요.
남 교통사고가 났었어요!
여 뭐라고요?
남 회사 오는 길에 교통사고를 목격했어요, 그래서 도와주기 위해 멈췄어요. 부상을 입은 한 여자를 치료받게 해 주기 위해 병원까지 차로 데려다 줬어요. 제가 그녀의 생명을 구해 준 것일지도 몰라요.
여 아… 그런 경우라면, Jones 씨, 제가 말한 것은 모두 취소하죠. 옳은 일을 하셨군요.
남 고맙습니다.

●●
excuse 변명, 핑계 **responsible** 책임이 있는 **injured** 부상을 입은 **attention** 치료, 보살핌

---

10 대화를 듣고, 여자가 대화 직후에 할 일로 가장 적절한 것을 고르시오.

① 화장실 가기
② 과일 구매하기
③ 후식 주문하기
④ 식사비 지불하기
⑤ 케이크 예약하기

W Let's order some more food!
M I don't think so. I don't think I can eat another bite.
W Okay. That was a great meal, wasn't it?
M It sure was.
W I can't remember when I ate so much. We have to eat dessert.
M Dessert? I will explode if I eat another bite.
W Why don't you have something like some sliced fruit?
M No, thank you. You really like sweets, don't you?
W Yeah, it's my weakness. I'll order something for myself then.

여 음식을 좀 더 주문하자!
남 난 괜찮은데. 더 이상은 못 먹을 것 같아.
여 알았어. 훌륭한 식사였어, 그렇지 않니?
남 확실히 그랬어.
여 내가 언제 그렇게 많이 먹은 건지 기억이 안 난다. 우리 후식은 먹어야지.
남 후식? 한 입만 더 먹으면 터질 것 같아.
여 얇게 썬 과일 같은 거라도 먹지 그래?
남 아냐, 괜찮아. 넌 정말로 단것을 좋아하는 구나, 그렇지 않니?
여 응, 내 약점이지. 그럼 내 것만 주문할게.

●●
bite 음식; 한 입 **explode** 터지다, 폭발하다 **weakness** 약점

11 대화를 듣고, 남자가 여자에게 요청한 일로 가장 적절한 것을 고르시오.

① 보고서 타이핑하기
② 약속 시간 변경하기
③ 보고서의 오탈자 수정하기
④ Anne을 사무실로 불러오기
⑤ Anne에게 보고서 가져다 주기

M Oh, Ms. Green, can you <u>do some typing</u> for me? Anne is busy now.
W Certainly, sir. I would be glad to.
M I must have <u>a copy of</u> this <u>report</u> by 4 o'clock.
W Let's see. There are ten pages. It should take me <u>about an hour</u>. That will be 4:10.
M Can you finish it before that?
W I can try.
M Good. It's very important. You <u>should bring it</u> right to my office.
W Yes, sir.
M And, Ms. Green, it must be <u>absolutely correct</u>. There mustn't be any mistakes in it at all.
W I don't usually <u>make mistakes</u> when I'm typing.

남 아, Green 씨, 저 대신 타이핑을 좀 해 줄 수 있나요? Anne이 지금 바빠서요.
여 물론이죠. 기꺼이 그러죠.
남 이 보고서의 복사본이 4시까지 필요해요.
여 어디 볼게요. 열 페이지군요. 한 시간 정도 길릴 덴데요. 4시 10분이 되겠네요.
남 그 전까지 마칠 수 있나요?
여 해 보죠.
남 좋아요. 이건 매우 중요하거든요. 제 사무실로 바로 가져오셔야 해요.
여 예.
남 그리고, Green 씨, 굉장히 정확해야 해요. 어떤 실수도 없어야 합니다.
여 전 타이핑할 때는 보통 실수 안 해요.

●●
Certainly. 물론이죠. **copy** 복사(본)
absolutely 굉장히 **correct** 정확한

12 대화를 듣고, 대화 내용과 일치하지 <u>않는</u> 것을 고르시오.

① 남자는 수업을 들으러 가는 중이다.
② 남자가 들으려 하는 수업은 10시에 시작한다.
③ 지금 시각은 9시 15분이다.
④ 남자의 시계는 항상 빠르게 간다.
⑤ 남자는 아래층에 있는 수리점에 시계를 맡기지 않을 것이다.

W Where are you going?
M I'm going to class.
W You're too early. It <u>doesn't begin until</u> 10 o'clock.
M What time is it now?
W It's only <u>a quarter past 9</u>.
M Oh, my watch is wrong. It doesn't work very well. Sometimes it runs too fast, and sometimes it runs too slow.
W There's a watch <u>repair shop downstairs</u>.
M I don't want to take my watch there.
W Why not?
M He <u>charges too much</u>. Do you know another place?
W No, I don't.

여 어디 가니?
남 수업에 들어가.
여 너무 빠르다. 10시 전까지는 시작 안 하는데.
남 지금 몇 신데?
여 겨우 9시 15분이야.
남 어, 내 시계가 틀렸네. 이거 잘 안 맞거든. 어떤 때는 너무 빨리 가고, 어떤 때는 너무 느리게 가.
여 아래층에 시계 수리점이 있어.
남 난 내 시계를 거기에 맡기고 싶지 않아.
여 왜?
남 그는 수리비를 너무 많이 불러. 다른 곳 아니?
여 아니, 몰라.

●●
downstairs 아래층에

13 대화를 듣고, 여자의 마지막 말에 이어질 남자의 말로 가장 적절한 것을 고르시오.

① They know what they're doing.
② You should quit worrying about them.
③ They bought a new car without telling me.
④ They don't want to get divorced because of their children.
⑤ They should have bought the apartment when they were financially ready.

M I'm a bit worried about our son and daughter-in-law.
W Is their marriage going badly?
M No, not at all. But they just bought a new apartment next to the park.
W It must be very expensive. How could they afford a new apartment?
M They've both got to be working to afford the monthly payments on their mortgage.
W I think they can handle it. Why are you worried?
M What I'm worried about is what would happen if either of them lost their jobs.
W If that happened, they would have to try to keep up the monthly payments.
M They should have bought the apartment when they were financially ready.

남 난 우리 아들과 며느리가 조금 걱정이에요.
여 그들의 결혼 생활이 나빠지고 있나요?
남 아뇨, 전혀요. 하지만 그들은 이제 막 공원 옆 새 아파트를 샀어요.
여 매우 비싸겠네요. 어떻게 새 아파트를 살 여유가 있었을까요?
남 그들은 대출금을 매월 상환하기 위해 둘 다 일해야 해요.
여 그들이 감당할 수 있을 것 같은데요. 왜 걱정하세요?
남 제가 걱정하는 것은 만약 둘 중 하나가 직장을 잃을 경우 어떻게 될지예요.
여 그렇게 된다면 그들은 계속해서 매달 상환하기 위해 노력해야겠군요.
남 난 그들이 재정적으로 준비되었을 때 새 아파트를 샀어야 했다고 생각해요.

●●
daughter-in-law 며느리 **mortgage** (담보) 대출(금) **financially** 재정적으로

---

14 대화를 듣고, 남자의 마지막 말에 이어질 여자의 말로 가장 적절한 것을 고르시오.

① Fried foods don't agree with me.
② That sounds nice. I've eaten it here before.
③ That'd be great. I really recommend the oyster soup.
④ That sounds good. Then I'll have the beefsteak tonight.
⑤ Are you done with that beefsteak? Mind if I finish it off for you?

M Let's take the one in the corner over there, shall we?
W Okay. Let's take that one.
M I used to come to this restaurant when I was in college. It wasn't very expensive, and it served very good food.
W Did you? I've never been here before. Did you eat dinner here very often?
M Yes, I ate here often.
W Then you're very familiar with this restaurant, aren't you?
M Yes, I am.
W What is this restaurant famous for?
M Well, the beefsteak is excellent. It was very popular with students in my time.
W That sounds good. Then I'll have the beefsteak tonight.

남 저기에 있는 구석 자리에 앉지요, 괜찮아요?
여 좋아요. 저기에 앉지요.
남 저는 대학에 다닐 때 이 식당에 오곤 했어요. 그다지 비싸지 않았고, 음식이 아주 괜찮았어요.
여 그랬나요? 저는 전에 여기 와 본 적이 없어요. 당신은 이곳에서 자주 저녁을 드셨나요?
남 예, 저는 여기서 자주 식사했어요.
여 그러면 이 식당에 대해 아주 잘 알고 계시겠군요, 그렇지 않아요?
남 예, 그래요.
여 이 식당은 뭘로 유명한가요?
남 음, 쇠고기 스테이크가 훌륭해요. 옛날에 학생들에게 아주 인기 있었어요.
여 좋아요. 그럼 오늘 밤에는 쇠고기 스테이크로 하죠.

●●
college 대학

15 다음 상황 설명을 듣고, Paul이 경찰관에게 할 말로 가장 적절한 것을 고르시오.

① I was trying to feed the cat on my way home.
②✓ The cat caused the accident. It wasn't my fault.
③ Send an ambulance here, please. It seems very serious.
④ I missed your call because my phone was switched to vibration mode.
⑤ The accident occurred right across from here. It was the bus driver's fault.

A few months ago, Paul had an accident. He was <u>driving to work</u> when a cat ran in front of his car. He <u>turned</u> <u>sharply</u> and missed the cat. But his car <u>hit a guardrail</u>. A policeman was standing on the corner when the accident happened. He <u>called an ambulance</u> immediately. The <u>ambulance came</u> and took Paul to the hospital with the policeman. While they were going to the hospital, Paul wanted to talk to the policeman about <u>how</u> the accident <u>took place</u>. In this situation, what would Paul say to the policeman?

Paul: <u>The cat caused the accident. It wasn't my fault.</u>

몇 달 전, Paul은 사고를 당했습니다. 그는 차로 출근하던 중이었는데, 그때 고양이 한 마리가 그의 차 앞으로 달려들었습니다. 그는 재빨리 차를 돌려서 고양이를 피했습니다. 하지만 그의 차는 가드레일을 들이받았습니다. 사고 발생 시에 코너에 경찰관이 서 있었습니다. 그는 즉시 구급차를 불렀습니다. 구급차가 와서 경찰관과 함께 Paul을 병원에 데리고 갔습니다. 그들이 병원에 가는 동안 Paul은 경찰관에게 어떻게 사고가 발생했는지에 관해 이야기하고 싶었습니다. 이런 상황에서, Paul은 경찰관에게 뭐라고 말하겠습니까?

Paul: <u>고양이가 사고의 원인입니다. 제 잘못이 아녜요.</u>

●●
sharply 재빨리 **immediately** 즉시 **take place** (일·문제 등이) 일어나다

◗ REVIEW TEST p. 47

A ① rent, 임차료, 집세 ② create, 만들다 ③ recipe, 요리법 ④ international, 국제적인 ⑤ correct, 정확한
⑥ passport, 여권 ⑦ plot, 줄거리 ⑧ receive, 받다 ⑨ weakness, 약점
⑩ responsible, 책임이 있는 ⑪ immediately, 즉시 ⑫ take place, (일·문제 등이) 일어나다

B ① ripped off ② I'd rather ③ have your autograph
④ have a point ⑤ hear any excuses ⑥ take, into account
⑦ is not separate ⑧ There is one exception

TEST 06 p. 48

문제 및 정답	받아쓰기 및 녹음내용	해석

01

다음을 듣고, 그림의 상황에 알맞은 대화를 고르시오.

① ② ③ ④ ⑤

① W Where are those reports you promised me?

M I'll finish them by tomorrow. I promise.

② W Do you have any baggage to check?

M Yes, I'd like to check this suitcase.

③ W Where are you going?

M I'm just walking to the store.

④ W Let's play basketball.

M No, not today. I'm too tired.

⑤ W Hi. I'm Carrie White.

M It's a pleasure to meet you. I've heard so much about you.

① 여 제게 약속하신 보고서는 어디에 있죠?
남 내일까지 끝낼게요. 약속드려요.

② 여 부치실 수화물이 있으세요?
남 네, 이 여행 가방을 부치고 싶어요.

③ 여 어디 가세요?
남 그냥 가게에 걸어가는 중이에요.

④ 여 우리 농구 하자.
남 안돼, 오늘 말고. 나 너무 피곤해.

⑤ 여 안녕하세요. 저는 Carrie White예요.
남 만나게 돼서 기뻐요. 당신에 대한 말씀 많이 들었어요.

●●
promise 약속하다 **baggage** 수하물

02

대화를 듣고, 두 사람이 대화하는 장소로 가장 적절한 곳을 고르시오.

① 호텔
② 세탁소
③ 문구점
④ 헬스클럽
⑤ 스포츠 용품 가게

W Hi. Can I help you find anything?

M Yes, actually, I'm looking for a pair of exercise pants.

W Do you have any particular style in mind?

M Something not too tight looking, I guess.

W All right. What size do you wear?

M A medium.

W How about this in navy blue? It would be perfect for you.

M That looks pretty good. I like it. Where can I try it on?

W The fitting rooms are right over there by the counter.

여 안녕하세요. 찾는 것을 도와드릴까요?
남 네, 사실은, 운동용 바지 한 벌을 찾고 있는데요.
여 찾고 계시는 특별한 스타일이 있나요?
남 제 생각에는 너무 꽉 껴 보이지 않는 것으로요.
여 알겠습니다. 어떤 사이즈를 입으시나요?
남 중간 사이즈요.
여 이 짙은 남색 옷은 어떠신가요? 잘 어울릴 것 같아요.
남 아주 괜찮아 보이네요. 마음에 들어요. 어디에서 입어 볼 수 있지요?
여 탈의실은 바로 저쪽 계산대 옆에 있습니다.

●●
particular 특별한 **medium** 중간; 중간의

03 다음을 듣고, 남자의 직업으로 가장 적절한 것을 고르시오.

① 기자 　　　② 군인
③ 경찰 　　　④ 판매원
⑤ 회사 부서장

I'm in charge of the Marketing Department. There are 20 people in the department besides myself, so I can be fairly busy at times. The people reporting to me all work forty hours a week, but I almost always work over fifty hours a week. Still, I like it. I like being in control, and I like being in a position where I can have some influence over the direction the company takes.

저는 마케팅 부서를 책임지고 있습니다. 이 부서에는 저를 제외하고 20명의 사람들이 있고, 그래서 저는 가끔 아주 바쁩니다. 저에게 보고하는 사람들은 모두 일주일에 40시간을 일하지만, 저는 거의 항상 일주일에 50시간 이상을 일합니다. 그렇지만 저는 이 일이 좋아요. 제가 관리하고 회사가 취하는 방향에 영향을 줄 수 있는 위치에 있는 것이 좋아요.

●●
be in charge of ~을 책임지고[담당하고] 있다
department 부서 　**fairly** 아주, 완전히
be in control 관리[통제]하다 　**influence** 영향
direction 방향

---

04 대화를 듣고, 두 사람의 관계로 가장 적절한 것을 고르시오.

① 경찰 - 시민
② 승무원 - 승객
③ 호텔 직원 - 투숙객
④ 관광 가이드 - 여행객
⑤ 출입국 관리원 - 입국 승객

M Good afternoon.
W May I see your passport, please?
M Yes, here it is, and here's my visa.
W Thank you. Business or pleasure?
M Pleasure.
W All right. You have a tourist visa good for three months.
M Yes, that's correct. I plan to travel some in Canada.
W Where are you going?
M I'm going to spend some time in Quebec. After that, I'm going to Ottawa and Ontario.
W All right. Enjoy your stay!
M Thank you. Have a nice day.

남 안녕하세요.
여 여권을 볼 수 있을까요?
남 네, 여기 있어요, 그리고 제 비자는 여기 있어요.
여 감사합니다. 사업차인가요, 관광차인가요?
남 관광차입니다.
여 알겠습니다. 석 달 동안 유효한 관광 비자를 받으셨군요.
남 네, 맞아요. 캐나다의 몇 곳을 여행할 계획입니다.
여 어디에 가실 거죠?
남 퀘벡에서 시간을 좀 보낼 거예요. 그런 다음에 오타와 온타리오에 갈 예정이에요.
여 좋습니다. 즐거운 여행 되세요!
남 감사합니다. 좋은 하루 보내세요.

05 대화를 듣고, 여자가 찾고 있는 동물을 고르시오.

①
②
③
④
⑤

M We finally <u>made it to</u> the zoo, Hanna.

W Yeah, Daddy. I am looking around here for an animal that I need to <u>make</u> a <u>presentation</u> about in class.

M Is this the animal that you are looking for?

W No, it's not. That one is too fat. It looks like a <u>hippo</u>.

M What about that animal over there?

W No, its neck is too long. That looks like a <u>giraffe</u>.

M Exactly what kind of animal do you want to find?

W I am looking for an animal with <u>short</u>, <u>fat</u> <u>legs</u> and two <u>horns</u> growing from its nose. It looks like an elephant, but the elephant has <u>a</u> <u>long</u> <u>nose</u>. However, this animal does not.

M Look over there. Is that the animal you are looking for?

W Yes, that's right. That's the one. It's a rhinoceros. Let's <u>go</u> and <u>look</u> <u>carefully</u> at it.

남 우리가 드디어 동물원에 왔구나, 한나야.

여 네, 아빠. 저는 여기서 수업 시간에 발표해야 할 동물을 찾고 있어요.

남 이게 네가 찾고 있는 동물이니?

여 아뇨, 그건 아녜요. 그건 너무 뚱뚱해요. 하마 같은데요.

남 저기 있는 동물은 어떠니?

여 아니에요. 목이 너무 길어요. 저것은 기린 같은데요.

남 정확히 어떤 종류의 동물을 찾고 싶은 거니?

여 통통하고 짧은 다리에 두 개의 뿔이 코에서 자라나 있는 동물을 찾고 있어요. 코끼리처럼 생겼지만, 코끼리는 긴 코를 가지고 있어요. 하지만 이 동물은 없어요.

남 저기 좀 봐. 저게 네가 찾고 있는 동물이니?

여 네, 맞아요. 바로 저거예요. 코뿔소예요. 가서 자세히 살펴봐요.

presentation 발표 **hippo** 하마 **giraffe** 기린 **horn** (소·양 등의) 뿔 **rhinoceros** 코뿔소

---

06 대화를 듣고, 무엇에 관한 내용인지 가장 적절한 것을 고르시오.

① 지진 ② 쓰나미
③ 화산 폭발 ④ 건물 붕괴
⑤ 환경 오염

W Did you <u>hear</u> <u>about</u> the <u>earthquake</u>?

M What earthquake? What are you talking about? I didn't feel anything shaking.

W Well, it <u>originated</u> in Japan, and some <u>buildings</u> in Busan even <u>collapsed</u>. A lot of people were very frightened.

M I had no idea. I guess we are kind of safe in Seoul. Was anyone <u>seriously</u> <u>hurt</u>?

W I don't think so although there was a lot of property damage.

M I'm not sure how I would <u>react</u> if an earthquake <u>struck</u> Seoul.

W You would probably act just like everyone else and <u>hide</u> <u>under</u> your <u>desk</u>.

여 지진에 대해 들었니?

남 무슨 지진? 무슨 소리야? 흔들리는 것을 전혀 못 느꼈는데.

여 음, 진원지는 일본인데, 심지어 부산에서도 건물들이 무너졌어. 많은 사람들이 정말로 깜짝 놀랐어.

남 전혀 몰랐어. 서울은 그나마 안전하다고 생각하는데. 누군가가 심하게 다쳤니?

여 많은 재산 피해가 발생하긴 했지만, 그런 것 같지는 않아.

남 만약 지진이 서울에서 일어난다면 난 어떻게 반응할지 잘 모르겠어.

여 너도 아마 다른 모든 사람들처럼 행동하고 책상 밑에 숨겠지.

originate 시작되다, 일어나다 **collapse** 무너지다, 붕괴되다 **frightened** 깜짝 놀란, 겁이 난 **seriously** 심하게 **property** 재산, 소유물 **hide** 숨다

07 대화를 듣고, 마지막 말에서 느껴지는 남자의 태도로 가장 적절한 것을 고르시오.

① selfish   ② critical
③ positive   ④ cautious
⑤ indifferent

M What are you doing?

W I'm <u>searching</u> the Internet for a <u>part</u>-<u>time</u> <u>job</u>.

M What kind of job are you looking for?

W Anything.

M I <u>used</u> <u>to</u> <u>deliver</u> newspapers in the morning, but it was hard to get up early.

W I <u>can't</u> <u>work</u> in the mornings. I can never get up before nine o'clock.

M Maybe you could be a tutor.

W I have <u>no</u> <u>teaching</u> <u>experience</u>.

M Waitress?

W I <u>can't</u> do <u>heavy</u> <u>lifting</u>.

M Do you really want to find a part-time job? No job is easy.

남 뭐 하고 있니?

여 나는 아르바이트를 구하려고 인터넷을 살펴보는 중이야.

남 어떤 종류의 일을 찾고 있니?

여 아무거나.

남 나는 아침에 신문을 배달하곤 했는데, 일찍 일어나는 것이 힘들었어.

여 난 아침에는 일할 수 없어. 9시 전에는 절대 일어날 수가 없거든.

남 너는 가정 교사를 할 수도 있을 거야.

여 나는 가르쳐 본 경험이 없는데.

남 종업원은?

여 난 무거운 걸 들어 올리는 일은 할 수 없어.

남 아르바이트를 진짜 찾고 싶기는 한 거니? 어떤 일도 쉽지는 않다구.

●●

search 살펴보다, 찾아보다   **part-time job** 아르바이트, 시간제 일   **tutor** 가정 교사

08 대화를 듣고, 여자가 지불한 핸드백 가격을 고르시오.

① $20   ② $40
③ $60   ④ $80
⑤ $100

W Oh, my god! Where did you get that handbag?

M I <u>got</u> <u>it</u> <u>downtown</u> yesterday. I bought it for my wife. Why do you ask?

W I have the <u>exact</u> <u>same</u> <u>one</u>.

M Isn't it adorable? And what a price!

W How much did you pay for it?

M It was <u>on</u> <u>sale</u> for <u>40</u> dollars. Stephanie, what's wrong? Are you okay?

W I'm not okay. I <u>paid</u> <u>double</u> <u>that</u> <u>price</u> last week.

M Oh, I'm sorry to hear that. Bad luck.

여 어머나! 그 핸드백 어디서 샀어요?

남 어제 시내에서 샀어요. 아내를 위해서 샀어요. 왜 물으시나요?

여 저도 똑같은 것을 가지고 있거든요.

남 예쁘지 않나요? 그리고 가격도 얼마나 싼지!

여 얼마 주셨는데요?

남 할인해서 40달러요. Stephanie, 무슨 일이에요? 괜찮아요?

여 괜찮지 않아요. 저는 지난주에 그 가격의 두 배를 지불했거든요.

남 아, 유감이군요. 운이 없으셨네요.

●●

downtown 시내에서   **exact** 바로 그 ~   **adorable** 사랑스러운, 반할 만한   **double** 두 배의

09

대화를 듣고, 여자가 선물을 사는 이유로 가장 적절한 것을 고르시오.

① 친구의 생일을 축하하기 위해서
② 남편의 승진을 축하하기 위해서
③ 동생의 대학 입학을 축하하기 위해서
④ 친구에게 감사의 마음을 전하기 위해서
⑤ 부모님의 결혼 기념일을 축하하기 위해서

M Hi, Sally. What are you doing in this department store?

W I'm looking for a gift for my friend.

M Is it your friend's birthday?

W No.

M Then what is the occasion?

W She helped me a lot when we were university students, so I want to let her know I appreciate her effort. What about you?

M I am looking for a gift for my parents for their wedding anniversary. Do you have any ideas for a gift?

W How about a bottle of wine? I'm going to that section now. Let's go together.

M Good idea. Why didn't I think of that?

남 안녕, Sally. 이 백화점에서 뭐 하고 있니?

여 친구에게 줄 선물을 찾고 있어.

남 네 친구의 생일이니?

여 아니.

남 그럼 무슨 일인데?

여 우리가 대학생이었을 때 그 친구가 나를 많이 도와줘서, 내가 그녀의 노고가 고맙다는 걸 그 친구에게 알려 주고 싶어서. 너는 웬일이니?

남 나는 부모님의 결혼 기념일을 위한 선물을 찾고 있어. 선물에 대한 아이디어 있니?

여 와인 한 병은 어때? 나 지금 그 코너에 가는 중이야. 같이 가자.

남 좋은 생각이다. 왜 그걸 생각하지 못했지?

••

occasion (특정한) 일, 경우   effort 노력
anniversary 기념일   section 코너, 구역

10

대화를 듣고, 남자가 여자에게 조언한 것으로 가장 적절한 것을 고르시오.

① 평소에 자기계발을 꾸준히 해야 한다.
② 대학에 진학하는 것은 선택의 문제이다.
③ 자신의 마음이 가는 대로 행동해야 한다.
④ 다른 사람의 말에 항상 귀를 기울여야 한다.
⑤ 경영학 학위를 취득하면 취업에 도움이 된다.

M What are you thinking about, Melissa?

W I'm considering going back to university to get a more advanced degree.

M Why is that?

W Well, I don't like my job very much, so I want to upgrade my skills.

M What would you study?

W I think I would get an MBA. What do you think?

M I think you should follow your heart. If you think you should do it, then do it.

W That's really great advice. Thank you.

M Not at all.

남 Melissa, 무슨 생각하고 있니?

여 더 높은 학위를 따기 위해 대학에 다시 갈까 생각 중이야.

남 왜?

여 글쎄, 내 일이 그다지 마음에 들지 않아서, 내 능력을 향상시키고 싶어.

남 무슨 공부를 하려고?

여 경영학 석사를 딸까 생각 중이야. 어떻게 생각하니?

남 네가 마음 내키는 대로 해야 할 것 같아. 네가 그걸 해야 한다고 생각한다면, 그렇게 하도록 해.

여 진짜 좋은 조언이다. 고마워.

남 천만에.

••

consider 생각하다, 고려하다   advanced 고급의   degree 학위   upgrade (등급·품질 등을) 향상시키다, 높이다

11 대화를 듣고, 여자가 점검한 것으로 언급되지 <u>않은</u> 것을 고르시오.

① 메모장　　② 펜
③ 모니터　　④ 의자
⑤ 쓰레기통

M Did you set the <u>conference room</u> up for the meeting today?

W Yes, I did. There's a <u>memo pad</u> on each seat.

M What about pens?

W <u>There are pens</u> next to the pads.

M And monitors?

W I <u>checked all</u> the <u>monitors</u>, and there is no problem.

M Did you <u>put any extra chairs</u> in the room? There are going to be 12 men at the meeting.

W There are 15 chairs in the room.

M What about water?

W There is <u>a pitcher of water</u> and some glasses on the table in the corner.

M That sounds good.

남 오늘 회의를 위해 회의실을 준비했나요?

여 예, 했어요. 각 좌석마다 메모장을 두었어요.

남 펜은요?

여 메모장 옆에 펜을 두었어요.

남 모니터는요?

여 모든 모니터를 점검했는데, 아무 문제 없습니다.

남 회의실에 여분의 의자를 갖다 놨나요? 회의에는 12명이 참석할 거예요.

여 회의실에 15개의 의자가 있어요.

남 물은요?

여 구석에 있는 탁자 위에 물 한 병과 컵이 있어요.

남 좋군요.

●●

conference room 회의실　**extra** 여분의, 추가의　**pitcher** 병, 주전자

---

12 대화를 듣고, 대화 내용과 일치하지 <u>않는</u> 것을 고르시오.

① 남자는 침실이 1개인 아파트를 찾고 있다.
② 여자는 남자에게 역 근처의 아파트를 권해 주었다.
③ 여자가 권해 준 아파트의 집세에는 전기세가 포함되어 있다.
④ 여자가 권해 준 아파트의 계약 기간은 2년이다.
⑤ 여자는 남자에게 집을 보러 갈 것을 제안했다.

M I'm looking for an <u>inexpensive</u> one-bedroom apartment.

W Here's something you might like: a one-bedroom apartment near the station.

M That's a <u>good location</u>. What's the rent?

W 200 dollars a month plus one month's deposit.

M Does that <u>include utilities</u>?

W It includes everything <u>except electricity</u>.

M How long is the <u>lease</u>?

W 2 years.

M When is it available?

W At the end of the month. Let's go over and <u>take a look</u> at it now.

남 침실이 1개인 비싸지 않은 아파트를 찾고 있어요.

여 여기 고객님 마음에 들 만한 것이 있어요. 역 근처에 침실이 하나인 아파트예요.

남 위치가 좋네요. 집세는요?

여 월 200달러와 1개월분의 보증금이에요.

남 거기에는 공과금이 포함되나요?

여 전기세 외에는 모두 포함돼요.

남 계약 기간은 얼마나 되나요?

여 2년이에요.

남 언제 들어갈 수 있나요?

여 월말에요. 지금 가서 한번 봅시다.

●●

inexpensive 비싸지 않은　**location** 위치　**include** 포함하다　**utilities** 공과금, 공공 요금　**lease** 임대차 기간

13 대화를 듣고, 남자의 마지막 말에 이어질 여자의 말로 가장 적절한 것을 고르시오.

① He ought to get a job at a zoo.
② He'll give you a warning this time.
③ I think we have a misunderstanding.
④ I couldn't believe how hard the test was.
⑤ That's fantastic. What a great feeling that must be!

M I'm always a bit <u>afraid of</u> <u>visiting</u> Peter.
W Why's that? He's such a nice guy.
M He is, but he's <u>got a taste</u> for exotic pets.
W I didn't know that. What does he have?
M Well, last week when I was there, he had a baby iguana <u>running around</u> the place.
W A lizard? Ugh! That would <u>give me the creeps</u>.
M I hate that kind of pet. But that's not the only thing he's got.
W He has more pets?
M Yeah... He's <u>had a snake</u> for quite a while.
W <u>He ought to get a job at a zoo.</u>

남 난 Peter를 방문하는 것이 언제나 약간은 꺼려져.
여 왜 그런데? 그는 정말 좋은 사람이야.
남 그렇긴 하지만, 그는 색다른 반려동물을 좋아하거든.
여 난 몰랐는데. 그가 무엇을 기르는데?
남 음, 지난주에 내가 거기 갔을 때 그에게는 주변을 뛰어다니는 이구아나 새끼가 있었어.
여 도마뱀? 어휴! 섬뜩해지는데.
남 난 그런 종류의 반려동물은 싫어. 하지만 그게 그가 가진 유일한 건 아니야.
여 그에게 반려동물이 더 있니?
남 응… 그는 꽤 오랫동안 뱀을 키우고 있어.
여 <u>그는 동물원에서 일을 구해야겠다.</u>

●●
exotic 색다른, 별난 **give ~ the creeps** ~를 섬뜩하게 하다 **zoo** 동물원

---

14 대화를 듣고, 여자의 마지막 말에 이어질 남자의 말로 가장 적절한 것을 고르시오.

① Yes, that's why I'm so upset.
② I know this must be a shock to you.
③ Let me know if there is anything I can do for you.
④ That's great! I've got some good news to share with you.
⑤ No, she wasn't. I would never have imagined that to be true.

W What's the matter? You <u>look as if</u> you've been <u>crying</u>.
M I have. I've just come from the vet.
W What happened?
M We had to have our cat <u>put to sleep</u>.
W What do you mean?
M She was painlessly <u>killed by a vet</u>. She had a tumor which was incurable.
W Oh, dear! I'm really sorry to hear that. <u>How old</u> was she?
M She was 15, which is quite old for a cat.
W Your cat was like a member of the family, wasn't she?
M <u>Yes, that's why I'm so upset.</u>

여 무슨 일이니? 너 울고 있는 것처럼 보여.
남 울었어. 방금 동물 병원에서 오는 길이야.
여 무슨 일인데?
남 우리 고양이를 잠들게 해야 했어.
여 무슨 소리야?
남 우리 고양이는 수의사에게 안락사되었어. 치료할 수 없는 종양이 있었거든.
여 아, 저런! 정말 안됐구나. 고양이는 몇 살이었니?
남 15살이었는데, 고양이로서는 꽤 나이가 많았지.
여 네 고양이는 가족 중 한 사람 같았잖아, 그렇지 않니?
남 <u>응, 그래서 내가 무척 속상한 거야.</u>

●●
as if 마치 ~인 것처럼 **vet** 동물 병원; 수의사 **painlessly** 고통 없이 **tumor** 종양 **incurable** 치료할 수 없는

15 다음 상황 설명을 듣고, Daniel이 지선이의 친구에게 할 말로 가장 적절한 것을 고르시오.

① She is planting flowers.
② She is looking for her mother.
③ She is helping her mother now.
④ She is painting "Welcome" on a sign.
⑤ She is cleaning the room to put up decorations.

Last Saturday, Daniel's family was very busy at home. They <u>invited</u> about twenty people to Daniel's birthday party. Everybody had a <u>special job to do</u>. Daniel's wife was <u>preparing food</u> in the kitchen. His daughter Ji-sun was helping her mother. His son Su-ho was cleaning the room to <u>put up decorations</u>. While Daniel was <u>painting</u> "Welcome" on a <u>sign</u>, the telephone rang. It was from one of Ji-sun's friends. She asked him <u>what</u> Ji-sun <u>was doing</u>. In this situation, what would Daniel most likely say to her?

Daniel: <u>She is helping her mother now.</u>

지난 토요일 Daniel의 가족들은 집에서 매우 바빴다. 그들은 Daniel의 생일 파티에 20명가량을 초대했다. 모든 식구들은 특정한 일을 하고 있었다. Daniel의 아내는 부엌에서 음식을 준비하고 있었다. 그의 딸인 지선이는 어머니를 돕고 있었다. 그의 아들인 수호는 장식을 하려고 방을 청소하고 있었다. Daniel이 '환영'이라는 문구를 표지판에 그리고 있는 동안 전화벨이 울렸다. 지선이의 친구 중 한 명으로부터 온 전화였다. 그녀는 지선이가 무엇을 하고 있는지 그에게 물었다. 이런 상황에서, Daniel은 그녀에게 뭐라고 말했겠는가?

Daniel: <u>그 애는 지금 엄마를 돕고 있단다.</u>

• •

prepare 준비하다   **decoration** 장식

REVIEW TEST p. 55

A ① vet, 수의사 ② tutor, 가정 교사 ③ extra, 여분의, 추가의 ④ effort, 노력 ⑤ particular, 특별한 ⑥ baggage, 수하물 ⑦ medium, 중간; 중간의 ⑧ location, 위치 ⑨ direction, 방향 ⑩ consider, 생각하다, 고려하다 ⑪ inexpensive, 비싸지 않은 ⑫ frightened, 깜짝 놀란, 겁이 난

B ① include utilities ② preparing food ③ wedding anniversary ④ conference room ⑤ paid double, price ⑥ searching, part, time ⑦ look as if ⑧ I'm in charge of

문제 및 정답	받아쓰기 및 녹음내용	해석

01

다음을 듣고, 그림의 상황에 알맞은 대화를 고르시오.

① ② ③ ④ ⑤

① M I'm so glad you could come.
　W I <u>wouldn't</u> <u>have</u> <u>missed</u> this party for the world.
② M Could you <u>drive</u> <u>a</u> <u>little</u> <u>slower</u>? You're making me nervous.
　W Sorry. I'll slow down.
③ M Come on in. The water is fine.
　W No, thanks. I'll <u>take</u> <u>a</u> <u>swim</u> later.
④ M Happy birthday!
　W Wow! I can't believe you <u>bought</u> <u>me</u> <u>some</u> <u>perfume</u> for my birthday!
⑤ M That'll be 29 dollars and 90 cents, please.
　W Here's a 50.

① 남 당신이 오시게 돼서 정말 기뻐요.
　여 무슨 일이 있어도 이 파티를 놓칠 순 없죠.
② 남 조금 더 천천히 운전해 주시겠어요? 당신은 저를 불안하게 만들고 있어요.
　여 미안해요. 속도를 늦출게요.
③ 남 들어오세요. 물이 좋아요.
　여 아녜요, 괜찮아요. 나중에 수영할게요.
④ 남 생일 축하해!
　여 와! 내 생일에 향수를 사 주다니 믿을 수 없어!
⑤ 남 29달러 90센트입니다.
　여 여기 50달러 있어요.

●●
nervous 불안한　**perfume** 향수

02

대화를 듣고, 두 사람이 대화하는 장소로 가장 적절한 곳을 고르시오.

① 은행　　　② 동물원
③ 미술관　　④ 옷 가게 ✓
⑤ 분실물 보관소

W Hi. Can I help you find anything?
M Yes, I'm looking for some <u>shorts</u> and <u>socks</u>.
W Do you have any <u>particular</u> <u>style</u> <u>in</u> <u>mind</u>?
M Something not too wild looking, I guess.
W How about these gray ones?
M They look pretty good. Can I <u>try</u> <u>them</u> <u>on</u>?
W Of course. The fitting room is <u>right</u> <u>over</u> <u>there</u>. Please follow me.
M Thank you.

여 안녕하세요. 찾는 걸 도와드릴까요?
남 네, 전 반바지와 양말을 찾고 있어요.
여 생각하시는 특별한 스타일이 있나요?
남 너무 과감해 보이지 않는 걸로요.
여 이 회색은 어떠세요?
남 아주 괜찮아 보이네요. 입어 봐도 될까요?
여 물론이죠. 탈의실은 바로 저쪽이에요. 저를 따라오세요.
남 감사합니다.

●●
shorts 반바지　**fitting room** 탈의실

03 대화를 듣고, 두 사람의 관계로 가장 적절한 것을 고르시오.

① 요리사 – 손님
② 제빵사 – 수강생
③ 배달 기사 – 고객 ✓
④ 슈퍼마켓 점원 – 손님
⑤ 호텔 지배인 – 종업원

M Here you go — one large cheese pizza with <u>two</u> <u>extra</u> toppings.

W Wait. I <u>don't</u> <u>think</u> I <u>ordered</u> <u>this</u>. I ordered a pepperoni pizza.

M You did? Oh, just a second. I think it's in the delivery box on the bike. I <u>got</u> <u>confused</u>.

W Oh, good. I'm glad you have it. <u>I'm</u> <u>starving</u>.

M Sorry about that. Here's your pepperoni pizza.

W Thanks. Here's 20 dollars. <u>Keep</u> <u>the</u> <u>change</u>.

M Thanks. Have a good day.

W You, too.

남 여기 있어요. 두 가지 토핑을 추가한 라지 사이즈 치즈 피자 한 판이요.

여 잠깐만요. 제가 주문한 게 아닌 것 같아요. 전 페퍼로니 피자를 주문했어요.

남 그러셨어요? 아, 잠시만요. 오토바이의 배달함에 있는 것 같아요. 헷갈렸나 봐요.

여 아, 괜찮습니다. 갖고 계시다니 다행이에요. 전 배가 무척 고프거든요.

남 죄송합니다. 여기 페퍼로니 피자요.

여 감사합니다. 여기 20달러요. 잔돈은 가지세요.

남 고맙습니다. 좋은 하루 보내세요.

여 기사님도요.

•• confused 헷갈리는, 혼란스러운 starving 배가 아주 고픈 change 잔돈, 거스름돈

---

04 대화를 듣고, 남자의 직업으로 가장 적절한 것을 고르시오.

① 목수　　　② 경찰관
③ 수리 기사　④ 아파트 관리인 ✓
⑤ 이삿짐센터 직원

M Good afternoon, Ms. Smith! You called us this morning for some <u>work</u> <u>to</u> <u>be</u> <u>done</u>? How may I help you?

W Yes, I <u>can't</u> <u>clean</u> the windows <u>myself</u>. Please help me with the dirty windows in my house.

M Well, they get that way, but many people don't know how to clean them.

W It seems like such a <u>hard</u> and <u>dangerous</u> <u>job</u>. That's why I need your help.

M That's good. I just happen to have all the cleaning tools that I need.

W Can I <u>give</u> <u>you</u> <u>a</u> <u>hand</u>?

M Leave them to me, ma'am. I'll take care of them.

W How kind of you. It's dangerous. You <u>should</u> <u>be</u> <u>careful</u>.

M Don't worry. I'll give them the best of care.

남 안녕하세요, Smith 씨! 처리되어야 할 일 때문에 오늘 아침에 저희에게 전화하셨지요? 무엇을 도와드릴까요?

여 네, 제 스스로 창문을 닦을 수가 없어요. 저희 집에 있는 더러운 창문을 청소하는 것 좀 도와주세요.

남 음, 창문이 그렇게 되더라도, 많은 분들이 그것을 어떻게 청소하는지는 모르시더라구요.

여 너무 힘들고 위험한 일인 것 같아서요. 그래서 당신의 도움이 필요해요.

남 잘됐군요. 마침 필요한 청소 도구들이 모두 있거든요.

여 제가 도와드릴까요?

남 제게 맡겨 주세요. 제가 알아서 하겠습니다.

여 친절하기도 하시네요. 위험합니다. 조심하셔야 해요.

남 걱정하지 마세요. 최대한 주의를 기울일게요.

•• dangerous 위험한 tool 도구

05 다음을 듣고, 오늘의 기상도와 일기 예보가 일치하지 <u>않는</u> 도시를 고르시오.

① 서울
② 강원
③ 경기
④ 광주
⑤ 제주도

Good morning. Here is today's weather for some <u>places</u> <u>around</u> Korea. Today is going to be sunny in Seoul <u>with</u> <u>a</u> <u>high</u> of 28 degrees Celsius. It's going to be cloudy in Kangwon Province with a high of 19 degrees. There's going to be <u>rain</u> with <u>thunder</u> and <u>lightning</u> <u>storms</u> in Gwangju. On Jeju Island, it will be mostly <u>foggy</u>, and there will be <u>strong</u> <u>winds</u> from the south. Gyeonggi Province will enjoy sunny skies and <u>mild</u> <u>weather</u> with a high of 24 degrees.

안녕하세요. 한국의 일부 지역의 오늘 날씨를 말씀드리겠습니다. 오늘 서울은 최고 기온이 섭씨 28도로 화창하겠습니다. 강원도는 최고 기온이 19도로 구름이 많이 끼겠습니다. 광주에는 천둥과 번개를 동반한 폭풍과 함께 비가 내리겠습니다. 제주도에는 주로 안개가 끼겠고 강한 남풍이 불겠습니다. 경기도는 최고 기온이 24도로, 화창한 하늘과 온화한 날씨를 즐길 수 있겠습니다.

●●
Celsius 섭씨 **province** (행정 단위인) 도(道), 주(州) **thunder** 천둥 **lighting** 번개 **mild** 온화한

---

06 대화를 듣고, 무엇에 관한 내용인지 가장 적절한 것을 고르시오.

① 교통사고 후유증
② 자전거에 치였던 일
③ 다리에 난 상처 치료 방법
④ 교통사고로 인한 금전적 손해
⑤ 여자에게 어렸을 때 발생한 사고

M Where did you <u>get</u> <u>that</u> <u>huge</u> <u>scar</u> on your leg?

W When I was six, I was hit by a car, so I had to <u>have</u> <u>an</u> <u>operation</u>.

M Were you seriously hurt?

W My leg was broken, but there was no serious <u>long</u>-<u>term</u> <u>damage</u>.

M Getting hurt when you're a kid is a <u>scary</u> thing, isn't it?

W It sure is. Even my mother was crying. But pretty soon, life was fine again. <u>Has</u> anything bad ever <u>happened</u> <u>to</u> <u>you</u>?

M Not like that. I fell off my bike once or twice, but that was it.

W Well, you should <u>consider</u> <u>yourself</u> <u>lucky</u>.

남 네 다리에 난 그 큰 상처는 어디에서 입은 거니?

여 내가 여섯 살 때 차에 치여서 수술을 받아야 했어.

남 심하게 다쳤었니?

여 다리를 다치긴 했지만, 오랫동안 지속된 심각한 손상은 아니었어.

남 어렸을 때 다치는 건 무서운 일이야, 그렇지 않니?

여 물론이지. 우리 엄마도 우셨어. 그렇지만 얼마 안되어 생활이 다시 괜찮아졌어. 너한테도 전에 나쁜 일이 생긴 적 있니?

남 그런 사고는 아니고. 자전거에서 한두 번 떨어진 정도지, 그게 다야.

여 음, 넌 행운인 줄 알아야 해.

●●
huge 큰, 거대한 **scar** 상처 **operation** 수술 **long-term** 장기적인 **scary** 무서운 **happen** (일이) 생기다, 발생하다

07 다음을 듣고, 남자가 여행 중에 느낀 점으로 가장 적절한 것을 고르시오.

① 볼거리는 별로 없었다.
② 기대가 커서 실망도 컸다.
③ 교통이 불편해서 피곤했다.
④ 기대한 만큼 만족스러웠다.
⑤ 혼자 여행을 해서 조금 외로웠다.

My whole life, I dreamed of visiting England and seeing all its <u>amazing</u> <u>sights</u>. On my first day, I saw Big Ben, the <u>huge</u> <u>clock</u> in the middle of London, as well as the River Thames. I also had a chance to visit Buckingham Palace, where the queen lives. I also <u>had</u> <u>a</u> <u>chance</u> <u>to</u> visit some English pubs and meet some interesting people. Probably <u>the</u> <u>most</u> <u>interesting</u> <u>part</u> of my trip was seeing the double-decker buses. I <u>traveled</u> <u>alone</u>, but I was never lonely. My trip to England was something that I <u>won't</u> <u>forget</u>.

전 항상 영국을 방문해서 멋진 명소를 전부 구경하는 것에 대해 꿈꾸었습니다. 여행 첫날 저는 Thames강과 함께 런던의 중앙에 있는 대형 시계인 Big Ben도 보았습니다. 전 또한 여왕이 살고 있는 버킹엄 궁을 방문할 기회가 있었습니다. 전 또한 영국 선술집에 가서 재미있는 몇몇 사람들을 만날 기회가 있었습니다. 아마도 제 여행에서 가장 재미있었던 부분은 2층 버스를 구경한 것일 겁니다. 전 혼자 여행했지만 전혀 외롭지 않았습니다. 영국 여행은 제가 잊지 못할 일이었습니다.

•●
sight 명소, 관광지 **palace** 궁전, 왕실 **pub** 선술집

---

08 대화를 듣고, 여자의 심정으로 가장 적절한 것을 고르시오.

① nervous ② hopeful
③ delighted ④ concerned
⑤ disappointed

W Oh, a box of white chocolates. How sweet! <u>What's</u> <u>the</u> <u>occasion</u>?
M No particular reason. I was just thinking about you. That's all.
W What a kind gesture. You are <u>so</u> <u>considerate</u>. Thank you.
M It was nothing. I hope you like them.
W I get it now. Today is March 14. It's White Day. I <u>forgot</u> <u>all</u> <u>about</u> <u>it</u>.
M I never forget it. You mean the world to me, so I always remember special occasions.
W I think I'm <u>the</u> <u>luckiest</u> <u>woman</u> in the world.

여 오, 화이트 초콜릿 상자네. 다정하기도 해라! 무슨 일 때문이지?
남 특별한 이유는 없어. 그냥 네 생각이 났어. 그게 다야.
여 참 상냥하구나. 넌 정말 사려 깊어. 고마워.
남 별것 아니야. 네가 초콜릿을 좋아했으면 좋겠다.
여 이제 알겠다. 오늘이 3월 14일이네. 화이트데이구나. 완전히 잊고 있었네.
남 난 절대 안 잊어버리지. 너는 나에게 있어서 전부거든. 그래서 난 항상 특별한 날들을 기억해둬.
여 난 세상에서 가장 운이 좋은 여자라고 생각해.

•●
gesture 태도; 몸짓 **considerate** 사려 깊은

09 대화를 듣고, 남자의 시간당 수입이 얼마나 늘었는지 고르시오.

① $1.25 ② $1.50
③ $1.75 ④ $2.00
⑤ $8.25

W Hi, Mike. What's up?

M I just started a new job.

W Really? Do you like it better than your old one?

M The pay is much better. At my old job, I was making 8 dollars and 25 cents an hour. Now I'm making 10 dollars an hour. Plus, I get benefits like medical and dental insurance.

W Good for you. You deserve to have some good luck.

M Thanks. I've been searching for a better job for a while.

W I wonder if I should start looking for a better job, too.

M Maybe you should. There are jobs out there. You just have to find them.

여 안녕, Mike. 어떻게 지내?

남 나 막 새로운 일을 시작했어.

여 정말? 예전에 하던 일보다 더 마음에 드니?

남 보수가 훨씬 더 좋아. 전에 하던 일에서는 시간당 8달러 25센트를 벌었어. 지금은 시간당 10달러를 벌고 있어. 거기에다가, 의료 보험과 치과 보험 같은 혜택도 받아.

여 잘됐다. 너한테는 좋은 일이 생길 만하지.

남 고마워. 한동안 더 나은 일을 구하려고 했었어.

여 나도 더 나은 일을 구하기 시작해야 하려나.

남 그러는 게 좋아. 나와 있는 일자리는 있으니까. 일단은 그것들을 찾아 봐야 해.

●●
pay 보수, 급료 **benefit** 혜택, 이득 **dental** 치과의, 치아의 **deserve** ~할 만하다, ~할 가치가 있다

---

10 대화를 듣고, 여자가 다이어트를 하려는 이유로 가장 적절한 것을 고르시오.

① 원하는 옷을 입기 위해서
② 관절 건강을 지키기 위해서
③ 좋은 몸매를 유지하기 위해서
④ 건강에 좋은 음식을 먹기 위해서
⑤ 보디빌딩 대회에 참가하기 위해서

W Guess what? Today, I'm starting a diet.

M Really? Why do you need to go on a diet? You already seem very thin. Do you intend to be a contestant in a bodybuilding competition or something?

W It's not that I need to lose weight. I just need to eat healthier food.

M Oh, I see what you mean.

W No more doughnuts, cakes, ice cream, and potato chips.

M It takes a lot of will power to give up the things you like.

W It does, but I know I can do it.

여 있잖아. 오늘 나 다이어트를 시작하려고.

남 정말? 네가 왜 다이어트를 해야 하니? 넌 이미 매우 날씬한 것 같은데. 보디빌딩 대회 같은 데서 참가자로 나갈 작정이니?

여 살을 뺄 필요가 있는 건 아니야. 그냥 좀 더 건강에 좋은 음식을 먹을 필요가 있어서.

남 아, 무슨 뜻인지 알겠다.

여 더 이상 도넛, 케이크, 아이스크림, 그리고 감자칩은 안 먹을 거야.

남 네가 좋아하는 것들을 포기하려면 많은 의지력이 필요하지.

여 그렇지, 하지만 난 할 수 있다는 걸 알아.

●●
intend to ~할 작정이다 **contestant** 참가자 **competition** 대회 **will power** 의지력 **give up** ~을 포기하다

11 대화를 듣고, 여자가 대화 직후에 할 일로 가장 적절한 것을 고르시오.

① 전화를 건다. ✓
② Bill에게 간다.
③ 옷을 사러 간다.
④ 돈을 인출하러 간다.
⑤ 사무실까지 걸어간다.

M Good morning. You're <u>sweating a lot</u>.
W Yes, I know. I walked to the office.
M Is it <u>a long walk</u>?
W It's about a mile. And I stopped, too. I looked in all the store windows.
M Did you <u>look around</u> at <u>clothes</u>?
W Yes, I looked at coats.
M Did you like <u>any of them</u>?
W I liked a blue coat, but it was too expensive for me.
M That's always the way it is. By the way, Bill called a few minutes ago. He wanted you to <u>call him back</u>.
W Thanks. I'm going to call him right away.

남 좋은 아침이에요. 당신은 땀을 많이 흘리고 있군요.
여 네, 알아요. 사무실까지 걸어왔거든요.
남 걷기에 먼 거리인가요?
여 1마일 정도예요. 그리고 멈추기도 했어요. 가게 진열대들을 모두 들여다봤어요.
남 옷을 구경했나요?
여 네, 코트를 봤어요.
남 맘에 드는 게 있었나요?
여 전 푸른색 코트가 맘에 들었지만 너무 비싸더군요.
남 항상 그렇지요. 그런데, Bill이 몇 분 전에 전화했었어요. 그는 당신이 전화해 주길 바라더군요.
여 고마워요. 지금 당장 그에게 전화해 볼게요.

●●
sweat 땀을 흘리다

---

12 대화를 듣고, 대화 내용과 일치하지 <u>않는</u> 것을 고르시오.

① 여자의 오빠는 사업에 성공한 사람이다.
② 여자의 오빠가 선거에 출마하는 것은 이번이 두 번째이다. ✓
③ 여자의 오빠는 시장 선거에 출마할 것이다.
④ 여자의 오빠는 가족 친화적인 정책을 공약으로 내세울 것이다.
⑤ 여자의 오빠가 제시할 공약에 남자는 호의적이다.

W My brother has decided to <u>go into politics</u>.
M Really? Why is that? He's such <u>a successful businessman</u>.
W Well, he's gone as far as he wants to go in business and is looking for a new challenge.
M What is he aiming for?
W City Hall. He's going to <u>run for mayor</u> during the next mayoral election.
M What's he going to promise?
W He's going to promise to <u>introduce</u> many more <u>family-friendly policies</u> if he is elected.
M That's the most important thing for me. I hope he <u>wins the election</u>.

여 우리 오빠는 정치에 입문하기로 결정했어.
남 정말? 왜 그런 거니? 너희 오빠는 매우 성공적인 사업가잖아.
여 음, 그는 사업에서 원하는 곳까지 가 봐서 새로운 도전을 찾고 있어.
남 그가 목표하는 것이 뭔데?
여 시청. 그는 다음번 시장 선거에서 시장으로 입후보할 거야.
남 어떤 공약을 할 건데?
여 그는 당선된다면 가족 친화적인 정책들을 더욱 많이 도입할 것을 약속할 거야.
남 그건 나에게는 가장 중요한 일이야. 그가 선거에서 이기길 바라.

●●
politics 정치 **challenge** 도전 **aim for** ~을 목표로 하다 **run for** ~에 입후보하다 **mayor** 시장 **election** 선거 **introduce** 도입하다 **policy** 정책

13 대화를 듣고, 남자의 마지막 말에 이어질 여자의 말로 가장 적절한 것을 고르시오.

① I'd say she was impossible to please.
② I was put in such an awkward position.
③ Who's going to take responsibility?
④ That was the most embarrassing situation I've ever been in.
⑤ That would be great, but if she's asking too much, let me know.

M I've just had a terrible hour and a half.

W I can see. You look exhausted. What happened?

M Well, I had a lady customer who wanted to buy a pair of shoes come in. And you know we've got quite a good selection.

W We certainly do.

M She asked me to bring her every single pair we had in the shop.

W That's not a nice thing to do. Was she satisfied with them?

M Not at all. She complained about every single one.

W Did she buy a pair?

M No, after complaining about the shoes and the service, she just left.

W I'd say she was impossible to please.

남 1시간 반 동안 끔찍했어.

여 알 것 같다. 지쳐 보여. 무슨 일이니?

남 음, 난 신발 한 켤레를 사길 원하는 여자 손님을 맞았어. 그리고 너도 알다시피 우리는 상품 종류가 정말 많잖아.

여 분명 그렇지.

남 그녀는 나에게 가게에 있는 모든 신발을 가져올 것을 요청했어.

여 그리 좋은 행동은 아니구나. 그녀가 신발에 만족했니?

남 전혀. 그녀는 모든 신발들에 대해 불평했어.

여 그녀가 신발은 샀니?

남 아니, 신발과 서비스에 대해 불평한 다음에 그냥 가버렸어.

여 그녀는 만족시키는 것이 불가능한 사람이구나.

••

exhausted 지친, 기진맥진한 **selection** 선택 가능한 것들 **satisfied** 만족하는 **complain** 불평하다

---

14 대화를 듣고, 여자의 마지막 말에 이어질 남자의 말로 가장 적절한 것을 고르시오.

① I'm disappointed with your attitude.
② Are you sure you can get all your money back?
③ I'm sending this back to you, and I expect a full refund.
④ Don't forget to take the coupons with you to the store!
⑤ There's a 16-percent interest charge if you pay for this with monthly payments.

M Why are you talking to your computer? Is it lonely?

W No, don't be silly. I'm trying out some new speech recognition software.

M How does it work?

W Well, I just say what I want to type into the microphone, and my words appear on the screen.

M It's like magic. It must be very expensive.

W It's not cheap. But if I'm not satisfied with it, I can return it free of charge within 30 days.

M Are you sure you can get all your money back?

남 넌 왜 컴퓨터랑 대화하니? 컴퓨터가 외롭대?

여 아니, 엉뚱한 소리 하지 마. 나는 새로운 음성 인식 소프트웨어를 시험해 보는 중이야.

남 그건 어떻게 작동하는데?

여 음, 내가 타자 치고 싶은 것을 마이크에 대고 말하기만 하면, 내가 한 말들이 화면에 나타나.

남 마술 같구나. 아주 비싸겠다.

여 싸지는 않지. 하지만 만약 내가 그것에 만족하지 않으면, 30일 안에 그것을 무료로 반품할 수 있어.

남 확실히 돈을 다 돌려받을 수 있는 거니?

••

recognition 인식 **microphone** 마이크 **appear** 나타나다 **free of charge** 무료로

15 대화를 듣고, 남자의 마지막 말에 이어질 여자의 말로 가장 적절한 것을 고르시오.

① You have a gift for playing the drums.
② I'm looking forward to playing the violin.
③ I've been playing the drums since I was 13.
④ I wish I could go to your graduation concert.
⑤ Do you know anyone who can give me lessons?

M Thank you for coming to my graduation concert.
W It was a great concert. I wish I could play the violin like you.
M I'm sure you could if you tried. You should take some lessons.
W I took some when I was younger, but I was hopeless.
M Why was that?
W I found that I was tone-deaf, which really made it impossible.
M In that case, why don't you try learning the drums?
W That's a good idea. I'll try.
M Then being tone-deaf shouldn't matter.
W Do you know anyone who can give me lessons?

남 제 졸업 연주회에 와 주셔서 감사합니다.
여 대단한 연주회였어요. 나도 당신처럼 바이올린을 켤 수 있다면 좋겠어요.
남 당신도 노력하면 분명 할 수 있어요. 레슨을 좀 받으셔야 해요.
여 제가 어렸을 때 레슨을 받았었는데 가망이 없었어요.
남 왜 그랬나요?
여 제게 음감이 없다는 것을 알았거든요, 그래서 정말 불가능해졌고요.
남 그렇다면 드럼을 한번 쳐 보시는 것은 어때요?
여 좋은 생각이네요. 해 보죠.
남 그러면 음감이 없다는 것은 문제가 되지 않을 거예요.
여 저에게 레슨을 해 주실 수 있는 분을 아시나요?

●●

hopeless 가망 없는　**tone-deaf** 음감이 없는, 음치의　**impossible** 불가능한

REVIEW TEST p. 63

A
① scary, 무서운　② shorts, 반바지　③ policy, 정책　④ deserve, ~할 만하다, ~할 가치가 있다
⑤ starving, 배가 아주 고픈　⑥ satisfied, 만족하는　⑦ confused, 헷갈리는, 혼란스러운
⑧ considerate, 사려 깊은　⑨ exhausted, 지친, 기진맥진한　⑩ impossible, 불가능한
⑪ competition, 대회　⑫ fitting room, 탈의실

B
① making, nervous　② complained about　③ benefits, dental
④ huge scar　⑤ sweating a lot　⑥ free of charge
⑦ run for mayor　⑧ will power, give up

문제 및 정답	받아쓰기 및 녹음내용	해석

01

다음을 듣고, 그림의 상황에 알맞은 대화를 고르시오.

① ② ③ ④ ⑤

① W Do you want to eat some?
　M Yes, I'm starving.
② W I'd like a T-bone steak.
　M How would you like it done?
③ W This looks delicious, doesn't it?
　M Yes, let's order two servings.
④ W Is it for here or to go?
　M For here, please.
⑤ W How long will it take?
　M It will only take about five minutes.

① 여 좀 먹겠니?
　남 네, 전 몹시 배고파요.
② 여 티본 스테이크로 할게요.
　남 어떻게 해 드릴까요?
③ 여 이거 맛있어 보이네, 그렇지 않니?
　남 응, 2인분을 주문하자.
④ 여 여기서 드실 건가요, 아니면 가져가실 건가요?
　남 여기서 먹을 거예요.
⑤ 여 얼마나 걸릴까요?
　남 5분 정도밖에 안 걸릴 겁니다.

●●
serving (음식의) 1인분

02

대화를 듣고, 두 사람이 대화하는 장소로 가장 적절한 곳을 고르시오.
① 교실　　　② 상점
③ 사무실　　④ 도서관
⑤ 수리점

M Could you tell me the good things and the bad things about this computer?
W Sure. First of all, I can say that there aren't any bad points about this model.
M Hmm, are you sure?
W Yes. This is the best computer we've ever made.
M Sounds interesting. Tell me more.
W This model is almost three times as fast as our other models.
M Three times?
W Uh-huh, and with this computer, you can handle complex tasks.
M Sounds good.
W That's right. Would you like to buy this one?

남 이 컴퓨터에 관한 장점과 단점을 말씀해 주시겠어요?
여 물론이죠. 먼저, 이 모델에는 어떤 단점도 없다고 말씀드릴 수 있어요.
남 흠, 확실한가요?
여 네. 이것은 저희가 이제까지 만든 컴퓨터 중에 최고예요.
남 흥미롭네요. 좀 더 말씀해 주세요.
여 이 모델은 다른 모델들보다 거의 세 배나 더 빨라요.
남 세 배나요?
여 네, 그리고 이 컴퓨터로 복잡한 업무들을 처리할 수 있어요.
남 좋네요.
여 맞아요. 이 제품을 구입하시겠어요?

●●
interesting 흥미로운　**almost** 거의
complex 복잡한　**task** 업무

03 다음을 듣고, 남자의 직업으로 가장 적절한 것을 고르시오.

① 농부   ② 정원사
③ 과학자   ④ 요리사
⑤ 엔지니어

My family has been <u>working</u> <u>on</u> <u>this</u> <u>land</u> for five generations. We're really proud of that fact. Agricultural technology has changed a lot though, especially during my lifetime. These days, there are environmentally friendly <u>farm</u> <u>chemicals</u>, and some of our fields <u>have</u> <u>gone</u> completely <u>organic</u>. We also have new types of <u>seeds</u> and use high-tech <u>farming</u> <u>methods</u>. This means that the vegetables and the grains we produce today are <u>higher</u> <u>in</u> <u>quality</u> and cheaper than those produced in my parents' day.

우리 가족은 이 땅에서 5대째 일해 오고 있어요. 우리는 정말 그 사실이 자랑스러워요. 그런데 특히 제가 살아 오는 동안 농업 기술이 많이 변했어요. 요즘에는 친환경적인 농장용 화학 물질이 있고, 우리 논 중 일부는 완전히 유기농 재배를 하게 됐어요. 또한, 우리는 새로운 종류의 씨앗을 갖고 있고 첨단 기술의 농경법을 사용하죠. 이것은 오늘날 우리가 생산하는 채소와 곡물이 우리 부모님 때 생산되던 것들보다 품질이 더 높고 더 저렴하다는 걸 의미하죠.

●●
generation 세대 **agricultural** 농업의 **chemical** 화학 물질 **organic** 유기농의 **seed** 씨앗, 종자 **high-tech** 첨단 기술의 **method** 방법 **grain** 곡물 **produce** 생산하다 **quality** 품질

04 대화를 듣고, 두 사람의 관계로 가장 적절한 것을 고르시오.

① 의사 - 환자
② 경찰 - 운전자
③ 구급대원 - 학생
④ 수리 기사 - 고객
⑤ 택시 기사 - 승객

M Are you hurt?
W Luckily, I am fine. But my husband <u>needs</u> <u>an</u> <u>ambulance</u>.
M Okay. It's on the way now. May I see your driver's license, please?
W Yes. Here you are.
M <u>What</u> <u>exactly</u> <u>happened</u>?
W Well, a car went through the red light. I slammed on the breaks, and my car <u>went</u> <u>off</u> the road and <u>hit</u> <u>the</u> <u>sign</u>.
M Did the other driver stop?
W No, he didn't. He <u>didn't</u> even <u>slow</u> <u>down</u>.
M All right. Could you come to the police station after you and your husband get better? I have to <u>fill</u> <u>out</u> a <u>report</u>.
W Yes, I will.

남 다쳤나요?
여 다행히, 전 괜찮아요. 하지만 제 남편은 구급차가 필요해요.
남 알았어요. 구급차가 지금 오고 있습니다. 운전면허증을 볼 수 있을까요?
여 네. 여기 있어요.
남 정확히 무슨 일이 일어난 거죠?
여 음, 차 한 대가 빨간 불을 통과해서 갔어요. 저는 브레이크를 세게 밟았고, 제 차가 길에서 벗어나서 이정표를 들이받았어요.
남 다른 운전자는 멈췄나요?
여 아뇨, 멈추지 않았어요. 그는 속도를 줄이지도 않았어요.
남 알겠습니다. 당신과 남편분께서 호전되고 난 후에 경찰서로 와 주시겠어요? 제가 보고서를 작성해야 해서요.
여 네, 알겠습니다.

●●
slam (브레이크 등을) 세게 밟다 **get better** 호전되다, 좋아지다 **fill out** ~를 작성하다

05 대화를 듣고, 여자가 설명하고 있는 사람을 고르시오.

①   ②

③   ④

⑤

W This guy is so handsome! He's <u>one</u> <u>of</u> <u>my</u> <u>favorite</u> fashion models.

M Where? Who's handsome?

W This guy in the magazine. I like <u>tall</u> <u>men</u>.

M Let me see. I don't see any handsome men here.

W The one with the <u>short</u> <u>hair</u>. He has a <u>m(o)ustache</u>. He looks really sharp in this suit, doesn't he?

M There are a few guys wearing a suit.

W The one who's wearing the <u>vest</u> and the <u>striped</u> <u>pants</u>.

M Frankly speaking, I think I look much better than any of those guys.

여 이 남자 너무 잘생겼다! 내가 가장 좋아하는 패션 모델 중에 한 사람이야.

남 어디? 누가 잘생겼다고?

여 잡지에 나온 이 남자 말야. 나는 키 큰 남자가 좋아.

남 어디 보자. 여기에 잘생긴 남자는 한 명도 안 보이는데.

여 짧은 머리의 남자 말이야. 그는 콧수염이 나 있어. 이 정장을 입고 있으니까 정말 세련돼 보여, 그렇지 않니?

남 정장을 입은 남자들이 몇 명 있는데.

여 조끼와 줄무늬가 있는 바지를 입은 사람을 말하는 거야.

남 솔직히 말해서, 내 생각에는 이 남자들보다는 내가 훨씬 더 나아 보여.

●●

m(o)ustache 콧수염 vest 조끼 frankly speaking 솔직히 말해서

---

06 다음을 듣고, 고객 페이지를 통해서 할 수 있는 일로 언급되지 <u>않은</u> 것을 고르시오.

① 물품의 취소
② 물품의 반송
③ 물품의 재고 확인
④ 예상 배송일 확인
⑤ 물품의 배송 상태 추적

We'd like to let you know we <u>shipped</u> <u>your</u> <u>items</u> today. You can <u>track</u> the <u>status</u> of your <u>order</u> online by visiting the Your Account page at our website. There, you can track the order and shipment status, review estimated <u>delivery</u> <u>dates</u>, <u>cancel</u> unshipped items, and <u>return</u> items. Thanks for shopping at pamon.com, and we <u>hope</u> <u>to</u> <u>see</u> <u>you</u> again soon!

고객님의 물품을 오늘 보내드렸음을 알려드리고 싶습니다. 저희 웹사이트의 고객 페이지를 방문하심으로써 주문하신 물품의 상태를 온라인으로 추적하실 수 있습니다. 그곳에서 여러분들은 주문 및 배송 상태를 추적하고, 예상 배송일을 확인하고, 미출고된 물품을 취소하고, 물품을 반송하실 수 있습니다. pamon.com에서 물품을 구매해 주신 것에 감사드리며, 곧 다시 만나 뵙기를 기대하겠습니다!

●●

ship 보내다, 수송하다 track 추적하다 status 상태, 사정 estimated 예상[추측]의 cancel 취소하다

07 대화를 듣고, 남자의 심정으로 가장 적절한 것을 고르시오.

① proud ② fearful
③ lonely ④ grateful
⑤ disappointed

M You spent your entire day helping me <u>weed</u> <u>my</u> <u>garden</u>. Thank you.

W Don't mention it. I <u>had</u> <u>nothing</u> <u>to</u> <u>do</u> today anyway.

M I really <u>appreciate</u> your help. I don't know any other people who give their time like you.

W No, really, it's my pleasure to <u>lend</u> <u>a</u> <u>hand</u>.

M You have to let me know when I can <u>return</u> <u>the</u> <u>favor</u>.

W Certainly.

남 내 정원의 잡초 뽑는 것을 도와주는 데 하루 종일 걸렸구나. 고마워.

여 천만에. 어쨌든 오늘은 할 일이 없었거든.

남 도와줘서 정말로 고마워. 너처럼 자기 시간을 할애하는 사람을 못 봤거든.

여 아냐, 정말로, 내가 도움이 될 수 있어서 기쁜걸.

남 내가 은혜를 갚을 일이 있으면 내게 알려 줘야 해.

여 물론이지.

●●

weed 잡초를 뽑다 **lend a hand** 도움을 주다 **favor** 은혜, 친절한 행위

---

08 대화를 듣고, 여자가 구입할 비행기 표의 가격을 고르시오.

① 16만 원 ② 17만 원
③ 60만 원 ④ 70만 원
⑤ 80만 원

M Fly Away Travel Agency. May I help you?

W I would like to take a vacation to Hong Kong for <u>a</u> <u>couple</u> <u>of</u> <u>weeks</u>. How much will it cost?

M That depends. <u>When</u> are you <u>planning</u> <u>to</u> <u>leave</u>?

W On the 28th of the month.

M If you leave on the 28th of the month, the airline ticket will be 800,000 won.

W <u>What</u> <u>if</u> I leave on the 30th? Is it any cheaper?

M Let me have a look on the computer. Yes. In fact, the price <u>drops</u> <u>to</u> <u>700,000</u> won if you leave on that date.

W It's still steep for me.

M Well, if you leave on the 25th, it's only 600,000 won.

W But I can't leave that early because of my job. I guess I will <u>leave</u> on the <u>30th</u>. Can you book a ticket for me?

M Yes, I'll <u>book</u> <u>a</u> <u>ticket</u> on the 30th.

남 Fly Away 여행사입니다. 무엇을 도와드릴까요?

여 몇 주간 홍콩으로 여행을 가고 싶은데요. 비용이 얼마나 들까요?

남 경우에 따라 다릅니다. 언제 떠나실 계획이죠?

여 이번 달 28일이요.

남 이번 달 28일에 떠나시면 비행기 표는 80만 원입니다.

여 30일에 떠나면요? 조금이라도 더 싼가요?

남 컴퓨터로 한번 볼게요. 네. 사실, 그 날짜에 떠나시면 가격이 70만 원까지 떨어집니다.

여 저한테는 여전히 비싸군요.

남 음, 25일에 떠나시면 60만 원밖에 안 하는데요.

여 그렇지만 일 때문에 그렇게 일찍 떠날 수는 없어요. 30일에 출발하는 것으로 하겠습니다. 비행기 표를 예약해 주시겠어요?

남 네, 30일로 표를 예약해드리겠습니다.

●●

travel agency 여행사 **What if ~?** ~라면 어떻게 되는가? **in fact** 사실은 **steep** 너무 비싼

09

대화를 듣고, 남자가 도시로 이사하려는 이유로 가장 적절한 것을 고르시오.

① 자신의 꿈을 이루기 위해서
② 공개 댄스 오디션에 참가하기 위해서
③ 유명한 댄스 학교에 합격했기 때문에
④ 도시에 살고 있는 친구의 권유 때문에
⑤ 도시에 살아보는 것이 어릴 적 꿈이었기 때문에

M I've decided to leave this town and <u>move</u> <u>to</u> <u>the</u> <u>city</u>.

W What is the reason?

M There's nothing for me in this town. I want to <u>follow</u> <u>my</u> <u>dreams</u> in the city.

W What will you do there? Will you continue with your <u>dancing</u> <u>career</u>?

M Yes, I want to <u>enroll</u> <u>in</u> a dance school there.

W So you've absolutely decided to leave?

M I've totally decided. I <u>leave</u> <u>in</u> <u>one</u> <u>month</u>.

W I wish you luck even though I will miss you.

남 나 이 마을을 떠나서 도시로 이사 가기로 결심했어.

여 이유가 뭔데?

남 이 마을에서는 내가 할 일이 없어. 나는 도시에서 내 꿈을 좇고 싶어.

여 거기서 무얼 할 거니? 춤추는 일을 계속할 거니?

남 응, 거기에서 댄스 학교에 등록하고 싶어.

여 그럼, 너는 떠나기로 확실히 결심한 거구나?

남 확실히 결심했어. 한 달 후에 떠나.

여 비록 네가 보고 싶기는 하겠지만 잘 됐으면 좋겠다.

●●
decide 결심하다, 결정하다 **career** 직업, 경력
enroll in ~에 등록하다 **totally** 완전히

10

대화를 듣고, 여자의 의견으로 가장 적절한 것을 고르시오.

① 소수의 잘못 때문에 다수가 피해를 본다.
② 안전한 환경을 만들기 위해 소수만 노력한다.
③ 소수의 의견이라는 이유로 배척되어서는 안 된다.
④ 법이 모든 사람에게 공평하게 적용되는 것은 아니다.
⑤ 도서관 열람실 내에서의 휴대폰 사용은 금지되어야 한다.

W Did you hear that we're not permitted to <u>bring</u> cell phones <u>into</u> the <u>public</u> <u>bath</u>?

M That's good. I heard that someone was taking pictures in there.

W But why should everyone <u>be</u> <u>punished</u> for the actions of a few?

M To <u>ensure</u> a <u>safe</u> <u>environment</u>. That's why.

W You're right, but there must be a better way to <u>deal</u> <u>with</u> <u>the</u> <u>problem</u>.

M I agree with you.

여 공중 목욕탕에 휴대폰을 갖고 들어가지 못하게 되었다는 것을 들었니?

남 잘 됐네. 어떤 사람은 그 안에서 사진을 찍는다고 들었어.

여 그런데 왜 몇몇 사람들의 행동 때문에 모든 사람들이 처벌을 받아야만 하는 거야?

남 안전한 환경을 보장하기 위해서지. 그게 이유야.

여 네 말이 맞지만, 그 문제를 처리하기 위한 더 나은 방법이 분명히 있을 거야.

남 나도 그렇게 생각해.

●●
be not permitted to ~하는 것이 허용되지 않다
public bath 공중 목욕탕 **punish** 처벌하다
ensure 보장하다; 지키다, 보호하다 **deal with**
(문제 등을) 처리하다

11 대화를 듣고, 남자가 주말에 할 일로 가장 적절한 것을 고르시오.

① 속초에 간다.
② 늦잠을 잔다.
③ 공원에 간다.
④ 집안 청소를 한다.
⑤ 휴가 계획을 세운다.

M What are you going to <u>do over</u> <u>the</u> <u>weekend</u>, Sora?

W Oh, I really want to rest, <u>sleep</u> <u>late</u>, stay home, and read the Sunday paper. What are you going to do?

M My family and I are planning to <u>go</u> <u>on</u> <u>a</u> <u>picnic</u> to Bukhansan National Park. It may be hot in the city, but it's always cool there.

W That's a good idea. By the way, when are you going to <u>take</u> <u>your</u> vacation?

M Next month.

W That's August. It's still going to be warm then.

M That's right. So my family and I will have a great time in Sokcho.

W Oh, you are a <u>good</u> <u>planner</u>.

남 주말 동안 뭐 할 거니, 소라야?

여 어, 나는 정말로 쉬고, 늦잠 자고, 집에 있으면서, 일요 신문이나 읽고 싶어. 넌 뭐 할 건데?

남 나와 가족들은 북한산 국립 공원에 소풍을 갈 계획이야. 도시는 덥지만 그곳은 항상 서늘하거든.

여 그거 좋은 생각이다. 그런데, 휴가는 언제 갈 거니?

남 다음 달에.

여 8월이네. 그때도 여전히 덥겠구나.

남 맞아. 그래서 나와 가족들은 속초에서 아주 좋은 시간을 보낼 거야.

여 오, 너는 계획을 잘 세우는구나.

---

12 대화를 듣고, 대화 내용과 일치하지 <u>않는</u> 것을 고르시오.

① Laura는 두 사람과 함께 가기로 했다.
② 여자는 남자의 얼굴이 빨개졌다고 생각한다.
③ 남자는 Laura를 좋아한다.
④ Laura는 남자의 데이트 신청을 거절했다.
⑤ 남자는 여자의 격려에 고마워하고 있다.

M Hey, Rachel, is Laura going with us?

W Yes. Why?

M No reason. I'm just asking.

W Just asking? But why is your face <u>getting</u> <u>red</u>? Aha. Someone <u>has</u> <u>a</u> <u>crush</u> <u>on</u> Laura, doesn't he?

M Who has a crush?

W Come on, Sam. If you like her, you've got to tell her. Maybe she likes you.

M But I am afraid to <u>ask</u> <u>her</u> <u>out</u>.

W What are you so afraid of?

M I'd totally die if she <u>turned</u> <u>me</u> <u>down</u>.

W But that's better than <u>keeping</u> <u>everything</u> <u>to</u> <u>yourself</u>. You've got to let her know.

M I don't know... Well, maybe you're right. Thanks for <u>encouraging</u> me.

남 이봐, Rachel, Laura도 우리와 함께 가는 거니?

여 응. 왜?

남 아니야. 그냥 물어보는 거야.

여 그냥 물어보는 거라고? 그런데 왜 네 얼굴이 빨개지지? 아하. 누군가가 Laura에게 홀딱 반했구나, 그렇지 않니?

남 누가 홀딱 반해?

여 왜 이래, Sam. 네가 그녀를 좋아하면, 그녀에게 말해야 해. 아마 그녀는 너를 좋아할 거야.

남 하지만 나는 그녀에게 데이트 신청을 하기가 겁이 나.

여 뭐가 그렇게 두려운데?

남 그녀가 거절하면 난 정말 죽어버릴 거야.

여 하지만 모든 것을 마음 속에 담아두는 것보다는 그게 더 나아. 너는 그녀가 알게 해야 해.

남 난 모르겠어… 음, 어쩌면 네 말이 맞겠다. 격려해 줘서 고마워.

●●
have a crush on ~에게 홀딱 반하다 **ask out** ~에게 데이트를 신청하다 **turn down** ~을 거절하다 **keep to oneself** 마음 속에 담아두다

13 대화를 듣고, 남자의 마지막 말에 이어질 여자의 말로 가장 적절한 것을 고르시오.

① Thank you very much.
② Come this way, please.
③ I feel so lucky to meet you.
④ What do you want me to do?
⑤ I'm sure they won't have a problem.

M Excuse me, ma'am. I would like to go to the Sejong Center. How can I get there from here?

W I think the place is on line 5. Now we are on line 3. You need to transfer to line 5.

M At which station do I need to change?

W You have to get off at the next station. You should take the subway on line 5 headed for Bangwha.

M I really appreciate your help.

W Why don't you get off here with me? I'm getting off, too.

M Oh, really? I'm glad that we're heading in the same direction.

W Come this way, please.

남 실례합니다, 아주머니. 세종회관으로 가려고 하는데요. 여기에서 그곳까지 어떻게 가나요?

여 제 생각에 그곳은 5호선에 있는데요. 우리는 지금 3호선에 있고요. 5호선으로 갈아타셔야 해요.

남 어느 역에서 갈아타야 하나요?

여 다음 역에서 내리셔야 해요. 당신은 방화행 5호선 지하철을 타야 해요.

남 도와주셔서 정말 감사합니다.

여 여기서 저랑 같이 내리시죠. 저도 내리거든요.

남 오, 정말요? 저희가 같은 방향으로 간다니 다행이네요.

여 이쪽으로 오세요.

●●
transfer to ~로 갈아타다

---

14 대화를 듣고, 여자의 마지막 말에 이어질 남자의 말로 가장 적절한 것을 고르시오.

① She just seems to have a gift.
② She'll be by your side until the end.
③ I know these must be difficult times for you.
④ I don't know. I think I have an upset stomach.
⑤ I think she feels sorry about what she said to you.

W Did you go to Linda's housewarming party?

M Yes, the house is fabulous, and the food was so good. She cooked everything by herself.

W I'm so envious of Linda. She has a talent for cooking.

M I know. Everything she makes tastes perfect.

W I tried some of her recipes myself, but they just didn't seem to turn out right.

M You're not the only one. My sister tried to make her chocolate cake the other day. It tasted all right but was not half as good as Linda's.

W I wonder how she does it.

M She just seems to have a gift.

여 Linda의 집들이에 갔었니?

남 응, 집이 굉장하고 음식도 상당히 좋았어. 그녀는 모든 음식을 혼자 다 했어.

여 Linda가 참 부럽다. 그녀는 요리에 재능이 있어.

남 나도 알아. 그녀가 만드는 건 모두 맛이 훌륭해.

여 내가 그녀의 요리법 몇 개를 혼자 해 봤는데 잘 안 되는 것 같더라고.

남 너뿐만이 아니야. 내 누이도 며칠 전에 그녀의 초콜릿 케이크를 만들려고 노력했어. 맛은 괜찮았는데 Linda 것의 반밖에 되지 않았어.

여 그녀가 어떻게 그렇게 만드는지 궁금해.

남 그녀는 정말 재능이 있는 것 같아.

●●
housewarming party 집들이 **fabulous** 멋진, 굉장한 **envious** 부러운 **talent** 재능 **the other day** 며칠 전에

15 대화를 듣고, 여자의 마지막 말에 이어질 남자의 말로 가장 적절한 것을 고르시오.

① I wouldn't go in there right now.
② Why are you worried about going there?
③ Okay. I'm looking forward to meeting him.
④ Of course. There's nothing you can do about it.
⑤ Yes. You'd better do it now, or you'll be sorry later.

M I heard that you are planning to <u>visit</u> <u>the</u> <u>aquarium</u> this weekend.
W No, that <u>has</u> <u>been</u> <u>canceled</u>.
M Why?
W My brother and his family will be coming to town this weekend.
M Is he the one who <u>writes</u> <u>articles</u> for The *New York Times*?
W Right. Why don't you come over this Saturday and meet him?
M I'd love to, but I can't. Can I <u>take</u> <u>a</u> <u>rain</u> <u>check</u>?
W Sure. They'll be here for a week. So just <u>let</u> <u>me</u> <u>know</u> <u>when</u> you can come.
M <u>Okay. I'm looking forward to meeting him.</u>

남 난 네가 이번 주말에 수족관을 방문할 계획이 있다고 들었는데.
여 아냐, 그건 취소됐어.
남 왜?
여 오빠와 오빠네 식구들이 이번 주말에 우리 동네에 올 거야.
남 그는 *New York Times*에서 기사를 쓰는 분이지?
여 맞아. 이번 주 토요일에 와서 그를 만나보지 그러니?
남 그러고 싶지만 안돼. 다음을 기약해도 될까?
여 물론이지. 그들은 일주일 동안 여기에 있을 거야. 그러니 네가 언제 올 수 있는지 알려 주기만 해.
남 <u>좋아. 그분을 만나는 것이 기대된다.</u>

••

take a rain check 다음을 기약하다

◗ REVIEW TEST p. 71

A
① seed, 씨앗, 종자 ② vest, 조끼 ③ talent, 재능 ④ envious, 부러운 ⑤ method, 방법
⑥ punish, 처벌하다 ⑦ cancel, 취소하다 ⑧ quality, 품질 ⑨ m(o)ustache, 콧수염 ⑩ in fact, 사실은
⑪ turn down, ~을 거절하다 ⑫ the other day, 며칠 전에

B
① transfer to ② fill out ③ enroll in
④ track, status ⑤ complex tasks ⑥ deal with
⑦ has a crush on ⑧ are not permitted to

| 01 ④ | 02 ① | 03 ③ | 04 ② | 05 ④ | 06 ② | 07 ② | 08 ⑤ |
| 09 ③ | 10 ① | 11 ④ | 12 ③ | 13 ⑤ | 14 ③ | 15 ② |

문제 및 정답	받아쓰기 및 녹음내용	해석

01

다음을 듣고, 그림의 상황에 알맞은 대화를 고르시오.

① ② ③ ④ ⑤

① M How's this?

　W No good. You need to kick it harder if you want to <u>score a goal</u>.

② M How does this feel?

　W The drill feels okay.

③ M I can't wear these; they're too small.

　W Sorry, but we're <u>all out of</u> the larger sizes.

④ M Can't you give me some more time?

　W No, the report <u>must be finished</u> by tomorrow.

⑤ M I'm afraid you <u>have a cavity</u>.

　W Oh, no! Are you sure?

① 남 이건 어때요?

　여 별로네요. 골을 넣고 싶다면 그것을 더 세게 차야 해요.

② 남 이건 느낌이 어때요?

　여 이 드릴은 느낌이 괜찮네요.

③ 남 전 이것들을 입을 수가 없어요. 너무 작거든요.

　여 죄송합니다만, 더 큰 사이즈는 다 팔렸어요.

④ 남 제게 좀 더 시간을 주실 수는 없나요?

　여 안돼요, 보고서는 내일까지 꼭 끝내야 합니다.

⑤ 남 유감스럽게도 당신은 충치가 있으시네요.

　여 오, 이런! 확실한가요?

●●
score a goal 골을 넣다, 득점하다　**be out of** ~이 소진되다[바닥나다]　**cavity** 충치

02

대화를 듣고, 두 사람이 대화하는 장소로 가장 적절한 곳을 고르시오.

① 식당　　② 서점
③ 공항　　④ 은행
⑤ 버스 터미널

W Welcome. <u>How many</u> of you are there?

M Two. Can we sit by a window?

W I'll see what we have available.

M Thank you. If there are no window seats, maybe something in a <u>private corner</u> will do.

W Sir, all of the window seats are taken. Actually, we only have one table available right now.

M Where is it <u>located</u>?

W I'm afraid it's near the kitchen. It's not exactly the best seat in the house.

M I see. <u>How long</u> do you think it will be until another table <u>becomes available</u>?

W Another table will be ready in <u>20 minutes</u>.

M That sounds great. Then we'll wait for that table.

여 안녕하세요. 몇 명이십니까?

남 두 명이요. 창가에 앉을 수 있을까요?

여 빈 자리가 있는지 확인해 보겠습니다.

남 감사합니다. 창가 자리가 없다면, 조용한 구석 자리도 괜찮습니다.

여 손님, 창가 자리가 꽉 찼습니다. 사실, 지금은 한 테이블밖에 남은 곳이 없습니다.

남 그 자리는 어디에 있습니까?

여 죄송하지만 주방 근처입니다. 엄밀하게 말하면 저희 식당에서 가장 좋은 자리는 아닙니다.

남 알겠습니다. 다른 테이블에 앉으려면 얼마나 걸릴 것 같은가요?

여 다른 테이블은 20분 후에나 준비될 겁니다.

남 그거 좋네요. 그럼 그 테이블을 기다리지요.

●●
available 이용할 수 있는　**private** 조용히 있을 수 있는　**actually** 사실은, 실제로　**located** ~에 위치한　**exactly** 엄밀하게는, 정확하게

03 대화를 듣고, 남자의 직업으로 가장 적절한 것을 고르시오.

① 기자
② 의사
③ 변호사
④ 구급대원
⑤ 식당 지배인

W Thanks for seeing me today. I slipped and fell in the grocery store. I might need to talk to a lawyer.

M Thanks for coming in. Can you tell me what happened?

W Well, I was walking down the aisle in the store. I suddenly slipped and fell and landed on my back.

M That sounds terrible. Did the store do anything after that?

W The store manager just called an ambulance for me. I want to know if I can sue the grocery store for what happened to me.

여 오늘 저를 만나 주셔서 감사합니다. 제가 식료품점에서 미끄러져 넘어졌어요. 변호사와 얘기해 볼 필요가 있을 것 같아서요.

남 방문해 주셔서 감사합니다. 무슨 일이 있었는지 말씀해 주시겠어요?

여 음, 저는 가게 통로를 걷고 있었어요. 갑자기 미끄러져서 넘어져 제 등이 땅에 부딪쳤어요.

남 끔찍했겠군요. 가게에서는 그 이후에 어떤 조치라도 취했나요?

여 가게 매니저가 구급차를 불러 주기만 했을 뿐이에요. 제게 일어난 일에 대해 그 식료품점을 고소할 수 있는지 알고 싶어요.

•• land (땅에) 부딪치다, 떨어지다 sue 고소하다

---

04 대화를 듣고, 두 사람의 관계로 가장 적절한 것을 고르시오.

① 교수 – 학생
② 면접관 – 지원자
③ 회사 상사 – 직원
④ 수리 기사 – 고객
⑤ 관광 가이드 – 여행객

M Have a seat, please, Ms. Kim.

W Thank you very much.

M So you're looking for a job at our company. Are you interested in working full time or part time?

W I would like to work full time.

M And what university do you go to?

W The University of New York.

M Oh, yes. I see that on your application. When will you graduate?

W Next January. I only have one semester left.

M Do you have any interests or special skills?

W Well, I can use design software, and I know how to speak Japanese.

남 앉으세요, Ms. Kim.

여 대단히 감사합니다.

남 그래서 저희 회사에서 할 일을 찾고 계신다는 거죠. 정규직과 아르바이트 중에서 어느 것에 관심이 있으신가요?

여 정규직으로 일하고 싶습니다.

남 그리고 어느 대학에 다니시나요?

여 뉴욕대학교입니다.

남 오, 그래요. 지원서에 써 있군요. 언제 졸업하죠?

여 내년 1월에요. 한 학기만 남았습니다.

남 관심사나 특별한 기술이 있나요?

여 음, 디자인 소프트웨어를 사용할 줄 알고, 일본어를 할 줄 알아요.

•• full time 전일제의 semester 학기

05 대화를 듣고, 여자가 전화를 건 목적으로 가장 적절한 것을 고르시오.

① 길을 물어보려고
② 파티에 초대하려고
③ 음식을 주문하려고
④ 만남을 제안하려고
⑤ 일자리에 지원하려고

M Hello? This is Ken.

W Hello, Ken. This is Nancy.

M Hi, Nancy. <u>What</u> are you <u>calling</u> <u>about</u>?

W Listen. I was wondering… If you <u>don't</u> <u>have</u> <u>any</u> <u>plans</u> on Saturday night, would you like to go out with me? We could have dinner or go to the movies.

M Oh, Saturday… It's my mother's birthday, so the whole family is <u>getting</u> <u>together</u> on Saturday.

W Oh, I see.

M But I'm free on Friday night.

W Great. <u>Let's</u> <u>make</u> <u>it</u> Friday then.

M Okay. What time?

W Can I <u>pick</u> <u>you</u> <u>up</u> around 6 o'clock?

M Okay. That sounds good to me.

남 여보세요. 저는 Ken입니다.

여 안녕, Ken. 나 Nancy야.

남 안녕, Nancy. 무엇 때문에 전화했니?

여 들어 봐. 궁금한 게 있는데… 토요일 밤에 별다른 계획이 없다면, 나랑 밖에 나갈까? 저녁을 먹거나 영화를 보러 갈 수도 있어.

남 아, 토요일… 그날은 우리 어머니 생신이라서, 온 가족이 토요일에 모이기로 했어.

여 이런, 알았어.

남 그렇지만, 금요일 밤에는 한가해.

여 좋았어. 그럼 금요일에 만나자.

남 좋아. 몇 시에?

여 6시쯤 널 데리러 가도 될까?

남 그래. 나야 좋지.

---

06 대화를 듣고, 그림에서 Bobby가 누구인지 고르시오.

W Where's Bobby? I can't find him anywhere.

M He's down there <u>playing</u> <u>soccer</u> with the others.

W I still can't see him.

M He's right <u>next</u> to the <u>goalpost</u>, and he's <u>running</u> <u>toward</u> the <u>ball</u>.

W Oh, that one?

M Yes. I can only see the back of his head, but it looks like him.

W I'm surprised he's <u>not</u> <u>wearing</u> his <u>cap</u> as usual.

M Me, too.

여 Bobby는 어디에 있어? 어디에서도 그를 찾을 수가 없어.

남 저기 아래에서 다른 사람들과 축구를 하고 있어.

여 여전히 안 보이는걸.

남 그는 골대 바로 옆에 있고, 공을 향해 달리고 있잖아.

여 아, 저기 있는 사람?

남 응. 그 애의 뒤통수만 보이지만, 그 애인 것처럼 보여.

여 그가 평상시와는 달리 모자를 쓰고 있지 않아서 놀랍네.

남 나도 그래.

● ●

goalpost 골대 **as usual** 평상시처럼

07 다음을 듣고, 누가 누구에게 쓴 편지인지 고르시오.

① 아들이 엄마에게
② 남편이 아내에게
③ 남자가 여자 친구에게
④ 남자가 회사 동료에게
⑤ 남자가 자신의 팬들에게

There are many things that are difficult for me to understand sometimes. One of them is when I happen to <u>look</u> <u>at</u> <u>the ring</u> on my left hand. Images and feelings <u>rush</u> <u>over</u> <u>me</u>. Then comes the still unbelievable realization: <u>we</u> <u>are</u> married. If I close my eyes, I can see your smile. I still find it hard to believe that <u>you</u> <u>are</u> <u>with</u> <u>me</u>. I feel so fortunate. I believe no one could love me <u>the</u> <u>way</u> <u>you</u> <u>do</u>.

가끔 내가 이해하기 어려운 것들이 많이 있습니다. 그 중의 하나는 내가 내 왼손에 있는 반지를 우연히 쳐다볼 때입니다. 이미지와 감정들이 나에게 몰려듭니다. 그러고 나서 여전히 믿기 어려운 깨달음이 옵니다. 우리가 결혼했다는 것 말입니다. 눈을 감으면 나는 당신의 미소를 볼 수 있습니다. 나는 여전히 당신이 나와 함께 있다는 것을 믿기 어렵다고 생각합니다. 나는 너무 운이 좋다고 느낍니다. 아무도 당신처럼 나를 사랑할 수는 없을 거라고 믿습니다.

● ●

happen to 우연히 ~하다 **rush** (갑자기) 몰려들다, 돌진하다 **unbelievable** 믿기 어려운 **realization** 깨달음, 인식 **fortunate** 운 좋은

08 대화를 듣고, 남자의 태도로 가장 적절한 것을 고르시오.

① 친절하다 ② 이기적이다
③ 부주의하다 ④ 고집스럽다
⑤ 무관심하다

W So what do you want to do today?

M I <u>don't</u> <u>really</u> <u>care</u>. Do you have any ideas?

W We could go to the music concert. Do you like <u>classical</u> <u>music</u>?

M It's okay.

W Or how about a roller coaster ride? <u>Wouldn't</u> that <u>be</u> <u>exciting</u>?

M Sure. That sounds fine. It <u>doesn't</u> <u>matter</u> to me what we do.

W You must <u>have</u> <u>a</u> <u>preference</u>. Don't you like one idea over the other?

M Not at all. To be honest with you, I'm <u>not</u> <u>interested</u> <u>in</u> <u>anything</u> now.

여 그래서 오늘 뭘 하고 싶니?

남 난 정말 아무거나 괜찮아. 뭐 생각한 거라도 있어?

여 음악회에 가도 되고. 클래식 음악 좋아하니?

남 괜찮지.

여 아니면 롤러코스터 타는 건 어때? 재미있지 않을까?

남 물론. 좋은 것 같아. 우리가 뭘 하든 난 상관없어.

여 네가 더 좋아하는 것이 있을 텐데. 이것보다는 저것이 낫겠다 하는 것 없니?

남 전혀. 네게 솔직히 말하자면, 지금으로서는 어떤 것에도 흥미가 가질 않아.

● ●

preference 더 좋아하는 것, 선호

09

대화를 듣고, 여자가 비행기를 타려고 하는 날짜를 고르시오.

① April 10 ② May 10
③ June 22 ④ June 28
⑤ July 22

M Hi, Susan. Did you <u>book</u> a ticket to come here?

W Yes, I did. I just called a travel agency to <u>change</u> my <u>flight</u> from June 28 to <u>June 22</u>.

M I can't wait to see you again. Was there a seat available?

W No, I am <u>on</u> <u>the</u> <u>waiting</u> <u>list</u>.

M What if you can't get a ticket? It must be a <u>busy</u> <u>time</u> <u>of</u> <u>year</u>. Do you still have the June 28 ticket confirmed?

W No, that wasn't a confirmed seat. Besides, you told me to arrive there <u>as</u> <u>early</u> <u>as</u> <u>possible</u>.

M I know, but I thought the ticket you booked earlier <u>was</u> <u>confirmed</u>.

W No, it wasn't. But don't worry too much. It's only May 10 now. I still have a lot of time. There will be a seat for me.

M I hope so.

남 안녕, Susan. 여기 오는 표를 예매했니?

여 응, 했어. 방금 항공편 날짜를 6월 28일에서 6월 22일로 변경하기 위해 여행사에 전화했었어.

남 빨리 너를 다시 만나고 싶다. 자리가 있었어?

여 아니, 나 대기자 명단에 있어.

남 표를 못 구하면 어떻게 하지? 성수기일 텐데. 6월 28일 표는 아직 유효한 거야?

여 아니, 그건 확정된 좌석이 아니었어. 게다가, 네가 나더러 최대한 빨리 그곳에 오라고 말했잖아.

남 알아, 그렇지만 네가 전에 예매한 표는 확정된 것으로 생각했는데.

여 아냐. 그렇지만 너무 걱정하지는 마. 이제 겨우 5월 10일이잖아. 아직 시간이 많아. 내 자리 하나쯤은 날 거야.

남 그랬으면 좋겠다.

●●
confirmed 확정된, 확인된

10

대화를 듣고, 두 사람이 차를 세운 이유로 가장 적절한 것을 고르시오.

① 타이어에 문제가 생겼기 때문에
② 사고 현장을 신고해야 했기 때문에
③ 아버지에게 전화를 드려야 했기 때문에
④ 차가 고장이 나서 견인을 해야 했기 때문에
⑤ 이모네 집으로 가는 길을 잃어버렸기 때문에

M I think we have to <u>pull</u> <u>over</u>. There's a problem with the tire.

W I guess we'll be late for my aunt's dinner.

M We have no choice. I'd better <u>call</u> <u>a</u> <u>mechanic</u>.

W Look. All we have to do is <u>change</u> <u>the</u> <u>tire</u>.

M Do you know how to do that?

W Oh, yes. I've done it <u>several</u> <u>times</u>. Dad taught me how to do it.

M Go ahead. Here's the tire iron.

W There we go. Finished in five minutes.

M I have to say I'm <u>totally</u> <u>impressed</u>.

W It was really nothing. Let's go. We're late.

남 우리는 길 한쪽으로 차를 대야 할 것 같아. 타이어에 문제가 있어.

여 우리는 이모네 저녁 식사에 늦겠다.

남 어쩔 수 없지. 정비사를 부르는 것이 좋겠어.

여 봐. 우리가 해야 할 일은 타이어를 바꾸는 것뿐이잖아.

남 그걸 어떻게 하는지 아니?

여 어, 그럼. 그거 몇 번 해 봤어. 아빠가 하는 법을 가르쳐 주셨거든.

남 그럼 한번 해 봐. 여기 타이어용 지렛대.

여 다 됐다. 5분 안에 완료.

남 정말로 인상 깊다고 말해야겠어.

여 정말 별것 아니었어. 가자. 우리 늦었어.

●●
pull over 길 한쪽에 차를 대다 **mechanic** 정비사 **tire iron** 타이어를 떼어내는 지렛대

11 대화를 듣고, 무엇에 관한 내용인지 가장 적절한 것을 고르시오.

① 꿈　　　② 취미
③ 날씨　　④ 낚시
⑤ 물고기

M Have you ever gone fishing?
W I can't say that I have. What do you like about it?
M I stand by the water, and the silence is beautiful. It's just the fish and me. It's a wonderful sport.
W It's one of those things I've always wanted to try.
M You should try fishing sometime.
W Sure. I'll give it a try.
M How about this weekend? I hear the weather will be gorgeous.
W All right. Let's go fishing.

남 낚시하러 가 본 적 있어?
여 가 본 적 없어. 낚시하면 뭐가 좋은데?
남 물가에 서 있으면 그 침묵이 멋지지. 그냥 물고기와 나뿐이야. 정말 멋진 스포츠야.
여 내가 항상 해 보고 싶었던 것들 중의 하나야.
남 언젠가 너도 낚시 한번 해 봐.
여 물론이지. 한번 해 보려고.
남 이번 주말은 어때? 날씨가 아주 좋을 거라던데.
여 좋아. 낚시하러 가자.

●●
silence 침묵　**gorgeous** 아주 좋은[멋진]

---

12 대화를 듣고, 대화 내용과 일치하지 <u>않는</u> 것을 고르시오.

① 비행기 출발 시각이 날씨 때문에 미뤄졌다.
② 비행기는 오전 10시 30분에 출발할 예정이다.
③ 두 사람은 비행을 취소할 것이다.
④ 두 사람은 자판기 옆 좌석에서 휴식을 취할 것이다.
⑤ 여자는 간식을 사러 갈 것이다.

M When is the boarding time?
W They've just announced that our flight will be delayed for 4 hours due to poor weather conditions.
M What? Oh, no! That means it won't be leaving until 10:30 in the morning.
W I'm afraid so. What shall we do in the meantime?
M Let's find some seats so that we can stretch out and take a nap.
W Sounds like a good idea. We've had a busy day, and I'm pretty tired.
M Me, too. Look. There are some seats next to the vending machine. Let's go before somebody else gets to them.
W Save a seat for me, and I will buy some snacks.

남 탑승 시간이 언제니?
여 방금 우리 비행기가 나쁜 기상 조건 때문에 4시간 동안이나 연착될 거라는 방송이 나왔어.
남 뭐라고? 오, 안돼! 그 말은 오전 10시 30분까지 안 떠날 거라는 말이잖아.
여 유감이지만 그런 것 같아. 우리 그동안에 뭘 할까?
남 몸도 풀고 잠깐 잘 수 있도록 자리를 좀 찾아 보자.
여 좋은 생각이야. 우리는 바쁜 하루를 보냈고 난 정말 지쳤어.
남 나도. 봐. 저기 자판기 옆에 자리가 좀 있어. 다른 사람이 앉기 전에 가자.
여 내 자리를 맡아 줘, 그럼 내가 간식을 좀 사 올게.

●●
boarding time 탑승 시간　**announce** 방송으로 알리다, 발표하다　**delay** 지연시키다　**in the meantime** 그동안에　**vending machine** 자판기

13

대화를 듣고, 여자의 마지막 말에 이어질 남자의 말로 가장 적절한 것을 고르시오.

① It usually doesn't take long.
② I just sold it two months ago.
③ Let me arrange for you to meet him.
④ Do you want to buy another camera?
⑤ If it didn't work, you'd better call a technician.

W Why has the photocopier stopped?
M Oh, it probably stopped because the paper has jammed.
W What should I do? I have to photocopy these two documents.
M You'll have to open the door and look inside the machine to check.
W Oh, yes. I can see where a sheet of paper has gotten stuck.
M You need to follow the instructions printed inside the door to remove it and then restart the machine.
W I will try as you said.
M Did you do it?
W I did, but I can't take out the jammed paper at all.
M If it didn't work, you'd better call a technician.

여 왜 복사기가 멈췄지?
남 오, 아마도 종이가 걸려서 멈췄을 거야.
여 어떻게 해야 하지? 난 이 두 가지 서류를 복사해야 하는데.
남 덮개를 열고 기계 내부를 보고 점검해야 할 거야.
여 오, 알았어. 어디에 종이가 걸려 있는지 보이네.
남 그걸 제거해서 기계를 재작동시키려면 덮개 안쪽에 적혀 있는 지시 사항을 따라야 해.
여 네가 말한 대로 해 볼게.
남 해 봤어?
여 해 봤는데, 걸린 종이를 전혀 빼낼 수가 없네.
남 작동이 안 되면 수리 기사님께 전화를 하는 편이 나아.

●●
photocopier 복사기 jam (기계에) 걸리다, 끼이다 document 서류, 문서 instruction 지시, 설명 remove 제거하다

14

대화를 듣고, 남자의 마지막 말에 이어질 여자의 말로 가장 적절한 것을 고르시오.

① I wish I had one.
② You look better than I thought you would.
③ Oh, how thoughtful of you. You're the best.
④ We can pick up some flowers on the way over there.
⑤ I talked to the doctor, and she said everything was going to be okay.

M How's your leg?
W Much better, but I'm so tired of being stuck in the house all day.
M Well, you can't expect to be up and around so soon after breaking your leg.
W I suppose not, but it is very frustrating.
M When are you going to get the cast off?
W Next week. I can't wait to get it off.
M I know. I've brought something to cheer you up.
W What is it? I can't wait to see it.
M It's a bottle of the very latest French perfume.
W Oh, how thoughtful of you. You're the best.

남 네 다리는 어때?
여 훨씬 나아졌지만, 하루 종일 집안에 틀어박혀 있는 것에 너무 싫증이 나.
남 음, 다리가 부러진 후에 그렇게 빨리 걸어 다닐 수 있게 되리라고는 기대할 수 없어.
여 그럴 수 있다고 생각하지는 않지만 정말 절망적이야.
남 넌 언제 깁스를 풀게 되니?
여 다음 주에. 난 빨리 깁스를 풀고 싶어.
남 알아. 내가 네 기분을 좋게 해 주려고 뭘 좀 가지고 왔어.
여 뭔데? 빨리 보고 싶은걸.
남 이건 가장 최근에 나온 프랑스 향수야.
여 오, 넌 참 사려 깊구나. 네가 최고야.

●●
be stuck in ~에 갇혀 있다 be up and around (회복해서) 걸어 다닐 수 있게 되다 frustrating 좌절감을 주는 cast 깁스

15 다음 상황 설명을 듣고, 박 선생님이 George와 Julia에게 할 말로 가장 적절한 것을 고르시오.

① You don't have much choice.
② You have to focus on class.
③ You are invited to the party tonight.
④ You'd better study early in the morning.
⑤ You should write the answers on the blackboard.

This is the English classroom. The students are studying English and paying attention to Mrs. Park, the English teacher. She is now teaching the present continuous tense and is writing on the blackboard. Everyone except George and Julia is listening carefully and answering her. George is reading a detective story. Julia is looking out of the window and seems to be thinking about the party tonight. Mrs. Park wants them to concentrate on the class. In this situation, what would Mrs. Park most likely say to them?

Mrs. Park: You have to focus on class.

이곳은 영어 교실입니다. 학생들은 영어를 공부하고 있고 영어 선생님인 박 선생님에게 주의를 기울이고 있습니다. 선생님은 지금 현재진행형을 가르치는 중이고 칠판에 쓰고 있습니다. George와 Julia를 제외하고는 모두 주의 깊게 듣고 대답하고 있습니다. George는 탐정 소설을 읽고 있습니다. Julia는 창밖을 보고 있는데 오늘 밤 파티에 대해 생각하고 있는 것 같습니다. 박 선생님은 그들이 수업에 집중하기를 원합니다. 이 상황에서, 박 선생님은 그들에게 뭐라고 말하겠습니까?

박 선생님: 너희들은 수업에 집중해야 해.

●●
detective story 탐정 소설 **concentrate on** ~에 집중하다

▶ REVIEW TEST p. 79

A
① delay, 지연시키다 ② sue, 고소하다 ③ silence, 침묵 ④ fortunate, 운 좋은
⑤ mechanic, 정비사 ⑥ document, 서류, 문서 ⑦ available, 이용할 수 있는 ⑧ semester, 학기
⑨ announce, 방송으로 알리다, 발표하다 ⑩ unbelievable, 믿기 어려운 ⑪ preference, 더 좋아하는 것, 선호
⑫ concentrate on, ~에 집중하다

B
① Where, located ② boarding time ③ follow, instructions
④ pull over ⑤ vending machine ⑥ have a cavity
⑦ in the meantime ⑧ score a goal

문제 및 정답	받아쓰기 및 녹음내용	해석

01

다음을 듣고, 그림의 상황에 알맞은 대화를 고르시오.

① ② ③ ④ ⑤

① M How did you enjoy everything?

W It was just fine. Thanks. Can we have the bill, please?

② M There's a 10-year warranty on this.

W Really? I'll take it.

③ M Would you like to upgrade your seat?

W No, thanks.

④ M May I help you?

W Yes, I made a reservation under the name of Karen Jackson.

⑤ M I can't stand this place.

W Me neither. We should check out another place.

① 남 모든 게 즐거우셨나요?

여 괜찮았어요. 감사합니다. 계산서 좀 주시겠어요?

② 남 이것은 10년 동안 보증이 돼요.

여 정말요? 그걸로 하겠어요.

③ 남 좌석 등급을 높이시겠어요?

여 아뇨, 괜찮아요.

④ 남 도와드릴까요?

여 네, Karen Jackson이라는 이름으로 예약을 했는데요.

⑤ 남 이 장소를 참을 수가 없어.

여 나도 그래. 다른 장소를 확인해 봐야겠어.

● ●

bill 계산서 **warranty** (품질 등의) 보증, 보증서

02

대화를 듣고, 두 사람이 대화하는 장소로 가장 적절한 곳을 고르시오.

① 공원   ② 호텔
③ 집안   ④ 식당
⑤ 영화관

M You haven't been here before, have you?

W No, this is my first time. I'm getting excited.

M Well, this is the living room, and over there is the kitchen.

W What's upstairs? I would like to see it.

M Of course you would. I'll show you. Okay, here are the two bedrooms, and there's the bathroom.

W What a nice place you have! I envy you.

M Thanks. I decorated it myself.

남 너는 전에 여기 와 본 적 없지, 그렇지?

여 응, 이번이 처음이야. 기대된다.

남 음, 여기가 거실이고, 저쪽이 부엌이야.

여 위층에는 뭐가 있어? 위층을 보고 싶어.

남 물론 봐도 돼. 내가 보여 줄게. 좋아, 여기 침실이 두 개 있고, 저쪽에 화장실이 있어.

여 정말 멋진 집을 갖고 있구나! 네가 부러워.

남 고마워. 내가 직접 꾸몄어.

● ●

envy 부러워하다 **decorate** 꾸미다, 장식하다

03 대화를 듣고, 여자의 장래 희망으로 가장 적절한 것을 고르시오.

① 판사 　　② 경찰관
③ 수의사 　　④ 해양 생물학자
⑤ 동물원 사육사

M What do you want to be in the future?

W I am interested in rule, justice, and fairness. So I would like to help people at court.

M Wow, that's an interesting occupation. By the way, are there many women working in that field?

W Yes, there are a lot these days. How about you, Sean?

M I like science and love the ocean a lot. I've also studied whales, fish, and all the things in the sea. Thus, I want to be a marine biologist.

W You must go to the ocean a lot.

M That's right. It must be wonderful to work in the ocean.

W I hope you become a good scientist.

남 넌 미래에 무엇이 되고 싶니?

여 나는 규칙, 정의, 공정에 관심이 있어. 그래서 법정에서 사람들을 돕고 싶어.

남 와, 그거 흥미로운 직업이구나. 그런데, 그 분야에서 일하고 있는 여성들이 많니?

여 응, 요즘에는 많지. Sean, 너는 어때?

남 나는 과학을 좋아하고 바다를 너무나 사랑해. 나는 또한 고래와 물고기, 그리고 바다에 있는 모든 것들을 공부해 왔어. 그래서 나는 해양 생물학자가 되고 싶어.

여 너는 바다에 자주 가야겠네.

남 맞아. 바다에서 일하는 건 틀림없이 멋질 거야.

여 네가 좋은 과학자가 되길 바라.

● ●

justice 정의 　**fairness** 공정 　**court** 법정
occupation 직업 　**whale** 고래

---

04 대화를 듣고, 두 사람의 관계로 가장 적절한 것을 고르시오.

① 의사 - 환자
② 교수 - 학생
③ 약사 - 손님
④ 교사 - 학부모
⑤ 카페 주인 - 손님

M Hi. How are you?

W Fine. Thank you. Er, I'm here to tell you something.

M Okay. Would you like some coffee? There's a coffee vending machine over there.

W No, thanks. I already drank two cups of coffee.

M So what's up?

W Professor Fleming, I may be coming down with something.

M Do you have a cold?

W I think so. I have a terrible headache and need time to get some rest. Er, Professor, can I ask you for a big favor?

M I know what you have in mind. You haven't finished your paper yet, have you?

W No, I haven't. Could you give me a couple more days to finish it?

남 안녕하세요. 잘 지내죠?

여 잘 지냅니다. 고맙습니다. 저, 교수님께 드릴 말씀이 있어서 왔어요.

남 좋아요. 커피 좀 마실래요? 저쪽에 커피 자판기가 있거든요.

여 아뇨, 괜찮습니다. 저는 벌써 커피를 두 잔이나 마셨어요.

남 자, 무슨 일이죠?

여 Fleming 교수님, 제가 몸이 안 좋아서요.

남 감기에 걸렸나요?

여 그런 것 같아요. 두통이 아주 심해서 휴식을 취할 시간이 필요합니다. 어, 교수님, 어려운 부탁 좀 드려도 될까요?

남 뭘 생각하고 있는지 알아요. 아직 과제를 못 끝냈죠, 그렇죠?

여 네, 못 했어요. 과제를 끝낼 수 있도록 며칠만 더 시간을 주시겠어요?

● ●

come down with (병에) 걸리다

05 대화를 듣고, 남자가 전화를 건 목적으로 가장 적절한 것을 고르시오.

① 물품을 주문하려고
② 물품 주문을 취소하려고
③ 물품의 재고를 확인하려고
④ 물품의 배송일을 문의하려고
⑤ 물품의 배송 지연 사실을 알려 주려고

W Hello?
M Is this Mary Patrick?
W Yes, this is she.
M Hi, Ms. Patrick. This is G Shopping.
W Oh, hi. Has the <u>rice</u> <u>cooker</u> I ordered <u>come in</u>?
M That's why I'm calling. We've just received a message from the manufacturer. There <u>will</u> <u>be a</u> <u>delay</u> on your order. It's <u>out of stock</u>.
W Oh, no. I need it for a party I'm going to have this Friday.
M I'm afraid it will be <u>another</u> <u>week</u> before it's <u>available</u>.
W One week? That's not good.
M What would you like us to do? Do you want us to <u>cancel the</u> <u>order</u>?
W Well, I really want the rice cooker, so I'll wait for it.

여 여보세요?
남 Mary Patrick이신가요?
여 네, 전데요.
남 안녕하세요, Patrick 씨. G쇼핑입니다.
여 아, 안녕하세요. 제가 주문한 밥솥이 배달됐나요?
남 그것 때문에 전화 드렸는데요. 방금 제조사로부터 메시지를 받았습니다. 주문하신 물품이 늦어질 것 같습니다. 재고가 없습니다.
여 오, 이런. 이번 주 금요일에 열 파티에 그게 필요한데요.
남 죄송하지만 일주일이 더 지나야 배송이 가능해질 것 같습니다.
여 일주일이라고요? 큰일 났네요.
남 어떻게 해 드릴까요? 주문을 취소해 드릴까요?
여 흠, 전 그 밥솥이 꼭 필요하거든요. 그러니 기다리겠습니다.

●●
rice cooker 밥솥 **manufacturer** 제조자
out of stock 재고가 없는

---

06 대화를 듣고, 여자가 찾고 있는 지갑의 위치로 가장 적절한 곳을 고르시오.

W Jim, have you <u>seen</u> <u>my</u> <u>purse</u>? It's got to be somewhere in this room.
M I saw it next to the computer monitor this morning.
W No, it's not there. I just <u>looked</u> <u>over</u> <u>there</u>.
M <u>Have</u> <u>you</u> <u>checked</u> under the desk?
W Yes, I did, but it wasn't there <u>either</u>.
M Oh, sorry. I forgot. I moved it somewhere, but I <u>can't</u> <u>remember</u>.
W Try to think of where you put it. I have to go to work now.
M I got it! I put it <u>on top of the</u> <u>bookcase</u> so that the baby wouldn't get it.
W Oh, now I see it. Thanks.

여 Jim, 내 지갑을 봤나요? 이 방 어딘가에 있어야 하는데.
남 오늘 아침에 컴퓨터 모니터 옆에서 봤는데요.
여 아니, 거기에 없어요. 그곳을 방금 찾아봤어요.
남 책상 밑을 확인해 봤나요?
여 네, 확인해 봤지만, 그곳에도 없었어요.
남 오, 미안해요. 내가 깜빡했네요. 내가 어딘가로 옮겨 놓았는데, 기억이 안 나요.
여 어디에다 뒀는지 생각해 봐요. 난 지금 일하러 가야 해요.
남 생각났어요! 아기가 만지지 못하게 책장 위에 놓았어요.
여 오, 지금 그걸 봤어요. 고마워요.

●●
bookcase 책장

07 다음을 듣고, 남자의 상황으로 가장 적절한 것을 고르시오.

① 지금 서울에 있다.
② 미나에게서 이메일을 받았다.
③ 미나의 생일 파티에 참석할 것이다.
④ 수업 시간에 적극적인 편이다.
⑤ 토론토에서 오랫동안 공부하고 있다.

Hi, Mina! It's your friend, Jinsu. I'm in Toronto. I just <u>read</u> your email. Thanks. I am sorry I <u>won't</u> <u>be</u> <u>able</u> <u>to</u> make it to your birthday party. Things are fine here. I just had my first class on Monday. After my first class, I wished I could <u>actively</u> <u>participate</u> <u>in</u> the class. But I know I will <u>survive</u> <u>here</u> somehow, so don't worry about me too much. I hope you enjoy your birthday with our other friends. I already <u>miss</u> <u>spending</u> <u>time</u> with you guys in Seoul.

안녕, 미나야! 네 친구 진수야. 난 토론토에 있어. 나 방금 전에 네 이메일을 읽었어. 고마워. 네 생일 파티에 참석할 수 없어서 아쉽다. 여기서는 모든 게 괜찮아. 월요일에 첫 수업을 들었어. 첫 수업을 마치고 내가 수업 시간에 적극적으로 참여할 수 있기를 바랐어. 그렇지만 내가 여기서 어떻게든 살아남을 거라는 것을 난 알아, 그러니까 나에 대해 너무 많이 걱정하지는 마. 다른 친구들과 생일 잘 보내길 바라. 너희들이랑 서울에서 보낸 시간들이 벌써 그립다.

● ●
participate in ~에 참여하다 **survive** 살아남다, 생존하다

---

08 대화를 듣고, 여자의 심정으로 가장 적절한 것을 고르시오.

① bored   ② jealous
③ amazed   ④ pleased
⑤ concerned

W Where were you today, Martin?
M I just <u>hung</u> <u>out</u> at the shopping mall.
W Really? Someone told me <u>you</u> <u>were</u> <u>there</u> with another woman. Is that true?
M Well, yes and no.
W So it is true. I can't believe you were spending time <u>with</u> <u>another</u> <u>woman</u>.
M No, it's not like that. You see...
W What? You'd better have a <u>good</u> <u>excuse</u>.
M It was my <u>cousin</u> that <u>I</u> <u>was</u> <u>with</u>. She was in town for the day, so we had coffee.

여 오늘 어디에 있었니, Martin?
남 그냥 쇼핑몰에서 많은 시간을 보냈는데.
여 정말? 누가 나한테 네가 다른 여자랑 거기에 있었다고 말하는 거야. 사실이니?
남 음, 맞기도 하고 아니기도 하고.
여 그럼 사실이구나. 네가 다른 여자랑 시간을 보내고 있었다니 믿을 수가 없다.
남 아냐, 그런 거 아니야. 너도 알잖아…
여 뭐? 그럴싸한 변명거리가 있어야 할 거야.
남 나랑 같이 있었던 건 내 사촌이었어. 그 애가 오늘 동네에 와서 우리는 커피를 마셨어.

● ●
hang out 많은 시간을 보내다

09 대화를 듣고, 남자가 학교에 도착하는 시각을 고르시오.

① 7:15 a.m. ② 7:30 a.m.
③ 8:15 a.m. ④ 8:30 a.m.
⑤ 9:15 a.m.

W You are a very <u>diligent</u> student, aren't you, Billy? You always arrive at school early.

M That's right, Ms. Johnson.

W Well, <u>arriving an hour early</u> for your 9:15 class every day gives you <u>extra time to study</u>. You are a model student.

M Thanks, Ms. Johnson.

W Do your parents encourage you to study <u>as much as possible</u>?

M Yes, they're always telling me I can do <u>anything I want</u> as long as I study hard.

W They are right. If you study hard, you will <u>have more choices</u> in your life.

M Thanks for the encouragement.

여 넌 매우 성실한 학생이구나, 그렇지, Billy? 넌 항상 학교에 일찍 도착하잖니.

남 맞아요, Johnson 선생님.

여 음, 9시 15분 수업을 위해 매일 1시간씩 일찍 도착하면 더 공부할 시간이 있겠구나. 넌 모범생이야.

남 고맙습니다, Johnson 선생님.

여 너희 부모님께서는 네가 가능한 한 많이 공부하도록 격려해 주시니?

남 네, 부모님께서는 항상 제가 열심히 공부하기만 하면 원하는 것을 뭐든 할 수 있다고 말씀하세요.

여 그분들 말씀이 맞아. 네가 열심히 공부하면, 인생에서 더 많은 선택의 기회를 갖게 될 거야.

남 격려해 주셔서 감사합니다.

●●
diligent 성실한, 부지런한 **model student** 모범생

---

10 대화를 듣고, 두 사람이 Steve를 걱정하는 이유로 가장 적절한 것을 고르시오.

① 부모에게 반항해서
② 성적이 너무 저조해서
③ 선생님께 항상 야단을 맞아서
④ 친구들과 잘 어울리지 못해서
⑤ 남들 앞에서 말하는 것을 부끄러워 해서

W This is the second time Steve's teacher <u>has called</u> this year.

M What happened?

W The teacher said he didn't seem to <u>get along with</u> the other kids. I don't know what to do.

M You and I work all day long, and he always plays by himself after class. Maybe he <u>feels lonely</u>.

W I know, but what can we do for him? <u>Even though I try</u> to talk with him, he doesn't say very much.

M We need to do something about him. This weekend, I will take him to the mountain we <u>used to climb</u> together. He really liked that.

W That's a good idea. I will talk to my boss about <u>taking several days off</u> to stay with him at home next week.

여 Steve의 선생님이 전화하신 것이 올해 들어서 이번이 두 번째예요.

남 무슨 일이 있었나요?

여 선생님이 그러시는데 그 애가 다른 아이들이랑 잘 지내지 못하는 것 같다고 해요. 어떻게 해야 할지 모르겠어요.

남 당신이나 나나 하루 종일 일하니, 그 애가 방과 후에 항상 혼자 놀잖아요. 아마도 외로운가 봐요.

여 알아요, 그렇지만 그 애를 위해 우리가 뭘 해 줄 수 있을까요? 얘기를 하려고 해도 그 애가 말을 그리 많이 하지 않아요.

남 우리가 그 애에 대해 뭔가를 해야겠어요. 이번 주말에는 내가 그 애와 함께 오르던 산에 그 애를 데리고 갈게요. Steve가 정말 등산을 좋아했었거든요.

여 좋은 생각이에요. 전 다음 주에 그 애와 집에 같이 있을 수 있도록 며칠 휴가를 내겠다고 사장님한테 이야기해 볼게요.

●●
get along with ~와 잘 지내다 **by oneself** 혼자서 **take ~ off** ~ 동안 쉬다

11 대화를 듣고, 무엇에 관한 내용인지 가장 적절한 것을 고르시오.

① 택시 잡기의 어려움
② 도로 위 차량의 속도 위반
③ 자동차 경적의 지나친 사용
④ 차량 운전자들의 신경질적인 태도
⑤ 자동차 배기가스로 인한 대기 오염

M I think drivers honk too much in Seoul.

W You're telling me.

M In most of Europe's large cities, the use of the car horn is strictly restricted.

W Oh, really?

M Yes. Motorists who use their horns in situations other than emergencies get fined.

W Is that right? I think that's a very good policy.

M It sure is. Honking not only adds to street noise but also makes people nervous.

W That's right. I hope the Korean authorities do something about this excessive use of car horns.

M So do I.

남 서울의 운전자들은 경적을 너무 많이 울리는 것 같아요.

여 맞아요.

남 대부분의 유럽 대도시에서는 자동차 경적의 사용이 엄격히 제한되어 있답니다.

여 아, 그런가요?

남 네. 비상 사태 이외의 상황에서 경적을 사용하는 운전자들에게는 벌금을 물립니다.

여 그래요? 그건 아주 좋은 정책인 것 같네요.

남 그렇고 말고요. 경적을 울리면 거리의 소음이 증가할 뿐만 아니라 사람들을 불안하게 만들어요.

여 그렇지요. 자동차 경적을 이렇게 지나치게 사용하는 것에 대해서 한국 정부가 무슨 조치를 취했으면 좋겠어요.

남 동감이에요.

honk (자동차 경적을) 울리다 **strictly** 엄격하게 **restricted** 제한된 **motorist** 운전자 **emergency** 비상 사태 **fine** 벌금을 물리다 **authorities** 당국 **excessive** 지나친, 과도한

---

12 대화를 듣고, 대화 내용과 일치하지 않는 것을 고르시오.

① 교황의 장례식이 언론에 보도되었다.
② 남자는 로마에 가서 직접 교황의 장례식을 봤다.
③ 백만 이상의 사람들이 오늘 로마에 모였다.
④ 수많은 가톨릭 신자들이 교회 미사에 참석하고 있다.
⑤ 교황은 St. Peter의 묘실에 묻힐 것이다.

M The papers, TV, and radio are all full of news about the pope's funeral today.

W Did you see the funeral mass in Rome for Pope John Paul?

M Yes, I watched it all on TV. It was a very solemn occasion.

W I know. One report said that more than a million people are in Rome today to mourn the pope's death.

M And it's not just in Rome. All over the world, millions of Catholics are mourning the pope's death.

W Yes, many of them are attending church services for the pope.

M Where will the pope be buried?

W He will be buried in a crypt in St. Peter's. That's where many of his predecessors were buried before him.

남 오늘은 신문, TV, 그리고 라디오 모두 교황의 장례식에 대한 소식으로 가득해.

여 로마에 온 교황 요한 바오로의 장례식 군중들을 봤니?

남 응, TV에서 모두 봤어. 매우 엄숙한 광경이었어.

여 나도 알아. 한 보도에 따르면 백만 이상의 사람들이 교황의 죽음을 애도하기 위해 오늘 로마에 왔대.

남 그리고 로마에서만 그런 게 아니야. 전 세계의 수백만의 가톨릭 신자들이 교황의 죽음을 애도하고 있어.

여 맞아, 그들 중 다수가 교황을 위해 교회 미사에 참석하고 있지.

남 교황은 어디에 묻힐까?

여 그는 St. Peter의 묘실에 묻히게 될 거야. 거기는 그 이전에 그의 많은 전임자들이 묻혔던 곳이야.

pope 교황 **funeral** 장례식 **mass** 군중 **solemn** 엄숙한, 근엄한 **mourn** 애도하다 **service** 미사, 예배 **bury** 묻다, 매장하다 **crypt** 묘실 **predecessor** 전임자

13 대화를 듣고, 남자의 마지막 말에 이어질 여자의 말로 가장 적절한 것을 고르시오.

① Don't give away the ending!
② There's absolutely no smoking in the theater!
③ It's much better to watch it on the big screen.
④ Don't get the first row. My neck will hurt if I sit there.
✓⑤ The next movie I go to see will be a romantic comedy.

M How was the movie?
W It was a really <u>violent</u> <u>movie</u>.
M It certainly was. There seemed to be one killing about <u>every</u> <u>10 minutes</u>.
W I know. I began to <u>get sick of</u> it long before the end.
M Why are so many movies full of violence?
W I suppose the reason is that violent movies <u>make</u> <u>a lot of money</u>.
M You must be right.
W <u>The next movie I go to see will be a romantic comedy.</u>

남 영화는 어땠어?
여 매우 폭력적인 영화였어.
남 확실히 그랬어. 대략 10분마다 한 명 꼴로 죽는 것 같더라.
여 알아. 나는 끝나기 오래 전부터 기분이 안 좋아지기 시작했어.
남 왜 그렇게 많은 영화들이 폭력으로 가득하지?
여 내 생각에는 폭력적인 영화가 돈을 많이 벌어들이니까 그런 것 같은데.
남 네 말이 맞을 거야.
여 <u>내가 다음에 보러 가는 영화는 로맨틱 코미디 영화가 될 거야.</u>

●●
violent 폭력적인

---

14 대화를 듣고, 여자의 마지막 말에 이어질 남자의 말로 가장 적절한 것을 고르시오.

✓① I'm sure you'll get the job.
② I feel like the world is coming to an end.
③ I think there'll be a position opening up soon.
④ Thank you for applying, but you're not the right fit.
⑤ They said you weren't exactly the man they were looking for.

M You <u>look</u> <u>relieved</u>. What have you been doing?
W I just <u>had an interview</u> for a reporter's job.
M I didn't know you were moving to another company.
W I told you I had a problem with my boss. That's why I've <u>decided to quit</u>.
M Anyway, how did the interview go? Did they <u>go through</u> your résumé <u>in detail</u>?
W Yes, they did, especially since I'm working for their main competitor.
M What's your overall feeling about <u>how</u> it <u>went</u>?
W I think I made a good impression. But I'm <u>not sure</u> if I <u>can pass</u> the interview.
M <u>I'm sure you'll get the job.</u>

남 한숨 돌린 것 같네. 무얼 하고 있었니?
여 난 방금 리포터 자리에 면접을 봤어.
남 난 네가 다른 회사로 옮기려는 걸 몰랐어.
여 내가 상사와 문제가 있다고 말해 줬잖아. 그게 그만두기로 결심한 이유야.
남 어쨌든 면접은 어땠니? 그들이 네 이력서를 상세히 살펴보던?
여 응, 그러던데, 특히 내가 그들의 주 경쟁사에서 일하기 때문에 말야.
남 면접 진행에 대한 네 전체적인 느낌은 어때?
여 내가 좋은 인상을 준 것 같아. 하지만 내가 면접에 통과할 수 있을지 잘 모르겠어.
남 <u>난 네가 그 직장을 얻을 거라 믿어.</u>

●●
relieved 안도한 **go through** ~를 살펴보다
competitor 경쟁자 **overall** 전체적인
impression 인상, 감명

15 다음 상황 설명을 듣고, Bill이 부동산 중개인에게 할 말로 가장 적절한 것을 고르시오.

① I'm pretty sure it's going to work out.

② Do you want to take a look at the house?

③ I was lucky to buy the house very cheaply.

④ I'd like to see the one on Broadway Avenue.

⑤ Let's go back to my office and take care of the paperwork.

Bill is looking for a new apartment. He has to move to a new city in order to begin his studies at a university. He wants to live somewhere near the university or at least on a bus line. And he needs to move in by the first of next month. He is at a real estate agency in the new city. The agent is showing him photos of the apartments they have available and which fit his preferences. He just found the one he likes. In this situation, what would Bill most likely say to the agent?

Bill: I'd like to see the one on Broadway Avenue.

Bill은 새 아파트를 구하고 있다. 그는 대학에서 공부를 시작하기 위해 새 도시로 이사 가야 한다. 그는 대학 근처 어딘가에, 혹은 적어도 버스가 닿는 곳에 살기를 원한다. 그리고 그는 다음 달 초까지 이사해야 한다. 그는 새 도시의 부동산 중개소에 있다. 중개인은 그에게 그의 취향에 맞는 임대 가능한 아파트들의 사진을 보여 주고 있다. 그는 방금 마음에 드는 곳을 발견했다. 이런 상황에서 Bill이 중개인에게 뭐라고 말하겠는가?

Bill: Broadway Avenue에 있는 아파트를 보고 싶은데요.

●●
real estate agency 부동산 중개소

REVIEW TEST p. 87

A   ❶ bill, 계산서   ❷ envy, 부러워하다   ❸ bury, 묻다, 매장하다   ❹ diligent, 성실한, 부지런한

❺ motorist, 운전자   ❻ survive, 살아남다, 생존하다   ❼ funeral, 장례식   ❽ relieved, 안도한

❾ competitor, 경쟁자   ❿ emergency, 비상 사태   ⓫ excessive, 지나친, 과도한   ⓬ by oneself, 혼자서

B   ❶ violent movie   ❷ good impression   ❸ participated in

❹ justice, fairness   ❺ top, bookcase   ❻ out of stock

❼ real estate agency   ❽ get along with

| 01 ③ | 02 ⑤ | 03 ⑤ | 04 ④ | 05 ② | 06 ① | 07 ② | 08 ② |
| 09 ② | 10 ① | 11 ② | 12 ③ | 13 ① | 14 ③ | 15 ② | |

문제 및 정답	받아쓰기 및 녹음내용	해석

01

다음을 듣고, 그림의 상황에 알맞은 대화를 고르시오.

① ② ③ ④ ⑤

① W Is it okay now?

M Will you <u>move</u> <u>back</u> a little more, please?

② W I would like to take a picture.

M Why not? I <u>would</u> <u>love</u> <u>to</u>.

③ W I'm thirsty. Can I have something to drink?

M Sure. Here you go. Why don't we <u>take</u> <u>a</u> <u>break</u>?

④ W Can you <u>lower</u> <u>the</u> <u>price</u> a bit?

M I have to sell it according to what's on the <u>price</u> <u>tag</u>.

⑤ W How much is this drink?

M It's only two dollars.

① 여 이젠 괜찮습니까?

남 뒤로 약간만 더 물러나 주시겠어요?

② 여 사진을 찍고 싶어요.

남 안될 것 없지요. 저도 좋아요.

③ 여 목말라. 뭐 좀 마실 수 있을까?

남 그럼. 여기 있어. 우리 쉬는 게 어때?

④ 여 가격을 조금만 깎아 주실 수 있나요?

남 가격표에 나와 있는 가격에 따라 판매해야 합니다.

⑤ 여 이 음료수 얼마이지요?

남 단돈 2달러입니다.

• •

thirsty 목마른 lower 내리다. 낮추다
according to ~에 따라서 price tag 가격표

02

대화를 듣고, 두 사람이 대화하는 장소로 가장 적절한 곳을 고르시오.

① 공항 ② 식당
③ 호텔 ④ 슈퍼마켓
⑤ 극장 매표소

M Hi. Two tickets for *Love Me Tender*, please.

W I'm afraid we're <u>sold</u> <u>out</u> for the 7:30 show.

M Oh, no. I <u>should</u> <u>have</u> <u>come</u> earlier.

W We still have seats for the 9:35 show though.

M No, that's okay. What else is playing right now?

W Well, *Moon War* still <u>has</u> <u>seats</u> <u>available</u>.

M Give me two tickets to that then.

W Here you are, sir. That'll be 20 dollars.

남 안녕하세요. 'Love Me Tender' 표 두 장 주세요.

여 죄송합니다만 7시 30분 상영분은 매진됐어요.

남 오, 이런. 좀 더 일찍 올 걸 그랬네요.

여 그래도 9시 35분 상영분 좌석은 아직 있어요.

남 아뇨, 괜찮아요. 지금 다른 건 뭐가 상영 중이죠?

여 음, 'Moon War'는 아직 예매 가능한 좌석이 있어요.

남 그럼 그걸로 두 장 주세요.

여 여기 있습니다, 손님. 20달러입니다.

03 대화를 듣고, 여자의 직업으로 가장 적절한 것을 고르시오.

① 의사
② 변호사
③ 패션 디자이너
④ 부동산 중개인
⑤ 컴퓨터 프로그래머

M Hi, June. It's been a long time. How do you like your new office?

W Actually, I don't like it. So I've <u>decided</u> to look for <u>another place</u>.

M What's the matter with your office now?

W It's a little far from my home, and it's <u>too noisy</u> for me <u>to focus</u> on my work. I have to create a software program by this month.

M Oh, really? Then why don't you move near my place? The <u>neighbors</u> are <u>quiet</u>. And there is a big parking lot in the area.

W That sounds nice.

M Do you want to go and <u>find a place</u>?

W Sure. I hope I can find a good place.

남 안녕, June. 오랜만이야. 새로운 사무실은 어떠니?

여 사실, 마음에 들지 않아. 그래서 다른 곳을 찾기로 결심했어.

남 지금 사무실에 무슨 문제가 있는데?

여 우리 집에서 조금 멀고, 너무 시끄러워서 내 일에 집중할 수가 없어. 이번 달까지 소프트웨어 프로그램을 만들어야 하는데 말야.

남 오, 정말? 그럼 우리 집 근처로 이사 오면 어떨까? 이웃 사람들은 조용해. 그리고 그곳에는 대형 주차 공간이 있어.

여 좋은 것 같구나.

남 가서 찾아 볼래?

여 좋아. 적당한 곳을 찾을 수 있다면 좋겠다.

● ●
focus on ~에 집중하다 **neighbor** 이웃 사람

04 대화를 듣고, 두 사람의 관계로 가장 적절한 것을 고르시오.

① 판매원 - 고객
② 은행원 - 고객
③ 버스 기사 - 승객
④ 호텔 직원 - 투숙객
⑤ 식당 종업원 - 손님

M How may I help you?

W I'd like to make an international call, please.

M You can dial <u>directly</u> <u>from your room</u> if you like.

W I'm sorry. I don't understand what to do.

M Just pick up. Then dial 011, your <u>country</u> and <u>city</u> <u>codes</u>, and your number.

W Okay. Thanks for your help.

M You're welcome. Would you like us to <u>charge</u> <u>the</u> <u>call</u> to your room?

W Yes, please.

M All right. I'll take care of it for you.

W Thank you.

남 무엇을 도와드릴까요?

여 저는 국제 전화를 걸고 싶은데요.

남 고객님이 원하시면 방에서 직접 거실 수도 있어요.

여 죄송합니다. 어떻게 해야 할지 모르겠어요.

남 그냥 수화기를 드세요. 그러고 나서 011을 누르고, 국가 번호, 도시 번호, 그리고 전화번호를 누르세요.

여 알겠어요. 도와주셔서 감사합니다.

남 천만에요. 저희가 전화 요금을 숙박비로 청구할까요?

여 예, 부탁드려요.

남 좋아요. 처리해 드리겠습니다.

여 감사합니다.

● ●
international 국제의, 국제적인 **dial** 전화를 걸다 **charge** (요금·값을) 청구하다

05

대화를 듣고, 남자가 전화를 건 목적으로 가장 적절한 것을 고르시오.

① 택배를 배달하려고
② 인터뷰를 요청하려고
③ 신문 구독을 신청하려고
④ 과외 일자를 조정하려고
⑤ 에어컨 수리를 의뢰하려고

W Hello. This is Kristin speaking.

M Hello, Kristin Gray. My name is Bob White. I'm a reporter from the *Times*.

W I see. What are you calling about?

M I have read your post that your five-year-old boy can speak English fluently. Could I come and talk to you about how your son has learned English?

W Yes. It certainly would make an interesting story! Can you come this Friday at 2 p.m.?

M Sounds great. May I ask your address?

W Sure. It's 1580 Robinson Street, Apartment #1202.

M I got it. Thank you very much.

W You're welcome. I'll see you then.

여 여보세요, Kristin입니다.

남 안녕하세요, Kristin Gray 씨. 제 이름은 Bob White입니다 'Times'의 기자예요.

여 알겠습니다. 무엇 때문에 전화하셨나요?

남 댁의 5살짜리 아드님이 영어를 유창하게 할 수 있다는 게시글을 읽었습니다. 제가 가서 아드님이 어떻게 영어를 배웠는지에 대해 이야기를 나눌 수 있을까요?

여 예. 확실히 재미있는 기사가 되겠네요! 이번 주 금요일 오후 2시에 오실 수 있나요?

남 좋습니다. 주소를 여쭤 봐도 될까요?

여 그럼요. Robinson Street 1580번지 아파트 1202호입니다.

남 알겠습니다. 정말로 감사합니다.

여 천만에요. 그때 뵙도록 하겠습니다.

● ●

reporter 기자 **post** 게시글 **fluently** 유창하게

06

대화를 듣고, 남자가 이번 주말에 할 일로 가장 적절한 것을 고르시오.

① ②

③ ④

⑤

W Hi, James. Hey, are you okay? You don't look so good.

M Oh, hi, Laura. I'm okay. I just feel heavy and sluggish.

W You know... You'd feel better if you exercised. Why don't you try swimming? Or maybe we could play some tennis.

M No, I just want to get some sleep this weekend.

W Well, okay, if that's what you want. However, you should try to eat well and get some rest.

M Thank you for your advice.

W Sure. If you feel better in a couple of days, give me a call. We can play some tennis or go swimming.

M Okay. I'll do that.

여 안녕, James. 이봐, 너 괜찮니? 안색이 안 좋아 보여.

남 오, 안녕, Laura. 난 괜찮아. 그냥 몸이 무겁고 나른할 뿐이야.

여 너도 알잖아… 운동을 하면 기분이 더 나아질 거야. 수영을 해 보면 어때? 아니면 우리가 어쩌면 테니스를 칠 수도 있고.

남 아니, 이번 주말에는 그냥 잠을 좀 자고 싶어.

여 그래, 그게 네가 원하는 거라면 알겠어. 그런데 잘 먹고 쉬려고 노력해야 해.

남 조언해 줘서 고마워.

여 천만에. 이틀 후쯤 괜찮아지면 전화 줘. 우리는 테니스를 치거나 수영하러 갈 수 있어.

남 좋아. 그렇게 할게.

● ●

sluggish 나른한, 둔한

07 대화를 듣고, 여자의 고민으로 가장 적절한 것을 고르시오.

① 이웃에게 한 거짓말이 탄로 났다.
② 이웃과의 점심 식사를 원하지 않는다.
③ 친구 때문에 이웃에게 선의의 거짓말을 했다.
④ 친구에게 한 거짓말 때문에 죄책감을 느낀다.
⑤ 병원 진료 때문에 이웃과의 점심 식사를 못하게 되었다.

W Hey, Jacob. Can you <u>help</u> me <u>with a problem</u>?
M Sure. What is it?
W My neighbor <u>asked me if</u> we could eat lunch together today.
M So what's wrong with that?
W Well, I told her I would, but I <u>don't want to</u>.
M Just tell her a <u>white lie</u>. Tell her you have a doctor's appointment or something.
W But I would <u>feel guilty</u> about that.
M Look. A white lie is not a big deal.
W White or not, it is still lying. I'll have to <u>think</u> <u>of</u> <u>another way</u>.

여 안녕, Jacob. 내게 문제가 있는데 좀 도와 줄래?
남 물론이지. 뭔데?
여 내 이웃이 오늘 점심 식사를 같이 할 수 있는지 내게 물어보는 거야.
남 그래서 그게 뭐가 문제인데?
여 음, 그렇게 하겠다고는 말했는데, 별로 그렇게 하고 싶지 않아서.
남 그냥 그녀한테 선의의 거짓말을 해. 진료 예약이나 그런 것이 있다고 말해.
여 하지만 그렇게 하는 것에 대해 죄책감을 느낄 거야.
남 이봐. 선의의 거짓말은 큰 문제는 아니잖아.
여 선의든 아니든, 어쨌든 거짓말하는 거잖아. 다른 방법을 생각해 봐야 할 것 같아.

●●
guilty 죄책감을 느끼는 **big deal** 큰 문제, 대단한 것

---

08 Melissa의 가족에 관한 다음 내용을 듣고, 일치하는 것을 고르시오.

① 엄마는 하루 종일 청소를 하신다.
② 아빠가 매일 아침 아이들을 깨우신다.
③ 엄마는 요리사이다.
④ 아빠는 회사에서 늦게까지 일하신다.
⑤ 아이들이 집으로 돌아오면 엄마가 요리를 하고 계신다.

My name is Melissa. Every morning, my father <u>wakes</u> my brother and me <u>up</u> and makes breakfast. Then, my mother goes to work, and my father <u>stays home</u>. He cooks and cleans all day. He is an <u>amazing cook</u> and makes wonderful pizza and cakes. Whenever we <u>get home</u> <u>from school</u>, we can smell food cooking in the kitchen. I know a lot of families <u>where</u> the mother stays home and the father works. But our family is <u>special</u>, and I think it's <u>quite cool</u>.

제 이름은 Melissa입니다. 매일 아침 아빠는 제 남동생과 저를 깨워 주시고 아침 식사를 만드십니다. 그러고 나서, 엄마는 회사에 가시고 아빠는 집에 계십니다. 아빠는 하루 종일 요리하고 청소하십니다. 아빠는 요리를 굉장히 잘하시고 아주 맛있는 피자와 케이크를 만들어 주십니다. 우리가 학교에서 집에 돌아올 때마다 부엌에서 나는 요리 냄새를 맡을 수 있습니다. 저는 엄마가 집에 계시고 아빠가 일하시는 많은 가정을 알고 있습니다. 그러나 우리 가족은 특별하고, 저는 그것이 아주 멋지다고 생각합니다.

●●
stay 계속 있다, 머무르다 **amazing** 굉장한, 놀라운 **quite** 아주, 정말

09

대화를 듣고, 남자가 돈을 갚는 데 걸리는 기간을 고르시오.

① 1개월　　　✓② 3개월
③ 5개월　　　④ 7개월
⑤ 9개월

M Let's go to the computer store.

W What for?

M I've had my eye on a laptop computer there. It's on sale for only 900 dollars. The regular price is 1,200 dollars.

W Have you saved any money?

M So far I've saved 600 dollars, and my father lent me the rest of the money that I need.

W You borrowed money from your father? How will you pay it back?

M Well, I am making 200 dollars every month at my part-time job. If I am really thrifty, then I can pay him back 100 dollars every month.

W Are you confident about that?

M Oh, yeah. I will keep my promise to my father.

W Wow, you are a good son.

남 우리 컴퓨터 매장에 가자.

여 무슨 일로?

남 내가 거기에 있는 노트북 컴퓨터를 눈여겨봤거든. 할인 중이라서 900달러밖에 안 해. 정가는 1,200달러야.

여 돈이라도 모았니?

남 지금까지 600달러를 모았고, 아빠가 나머지 필요한 돈을 빌려주셨어.

여 아빠한테서 돈을 빌렸다고? 어떻게 갚으려고?

남 글쎄, 내가 아르바이트로 매달 200달러를 벌고 있거든. 내가 정말로 절약하면 매달 100달러는 갚을 수 있어.

여 자신 있니?

남 어, 그럼. 나는 아빠와의 약속은 지킬 거야.

여 와, 넌 훌륭한 아들이구나.

●●

have one's eye on ~을 눈여겨보다
regular price 정가　**so far** 지금까지
thrifty 절약하는　**confident** 자신이 있는

10

대화를 듣고, 여자의 기분이 좋지 않은 이유로 가장 적절한 것을 고르시오.

✓① 체중이 늘어서
② 독감에 걸려서
③ 엄마에게 야단을 맞아서
④ 주문한 요리가 맛이 없어서
⑤ 남자가 비꼬면서 이야기해서

M What's wrong, Kate?

W I hate weighing myself. I've gained weight.

M When I met you a month ago, you said you had lost weight.

W Well, I had had a bad cold for a month, so I lost almost three kilos.

M Losing three kilograms is quite a lot, don't you think?

W Yeah, but I soon gained it back.

M I can't tell. You still look good.

W Anyway, this is my mother's fault.

M What are you talking about?

W My mom cooks tasty food every evening. My mom's food is really good, so I have no choice but to eat a lot.

M Ha-ha. I think your mother would be offended if she heard what you said.

남 Kate, 무슨 일 있니?

여 몸무게 재는 거 너무 싫어. 몸무게가 늘었단 말이야.

남 한 달 전에 만났을 때 너는 살이 빠졌다고 말했잖아.

여 음, 한 달 동안 심한 감기에 걸려 있어서 거의 3kg이 빠진 거였어.

남 3kg 빠진 거면 꽤 많은 것 아니니?

여 응, 그런데 곧 다시 살이 쪘어.

남 난 잘 구별 못하겠는데. 여전히 좋아 보이거든.

여 어쨌든, 우리 엄마 때문이야.

남 무슨 소리야?

여 엄마가 매일 저녁마다 맛있는 요리를 해 주시거든. 엄마가 해 주신 음식은 너무 맛있어서 많이 먹을 수밖에 없다니까.

남 하하. 너희 어머니가 네 말을 들으면 억울해하시겠는걸.

●●

fault 책임, 잘못　**have no choice but to ~**
할 수밖에 없다　**offended** 기분이 상한

11 다음을 듣고, 무엇에 관한 안내 방송인지 고르시오.

① 분실물 　　②✓ 할인 판매
③ 인테리어 강좌 　④ 도로 통행 제한
⑤ 마트 연장 영업

Attention, Buymart shoppers! Let me direct your attention to the sale going on in aisle nine. This is your chance to save big on famous name brands. All fitted sheets are 20% off. Towels and bath mats are 30% off, and curtains are 50% off. Ralph Laurel, Pierre Cardini, Lori Ashley, and dozens of other top brands are available. Be sure to stop by aisle nine and check out these bargains before they're all gone!

주목해 주세요, Buymart 쇼핑객 여러분! 9번 통로에서 진행 중인 할인 판매에 주목해 주세요. 유명 브랜드의 제품을 크게 할인된 가격으로 구입할 수 있는 기회입니다. 모든 맞춤 시트들은 20% 할인입니다. 수건과 욕실용 매트들은 30% 할인이며, 커튼은 50% 할인입니다. Ralph Laurel, Pierre Cardini, Lori Ashley, 수십 개의 다른 유명 브랜드의 제품들도 있습니다. 제품들이 다 팔리기 전에 9번 통로에 꼭 들러서 이 특가품들을 확인해 보세요!

●●
direct (주의 등을) 돌리다, 향하게 하다　**aisle** 통로　**sheet** 시트, 얇은 천　**be sure to** 꼭 ~을 하다　**stop by** ~에 (잠깐) 들르다　**bargain** 특가품, 싼 물건

12 대화를 듣고, 대화 내용과 일치하지 <u>않는</u> 것을 고르시오.

① 남자는 유럽으로 여행을 갔었다.
② 남자는 런던에서 자신의 짐이 없어졌음을 알았다.
③✓ 누군가가 남자의 짐을 실수로 가져갔다.
④ 남자의 짐은 파리로 보내졌다.
⑤ 남자가 자신의 짐을 되찾는 데 이틀이 걸렸다.

W How was your trip?
M I had a terrible time on my trip to Europe.
W Why? What happened? Did you have an accident?
M No, my luggage got lost. When I arrived in London and went to collect my bag from the baggage carousel, it never arrived.
W Somebody must have taken it by mistake, right?
M No, it had been sent to Paris by mistake.
W Did you get it back?
M Yes, I did, but it took two whole days. I was so upset.
W I'm sorry to hear that.

여 여행은 어땠어?
남 유럽으로 여행하는 동안은 끔찍한 시간을 보냈어.
여 왜? 무슨 일 있었니? 사고라도 났었어?
남 아니, 짐을 잃어버렸거든. 런던에 도착해서 회전식 원형 컨베이어에서 짐을 찾기 위해 갔는데, 짐은 도착하지 않았어.
여 어떤 사람이 실수로 가져갔구나, 그렇지?
남 아냐, 그것은 실수로 파리로 보내졌어.
여 짐을 되찾았니?
남 응, 되찾긴 했는데, 꼬박 이틀이나 걸렸어. 난 정말 화가 났어.
여 정말 안됐구나.

●●
carousel 회전식 원형 컨베이어

13 대화를 듣고, 남자의 마지막 말에 이어질 여자의 말로 가장 적절한 것을 고르시오.

① You really ought to have a talk with him.
② You have to wash his clothes the next time.
③ You can express your appreciation to Paul.
④ You'd better put the dishes away right after a meal.
⑤ You should go to the supermarket to get some more towels.

W Do you get along with your new roommate?

M Well, to be honest with you, I need some advice about how to handle a problem with your brother, my new roommate.

W What's the problem?

M Paul is a good roommate overall, but he does some things that drive me crazy.

W Can you be more specific?

M Well, he's kind of lazy. He leaves his wet towels everywhere, and he never cleans off the kitchen counter after he uses it.

W That sounds like Paul.

M What do you mean?

W He really is a good guy, but he is not used to doing anything for himself.

M Hmm, then what should I do?

W You really ought to have a talk with him.

여 네 새로운 룸메이트와 잘 지내고 있니?

남 글쎄, 네게 솔직히 말하자면 나는 새 룸메이트인 네 남동생과의 문제를 어떻게 다루어야 할지에 관해서 조언이 좀 필요해.

여 문제가 뭐니?

남 Paul은 전반적으로는 좋은 룸메이트지만, 나를 못 견디게 만드는 행동을 해.

여 좀 더 구체적으로 말해 줄래?

남 음, 그는 게으른 편이야. 그는 젖은 수건을 아무데나 놓고, 부엌 조리대를 사용하고 난 다음에 결코 치우지 않아.

여 Paul답구나.

남 무슨 소리니?

여 그는 실제로는 착한 애지만, 혼자서 무언가를 하는 데는 익숙하지가 않아.

남 흠, 그럼 나는 어떻게 해야 하지?

여 넌 정말 그와 이야기해 봐야 해.

●●

advice 조언, 충고 **overall** 전반적으로 **drive** ∼하게 만들다 **specific** 구체적인 **for oneself** 혼자서

14 대화를 듣고, 여자의 마지막 말에 이어질 남자의 말로 가장 적절한 것을 고르시오.

① How do I know where I am?
② I don't want to think about it.
③ Umm, I see the Watson Discount Mall.
④ I would like to let you know where I am.
⑤ You should ask someone who can help you right now.

W Hello. This is the 911 operator.

M Help. Please help me!

W Yes, sir. Please calm down and explain exactly what is happening.

M Okay. My car broke down on the road. I have a lady passenger, and she's going into labor.

W Now take it easy, sir. Explain exactly where you are.

M I'm... I'm in the right lane of the Lincoln Expressway about 15 miles from City Hall, and this lady isn't going to wait.

W Okay, now what's the nearest landmark to your location?

M Umm, I see the Watson Discount Mall.

여 여보세요. 911 교환원입니다.

남 도와주세요. 제발 절 도와주세요!

여 예, 선생님. 진정하시고 정확하게 무슨 일인지 설명해 주세요.

남 알겠어요. 내 차가 도로에서 고장 났어요. 여자 승객을 태웠는데 그녀가 지금 아기를 낳으려고 해요.

여 자, 진정하세요, 선생님. 정확하게 어디에 계신지 설명해 주세요.

남 저는… 저는 시청에서 15마일 정도 떨어진 Lincoln 고속도로의 오른쪽 차선에 있고요, 이 여자분은 기다릴 시간이 없어요.

여 예, 그럼 선생님이 계신 곳에서 가장 가깝게 눈에 띄는 건물이 뭔가요?

남 음, Watson 할인점이 보여요.

●●

passenger 승객 **go into labor** 출산이 임박하다 **lane** 차선 **expressway** 고속도로 **landmark** 주요 지형지물

15 다음 상황 설명을 듣고, Addy가 아버지에게 할 말로 가장 적절한 것을 고르시오.

① I'd like to try it sometime.
② Did you have a good trip?
③ How was your trip to France?
④ I really appreciate your coming over.
⑤ I'm expecting you to have lots of gifts for me.

Addy's father went to the United States a month ago. He came back yesterday afternoon. Her whole family went to the international airport to meet him. Her younger brother spotted him first and said, "Daddy is over there." They all looked at him. He looked fine. He had a big suitcase in each of his hands. Addy thought he must have brought plenty of gifts for them. She wanted to ask him, but she didn't. Instead, she was about to ask him about how his trip was. In this situation, what would Addy most likely say to him?

Addy: Did you have a good trip?

Addy의 아버지는 한 달 전에 미국으로 갔다. 그는 어제 오후에 돌아왔다. 그녀의 가족 모두는 그를 맞으러 국제 공항에 갔다. 그녀의 남동생이 먼저 그를 발견하고 말했다. "아빠가 저기 오신다." 그들은 모두 그를 보았다. 그는 좋아 보였다. 그는 양손에 커다란 여행 가방을 가지고 있었다. Addy는 아빠가 가족들을 위한 선물을 많이 가져오셨음이 틀림없다고 생각했다. 그녀는 아빠에게 물어보고 싶었지만 그렇게 하지 않았다. 대신에, 그녀는 아빠에게 여행이 어땠는지에 대해서 막 물어보려는 참이다. 이 상황에서, Addy는 아빠에게 뭐라고 말하겠는가?

Addy: 여행은 좋으셨어요?

●●
spot 발견하다, 알아채다 **plenty of** 많은
instead 대신에 **be about to** 막 ~하려는 참이다

REVIEW TEST p. 95

A
① spot, 발견하다, 알아채다 ② lower, 내리다, 낮추다 ③ charge, (요금·값을) 청구하다
④ guilty, 죄책감을 느끼는 ⑤ thrifty, 절약하는 ⑥ thirsty, 목마른 ⑦ overall, 전반적으로
⑧ specific, 구체적인 ⑨ expressway, 고속도로 ⑩ so far, 지금까지 ⑪ price tag, 가격표
⑫ according to, ~에 따라서

B
① regular price ② focus on ③ get along with
④ need some advice ⑤ stop by aisle ⑥ have no choice but
⑦ make an international call ⑧ Instead, was about to

문제 및 정답	받아쓰기 및 녹음내용	해석

01

대화를 듣고, 남자가 찾고 있는 메모지의 위치로 가장 적절한 곳을 고르시오.

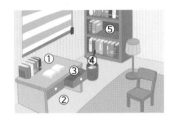

M Ms. Jones, where is that memo from Mr. Horner?

W I left it <u>on top of</u> your desk this morning, sir.

M Hmm… I can't find it. Where is it?

W Did you <u>check</u> <u>your</u> <u>drawers</u>?

M Yes, but it's not there either.

W Could it have dropped on the floor?

M Do you mean <u>underneath</u> <u>my</u> <u>desk</u>? Oh, here it is.

W Where is it?

M It <u>fell</u> in the <u>trash</u> <u>bin</u>.

남 Jones 씨, Horner 씨가 남긴 메모는 어디에 있나요?

여 오늘 아침에 책상 위에 놓아두었는데요, 선생님.

남 흠… 못 찾겠는데요. 어디에 있죠?

여 서랍은 확인해 보셨나요?

남 네, 하지만 거기에도 없어요.

여 바닥에 떨어졌을 수도 있죠?

남 내 책상 밑을 말하시는 건가요? 오, 여기에 있네요.

여 어디에 있나요?

남 쓰레기통 속에 떨어져 있었어요.

••
drawer 서랍 **underneath** ~의 밑에
trash bin 쓰레기통

02

대화를 듣고, 두 사람이 대화하는 장소로 가장 적절한 곳을 고르시오.

① 식당 ② 서점
③ 박물관 ④ 유치원
⑤ 교수실

W Good morning. May I <u>come</u> <u>in</u>?

M Sure, please. Have a seat here.

W You're the <u>new</u> <u>professor</u>, right?

M Yes, my name is Daniel, but you can call me Dan.

W Nice to meet you, Dan. I'm Nancy.

M <u>It's</u> <u>a</u> <u>pleasure</u> to meet you.

W I've heard many great things about you.

M That's a relief.

W Professor Kim <u>speaks</u> <u>very</u> <u>highly of</u> you. He says you're great at doing research.

M Thank you. I'm new here, so you'll have to <u>help</u> <u>me</u> <u>out</u>.

W I'll be more than happy to help you. Just let me know when.

M Thanks.

여 안녕하세요. 들어가도 될까요?

남 네, 들어오세요. 여기에 앉으세요.

여 당신이 새로 온 교수님이시군요, 맞죠?

남 네, 제 이름은 Daniel이에요, 그렇지만 Dan이라고 부르셔도 돼요.

여 만나서 반가워요, Dan. 저는 Nancy예요.

남 만나서 반갑습니다.

여 당신에 대한 매우 좋은 이야기를 많이 들었어요.

남 안심이 되네요.

여 김 교수님께서는 당신을 아주 극찬하세요. 당신이 조사를 굉장히 잘하신다고 말씀하시던데요.

남 감사합니다. 제가 이곳은 처음이라서, 저를 도와주셔야 해요.

여 당신을 돕는다면 더할 나위 없이 기쁠 겁니다. 제가 언제 도와드리면 될지 알려 주세요.

남 고맙습니다.

••
relief 안심, 안도 **speak highly of** ~를 극찬하다

03 다음을 듣고, 여자의 직업으로 가장 적절한 것을 고르시오.

① 교수　　　　② 정치인
③ 건축가　　　④ 뉴스 진행자
⑤ 영화 제작자

There are <u>growing</u> <u>concerns</u> about the cost of living, housing, and rising inflation. Let me <u>rebuild</u> <u>the</u> <u>country</u> <u>by</u> focusing on the economy. I <u>promise</u> <u>to</u> <u>cut</u> <u>taxes</u>, reform the welfare system, and restore moral leadership to this country. The people of this country <u>want</u> <u>action</u>! They want a leader they can <u>depend</u> <u>on</u>, and that's what this campaign is all about: leadership. I <u>stand</u> <u>up</u> <u>for</u> my beliefs, and I stand by my convictions.

생활비, 주거, 인플레이션 상승에 대한 우려가 커지고 있습니다. 경제에 주력하여 나라를 재건하겠습니다. 저는 세금을 줄이고, 복지 제도를 개혁하고, 우리나라에 도덕적인 지도력을 복원할 것을 약속드립니다. 우리나라의 국민들은 행동을 원합니다! 국민들은 의지할 수 있는 지도자를 원하며, 지도력이야말로 이 선거 유세의 모든 것입니다. 저는 제 믿음을 위해서 일어서고, 제 신념으로 일어섭니다.

◦◦
concern 우려　**tax** 세금　**reform** 개혁하다
welfare system 복지 제도　**restore** 복원하다
moral 도덕적인　**conviction** 신념, 확신

---

04 대화를 듣고, 두 사람의 관계로 가장 적절한 것을 고르시오.

① 간호사 - 환자
② 판매원 - 고객
③ 호텔 접수원 - 투숙객
④ 식당 지배인 - 종업원
⑤ 관광 가이드 - 여행객

W Welcome to the Happy Plaza. Do you <u>have</u> <u>a</u> <u>reservation</u>?
M Yes, I do. I'll be <u>staying</u> <u>for</u> three nights.
W What is your name?
M Andrew Smith.
W <u>Would</u> <u>you</u> <u>prefer</u> <u>to</u> have a room with a view of the ocean?
M I would love to <u>have</u> <u>an</u> <u>ocean</u> <u>view</u>.
W Here is your key for room 212. To get to your room, <u>take</u> <u>the</u> <u>elevator</u> on the right up to the second floor.
M Great. Thanks.
W If you have any questions or requests, please <u>dial</u> <u>0</u> <u>from</u> <u>your</u> <u>room</u>. There is also wi-fi available 24 hours a day.
M Thanks.

여 Happy Plaza에 오신 걸 환영합니다. 예약하셨나요?
남 네, 했어요. 3박 4일 동안 묵을 거예요.
여 성함이 어떻게 되시죠?
남 Andrew Smith입니다.
여 바다가 보이는 객실을 원하시나요?
남 바다가 보이는 객실이면 정말 좋겠습니다.
여 여기 212호실 열쇠입니다. 객실에 가기 위해서는 오른쪽에 있는 엘리베이터를 타고 2층으로 올라가시면 됩니다.
남 좋아요. 감사합니다.
여 문의 사항이나 요청 사항이 있으시면 객실에서 0을 누르시면 됩니다. 또한, 하루 24시간 동안 와이파이 이용 가능합니다.
남 감사합니다.

◦◦
request 요청, 부탁

대화를 듣고, 남자가 전화를 건 목적으로 가장 적절한 것을 고르시오.

① 진료 예약을 하려고
② 취업 상담을 신청하려고
③ 선생님에게 문병을 가려고
④ 수강 신청 일자를 문의하려고
⑤ 아들의 결석 사실을 알리려고

W Saint Andrew Elementary School. How can I help you?

M Hi. Is this the <u>school secretary</u>?

W Yes, it is. What can I do for you?

M I'm Gino Arlington, and my boy Louis is sick. He <u>won't</u> be able to <u>go</u> to <u>school</u> today. He is in the third grade in Mrs. Smith's class.

W Aw, that's too bad. Has he <u>got a cold</u>?

M No, I'm afraid it's an ear infection.

W Poor Louis. <u>Remind</u> me who his teacher is.

M Becky Smith. Please let her know <u>he'll</u> <u>be</u> <u>absent</u>.

여 Saint Andrew 초등학교입니다. 무엇을 도와드릴까요?

남 안녕하세요. 학교 비서이신가요?

여 네, 그렇습니다. 무엇을 도와드릴까요?

남 저는 Gino Arlington인데, 제 아들인 Louis가 아픕니다. 오늘 학교에 못 갈 것 같아요. 그 애는 3학년이고 Smith 선생님 반이에요.

여 저런, 참 안됐군요. 감기에 걸렸나요?

남 아뇨, 귓병인 것 같아요.

여 가여운 Louis. 선생님이 누구이신지 다시 한 번 알려 주시겠어요?

남 Becky Smith예요. 제 아들이 결석할 거라고 그분께 알려 주세요.

secretary 비서 **ear infection** 귓병
remind 다시 한 번 알려 주다 **absent** 결석한

대화를 듣고, 그림에서 여자의 딸이 누구인지 고르시오.

W That's my daughter over there. Her name is Candy.

M Where is she? She must be beautiful like you.

W She is <u>by</u> <u>the</u> <u>window</u> with the other kids.

M Which one is she?

W She's <u>wearing</u> <u>a</u> <u>white</u> <u>dress</u>. Can you see her?

M Do you mean the one playing with the blocks?

W No, the one <u>waving</u> <u>to</u> <u>us</u>.

M Oh, I see her now. What a cute hairstyle!

W I <u>braid</u> <u>her</u> <u>hair</u> like that every morning.

여 내 딸이 저기에 있어. 그 애의 이름은 Candy야.

남 어디에 있는데? 너를 닮아서 예쁘겠구나.

여 그 애는 다른 아이들과 함께 창가에 있어.

남 누가 네 딸인데?

여 내 딸은 흰색 드레스를 입고 있어. 내 딸이 보이니?

남 블록을 가지고 놀고 있는 아이를 말하는 거니?

여 아니, 우리에게 손을 흔들고 있는 아이야.

남 아, 이제 알겠다. 머리 모양이 참 귀엽구나!

여 내가 매일 아침 그 애의 머리카락을 그렇게 땋아 준다구.

wave 손을 흔들다 **braid** (머리 등을) 땋다

07 대화를 듣고, 무엇에 관한 내용인지 가장 적절한 것을 고르시오.

① 다양한 운동 방법
② 하루의 적정 운동량
③ 스트레스를 받는 이유
④ 스트레스로 유발되는 병
⑤ 스트레스를 해소하는 방법

W What do you do to <u>relieve</u> your <u>stress</u>?

M Well, I don't do anything. That's the problem. What do you do?

W I have a <u>regular</u> <u>exercise</u> <u>routine</u>, so that relieves a lot of my stress.

M That's a really smart idea. Sometimes I <u>get</u> <u>so</u> <u>much</u> <u>stress</u>.

W You need to do something about that. Why don't you <u>go to the gym</u> with me tomorrow?

M All right. What time do you go there?

W 6 a.m. Do you still want to go?

M I think <u>that's</u> <u>too</u> <u>early</u>.

여 스트레스를 해소하기 위해서 넌 무얼 하니?

남 음, 아무것도 안 해. 그게 문제야. 넌 무얼 하는데?

여 나는 규칙적인 운동 일과를 갖고 있어서 스트레스를 많이 풀지.

남 정말로 현명한 생각이다. 가끔 난 스트레스를 너무 많이 받거든.

여 그것에 대해 뭔가를 할 필요는 있어. 내일 나랑 체육관에 같이 갈래?

남 좋아. 너는 그곳에 몇 시에 가니?

여 오전 6시. 그래도 가고 싶니?

남 그건 너무 이르다고 생각해.

●●

relieve (고통 등을) 없애 주다, 완화하다
routine (매일 하는) 일과 **gym** 체육관

---

08 다음을 듣고, 다음 주의 날씨로 가장 적절한 것을 고르시오.

① strong winds
② sunny and hot
③ cloudy and rainy
④ cloudy and warm
⑤ rain showers and thunderstorms

The weather forecast is next on *Channel Six News*. It looks as though the forecast for the next week will be <u>outstanding</u>. The clouds and rain over the last few days <u>will</u> <u>disappear</u> in the next 24 hours. <u>The</u> <u>next</u> <u>seven</u> <u>days</u> promise to be gloriously <u>sunny</u> with temperatures in the early to mid-thirties. Make sure to <u>wear</u> <u>plenty</u> <u>of</u> <u>sunscreen</u> if you're going to the beach this week. Enjoy it while you have it because this great weather <u>will</u> <u>be</u> <u>followed</u> again <u>by</u> rain showers and thunderstorms.

다음은 채널 6번 뉴스에서 알려드리는 일기 예보입니다. 다음 한 주 동안은 매우 좋은 날씨가 될 것으로 보입니다. 지난 며칠 동안의 구름과 비는 앞으로 24시간 이내에 사라질 것입니다. 다음 7일간은 기온이 30도를 웃도는 기분 좋게 쾌청한 날씨가 될 것 같습니다. 이번 주에 해변에 가신다면 반드시 자외선 차단제를 듬뿍 바르세요. 이 멋진 날씨에 이어 다시 소나기와 뇌우가 이어질 것이므로, 좋은 날씨일 때 즐기세요.

●●

as though ~인 것처럼 **outstanding** 매우 좋은, 뛰어난 **disappear** 사라지다 **gloriously** 기분 좋게, 멋지게 **make sure to** 반드시 ~하다 **sunscreen** 자외선 차단제 **thunderstorm** 뇌우(천둥과 번개를 동반한 비)

09 대화를 듣고, 여자가 지불한 금액을 고르시오.

① $5 ② $25
③ $30 ④ $35 ✓
⑤ $40

M Please put your suitcase <u>on the scale</u>.

W Okay. Is it too heavy?

M <u>Our limit</u> for each bag is <u>25</u> kilograms.

W How heavy is mine?

M It is 32 kilograms. You have to pay <u>five dollars for every kilogram</u> over the limit.

W That seems a little excessive.

M I'm sorry, but <u>that's our policy</u>.

W Well, then here's the cash.

M Thank you. Enjoy your flight.

남 저울 위에 당신의 여행 가방을 놓으세요.

여 네. 너무 무거운가요?

남 각 가방에 대한 제한 무게는 25kg입니다.

여 제 건 얼마나 무거운가요?

남 32kg입니다. 제한 무게 초과로 각 kg당 5달러를 내셔야 합니다.

여 좀 과한 것 같은데요.

남 죄송하지만 그것이 저희의 방침입니다.

여 흠, 그렇다면 여기 현금이요.

남 감사합니다. 즐거운 비행 되십시오.

●●

scale 저울 **limit** 제한, 한도

---

10 대화를 듣고, 남자가 벌금을 급히 내러 가는 이유로 가장 적절한 것을 고르시오.

① 양심적인 운전자가 되기로 결심해서
② 여자가 서둘러 내야 한다고 독촉해서
③ 다음에 내러 갈 시간이 없을 것 같아서
④ 벌금을 내지 않아 면허가 정지된 적이 있어서
⑤ 기한 내에 내지 못하면 벌금이 두 배가 되어서 ✓

W Where are you going in such a hurry, Jake?

M I have to <u>pay</u> this <u>speeding ticket</u> within two days, or the <u>fine doubles</u>.

W Really? I've never heard of something like that.

M It's true. The ticket is 25 dollars, but if I <u>don't pay it soon</u>, it will be 50 dollars.

W I suppose that's a good way to get people to pay on time.

M You're probably right about that. It just never feels good <u>to be fined twice</u>.

W I don't drive that often, so it's not a big problem for me.

M I drive everywhere, so I have to be <u>a very cautious driver</u>.

여 Jake, 어디를 그렇게 급히 가는 중이니?

남 이틀 안에 이 과속 딱지 벌금을 내야만 해, 그렇지 않으면 두 배가 되거든.

여 정말? 난 그런 얘기를 한 번도 들어 본 적이 없는데.

남 사실이야. 벌금이 25달러이지만 곧 내지 않으면 50달러가 될 거야.

여 제시간에 사람들이 벌금을 내도록 하는 좋은 방법인 것 같다.

남 그것에 관한 네 말이 아마 맞을 거야. 벌금을 두 배로 내는 게 결코 기분 좋은 일은 아닐 뿐이야.

여 난 운전을 그렇게 자주 하지는 않아서, 나한테는 그게 큰 문제는 아니야.

남 난 어디든지 운전해서 가니까 매우 조심성 있는 운전자가 되어야만 해.

●●

speeding ticket 과속 딱지 **double** 두 배로 되다 **on time** 제시간에 **cautious** 조심성 있는, 신중한

11 대화를 듣고, 여자가 파티에 갖고 가야 할 것으로 가장 적절한 것을 고르시오.

① 없음　　②풍선
③ 피자　　④양초
⑤ 음료

W Hello, Paul. It's Cindy. I just received the invitation to your party.

M Can you make it?

W Well, let me see. It's next Saturday evening at 7:00 at your apartment, right?

M That's right. I hope you can come.

W It would be my pleasure. Can I bring anything?

M Just yourself.

W Okay. I'll be glad to go. I'm looking forward to it.

M I'm looking forward to seeing you then.

W See you then.

여 안녕, Paul. 나 Cindy야. 나는 방금 네 파티 초대장을 받았어.

남 올 수 있니?

여 글쎄, 어디 보자. 다음 주 토요일 저녁 7시에 네 아파트에서 하는 거 맞지?

남 맞아. 난 네가 올 수 있길 바라.

여 내가 더 좋지. 내가 뭐라도 가져갈까?

남 너만 오면 돼.

여 알았어. 기꺼이 갈게. 파티가 몹시 기대돼.

남 널 그때 보길 손꼽아 기다릴게.

여 그때 봐.

••
invitation 초대장

---

12 대화를 듣고, 대화 내용과 일치하지 <u>않는</u> 것을 고르시오.

① 남자의 어머니가 아버지에게 화를 내셨다.
② 남자의 어머니는 요리를 잘하신다.
③ 남자의 아버지는 어제 집에 늦게 들어오셨다.
④ 남자의 아버지가 TV 채널을 계속 돌리셨다.
⑤ 여자는 남자의 어머니에게 공감하고 있다.

M My mother got really annoyed with my father yesterday evening.

W Why? Did he complain about her cooking?

M Oh, no. She's a great cook.

W Did he come home late?

M No. It was when they were watching television.

W While watching TV? What made her so upset?

M My father kept changing the channels with the remote control.

W That can be irritating. My younger brother does it all the time.

남 우리 어머니가 어제 저녁에 아버지께 매우 화를 내셨어.

여 왜? 아버지가 어머니의 요리에 대해 불평이라도 하셨니?

남 오, 아냐. 어머니는 요리를 매우 잘하셔.

여 아버지가 집에 늦게 오셨니?

남 아니. 부모님이 텔레비전을 보고 계실 때였어.

여 TV를 보고 계실 때? 어머니가 무엇 때문에 그렇게 화가 나신 거야?

남 아버지가 리모컨으로 채널을 계속 돌리셨거든.

여 짜증이 날 만하지. 내 남동생도 항상 그래.

••
annoyed 화가 난　remote control 리모컨
irritating 짜증나게 하는

13 대화를 듣고, 여자의 마지막 말에 이어질 남자의 말로 가장 적절한 것을 고르시오.

① I can't follow you.
② That's very kind of him.
③ I promise it won't happen again.
④ Just around the corner on your left.
⑤ I would appreciate it if you did that.

W Mike, the light in the basement has gone out.
M I'll replace the bulb in a minute.
W No, no. I already tried that, but it still doesn't work.
M Maybe there's a short. Did you try the fuse box?
W Yes, and that didn't help either.
M Then we should call an electrician, shouldn't we?
W Do you have his number?
M It's on the bulletin board.
W I'll call an electrician right away.
M I would appreciate it if you did that.

여 Mike, 지하실에 전등이 나갔어요.
남 내가 금방 전구를 갈게요.
여 아니에요. 제가 벌써 해 봤지만, 여전히 불이 안 들어와요.
남 아마 단선이 된 모양이에요. 두꺼비집은 열어 봤어요?
여 네, 그런데 그것도 소용없었어요.
남 그렇다면 전기 기사를 불러야겠네요, 그렇지 않아요?
여 전화번호를 갖고 있어요?
남 게시판에 적혀 있어요.
여 제가 바로 전기 기사에게 전화할게요.
남 그렇게 해 준다면 고맙겠어요.

●●
basement 지하실 **replace** 갈다. 교체하다
bulb 전구 **fuse box** 두꺼비집 **electrician** 전기 기사 **bulletin board** 게시판

14 대화를 듣고, 남자의 마지막 말에 이어질 여자의 말로 가장 적절한 것을 고르시오.

① Why are you so upset?
② Mind your own business.
③ You shouldn't give up so easily.
④ Relax. It could be worse, you know.
⑤ You must feel on top of the world now.

W What's the matter? You look really depressed.
M I just got my exam results. I failed.
W You flunked? How could that be? You studied night and day for months.
M Apparently, that wasn't enough.
W I'm really sorry to hear that.
M So am I.
W You can try again next year. Cheer up.
M I don't know. Maybe I wasn't meant to be a lawyer.
W You shouldn't give up so easily.

여 무슨 일이야? 너 굉장히 의기소침해 보이는데.
남 방금 시험 결과를 받았어. 나 떨어졌어.
여 떨어졌어? 어떻게 그런 일이? 몇 개월 동안이나 밤낮으로 공부했는데.
남 분명 그것만으로는 충분하지 않았던 것 같아.
여 정말 유감스럽구나.
남 나도 그래.
여 내년에 다시 하면 되지. 기운 내.
남 모르겠어. 아마 애초부터 변호사가 될 운명은 아니었나 봐.
여 그렇게 쉽게 포기할 일은 아니야.

●●
depressed 의기소침한, 우울한 **flunk** (시험에) 떨어지다 **apparently** 분명히

15 대화를 듣고, 남자의 마지막 말에 이어질 여자의 말로 가장 적절한 것을 고르시오.

① It was an earthquake under the sea, wasn't it?

✓② That's amazing. He was one of the few lucky ones.

③ I've never heard of an earthquake of that magnitude.

④ He was the bravest and strongest man I have ever known.

⑤ You don't have to look too far back in history to realize that.

M Have you seen the reports on TV from the countries affected by the tsunami disaster?

W Yes, I've been really depressed by all the sad stories.

M Me, too. Many of the people who live there have lost their entire families, and the survivors seem to be stunned by the disaster.

W I know. If that had happened to me, I don't know what I would have done.

M On the other hand, there have been some incredible survival stories.

W I haven't heard any of those.

M There was one man who managed to hang on to the top of a tree after the tsunami carried him inland.

W That's amazing. He was one of the few lucky ones.

남 해일 재앙이 닥친 나라들에서 찍어 온 TV 보도를 봤니?

여 응, 그 모든 슬픈 소식들 때문에 정말 기운이 없었어.

남 나도 그랬어. 그곳에 사는 많은 사람들이 가족 모두를 잃었고, 생존자들은 재앙으로 인해 망연자실한 것처럼 보여.

여 알아. 그런 일이 나에게 발생했다면 난 어떻게 할지 모르겠어.

남 반면에 몇 개의 놀라운 생존 소식들이 있었지.

여 난 그건 듣지 못했는데.

남 해일 때문에 오지로 쓸려간 후에 간신히 나무 꼭대기를 꽉 붙잡고 있던 사람이 한 명 있었어.

여 놀랍구나. 그는 운 좋은 몇 사람들 중 하나였네.

● ●
stunned 망연자실한 **on the other hand** 반면에 **manage to** 간신히 ~하다 **hang on to** ~을 꽉 붙잡다 **inland** 오지로, 내륙으로

⏵ REVIEW TEST p. 103

A ① limit, 제한, 한도 ② moral, 도덕적인 ③ drawer, 서랍 ④ concern, 우려 ⑤ disappear, 사라지다
⑥ secretary, 비서 ⑦ cautious, 조심성 있는, 신중한 ⑧ sunscreen, 자외선 차단제
⑨ depressed, 의기소침한, 우울한 ⑩ underneath, ~의 밑에 ⑪ trash bin, 쓰레기통
⑫ bulletin board, 게시판

B ① relieve, stress ② remote control ③ regular exercise routine
④ replace the bulb ⑤ he'll be absent ⑥ braid her hair
⑦ speaks very highly of ⑧ On the other hand

문제 및 정답	받아쓰기 및 녹음내용	해석

01 대화를 듣고, 두 사람이 만나기로 한 시각을 고르시오.

① ②

③ ④

⑤

W Hello.

M Hi, Jill. It's me again.

W Oh, hi. Did you <u>forget</u> <u>something</u>?

M Yeah. Are we meeting at seven or eight?

W We're going to <u>meet</u> <u>at</u> <u>eight</u>.

M Ah, now I remember. Okay, see you tomorrow night.

W No, wait. It's <u>eight</u> <u>in</u> <u>the</u> <u>morning</u>, not eight at night!

M It is? Wow! I am all <u>mixed</u> <u>up</u>, aren't I?

여 여보세요.

남 안녕, Jill. 또 나야.

여 아, 안녕. 뭐 잊었어?

남 응. 우리가 7시에 만나기로 했던가, 아니면 8시에 만나기로 했던가?

여 8시에 만나기로 했어.

남 아, 이제 기억 난다. 알겠어, 내일 밤에 보자.

여 아니야, 잠깐. 밤 8시가 아니고 아침 8시야!

남 그래? 와! 내가 완전히 헷갈리고 있었네, 안 그래?

•• **be mixed up** 헷갈려 하다, 혼동하다

---

02 대화를 듣고, 두 사람이 대화하는 장소로 가장 적절한 곳을 고르시오.

① 학교 ② 병원
③ 사무실 ④ 기차역
⑤ 슈퍼마켓

M Good morning, Kate!

W Oh, hi. How are you doing?

M Pretty good. And you?

W I'm just a little tired. Anyway, I <u>haven't</u> <u>seen</u> <u>you</u> <u>around</u> lately.

M Well, I was away for a week. I had <u>several</u> <u>business</u> <u>meetings</u> in Asia last week.

W Oh, how did they go?

M Great! I made some <u>big</u> <u>deals</u> on that trip.

W Good for you. But you must be exhausted.

M Yes, I still have jet lag, so I'm going to <u>work</u> only <u>half</u> <u>a</u> <u>day</u> today. By the way, are we going to have a sales meeting at 10:30?

W That's right. We <u>had</u> <u>better</u> <u>take</u> a look at this sales document <u>before</u> <u>the</u> <u>meeting</u>.

남 좋은 아침이에요, Kate!

여 어, 안녕하세요. 잘 지냈어요?

남 잘 지냈어요. 당신은요?

여 저는 조금 피곤할 뿐이에요. 그나저나 요 근래에 당신을 못 본 것 같아요.

남 음, 일주일 동안 멀리 갔었어요. 지난주에 아시아에서 몇 개의 사업 회의가 있었거든요.

여 아, 어떻게 됐는데요?

남 아주 잘됐어요! 저는 그 여행에서 몇 개의 큰 거래를 성사시켰어요.

여 잘됐네요. 그런데 당신은 무척 피곤하겠어요.

남 네, 아직은 시차로 인한 피로감이 있어서, 오늘은 반나절만 일할 거예요. 그런데 우리 10시 30분에 판매 회의가 있죠?

여 맞아요. 회의 전에 이 판매 서류를 살펴보는 게 좋을 것 같아요.

•• **deal** 거래 **jet lag** 시차로 인한 피로

03 다음을 듣고, 남자가 설명하고 있는 운동 종목으로 가장 적절한 것을 고르시오.

① 축구, 야구 ② 배구, 축구
③ 배구, 농구 ④ 농구, 테니스
⑤ 테니스, 배구

I'm going to talk about sports. Men, women, and children like sports. Some like tennis or volleyball. Others like soccer or baseball. I'm going to tell you first about two sports. One uses a ball and a high net. Six players hit the ball over the net with their hands. The other team hits it back. The other sport uses a ball and two baskets. Five players on each team use their hands to bounce and throw the ball. Each team tries to throw the ball in the other's basket.

나는 스포츠에 대해 이야기하고자 합니다. 남자들, 여자들, 그리고 아이들은 스포츠를 좋아합니다. 어떤 사람들은 테니스나 배구를 좋아합니다. 다른 사람들은 축구나 야구를 좋아합니다. 나는 당신에게 먼저 두 가지 스포츠에 대해 이야기하겠습니다. 하나는 공과 높은 네트를 사용합니다. 6명의 선수들이 손으로 공을 쳐서 네트 위로 넘깁니다. 상대 팀은 그것을 되받아 칩니다. 다른 하나는 공과 두 개의 바스켓을 사용합니다. 각 팀의 5명의 선수들이 손을 사용해서 공을 튀기고 던집니다. 각 팀은 공을 상대의 바스켓에 던져 넣으려고 합니다.

•• volleyball 배구

04 대화를 듣고, 두 사람의 관계로 가장 적절한 것을 고르시오.

① 승무원 - 승객
② 교통경찰 - 시민
③ 변호사 - 의뢰인
④ 자동차 판매원 - 고객
⑤ 렌터카 회사 직원 - 고객

M I'd like to rent a car for several weeks.

W Do you have a reservation?

M No, I don't.

W All right. I'll see what we have available. Would you like a subcompact, compact, mid-size, or luxury car?

M I don't need much room, just good fuel economy and safety. What do you recommend?

W I have a minivan ready. Would that be all right with you?

M Fine. How much does it cost?

W Well, if you rent it for a week or more, I would recommend the unlimited mileage plan.

M How does it work?

W You pay a flat rate for a week, and then you can drive as much as you want.

M Okay. I'll take it.

남 몇 주 동안 차를 빌리고 싶습니다.

여 예약하셨나요?

남 아뇨, 안 했어요.

여 좋습니다. 우리가 가진 것 중에서 어떤 차가 가능한지 알아보지요. 경차, 소형차, 중형차, 고급 대형 승용차 중에서 뭘 원하세요?

남 공간은 많이 필요 없고, 연비가 좋고 안전하기만 하면 됩니다. 뭘 추천하시겠어요?

여 미니밴이 준비되어 있는데요. 괜찮으시겠어요?

남 좋아요. 얼마죠?

여 음, 일주일이나 그 이상을 빌리신다면, 무제한 마일리지 플랜을 추천해드리겠습니다.

남 어떻게 되는 건데요?

여 일주일 동안 고정 요금을 내시고, 손님께서 원하는 만큼 운전하실 수 있는 거예요.

남 좋아요. 그걸로 하죠.

•• subcompact car 경차 mid-size car 중형차 luxury car 고급 대형 승용차 fuel economy (자동차) 연비 safety 안전 recommend 추천하다 unlimited 무제한의 flat rate 고정 요금

05

대화를 듣고, 남자가 전화를 건 목적으로 가장 적절한 것을 고르시오.

① 자신의 아들을 찾으려고
② 여자의 출장 일자를 확인하려고
③ John이 집에 있는지 알아보려고
④ John의 휴대폰 번호를 물어보려고
⑤ 축구 경기를 보러 갈 것을 제안하려고

M Hello? Is this John's home?

W Yes, it is. May I <u>ask</u> <u>who's</u> <u>calling</u>? My son isn't home right now.

M Hello, Mrs. Mester. I'm Scott Myers' father.

W Oh, hello, Mr. Myers. How is your wife doing?

M She's out of town on a business trip. I am just <u>wondering</u> if Scott is <u>at your</u> <u>place</u>.

W Yes, he was. But he and John <u>went</u> <u>out</u> to play soccer.

M Oh, I see. I just came home and found that Scott <u>was</u> <u>not</u> <u>here</u>.

W When they come back, I'll tell him <u>to</u> <u>call</u> <u>you</u>.

M Thank you.

W Sure. I'll see you around.

남 여보세요? 거기 John네 집인가요?

여 예, 그런데요. 누구시죠? 저희 아들은 지금 집에 없는데요.

남 안녕하세요, Mester 부인. 저는 Scott Myers의 아버지입니다.

여 아, 안녕하세요, Myers 씨. 부인은 어떻게 지내세요?

남 제 아내는 도시를 떠나 출장을 갔답니다. 혹시 Scott이 당신의 집에 있는지 그냥 궁금해서요.

여 예, 있었어요. 그런데 John과 함께 축구하러 나갔어요.

남 아, 알겠습니다. 제가 방금 집에 왔는데 Scott이 여기에 없다는 걸 알게 돼서요.

여 애들이 돌아오면 아버지께 전화하라고 Scott에게 말할게요.

남 감사합니다.

여 천만에요. 나중에 뵐게요.

●●
business trip 출장

06

대화를 듣고, 머그잔의 위치로 가장 적절한 곳을 고르시오.

M Where do you <u>keep</u> <u>the</u> <u>mugs</u>? I need a cup of coffee.

W They're <u>in</u> <u>the</u> <u>cabinet</u> over there.

M Which cabinet? Your kitchen is full of cabinets.

W You're right. Sorry. It's the cabinet <u>over</u> <u>the</u> <u>sink</u>.

M You have to be more specific than that.

W It's the <u>second</u> one <u>from</u> <u>the</u> <u>left</u>, and it's directly over the sink.

M Aha. Now I've found it.

남 머그잔들을 어디에다 보관해요? 커피를 마셔야겠는데요.

여 저기에 있는 수납장 안에 있어요.

남 어떤 수납장이요? 당신의 부엌은 수납장으로 가득 차 있잖아요.

여 당신 말이 맞아요. 미안해요. 싱크대 위에 있는 수납장이요.

남 그보다 더 구체적으로 말해 주셔야 해요.

여 왼쪽에서 두 번째 수납장이고, 싱크대 바로 위에 있어요.

남 아하. 이제 찾았어요.

●●
cabinet 수납장

07 대화를 듣고, 무엇에 관한 내용인지 가장 적절한 것을 고르시오.

① 방과 후 활동
② 동물원 방문 계획
③ 토끼와 개의 다른 점
④ 반려동물 키우기의 어려움
⑤ 어린 시절 키우던 반려동물

M Look at those rabbits over there! Aren't they cute? The kids seem very excited.

W Did you ever have any pets when young?

M Yeah, I had a pet rabbit called Mary. I was excited to go home after class every day because I was always thinking about my rabbit.

W What happened to her?

M Well, she lived for about a year, and then she died. She was really cute.

W That's too bad. I used to have a dog when I was little.

M Did you have fun with him?

W Oh, yeah. I had the greatest time playing with him.

M Pets seem to really make our childhood happy.

남 저기 있는 저 토끼들 좀 봐! 귀엽지 않니? 아이들이 정말 신나 보인다.

여 어릴 때 반려동물을 키워 본 적 있니?

남 응, Mary라는 이름의 애완용 토끼를 키웠어. 항상 내 토끼에 대해 생각했기 때문에 방과 후에 집에 갈 때면 매일 신이 났었어.

여 그 토끼는 어떻게 됐니?

남 음, 약 1년 정도 살다가 죽었어. 정말로 귀여웠는데.

여 안됐다. 내가 어렸을 때는 개를 키웠었는데.

남 그 개랑 잘 놀았었니?

여 오, 그럼. 같이 놀면서 정말 멋진 시간을 보냈었지.

남 반려동물들은 정말 우리의 어린 시절을 행복하게 해 주는 것 같아.

••
childhood 어린 시절

---

08 대화를 듣고, 여자의 심정으로 가장 적절한 것을 고르시오.

① upset　　② hopeful
③ relieved　　④ ashamed
⑤ depressed

W Where were you yesterday? We were supposed to meet for lunch.

M I know, but something came up.

W Something came up? You could have at least called to tell me.

M There was no telephone around.

W What about your cell phone?

M Sorry. The battery was dead.

W It seems you have an excuse for everything. I don't even want to have you as a friend.

여 너 어제 어디에 있었니? 우리 점심 식사를 위해 만나기로 했잖아.

남 알아, 그런데 일이 생겨서.

여 일이 생겼었다고? 적어도 전화해서 나한테 말해 줄 수 있었잖아.

남 주변에 전화가 없어서.

여 네 휴대폰은 어쩌고?

남 미안해. 배터리가 나가서.

여 넌 무슨 일에든 변명거리가 있는 것 같구나. 난 널 친구로 두고 싶지도 않아.

09 대화를 듣고, 남자와 아들의 나이 차이로 가장 적절한 것을 고르시오.

① 15살 ② 19살
③ 20살 ④ 30살
⑤ 35살

W Can I look at your high school <u>yearbook</u>, honey?

M Sure. Why not?

W <u>How</u> <u>old</u> <u>were</u> <u>you</u> in this picture? You look really young here.

M I was 19 years old. That was such a crazy time in my life.

W High school was fun, wasn't it? But now we're <u>in</u> <u>our</u> <u>forties</u>. Time really flies.

M <u>Don't</u> <u>remind</u> me that I am already <u>45</u>.

W They say that the older you get, the <u>faster</u> <u>time</u> <u>goes</u> <u>by</u>. Now our son is <u>15</u> years old.

M This is depressing. Let's change the subject.

여 여보, 제가 당신의 고등학교 졸업 앨범을 봐도 돼요?

남 그럼요. 왜 안 되겠어요?

여 이 사진 찍었을 때 당신 몇 살이었죠? 여기서는 정말로 어려 보이네요.

남 19살이었어요. 그때가 내 인생에서 정말이지 최고의 시간이었죠.

여 고등학교 때는 재미있었어요, 그렇지 않아요? 그런데 지금 우리가 40대라뇨. 시간 참 빨라요.

남 내가 벌써 마흔다섯 살이라는 걸 상기시켜 주지 말아요.

여 나이를 먹으면 먹을수록 시간이 더 빨리 간다고 하잖아요. 지금 우리 아들이 열다섯 살이에요.

남 울적한 걸요. 화제를 바꿔 보아요.

yearbook 졸업 앨범

---

10 대화를 듣고, 여자가 남자에게 충고한 것으로 가장 적절한 것을 고르시오.

① 부모님의 입장에서 생각해 보아야 한다.
② 부모로서 자녀에게 모범을 보여야 한다.
③ 항상 다음 기회가 있음을 기억해야 한다.
④ 자신을 위해서는 조금 이기적일 필요가 있다.
⑤ 목표를 이루려면 시간을 효율적으로 사용해야 한다.

W How was your <u>graduation</u> <u>ceremony</u>?

M Well, I guess it was just okay.

W What do you mean by "just okay"? <u>You</u> <u>were</u> <u>with</u> your parents. They must have been very proud of you.

M But I <u>didn't</u> actually <u>want</u> <u>to</u> <u>attend</u> my ceremony.

W Why is that?

M As you know, I <u>have</u> <u>an</u> <u>important</u> exam next week. If I fail it this time, then I have to spend the entire year studying again.

W <u>Think</u> about it from your parents' <u>point</u> <u>of</u> <u>view</u>. Your graduation ceremony must be very important to them.

M I know, but I <u>wasted</u> three <u>important</u> <u>days</u> flying there and back.

W Come on. I'm sure you will get a good result on the exam.

여 네 졸업식 어땠니?

남 글쎄, 그냥 괜찮았던 것 같아.

여 "그냥 괜찮았다"라니 무슨 뜻이야? 네 부모님과 함께 있었잖아. 부모님이 틀림없이 널 매우 자랑스러워하셨을 텐데.

남 그렇지만 난 사실 졸업식에 별로 참석하고 싶지 않았거든.

여 왜?

남 너도 알다시피, 난 다음 주에 중요한 시험이 있어. 이번에 떨어지면 꼬박 1년을 다시 공부하는 데 써야 해.

여 네 부모님의 입장에서 그것에 대해 생각해 봐. 네 졸업식은 그분들에게 매우 중요한 것일 거야.

남 알아, 그렇지만 난 비행기 타고 왔다 갔다 하느라 중요한 3일을 허비했다구.

여 이봐. 너는 분명 시험에서 좋은 결과를 얻을 거야.

attend 참석하다 **point of view** 입장, 관점

11 대화를 듣고, 여자가 응급 전화를 건 이유로 가장 적절한 것을 고르시오.

① 여자가 아파서
② 여자의 여동생이 아파서
③ 여자가 교통사고를 목격해서
④ 여자의 집이 홍수로 침수되어서
⑤ 여자의 집에 야생 동물이 들어와서

M 911. Where's the emergency?

W 35 Oakhurst Lane.

M What's your name?

W Jenny Tyler. Please hurry. It's my little sister. She drank some kitchen cleaner by mistake, and now she's very sick. I don't know what to do!

M Just calm down. A rescue team is on the way.

W Tell the team to hurry, please!

남 911입니다. 응급 사태가 난 곳은 어디인가요?

여 Oakhurst Lane 35예요.

남 성함이 어떻게 되시죠?

여 Jenny Tyler예요. 서둘러 주세요. 제 여동생이에요. 그녀는 실수로 부엌용 세제를 조금 마셨는데 지금 매우 아파해요. 저는 어떻게 해야 할지 모르겠어요!

남 진정하세요. 구조 팀이 가고 있어요.

여 구조 팀에게 서둘러 달라고 말해 주세요!

●●
cleaner 세제   rescue 구조, 구출

12 대화를 듣고, 대화 내용과 일치하지 <u>않는</u> 것을 고르시오.

① Mary는 사람들과 대화하는 중이다.
② Mary는 예전에는 모든 사람들에게 친절했었다.
③ Mary는 협회 부회장으로 선출되었다.
④ 여자는 Mary의 행동이 바람직하다고 생각한다.
⑤ 남자는 Mary가 행동 방식을 바꿔야 한다고 생각한다.

W Do you see Mary over there?

M Yeah. She's been acting weird these days.

W Look at her! She only seems to be interested in talking to the important people here.

M I know, but she wasn't always like that. She used to be friendly with everybody.

W What made her change?

M This started after she was elected vice president of the association. It seems that she wants to communicate only with important people.

W That's not the best way to behave if you need everybody's cooperation.

M That's true. She should realize what she's doing and change the way she behaves.

W That's what I'm saying.

여 저기 Mary 보이니?

남 응. 그녀는 요즘 별나게 행동하더라.

여 그녀를 봐! 그녀는 여기에 있는 중요한 사람들과 대화하는 것에만 흥미가 있는 것 같아.

남 나도 알지만 그녀가 항상 그렇지는 않았어. 그녀는 모든 사람들에게 친절했었어.

여 왜 그녀는 변했지?

남 그녀가 협회의 부회장으로 선출된 후부터 그랬어. 그녀는 중요한 사람들하고만 소통하기를 원하는 것 같아.

여 모든 사람의 협력을 필요로 한다면 그렇게 행동하는 것이 최선의 방법은 아니야.

남 맞아. 그녀는 자신이 무얼 하고 있는지 깨달아서 행동하는 방식을 바꿔야만 해.

여 내 말이 그 말이야.

●●
weird 별난, 이상한 vice president 부회장
association 협회 communicate 의사소통하다 behave 행동하다 cooperation 협력

13 대화를 듣고, 남자의 마지막 말에 이어질 여자의 말로 가장 적절한 것을 고르시오.

① You must be happy.
② They all know what to do.
③ I'll do my best to save you.
④ We should be very careful all the time.
⑤ I could have helped you if I had been there.

W I saw a traffic accident on my way to school.
M How did it happen?
W A truck driver was driving too fast and hit an oncoming car.
M I wonder what happened to the people.
W I heard that one person died and that the truck driver was badly injured and sent to a nearby hospital.
M The other day, I failed to use my turn signal, and I almost got in a terrible accident. I was really lucky.
W We should be very careful all the time.

여 나는 학교 가는 길에 교통사고를 봤어.
남 어떻게 일어났는데?
여 트럭 운전사가 과속하다가 마주 오는 차와 충돌했지.
남 사람들이 어떻게 되었는지 궁금하다.
여 한 사람은 죽고 트럭 운전사는 심하게 부상을 입어서 근처 병원으로 옮겨졌대.
남 예전에 나도 방향 지시등을 사용하지 못해서 끔찍한 사고를 당할 뻔했어. 난 정말 운이 좋았지.
여 우리는 항상 매우 조심해야만 해.

● ●
oncoming 다가오는 injured 부상을 입은
turn signal 방향 지시등

---

14 대화를 듣고, 여자의 마지막 말에 이어질 남자의 말로 가장 적절한 것을 고르시오.

① Of course I do. There is a jazz dance club.
② No, I don't. Could you fill out this application?
③ The speech club will give you a lot of opportunities.
④ You don't have to worry about making a lot of speeches.
⑤ Yes, I do. There are two clubs that teach you foreign languages.

M Have you decided which club you're going to join?
W No. Because I'm a freshman, I don't know what clubs are on campus.
M Well, why don't you join the speech club?
W What's that for? Do you get to make a lot of speeches?
M That's right. It helps you develop confidence in public speaking.
W But I'm afraid of talking in front of many people. I think it's a bit challenging.
M Then how about the yoga club? That will help you relax.
W Sounds boring. Do you know any club that teaches you how to dance?
M Of course I do. There is a jazz dance club.

남 어떤 동아리에 가입할지 결정했니?
여 아니. 난 신입생이라 학교에 어떤 동아리가 있는지 모르겠어.
남 음, 연설 동아리에 가입하는 게 어때?
여 뭘 하는 곳인데? 연설을 많이 하게 되니?
남 맞아. 그곳은 네가 사람들 앞에서 연설을 하는 데 자신감을 키우도록 도와줘.
여 하지만 나는 여러 사람들 앞에서 말하기가 겁이 나. 약간 힘들 것 같은데.
남 그럼 요가 동아리는 어때? 그건 긴장을 풀도록 도와줄 거야.
여 지루하게 들린다. 춤추는 법을 가르쳐 주는 동아리를 아니?
남 물론 알지. 재즈 댄스 동아리가 있어.

● ●
freshman (대학의) 신입생, 1학년생 public 대중의 challenging 힘든 boring 지루한

15 다음 상황 설명을 듣고, Ben이 Paul에게 할 말로 가장 적절한 것을 고르시오.

① It makes me so mad when I do that!

② I'm really displeased with his behavior.

③ Let's go to the Customer Service Department to complain.

④ I can't sleep. There's something that is really bothering me.

⑤ Stop thinking about work and take it easy as much as possible.

Paul has been <u>tossing</u> <u>and</u> <u>turning</u> all night. He can't sleep because he's <u>worried</u> <u>about</u> <u>work</u>. There was a new guy last week. The boss assigned the guy to help Paul on the <u>new</u> <u>project</u> that he's been <u>working</u> <u>on</u>. The guy is supposed to be Paul's assistant. But he <u>started</u> <u>criticizing</u> all of Paul's work and making a whole bunch of suggestions. Paul's so <u>upset</u> that he <u>can't</u> <u>sleep</u>. His old friend Ben wants to advise him to <u>take</u> <u>work</u> <u>off</u> his <u>mind</u> and to take things easy. In this situation, what would Ben most likely say to Paul?

Ben: <u>Stop thinking about work and take it easy as much as possible.</u>

Paul은 밤새 잠이 안 와서 몸을 뒤척이고 있다. 그는 일 때문에 걱정이 되어서 잠을 잘 수가 없다. 지난주에 새로운 남자가 왔다. 사장은 그가 Paul이 진행하고 있는 새 프로젝트를 돕도록 그를 선임했다. 그 사람은 Paul의 보조원이 되어야 한다. 하지만 그는 Paul의 모든 일을 비판하고 굉장히 많은 제안을 하기 시작했다. Paul은 너무 기분이 상해서 잠을 잘 수가 없다. 그의 오랜 친구인 Ben은 그에게 일에 대해 생각하지 말고 마음을 편히 하라고 조언하기를 원한다. 이런 상황에서 Ben은 Paul에게 뭐라고 말하겠는가?

Ben: <u>일에 대해 생각하는 걸 멈추고, 가능한 한 마음을 편하게 가져 봐.</u>

●●
toss and turn 잠이 안 와서 몸을 뒤척이다 **assign** 선임하다, 맡기다 **assistant** 보조원, 조수 **criticize** 비판하다 **suggestion** 제안 **take things easy** 마음을 편히 하다

▶ REVIEW TEST p. 111

A
① weird, 별난, 이상한　② safety, 안전　③ public, 대중의　④ behave, 행동하다

⑤ injured, 부상을 입은　⑥ oncoming, 다가오는　⑦ cabinet, 수납장　⑧ assistant, 보조원, 조수

⑨ freshman, (대학의) 신입생, 1학년생　⑩ communicate, 의사소통하다　⑪ cooperation, 협력

⑫ suggestion, 제안

B
① jet lag　② rescue team　③ business trip

④ big deals　⑤ take, easy　⑥ vice president

⑦ high school yearbook　⑧ point of view

01 ③	02 ②	03 ⑤	04 ⑤	05 ④	06 ⑤	07 ②	08 ③
09 ②	10 ③	11 ①	12 ③	13 ③	14 ②	15 ④	

문제 및 정답	받아쓰기 및 녹음내용	해석
01 대화를 듣고, 남자가 예약한 시각을 고르시오. ① ② ③ ④ ⑤	W Endicott Beauty Salon. How may I help you? M Hi. I <u>wonder if I could</u> go there without making an appointment. W No, sorry. We work strictly by appointment. M Well, when is <u>the soonest</u> I could make an appointment? W You could come in tomorrow at 2:30, 4:30, or 6:00. M <u>Couldn't I go</u> there in the morning? Say, 8:00 or so? W I'm sorry, but that time <u>is not available</u>. M Then I'd like to <u>make an appointment</u> for 2:30 p.m. W Okay. I'll see you tomorrow at 2:30.	여 Endicott 미용실입니다. 무엇을 도와드릴까요? 남 안녕하세요. 예약하지 않고 그곳에 가도 되는지 궁금해서요. 여 아뇨, 죄송합니다. 저희는 엄격히 예약제로만 운영합니다. 남 음, 제가 예약을 할 수 있는 가장 빠른 때는 언제인가요? 여 내일 2시 30분, 4시 30분, 아니면 6시에 오실 수 있습니다. 남 오전에 가면 안될까요? 말하자면, 8시쯤에는요? 여 죄송하지만, 그 시간은 안 됩니다. 남 그러면 오후 2시 30분에 예약을 하고 싶습니다. 여 알겠습니다. 내일 2시 30분에 뵙겠습니다. ●● **appointment** (병원·미용실 등의) 예약
02 대화를 듣고, 두 사람이 대화하는 장소로 가장 적절한 곳을 고르시오. ① 버스 안 ② 거리 위 ③ 전철 안 ④ 비행기 안 ⑤ 엘리베이터 안	W Could you tell me <u>how</u> to <u>get to</u> Jongno? M Are you going to drive? W I am going to <u>use public transportation</u>. M Well, you had better take the subway. First, you <u>ought to take</u> a bus at the bus stop <u>across the street</u>. W Which number should I take? M Number 160. And <u>get off</u> at Sindorim Station. W Get off at Sindorim Station? M Yes, and then take the subway there. W The green line? M No, the blue line. Oh, you should be careful. Don't <u>take the trains for</u> Incheon or Suwon.	여 종로에 어떻게 가야 하는지 알려 주시겠어요? 남 운전하실 건가요? 여 대중교통을 이용할 거예요. 남 음, 지하철을 타는 편이 좋아요. 먼저, 길 건너 버스 정류장에서 버스를 타셔야 해요. 여 몇 번을 타야 하죠? 남 160번이요. 그리고 신도림역에서 내리세요. 여 신도림역에서 내리라고요? 남 네, 그런 다음 거기서 지하철을 타세요. 여 녹색 노선이요? 남 아뇨, 파란색 노선이요. 아, 조심하셔야 해요. 인천이나 수원으로 가는 열차는 타지 마세요. ●● **ought to** ~해야 하다

03 다음을 듣고, 여자의 직업으로 가장 적절한 것을 고르시오.

① 군인　　　② 교사
③ 언어학자　④ 택시 기사
⑤ 기계 설계 기사 ✓

I could have done a lot of different things, but I chose to work for Tectonics. It's a challenging job. You see, my company manufactures industrial-use mechanical equipment. It's too technical for most people, so I won't bore you with the details. Basically, I design the machines and redesign them every time a new model comes out. There are a lot of experts in this field.

다른 많은 일들을 해 볼 수도 있었지만, 전 Tectonics에서 일하는 것을 선택했습니다. 그것은 도전적인 일입니다. 아시다시피, 우리 회사는 공업용 기계 장치를 제조합니다. 대부분의 사람들에게는 너무 기술적이라서, 세부 사항들을 말해서 당신을 지루하게 하지는 않겠습니다. 기본적으로, 저는 기계들을 디자인하고 신형이 나올 때마다 그것들을 다시 디자인합니다. 이 분야에는 전문가들이 많습니다.

●●

manufacture 제조하다　**industrial-use** 공업용의　**mechanical** 기계의　**equipment** 장치　**technical** 기술적인　**bore** 지루하게 하다　**basically** 기본적으로　**redesign** 다시 디자인하다　**expert** 전문가

---

04 대화를 듣고, 두 사람의 관계로 가장 적절한 것을 고르시오.

① 은행원 – 고객
② 세입자 – 집주인
③ 택시 기사 – 승객
④ 이삿짐 센터 직원 – 고객
⑤ 부동산 중개업자 – 고객 ✓

W Hello?

M Hello, Mrs. Andrews? This is Tommy from ABC Real Estate.

W Hi. Have you found an apartment for me yet?

M Yes, I have a great place to show you on Park Avenue. It's 150,000 dollars.

W Oh, that's too expensive for me.

M Well, I have another one on Cook Street. It's only 95,000 dollars. But it only has one bedroom.

W Oh, that's not big enough.

M Well, how about getting a mortgage?

W I think that's worth considering.

여 여보세요?

남 여보세요, Andrews 부인? 전 ABC 부동산의 Tommy입니다.

여 안녕하세요. 벌써 아파트를 찾으셨나요?

남 예, Park Avenue에 당신에게 보여드릴 매우 좋은 집이 있어요. 15만 달러입니다.

여 아, 저에게는 너무 비싸네요.

남 그러면, Cook Street에 하나 더 있어요. 그건 9만 5천 달러밖에 하지 않아요. 하지만 침실이 하나뿐이죠.

여 아, 그것은 충분히 크지 않네요.

남 그럼, 대출을 받는 건 어떠세요?

여 그것도 고려해 볼 만한 것 같네요.

●●

avenue (도시의) ~가(街), 대로

05 대화를 듣고, 여자가 전화를 건 목적으로 가장 적절한 것을 고르시오.

① 쇼핑을 같이 가려고
② 운동을 같이 하려고
③ 불만을 이야기하려고
④ 점심 식사에 초대하려고 ✓
⑤ 일요일에 교회에 같이 가려고

M Hello?

W Oh, hello, Ken. How are you doing?

M Just fine. Thanks. How about you, Cathy?

W Can't complain. Well, Tony and I were wondering... Are you and Rosa <u>free</u> <u>this</u> <u>Sunday</u>?

M Sunday? Oh... We were <u>planning</u> <u>to</u> <u>go</u> shopping on Sunday. Why? What's going on?

W Oh, we just thought it would be nice to <u>have</u> you <u>over</u> <u>for</u> <u>lunch</u>.

M Well, let me talk about it with Rosa. I'll let you know for sure tonight. Is that all right?

W Okay. I'll be <u>waiting</u> <u>for</u> <u>your</u> <u>call</u>.

M Sure. Talk to you later.

남 여보세요?

여 아, 안녕, Ken. 어떻게 지내니?

남 잘 지내. 고마워. 넌 어떠니, Cathy?

여 그럭저럭 지내. 음, Tony와 내가 궁금한 게 있어서… 이번 주 일요일에 너와 Rosa는 시간이 있니?

남 일요일? 아… 우리는 일요일에 쇼핑하러 가기로 계획했어. 왜? 무슨 일 있어?

여 아, 우리는 그냥 너희 부부를 점심 식사에 초대하면 좋겠다고 생각했거든.

남 그러면, 그것에 관해 Rosa와 이야기해 볼게. 오늘 밤에 확실히 말해 줄게. 괜찮겠어?

여 좋아. 네 전화를 기다리고 있을게.

남 알았어. 나중에 이야기하자.

●●
for sure 확실히

---

06 다음 표를 보면서 대화를 듣고, Olivia가 탑승한 비행기로 가장 적절한 것을 고르시오.

	Flight Number	Arrival Time	From	Status
①	053	8:00	San Francisco	Delayed
②	694	8:20	Salt Lake City	On Time
③	705	8:35	Portland	On Time
④	950	9:00	Phoenix	Arrived
⑤	821	9:20	Los Angeles	Arrived

M <u>Which</u> <u>flight</u> is Olivia coming in on?

W I can't remember. It's <u>eight</u> <u>hundred</u>... something.

M Anyway, she's coming in from Phoenix, right?

W No, actually, her flight <u>originated</u> <u>in</u> L.A.

M I thought she lived in Phoenix.

W She does, but she <u>stopped</u> <u>off</u> in L.A. to visit a friend on the way.

M Oh! Hey, is that her flight?

W You're right. <u>That</u> <u>must</u> <u>be</u> <u>it</u>. Let's hurry and meet her.

남 Olivia는 어느 비행기로 오고 있는 거야?

여 기억이 안 나. 800… 몇 번인데.

남 어쨌든, Phoenix에서 오고 있는 거 맞지?

여 아니, 사실, 그녀의 비행기는 L.A.발이야.

남 그녀는 Phoenix에 살았던 것 같은데.

여 맞아, 그렇지만 그녀는 오는 길에 친구를 방문하려고 L.A.에 잠시 들렀어.

남 오! 이봐, 저거 그녀가 탄 비행기 아냐?

여 맞아. 그게 분명해. 서둘러 가서 그녀를 만나자.

●●
stop off 잠시 들르다

07 대화를 듣고, 무엇에 관한 내용인지 가장 적절한 것을 고르시오.

① 영화　　　② 음악
③ 잡지　　　④ 철학
⑤ 화가

W Do you like Mozart?

M Yes, Mozart is <u>one of my favorites</u>, especially his *Marriage of Figaro*.

W It's very moving, isn't it? What about <u>other</u> <u>styles</u> <u>of</u> <u>music</u>, for example, jazz?

M I also really like jazz. Miles Davis and Charlie Parker are the best.

W I didn't know you <u>were a music fan</u>.

M I think everyone loves music. It's part of being human, I think.

W And a philosopher, too. You seem to be a very <u>interesting person</u>.

M I don't think so, but thanks for the <u>compliment</u>.

여 너 모차르트 좋아하니?

남 응, 내가 가장 좋아하는 사람 중의 하나가 모차르트야, 특히 그의 '피가로의 결혼'을 좋아해.

여 그 곡은 매우 감동적이지, 그렇지 않니? 다른 종류의 음악은 어때, 예를 들면 재즈 같은 건?

남 난 재즈도 정말 좋아해. Miles Davis랑 Charlie Parker가 최고지.

여 난 네가 음악 팬인지 몰랐어.

남 난 모든 사람들이 음악을 사랑한다고 생각해. 음악은 인간 생활의 일부분이라고 생각하거든.

여 게다가 철학자이기까지. 넌 참 흥미로운 사람인 것 같다.

남 난 그렇게 생각하지 않지만, 칭찬은 고마워.

●●
especially 특히　**moving** 감동적인
for example 예를 들면　**philosopher** 철학자
compliment 칭찬

08 다음을 듣고, 남자의 의견으로 가장 적절한 것을 고르시오.

① 스트레스는 만병의 근원이다.
② 휴식은 현대인들에게 필수이다.
③ 운동으로 삶의 질을 높일 수 있다.
④ 규칙적인 생활은 건강에 유익하다.
⑤ 현대인들은 운동할 시간이 없을 만큼 바쁘다.

Fifteen to <u>thirty</u> <u>minutes</u> <u>of</u> <u>exercise</u> three days a week could perhaps <u>save</u> <u>your</u> <u>life</u>. Yet many of us don't get any exercise at all. We work or go to school, come home, eat, watch television, and go to bed. The next day, we <u>repeat</u> <u>this</u> <u>routine</u>. Exercise makes us <u>more</u> <u>relaxed</u>. We sleep better. We have more energy. We are happier in general. Once we finally decide to <u>take</u> <u>good</u> <u>care</u> <u>of</u> ourselves, our lives can <u>change</u> for the better <u>immediately</u>.

일주일에 3일, 15분에서 30분의 운동은 어쩌면 당신의 생명을 구할지도 모릅니다. 그러나 많은 사람들이 운동을 전혀 하지 않습니다. 우리는 일하거나 학교에 가고, 집에 와서 먹고, 텔레비전을 보고, 잠자리에 듭니다. 그 다음날 이러한 일과를 반복합니다. 우리는 운동으로 긴장을 더욱 풀 수 있습니다. 잠을 더 잘 잡니다. 더 많은 에너지를 얻기도 합니다. 일반적으로 기분이 더 좋습니다. 일단 우리가 마침내 스스로를 잘 챙기기로 결심한다면, 우리의 삶은 즉시 더 나은 쪽으로 바뀔 수 있습니다.

●●
relaxed 편안한, 긴장을 푼　**in general** 일반적으로　**for the better** 더 나은 쪽으로

09

대화를 듣고, 여자가 생각하는 남자는 어떤 사람인지 고르시오.

① 게으른 사람
② 안전을 중시하는 사람 ✓
③ 자기 안전만 생각하는 사람
④ 자기보다 남을 먼저 생각하는 사람
⑤ 쓸데없는 일에 시간을 낭비하는 사람

W What is that noise?

M It's the new smoke alarm I installed. It will tell us if there's a fire in the house.

W That's a great idea. Everyone should have one.

M It's important to test it once a month to make sure it works.

W You really think a lot about safety, don't you?

M Safety is so important. We can avoid a lot of unnecessary pain if we are smart.

W I agree completely.

M I also check our door locks once a week to make sure they're functional. Better safe than sorry.

여 저 소리는 뭐지?

남 내가 설치한 새 연기 경보기야. 집에 불이 났는지 알려 줄 거야.

여 아주 좋은 생각이다. 모든 사람들이 하나쯤 가지고 있어야 하는데.

남 그것이 작동함을 확인하기 위해 한 달에 한 번 그것을 점검하는 것이 중요해.

여 넌 정말로 안전에 대해서 많이 생각하는구나, 그렇지 않니?

남 안전은 정말로 중요해. 우리가 현명하면 불필요한 고통을 많이 피할 수 있으니까.

여 전적으로 동의해.

남 난 문 잠금 장치도 가동되는지 확인하기 위해서 일주일에 한 번씩 점검해. 나중에 후회하는 것보다는 미리 대비하는 편이 낫거든.

●●
install 설치하다 **important** 중요한 **make sure** ~임을 확인하다 **unnecessary** 불필요한 **functional** 가동되는

10

대화를 듣고, 남자가 표 값으로 지불한 총금액을 고르시오.

① $30　　② $70
③ $90 ✓　　④ $120
⑤ $150

M Guess what I bought today.

W Give me a hint!

M It's something you have always wanted to see.

W I don't know. I give up. Just tell me.

M I bought three tickets for *The Phantom of the Opera* tomorrow night. The tickets were only 30 dollars each.

W Wow! Are you going to take me with you?

M Of course! Why do you think I bought many tickets?

W Thanks. Can I ask you who the last one is for?

M It's for your sister. You once said she was crazy about that musical, too.

W How thoughtful of you! Thanks. Really, thanks.

남 오늘 내가 뭘 샀는지 맞춰 봐.

여 힌트 좀 줘!

남 네가 항상 보고 싶어 했던 거야.

여 모르겠어. 포기할래. 그냥 말해 줘.

남 내일 밤 '오페라의 유령' 표를 세 장 샀어. 표 값도 한 장에 30달러밖에 안 하더라.

여 와! 나 데려가 줄 거지?

남 물론이지! 왜 내가 표를 여러 장 샀겠어?

여 고마워. 남은 표 한 장은 누굴 위한 건지 물어봐도 되니?

남 네 여동생을 위한 거야. 그녀도 그 뮤지컬에 푹 빠져 있다고 네가 예전에 말했잖아.

여 넌 정말 사려 깊구나! 고마워. 정말 고마워.

●●
phantom 유령 **each** 각각 **be crazy about** ~에 푹 빠져 있다 **thoughtful** 사려 깊은

11 대화를 듣고, 남자가 여자에게 소리를 줄여 달라고 말한 이유로 가장 적절한 것을 고르시오.

① 에세이를 써야 해서
② 다른 음악을 듣고 있어서
③ 랩 음악을 좋아하지 않아서
④ 엄마가 소리를 줄이라고 해서
⑤ 옆집에서 시끄럽다고 연락이 와서

M Julia!

W What?

M Turn down the music, please.

W What's the problem? Don't you like rap music?

M Yes, I do, but I can't write my essay and listen to music at the same time.

W Are you saying you can't do two things at the same time?

M Don't be sarcastic. Just turn it down, or I will call Mom.

W Okay, okay. Relax.

M Thank you. I'll finish my essay in an hour, so you can turn up your music then. Okay?

W All right.

남 Julia!

여 왜?

남 음악 소리 좀 줄여 줘.

여 뭐가 문제야? 랩 음악 안 좋아해?

남 좋아하지, 그렇지만 음악을 들으면서 동시에 에세이를 쓸 수는 없어.

여 두 가지 일을 동시에 할 수 없다는 말이야?

남 빈정대지 마. 그냥 소리 좀 줄여 줘, 안 그러면 엄마를 부를 거야.

여 알았어, 알았어. 진정해.

남 고마워. 한 시간 내에 에세이를 끝낼 테니까, 그때 음악 소리를 크게 해도 돼. 알았지?

여 알았어.

● ●
at the same time 동시에 **sarcastic** 빈정대는, 비꼬는

12 대화를 듣고, 대화 내용과 일치하지 <u>않는</u> 것을 고르시오.

① 여자는 차가 없어서 불편함을 느낀다.
② 남자는 작년에 차를 구입했다.
③ 여자는 새 차를 보러 갈 예정이다.
④ 남자는 여자가 차를 살펴보는 데 도움을 줄 것이다.
⑤ 두 사람은 오후 6시에 만나기로 했다.

W It's inconvenient not to have a car. I always have to ask around for a ride.

M I know what you mean. That's why I bought a car last year.

W So I'm going to look at a secondhand car this evening.

M That's great. You're going to have a car.

W But you know I don't know anything about cars.

M Hmm… Do you want me to go with you and have a look at it?

W Yes, it would be great if you could check whether there's nothing wrong with it.

M No problem. What time shall we meet?

W At 6 p.m. Are you okay with that?

M Sure. See you then.

여 차가 없는 것은 불편해. 난 항상 차를 태워 줄 수 있는지 이리저리로 알아보러 다녀야 하거든.

남 무슨 말인지 알아. 그것이 내가 작년에 차를 샀던 이유야.

여 그래서 난 오늘 저녁에 중고차를 하나 보려고 해.

남 잘됐구나. 차를 갖게 되겠네.

여 하지만 너도 알다시피 난 차에 대해 아는 것이 없어.

남 흠… 내가 같이 가서 차를 살펴봐 줄까?

여 응, 네가 차에 문제가 있는지 없는지 점검해 줄 수 있다면 좋겠어.

남 문제 없어. 우리 몇 시에 만날까?

여 오후 6시에. 괜찮겠니?

남 좋아. 그때 보자.

● ●
inconvenient 불편한 **That's why ~** 그것이 ~한 이유이다 **secondhand** 중고의

13

대화를 듣고, 남자의 마지막 말에 이어질 여자의 말로 가장 적절한 것을 고르시오.

① I'd like to learn yoga from him.
② Why don't you come over here?
③ Yeah, I started about two months ago.
④ How do you know about my yoga teacher?
⑤ He has never learned yoga before, hasn't he?

W Hi, Tom. I'm glad that you made it. Come on in.
M Wow! It looks like the party is in full swing.
W Yeah. Everybody is having fun. Oh, I'd like you to meet my sister, Jennifer.
M Which one is she?
W She's sitting on the sofa over there.
M Do you mean the woman wearing the red blouse with the long blond(e) hair?
W That's right.
M Uh, and who's the man sitting next to her? The man with the leather jacket?
W Oh, that's Bob, my yoga teacher.
M Yoga teacher! I never knew you were into yoga.
W Yeah, I started about two months ago.

여 안녕, Tom. 네가 와 줘서 기뻐. 안으로 들어와.
남 와! 파티가 한창 진행 중인 것 같네.
여 응. 모두가 즐거운 시간을 보내고 있어. 오, 네가 내 자매인 Jennifer를 만나 봤으면 해.
남 누가 그녀니?
여 그녀는 저기 소파에 앉아 있어.
남 긴 금발 머리에 빨간색 블라우스를 입은 여자 말이니?
여 맞아.
남 어, 그리고 그녀 옆에 앉아 있는 남자는 누구야? 가죽 재킷을 입고 있는 남자.
여 오, 그 사람은 내 요가 선생님이신 Bob이야.
남 요가 선생님! 난 네가 요가에 관심이 있는 줄 전혀 몰랐어.
여 응, 2개월 전쯤에 시작했어.

●●

in full swing 한창 진행 중인   leather 가죽
be into ~에 관심이 있다

14

대화를 듣고, 여자의 마지막 말에 이어질 남자의 말로 가장 적절한 것을 고르시오.

① It's too expensive.
② Well, they're a little tight.
③ I feel great this afternoon.
④ I want something cheaper.
⑤ You always sell good shoes.

W What kind of shoes would you like, sir? We have various kinds of shoes.
M Well, I'm looking for some walking shoes. Would suede shoes be good for that?
W Yes, they would, but perhaps calfskin shoes would be the best.
M Okay. Could you show me several pairs of each kind?
W Certainly, sir. What's your size, please?
M Nine and a half.
W Here's a pair in your size. They are very good for the price.
M Could I try them on?
W Certainly. How do they feel?
M Well, they're a little tight.

여 어떤 종류의 신발을 원하시나요? 우리는 다양한 종류의 신발을 가지고 있답니다.
남 음, 전 보행용 신발을 찾고 있어요. 스웨이드 신발이 좋을까요?
여 예, 그렇지요, 하지만 아마 송아지 가죽 신발이 가장 좋을 거예요.
남 좋아요. 각 종류로 몇 켤레 보여 주시겠어요?
여 물론이죠. 사이즈가 어떻게 되시나요?
남 9.5요.
여 여기 고객님 사이즈로 한 켤레 있습니다. 가격 면에서도 매우 좋습니다.
남 신어 봐도 될까요?
여 물론이죠. 느낌이 어떠세요?
남 음, 약간 끼는군요.

●●

various 다양한   casual 캐주얼의, 평상복의
perhaps 아마, 어쩌면   calfskin 송아지 가죽

15 다음 상황 설명을 듣고, Emma가 Jamie에게 할 말로 가장 적절한 것을 고르시오.

① You have to have medical examinations regularly.

② Keep your hospital gown on until after the surgery.

③ I don't think you'll be able to get through the night.

④ You're tough. You'll get back on your feet in no time.

⑤ Better than I thought I would. Thank you for coming by.

Jamie was <u>diagnosed</u> <u>with</u> <u>cancer</u>, and the news that she might only live up to six months was a <u>great</u> <u>shock</u> to her, her family, and her friends. However, she was determined to look into all <u>available</u> <u>treatments</u> that might cure her or extend her life because she didn't want to leave her husband and lovely little daughter. She decided to look up <u>every</u> <u>possible</u> <u>way</u> for hope of preserving her life. And Emma <u>wants</u> <u>to</u> <u>encourage</u> her friend Jamie. In this situation, what would Emma most likely say to Jamie?

Emma: <u>You're tough. You'll get back on your feet in no time.</u>

Jamie는 암을 진단받았고, 그녀가 6개월 정도밖에 못 산다는 소식은 그녀와 그녀의 가족과 그녀의 친구들에게 매우 큰 충격이었다. 하지만, 그녀는 자신의 남편과 사랑스러운 어린 딸을 남겨 두고 가기를 원하지 않았기 때문에, 치료하거나 생명을 연장시킬 모든 가능한 치료법을 찾아보기로 결심했다. 그녀는 삶을 보전하고자 하는 희망으로 가능한 모든 방법을 찾아보기로 결심했다. 그리고 Emma는 자신의 친구인 Jamie를 격려하기를 원한다. 이런 상황에서, Emma는 Jamie에게 뭐라고 말하겠는가?

Emma: 너는 강해. 넌 곧 회복될 거야.

● ●
be diagnosed with ~로 진단받다 **cancer** 암 **be determined to** ~하기로 결심하다 **treatment** 치료(법) **cure** 치료하다 **extend** (기간을) 연장하다, 늘이다 **preserve** 보전하다, 지키다

◗ REVIEW TEST p. 119

A ① cure, 치료하다 ② moving, 감동적인 ③ install, 설치하다 ④ expert, 전문가 ⑤ leather, 가죽 ⑥ cancer, 암 ⑦ extend, (기간을) 연장하다, 늘이다 ⑧ thoughtful, 사려 깊은 ⑨ secondhand, 중고의 ⑩ inconvenient, 불편한 ⑪ in general, 일반적으로 ⑫ for example, 예를 들면

B ① various kinds ② That's why ③ make sure ④ mechanical equipment ⑤ is crazy about ⑥ avoid, unnecessary pain ⑦ for the better ⑧ at the same time

문제 및 정답	받아쓰기 및 녹음내용	해석

01

대화를 듣고, 여자의 현재 몸무게를 고르시오.

① ②

③ ④

⑤

W My goal is to get down to 110 pounds by my twenty-fifth birthday.

M Isn't that <u>low</u> for someone <u>of your</u> height?

W I'm only five feet six and a half inches.

M Wait. How tall is that <u>in centimeters</u>?

W It's about 168 cm.

M Really? Then you definitely <u>shouldn't</u> <u>weigh</u> <u>below</u> 115 pounds.

W But that's how much <u>I weigh</u> right now!

M Exactly. And you look very good!

여 내 목표는 25번째 생일까지 110파운드로 몸무게를 줄이는 거야.

남 키가 너만 한 사람에게 그건 적지 않니?

여 내 키는 겨우 5'6피트 0.5인치야.

남 잠깐. 센티미터로는 키가 얼마야?

여 168cm 정도야.

남 정말? 그러면 확실히 몸무게가 115파운드 밑으로 가면 안 돼.

여 그렇지만 그게 지금 내 몸무게인걸!

남 바로 그래. 그리고 너 아주 보기 좋아!

● ●
goal 목표 **height** 키, 신장 **definitely** 확실히, 분명히

02

대화를 듣고, 두 사람이 대화하는 장소로 가장 적절한 곳을 고르시오.

① 식당 ② 병원
③ 시장 ④ 체육관
⑤ 영화관

M How's that pasta <u>of yours</u>?

W It's delicious. How's your dish?

M Not bad. But it's not as good as <u>I expected</u>.

W Do you <u>want</u> <u>to</u> <u>try</u> <u>some</u> of my pasta?

M Sure.

W Do you love pasta?

M Who doesn't like pasta?

W Well, it's <u>one of my</u> favorite <u>kinds</u> of food.

M It's not my favorite, but I like it. My favorite food is steak.

W Steak? I <u>don't</u> <u>care</u> <u>for</u> meat. I <u>prefer</u> <u>seafood</u> to meat.

M No seafood for me. It makes me sick.

W That's too bad.

남 네 파스타는 어때?

여 맛있어. 네 요리는?

남 나쁘지 않아. 하지만 내가 기대했던 것만큼 맛있지는 않아.

여 내 파스타 좀 먹어 볼래?

남 물론이지.

여 파스타 좋아하니?

남 누가 파스타를 안 좋아하겠어?

여 그래, 그건 내가 가장 좋아하는 음식 종류 중 하나야.

남 그건 내가 가장 좋아하는 건 아니지만, 나도 좋아하기는 해. 내가 가장 좋아하는 음식은 스테이크야.

여 스테이크? 난 고기를 좋아하지 않아. 나는 고기보다 해산물을 더 좋아해.

남 내겐 해산물이 맞지 않더라. 그건 나를 메스껍게 해.

여 정말 안됐다.

● ●
expect 기대하다 **care for** ~을 좋아하다
seafood 해산물

03 다음을 듣고, 남자의 직업으로 가장 적절한 것을 고르시오.

① 가수　　　✔② 군인
③ 교수　　　④ 경호원
⑤ 비행기 조종사

To be honest, I joined the military just to earn money for college. I wasn't even interested in national defense. Strangely enough though, after finishing my two-year commitment, I didn't want to leave. Of course, I was lucky to have really great officers who taught me a lot. I learned all about weapons, and I even got special training as a communications expert. You can't learn this sort of stuff anywhere else. That's for sure.

솔직히 말하자면, 저는 단지 대학에 갈 돈을 벌기 위해 군대에 갔어요. 저는 국방에는 관심조차 없었어요. 그런데 정말 이상하게도, 2년간의 복무를 마치고 나서도 떠나고 싶지 않았어요. 물론, 운이 좋게도 제게 많은 걸 가르쳐 주신 정말 훌륭한 장교분들이 계셨어요. 저는 무기에 관한 모든 걸 배웠고, 심지어 통신 전문가로서 특별 훈련을 받기도 했죠. 당신은 이런 종류의 것을 다른 어디에서도 배울 수 없어요. 그건 확실해요.

●●
to be honest 솔직히 말하자면　**national defense** 국방　**commitment** 복무, 책무　**weapon** 무기

---

04 대화를 듣고, 두 사람의 관계로 가장 적절한 것을 고르시오.

① 비서 - 사장　　✔② 기자 - 매니저
③ 면접관 - 지원자　④ 의사 - 운동선수
⑤ 배우 - 영화감독

M Hello?
W Hello? Is this Mia's phone?
M Yes. But I am her manager. She is busy at the moment. What can I do for you?
W My name is Sandra. I'm with *News Magazine*. My magazine has decided to do a story about her new album and wants an interview with her. If it's possible, can I see her today?
M Well, she just canceled something at 3 p.m., so if you don't mind, she can see you for half an hour. Is this enough?
W Yes. That's perfect.
M Then why don't we meet in her office in Gangnam?
W Great! I'm looking forward to seeing you and Mia there.

남 여보세요?
여 여보세요? Mia 씨의 전화인가요?
남 네. 하지만 저는 그녀의 매니저입니다. 그녀는 지금 바쁩니다. 무슨 일이신가요?
여 제 이름은 Sandra입니다. 저는 News Magazine에 근무합니다. 저희 잡지사에서는 그녀의 새 음반에 대한 기사를 싣기로 결정해서, 그녀와 인터뷰를 하고 싶은데요. 가능하다면, 그분을 오늘 뵐 수 있을까요?
남 글쎄요, 그녀의 오후 3시 약속이 지금 막 취소됐어요, 그래서 괜찮으시다면 그녀가 30분 정도는 당신을 만날 수 있겠네요. 그 정도면 충분한가요?
여 네. 아주 좋아요.
남 그러면 강남에 있는 그녀의 사무실에서 만나는 게 어떨까요?
여 좋습니다! 그곳에서 당신과 Mia 씨를 만나기를 기대하겠습니다.

●●
at the moment 지금, 현재

05 대화를 듣고, 여자가 전화를 건 목적으로 가장 적절한 것을 고르시오.

① 길을 물어보려고
② 소음에 항의하려고
③ 피자를 주문하려고
④ 부엌 리모델링을 의뢰하려고
⑤ 누수로 인해 도움을 요청하려고

M Hello? Management office. How may I help you?

W Hello, Mr. Smith? This is Ms. Cook.

M Uh, Ms. Cook... in apartment 1306?

W No, not 1306. 1308.

M Oh, right. What can I do for you? Is it the kitchen sink again?

W No, it's not the sink. The ceiling in the bedroom is leaking.

M All right. I'll be up sometime in the afternoon.

W I'd appreciate it if you could come up right now. There's water all over the floor.

M That's a bad leak. I'll be there soon.

W Thanks a lot.

남 여보세요? 관리 사무소입니다. 무엇을 도와드릴까요?

여 여보세요, Smith 씨인가요? 저는 Cook입니다.

남 아, 1306호에 사시는 Cook 씨인가요?

여 아뇨, 1306호가 아니라 1308호입니다.

남 아, 그렇군요. 무엇을 도와드릴까요? 또 부엌 싱크대입니까?

여 아뇨, 싱크대 문제가 아니에요. 침실의 천장에서 물이 새고 있어요.

남 알겠습니다. 오후 중에 한번 올라가겠습니다.

여 지금 바로 와 주실 수 있다면 감사하겠어요. 바닥 전체가 물바다예요.

남 심하게 새는군요. 곧 가겠습니다.

여 정말 감사합니다.

●●
ceiling 천장 **leak** (물·가스 등이) 새다; 누출

---

06 다음을 듣고, 오늘의 날씨로 가장 적절한 것을 고르시오.

①
②
③
④
⑤

Good morning. This is Lucy Scott with today's weather. It's a chilly 49°F out there right now, but that will change soon. Highs today are expected to reach all the way up to the mid-sixties before going back down again as evening sets in. Visibility will not be good today. The fog we're currently experiencing will not completely go away, and the hazy weather will continue until tomorrow.

안녕하세요. 오늘의 날씨의 Lucy Scott입니다. 지금은 바깥 기온이 화씨 49도로 쌀쌀하지만, 곧 바뀔 것입니다. 오늘의 최고 기온은 해가 저물어 다시 내려가기 전까지 60도 중반까지 오를 것으로 전망됩니다. 오늘 가시도는 좋지 않겠습니다. 현재 긴 안개가 완전히 개지 않을 것이고, 안개 낀 날씨는 내일까지 계속되겠습니다.

●●
chilly 쌀쌀한, 추운 **reach** 이르다, 도달하다
set in 시작되다 **visibility** 가시도, 시야
currently 현재 **hazy** 안개 낀, 흐린

07 대화를 듣고, 남자가 생각하는 가장 중요한 자질로 적절한 것을 고르시오.

① 관용 ② 친절
③ 공감 ④ 도덕성
⑤ 호기심

M My wife and I are going to have a baby.

W Congratulations! That's incredible.

M Thanks. I'm sure it's <u>difficult</u> to be a <u>parent</u>. We have to teach children the important things about life.

W I think generosity is <u>important to teach</u>. What do you think?

M That's important.

W Kindness is another thing. Teaching <u>how to share</u> is good, too.

M You're right again. But I think the most important thing is <u>empathy</u>.

W Why do you say that?

M A child should also learn to <u>understand</u> <u>other</u> <u>people's feelings</u>.

W That's a good point.

남 내 아내와 나에게 아기가 생길 거야.

여 축하해! 굉장한 소식이다.

남 고마워. 부모가 된다는 것은 분명 어려운 일이야. 애들한테 인생에 관한 중요한 것들을 가르쳐야 하니까.

여 관용을 가르치는 것이 중요한 것 같아. 넌 어떻게 생각해?

남 중요한 것이지.

여 친절은 또 하나의 덕목이지. 나누는 법을 가르치는 것도 좋고.

남 그 말도 맞아. 그렇지만 가장 중요한 것은 공감인 것 같아.

여 왜 그렇게 생각하는데?

남 아이들 역시 다른 사람들의 기분을 이해하는 것을 배워야만 하니까.

여 좋은 지적이야.

● ●

generosity 관용, 너그러움 **share** 나누다, 공유하다 **empathy** 공감

---

08 대화를 듣고, 대화의 마지막에 남자가 느꼈을 심정으로 가장 적절한 것을 고르시오.

① furious ② jealous
③ worried ④ relieved
⑤ embarrassed

W Hi. How are you?

M Where have you been? I <u>haven't</u> <u>seen</u> <u>you</u> in a month.

W I was in the hospital. I had to <u>get an operation</u>.

M An operation? What kind of operation?

W I had to <u>get</u> a large lump <u>removed</u> from my breast.

M Lump? Oh, my god. I can't believe it. Was it serious?

W No, the doctor said it <u>wasn't serious</u> and everything would be fine.

M <u>Thank goodness</u> it wasn't serious.

W Yes, I feel fine now. No need to worry.

M <u>I'm glad to hear</u> you're fine.

여 안녕하세요. 어떻게 지내셨어요?

남 어디에 계셨어요? 한 달 동안 안 보이시던데.

여 저는 병원에 있었어요. 수술을 받아야 했거든요.

남 수술요? 무슨 수술요?

여 가슴에서 큰 혹을 제거해야 했어요.

남 혹이요? 오, 이런. 믿을 수가 없군요. 심각한 거였나요?

여 아뇨, 의사가 그러는데 심각하지는 않고 괜찮아질 거래요.

남 심각하지 않았다니 천만 다행이네요.

여 네, 지금은 괜찮아요. 걱정하실 필요 없어요.

남 괜찮다고 하시니 다행이에요.

● ●

operation 수술 **lump** 혹 **remove** 제거하다 **breast** 가슴, 유방

09 대화를 듣고, 두 사람이 이번 학기에 책 값으로 지불한 총 금액을 고르시오.

① $200 ② $300
③ $500 ✓ ④ $600
⑤ $900

W I can't believe how expensive university books are.

M What do you mean?

W One of my books costs 100 dollars.

M I know. They are expensive. This semester, I spent 200 dollars on books.

W It seems they're getting far too expensive. I had to pay 300 dollars this semester.

M But you got a scholarship, didn't you?

W School still costs too much. I have other expenses, too.

M Like what?

W You live at home, but I live in a dormitory. I have to pay 600 dollars every month.

M I guess I see your point.

여 대학교 교재가 얼마나 비싼지 믿을 수가 없다.

남 무슨 소리야?

여 내 책 중의 하나는 가격이 100달러씩이나 해.

남 알아. 비싸지. 난 이번 학기에 책 값으로 200달러나 썼어.

여 너무 턱없이 비싸지는 것 같아. 이번 학기에 난 300달러나 써야 했어.

남 그렇지만 넌 장학금을 탔잖아, 그렇지 않니?

여 그래도 대학 생활에는 비용이 너무 많이 들어. 다른 데 쓸 데도 있고 말이야.

남 어디에?

여 너는 집에 살지만, 난 기숙사에서 살잖아. 난 매달 600달러를 내야 하거든.

남 무슨 말인지 알 것 같아.

●●
scholarship 장학금 expense 돈이 드는 일
dormitory 기숙사

---

10 대화를 듣고, 여자가 강아지를 싫어하는 이유로 가장 적절한 것을 고르시오.

① 대소변을 잘 가리지 못해서
② 강아지 털 알레르기가 있어서
③ 가끔 공격적인 행동을 보여서
④ 강아지에게서 특유의 냄새가 나서
⑤ 어렸을 때 개에게 물린 적이 있어서 ✓

W What is that, Eric?

M It's my new puppy.

W Keep it away from me, please!

M Relax. He is such a gentle dog.

W I really don't care how gentle you think he is.

M Why are you reacting like that?

W When I was a little girl, a dog bit me on my leg.

M Oh, that's why you are so scared of dogs. Don't worry. He won't bite you. I've trained him well.

여 그거 뭐니, Eric?

남 내 새 강아지야.

여 제발 나한테서 치워 줘!

남 진정해. 아주 순한 개야.

여 네가 생각하기에 이 개가 얼마나 순한가는 정말 상관없어.

남 왜 그런 반응을 보이는 거야?

여 내가 어렸을 때 어떤 개가 내 다리를 물었거든.

남 아, 그래서 그렇게 개를 무서워하는 거구나. 걱정 마. 이 개는 널 안 물 거니까. 내가 잘 훈련시켰거든.

●●
gentle 순한, 온화한 bite 물다

11 대화를 듣고, 남자가 해야 할 일로 언급되지 <u>않은</u> 것을 고르시오.

① 욕실 청소　　② 책상 정리
③ 부엌 청소　　④ 잠자리 정돈
⑤ 장난감 정리

M Mom, can I go outside to play?

W Well, did you get your <u>regular Saturday chores</u> done?

M Oh, Mom. Do I have to?

W You know the rules. No playing until your <u>work is done</u>.

M So what is my work?

W Well, first, you have to <u>clean the bathroom</u>, including the toilet. And don't forget to scrub the bathtub.

M Is there anything else?

W Don't forget to wipe the walls. After that, sweep and <u>mop the kitchen floor</u>, and be sure to polish the table in the living room.

M Okay, I will.

W And then <u>make your bed</u>, pick up all your toys, and <u>put them away</u>.

남 엄마, 밖에 나가서 놀아도 되나요?

여 글쎄, 토요일마다 하기로 한 일들은 다 했니?

남 오, 엄마. 제가 해야 해요?

여 규칙을 알잖니. 일을 끝내기 전까지는 놀지 않기.

남 그럼, 제 일이 뭔가요?

여 음, 첫째로 변기를 포함해서 욕실을 청소해야 해. 그리고 욕조를 문질러 씻는 것을 잊지 말고.

남 또 있나요?

여 벽을 닦는 걸 잊지 마. 그다음에는 부엌 바닥을 쓸고 대걸레로 닦고, 거실 테이블을 꼭 닦도록 해.

남 알았어요, 그렇게 할게요.

여 그러고 나서 네 잠자리를 정돈하고, 네 장난감은 모두 모아서 치워 두거라.

●●

chore (정기적으로 하는) 일, 가사　**scrub** 문질러 씻다　**sweep** (빗자루로) 쓸다　**mop** 대걸레로 닦다　**polish** (윤이 나도록) 닦다　**make one's bed** 잠자리를 정돈하다

12 대화를 듣고, 대화 내용과 일치하지 <u>않는</u> 것을 고르시오.

① 두 사람은 오랜만에 만났다.
② 여자는 요즘 피곤함을 느낀다.
③ 여자는 오늘 고객들을 만나기로 되어 있다.
④ 남자는 여자에게 할 일을 기록해 보라고 조언했다.
⑤ 남자는 여자가 일정을 기록하는 것을 도와주었다.

W Richard, I'm so lucky to see you!

M <u>It's been a while</u> since I saw you. How are you doing?

W I'm not doing very well. I'm so <u>tired these days</u>.

M What's the matter?

W I have so many things to do. I don't know <u>where to start</u>.

M Tell me what you have to do today.

W I have to make a reservation call. And I have to <u>meet my clients</u>. I also have to write a report to submit to my company.

M First, <u>write down</u> what you have to do <u>on paper</u>. You will know what to do first.

W You mean recording today's schedule, right?

M Yes, that's right. That way, you can <u>manage</u> your <u>busy schedule</u>.

W Thank you for your advice.

여 Richard 씨, 당신을 뵙게 되다니 전 정말 운이 좋군요!

남 오랜만에 만나 뵙는군요. 어떻게 지내세요?

여 그리 잘 지내지 못해요. 전 요새 너무 피곤하답니다.

남 무슨 일 있으세요?

여 저는 해야 할 일들이 너무 많아요. 어디서부터 시작해야 할지 모르겠어요.

남 당신이 오늘 해야 할 일을 얘기해 보세요.

여 예약 전화를 해야 해요. 그리고 고객들을 만나야 하고요. 회사에 제출할 보고서도 써야 해요.

남 우선, 당신이 해야 할 일을 종이에 적어 보세요. 무엇을 먼저 해야 할지 알 거예요.

여 오늘의 일정을 기록해 보라는 뜻이지요?

남 네, 맞아요. 그런 방식으로 당신은 바쁜 일정을 관리할 수 있어요.

여 조언해 주셔서 감사해요.

●●

client 고객, 의뢰인　**submit** 제출하다　**record** 기록하다　**manage** 관리하다

13 대화를 듣고, 남자의 마지막 말에 이어질 여자의 말로 가장 적절한 것을 고르시오.

① I wish I could do that.
② I can't believe you did this to me.
③ Try not to think about what she said.
④ I'm really uncomfortable about her behavior.
⑤ I'm sorry. I'll be more considerate in the future.

W I have a real problem.
M I'm shocked you said that. You're the one who <u>doesn't seem to have</u> any problems.
W Thank you for saying that but…
M What's the matter with you?
W I work so hard during the week that I'm <u>too</u> exhausted <u>to</u> do anything on the weekend.
M So <u>how late</u> do you <u>usually work</u> during the week?
W I work until 10 p.m.
M If I <u>were in your shoes</u>, I think I'd go home a little earlier and then <u>get</u> some <u>rest</u>.
W <u>I wish I could do that.</u>

여 진짜 문제가 생겼어.
남 네가 그런 말을 하다니 충격인데. 너는 문제라고는 없는 것처럼 보이는 사람이거든.
여 그렇게 말해 줘서 고마워, 그런데…
남 무슨 문제인데?
여 난 주중에 너무 열심히 일해서 주말에는 너무 지쳐서 아무것도 할 수 없어.
남 그래서, 주중에 보통 얼마나 늦게까지 일하니?
여 난 밤 10시까지 일해.
남 내가 네 입장이라면, 난 조금 더 일찍 집에 가서 휴식을 좀 취할 것 같아.
여 <u>나도 그렇게 할 수만 있다면 좋겠어.</u>

be in one's shoes ~의 입장에 처하다

---

14 대화를 듣고, 여자의 마지막 말에 이어질 남자의 말로 가장 적절한 것을 고르시오.

① Do you need anything else?
② I am sorry. I am not a pharmacist.
③ Why don't you go to a drugstore?
④ Oh, yeah. Why not? Show me your ID.
⑤ No, I can't give you any medicine without a prescription.

W Can I get some medicine here?
M Do you <u>have a prescription</u> from a doctor?
W Yes, I do.
M Let's see. I'll <u>fill</u> the prescription for you. Here you are.
W How should I take the medicine?
M You should take it three times a day <u>30 minutes after eating</u>.
W By the way, I have a terrible sore throat.
M How <u>long</u> have you <u>had it</u>?
W For three days I used a throat spray. But it didn't help me. Can you <u>give</u> me <u>some medicine</u>?
M <u>No, I can't give you any medicine without a prescription.</u>

여 여기서 약을 탈 수 있나요?
남 의사의 처방전이 있으신가요?
여 네, 있습니다.
남 어디 보죠. 약을 조제해 드리겠습니다. 여기 있습니다.
여 약을 어떻게 복용해야 하나요?
남 하루에 세 번, 식후 30분에 복용해야 합니다.
여 그런데, 저는 목이 몹시 아픕니다.
남 얼마나 오랫동안 아팠나요?
여 3일간 목에 뿌리는 스프레이를 사용했어요. 그런데 도움이 안됐어요. 약을 좀 주실 수 있나요?
남 <u>아뇨, 처방전 없이는 약을 드릴 수 없습니다.</u>

prescription 처방전, 처방 **sore throat** 인후통

15 다음 상황 설명을 듣고, Bob이 Laura에게 할 말로 가장 적절한 것을 고르시오.

① It's better if you don't get it wet for a couple of days.
② You have to know how to handle this kind of situation.
③ You should check who's out there before opening the door.
④ I think you should be more careful when you drive in the dark.
⑤ I don't appreciate your attitude. I'm so angry that I'm speechless.

Laura lives alone on the third floor of an apartment building. The front door has a peephole, a tiny piece of glass through which Laura can look out her door to check who is knocking on her door or ringing her doorbell. The peephole is a security device, but Laura never uses it. When someone knocks, she just opens the door. She thinks that she lives in a safe neighborhood, so security is not really a problem. But her friend Bob saw the news about burglars breaking into apartments where women live alone. He's worried about her. In this situation, what would Bob most likely say to Laura?

Bob: You should check who's out there before opening the door.

Laura는 아파트 건물의 3층에서 혼자 살고 있다. 현관문에는 작은 구멍이 있는데, 그 아주 작은 유리를 통해 Laura는 누가 그녀의 문을 두드리고 있는지 혹은 초인종을 누르고 있는지 확인하기 위해 문 밖을 볼 수 있다. 그 구멍은 안전 장치지만, Laura는 그것을 사용하지 않는다. 누군가가 문을 두드리면 그녀는 그냥 문을 열어 준다. 그녀는 안전한 지역에 살기에 안전은 실제로 문제가 안 된다고 생각한다. 그러나 친구인 Bob이 여자들이 혼자 사는 아파트에 침입한 강도들에 대한 뉴스를 보았다. 그는 그녀를 걱정하고 있다. 이런 상황에서, Bob은 Laura에게 뭐라고 말하겠는가?

Bob: 너는 문을 열어 주기 전에 밖에 누가 있는지를 확인해야 해.

● ●
peephole (문 등에 나 있는) 작은 구멍 **tiny** 아주 작은 **security** 안전, 보안 **device** 장치 **burglar** 강도, 절도범 **break into** ~에 침입하다

◗ REVIEW TEST p. 127

A
① hazy, 안개 낀, 흐린　② goal, 목표　③ reach, 이르다, 도달하다　④ sweep, (빗자루로) 쓸다
⑤ device, 장치　⑥ client, 고객, 의뢰인　⑦ remove, 제거하다　⑧ weapon, 무기　⑨ height, 키, 신장
⑩ dormitory, 기숙사　⑪ scholarship, 장학금　⑫ break into, ~에 침입하다

B
① scrub, bathtub　② ceiling, leaking　③ sore throat
④ at the moment　⑤ Make your bed　⑥ To be honest
⑦ manage your busy schedule　⑧ submit to my company

문제 및 정답	받아쓰기 및 녹음내용	해석

01

대화를 듣고, 여자가 남자에게 하지 말라고 충고한 것으로 가장 적절한 것을 고르시오.

① 　②

③ 　④

⑤

W It looks like you sprained your ankle.

M It's not that bad, is it?

W Well, you should be very careful.

M I know I can't jog.

W Mr. Johnson, I think it'll be difficult even to walk on your leg.

M Oh, dear. How am I going to drive?

W Well, you should avoid lifting any heavy objects. It might put too much strain on your ankle.

M Yes, I understand.

여 당신은 발목을 삔 것 같군요.

남 그렇게 심하지는 않죠, 그렇죠?

여 글쎄요, 아주 조심하셔야겠어요.

남 조깅을 할 수 없다는 건 알아요.

여 Johnson 씨, 다리로 걷는 것조차도 힘들 것 같아요.

남 오, 이런. 운전은 어떻게 하죠?

여 음, 무거운 물건을 드는 걸 피하셔야 해요. 발목에 무리가 너무 많이 가거든요.

남 네, 알겠습니다.

●●

sprain 삐다, 접질리다　**avoid** 피하다　**object** 물건, 물체　**strain** 무리, 부담

02

대화를 듣고, 두 사람이 대화하는 장소로 가장 적절한 곳을 고르시오.

① 병원　② 방송국
③ 백화점　④ 자동차 정비소
⑤ 중고차 판매장

W Hi. I have a problem with my car. I heard your ad on the radio, and I thought that maybe you could fix it.

M What's the matter with it?

W It's the transmission. It's making funny noises.

M Let's take a look at it. Is it parked outside?

W Yes. It's over there.

M Wow! What kind of car is that?

W It's a 1949 Peugeot.

M No kidding. Where did you get it?

W I bought it from a movie studio in Hollywood.

M Really? I've never seen one before. Anyway, let me see what's wrong with the transmission.

여 안녕하세요. 제 자동차에 문제가 있습니다. 라디오에서 광고를 들었는데, 아마도 당신이 고칠 수 있을 거라 생각했어요.

남 차에 무슨 문제가 있지요?

여 변속기에 문제가 있습니다. 이상한 소리를 내요.

남 한번 볼까요. 차가 밖에 세워져 있나요?

여 네. 저기에 있습니다.

남 와! 어떤 종류의 자동차입니까?

여 1949년형 Peugeot인데요.

남 설마. 어디에서 구입하셨어요?

여 할리우드에 있는 영화 촬영소에서 구입했어요.

남 정말요? 저는 전에 이런 종류의 차를 본 적이 없어요. 그건 그렇고, 변속기에 무슨 문제가 있는지 살펴보죠.

●●

ad 광고(= **advertisement**)　**transmission** (자동차의) 변속기

03 대화를 듣고, 남자의 직업으로 가장 적절한 것을 고르시오.

① 형사   ② 사진사
③ 과학자   ④ 요리사
⑤ 연극배우

M Mrs. Rose, you witnessed the convenience store robbery, didn't you?

W Yes, I did. I saw the robber when he went into the store and when he came out.

M Now, look at these pictures. Do you see that man?

W Yes, he's the one! He's the man I saw!

M He wasn't alone when he went into the store, was he?

W No, he wasn't. He was with a woman.

M Now, do you see the woman in these pictures?

W No... Sorry, but I can't remember her. The only thing that I can remember is that she was wearing a hat and sunglasses.

남 Rose 부인, 편의점 강도 사건을 목격하셨어요, 그렇지 않나요?

여 네, 그렇습니다. 저는 그 강도가 편의점 안으로 들어갈 때와 밖으로 나올 때 그를 봤습니다.

남 자, 이 사진들을 봐 주세요. 그 남자가 보입니까?

여 네, 이 남자예요! 이 사람이 제가 본 그 남자예요!

남 그가 편의점으로 들어갈 때 혼자가 아니었죠, 그렇죠?

여 네, 그래요. 한 여자와 함께 있었어요.

남 그럼, 이 사진들 중에 그 여자가 보입니까?

여 아니요… 죄송하지만 그 사람은 기억이 안 나요. 제가 기억하는 것은 그 여자가 모자와 선글라스를 쓰고 있었다는 것뿐이에요.

● ●

witness 목격하다   **convenience store** 편의점   **robbery** 강도, 도둑질

---

04 대화를 듣고, 두 사람의 관계로 가장 적절한 것을 고르시오.

① 약사 - 손님
② 의사 - 환자
③ 코치 - 운동선수
④ 면접관 - 지원자
⑤ 헬스 트레이너 - 고객

M Does this hurt?

W No.

M Or does this hurt?

W Yes. It's my leg — my left leg. I keep getting a strange pain in it.

M Could you describe this pain to me?

W It's like... like feeling pins and needles all over my left leg. I haven't been sleeping well at all.

M Do you mean the pain has been keeping you awake?

W Yes. It's been keeping me awake almost every night.

M Now, tell me... How long have you had this problem?

W The pain? For about a week now.

M I'd like you to rest for a few days and take this medicine. You should not walk for a long time or exercise for a couple of weeks.

남 여기가 아픕니까?

여 아뇨.

남 아니면 여기가 아픕니까?

여 네. 제 다리, 왼쪽 다리예요. 다리 속이 이상하게 계속 아파요.

남 그 통증을 제게 설명하실 수 있겠어요?

여 그건 마치… 왼쪽 다리 전체가 찌릿하는 느낌인 것 같아요. 잠을 제대로 자지 못하고 있어요.

남 통증 때문에 계속 잠을 설친다는 건가요?

여 예. 아파서 거의 매일 밤 잠을 못 자고 있어요.

남 그러면, 말씀해 주세요… 이 증세가 얼마나 오랫동안 계속됐나요?

여 통증이요? 이제 약 일주일 됐습니다.

남 며칠간 쉬시고 이 약을 드시는 게 좋겠어요. 몇 주 정도는 오랫동안 걷거나 운동하시면 안 됩니다.

● ●

describe 설명하다, 말하다   **pins and needles** 찌릿하는[저리는] 느낌   **awake** 자지 않는, 깨어 있는   **a couple of** 몇 개의, 두서너 개의

05 대화를 듣고, 남자가 예약한 요일과 시각을 고르시오.

① Thursday at 7:00
② Friday at 5:30
③ Friday at 6:00 ✓
④ Friday at 7:00
⑤ Saturday at 7:00

W Carlson's Ritzy Restaurant. How can I help you?

M Hi. I'd like to <u>reserve</u> a table for four <u>for Friday</u> evening.

W We already have quite a few reservations for Friday evening. What time do you want?

M I <u>was</u> <u>hoping</u> <u>for</u> sometime around 7:00.

W I'm so sorry, sir. We're <u>fully booked</u> for 7:00. Would 5:30 or 6:00 be all right?

M Yes, I suppose <u>6:00</u> would be <u>acceptable</u>.

W Wonderful. May I have your name, please?

M Sure. Please reserve it <u>under the name of</u> Noah.

W We'll see you then. Thank you for calling.

여 Carlson's Ritzy 식당입니다. 무엇을 도와 드릴까요?

남 안녕하세요. 저는 금요일 저녁에 네 명이 앉을 테이블을 예약하고 싶어요.

여 금요일 저녁은 벌써 예약이 꽤 많이 되어 있네요. 몇 시를 원하시는데요?

남 대략 7시쯤으로 예약하길 바랐는데요.

여 정말 죄송합니다, 손님. 7시는 예약이 다 찼군요. 5시 30분이나 6시도 괜찮으세요?

남 네, 6시라면 그런대로 괜찮을 것 같아요.

여 좋습니다. 성함을 말씀해 주시겠습니까?

남 네. Noah라는 이름으로 예약해 주세요.

여 그때 뵙겠습니다. 전화해 주셔서 감사합니다.

●●
reserve 예약하다 **acceptable** 그런대로 괜찮은

---

06 대화를 듣고, 여자 화장실의 위치로 가장 적절한 곳을 고르시오.

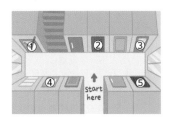

W Excuse me, but where's the <u>ladies' room</u>?

M Actually, we don't have any bathrooms in this office.

W <u>There</u> <u>must</u> <u>be</u> a bathroom somewhere in this building.

M You'll have to go out, turn left, and <u>walk</u> <u>down</u> <u>to</u> <u>the</u> <u>end</u> of the hall.

W The end of the hall. Okay.

M It's right <u>next</u> <u>to</u> <u>the</u> stairwell.

W All right. I know where that is.

여 실례합니다만, 여자 화장실이 어디죠?

남 사실은, 이 사무실 안에는 화장실이 없습니다.

여 분명히 이 건물 어딘가에는 화장실이 있을 텐데요.

남 밖으로 나가서, 왼쪽으로 돌아, 복도 끝까지 걸어가셔야 할 겁니다.

여 복도 끝이요. 알겠습니다.

남 계단통 바로 옆이에요.

여 알겠습니다. 어디에 있는지 알겠어요.

●●
ladies' room 여자 화장실 **hall** (건물 안의) 복도
stairwell 계단통

07

다음을 듣고, 약을 복용하지 말아야 할 경우로 가장 적절한 것을 고르시오.

① 휴식 중에   ② 식사 전에
③ 귀가 후에   ④ 취침 전에
⑤ 근무 중에

Please be careful not to take this medicine if you are required to be alert. This product can make you drowsy. Do not take this medicine if you intend to do something requiring concentration. It's better to take this medicine while you are resting or just before bed. You may experience other side effects from taking this medicine such as nausea, dizziness, and headaches.

당신이 정신을 차려야 할 필요가 있다면 이 약을 복용하지 않도록 주의하십시오. 이 제품은 당신을 졸리게 할 수 있습니다. 집중을 요하는 일을 하려면 이 약을 복용하지 마세요. 이 약은 휴식 중이거나 잠자리에 들기 바로 전에 복용하는 것이 더 좋습니다. 당신은 이 약의 복용으로 메스꺼움, 현기증, 두통과 같은 다른 부작용을 경험하실 수도 있습니다.

•●

be required to ~해야 하다, ~하도록 요구되다
alert 정신을 차리고 있는, 기민한   **drowsy** 졸리는
side effect 부작용   **nausea** 메스꺼움
dizziness 현기증

08

대화를 듣고, Kevin에 대한 여자의 심정으로 가장 적절한 것을 고르시오.

① angry   ② proud
③ envious   ④ worried
⑤ grateful

W I can't believe Kevin got a better mark than me on the exam. I saw him cheating with his friends.
M That's just the kind of guy he is. He doesn't care how many people he steps on.
W Once, I also saw him pick on a girl because she was overweight.
M Yeah, that sounds like him.
W I really can't stand him. We should do something about him.
M You're not the only one.
W He represents selfishness and indifference toward everyone else.
M You've got that right. Most people in our class would agree with you.

여 Kevin이 시험에서 나보다 더 좋은 점수를 받았다니 믿을 수가 없어. 나는 그가 친구들과 커닝하는 걸 봤어.
남 그 애는 그냥 그런 사람이잖아. 그 애는 자신이 얼마나 많은 사람들을 밟는지는 신경 쓰지 않아.
여 한번은 나도 그가 어떤 여자애를 뚱뚱하다는 이유로 괴롭히는 걸 봤어.
남 그래, 그 애답네.
여 그 애를 정말 못 봐주겠어. 우리는 그에 대해 무언가를 해야 해.
남 너만 그렇게 느끼는 것이 아니야.
여 그 앤 이기적이고 다른 모든 사람들에 대해서는 신경도 안 쓰는 사람의 표본이지.
남 네 말이 맞아. 우리 반 애들 대부분이 네 말에 동의할 거야.

•●

cheat (시험에서) 커닝하다, 부정 행위를 하다
pick on ~을 괴롭히다   **represent** (~의) 표본이
되다   **selfishness** 이기심   **indifference** 무
관심

09 대화를 듣고, 남자의 가방에 들어 있던 귀중품의 대략적인 가치가 얼마인지 고르시오.

① $350
② $500
③ $600
④ $700
⑤ $800

W Can I help you, sir?

M Yes, my suitcase seems to be lost.

W What does it look like?

M It's big and black with a silver handle.

W Did you have any valuables in it?

M Yes, I did. I had my clothes, worth around 250 dollars, some books worth around 100 dollars, and a gold necklace worth around 350 dollars.

W Did you buy insurance for your baggage?

M Yes, but the insurance is only for a loss of 500 dollars.

W Please fill out this form. We will look for your suitcase and will call you as soon as we find it.

M Thank you very much.

여 도와드릴까요, 선생님?

남 네, 제 여행 가방을 잃어버린 것 같습니다.

여 어떻게 생긴 것이죠?

남 크고 검은색에 은색 손잡이가 달려 있습니다.

여 그 안에 귀중품이 들어 있었습니까?

남 네, 그래요. 약 250달러 상당의 옷과 약 100달러 상당의 책 몇 권, 그리고 약 350달러 상당의 금 목걸이가 들어 있었어요.

여 수하물에 대한 보험은 드셨나요?

남 네, 하지만 보험으로는 500달러의 손실에 대해서만 보장받을 수 있습니다.

여 이 양식을 작성하세요. 저희가 여행 가방을 찾아보고 발견 즉시 연락 드리겠습니다.

남 정말 고맙습니다.

●●

valuables 귀중품

---

10 대화를 듣고, 여자가 퍼즐 맞추기를 좋아하는 이유로 가장 적절한 것을 고르시오.

① 생각하게 만들므로
② 공부에 도움이 되므로
③ 자신의 무지함을 깨닫게 하므로
④ 시간을 때우기에 가장 좋으므로
⑤ 다른 사람과 함께 맞춰 나가면서 친해지므로

W What is a three-letter word for a poisonous snake?

M Are you doing crossword puzzles again? Don't you ever get tired of them?

W On the contrary, I love them. Come on. Help me out.

M Cobra? No, that can't be it. Oh, boa! No, that's not poisonous.

W Do you see? Puzzles make you think.

M They frustrate me too much. They remind me how much I don't know.

W Oh, well. I give up finding the answer.

M Oh, now I have it: asp. What do I win?

W You win my admiration.

여 독이 있는 뱀을 뜻하는 세 글자로 된 단어가 뭐지?

남 너 또 크로스워드 퍼즐을 하고 있니? 지겹지도 않니?

여 그 반대야, 너무 좋아해. 이것 봐. 나 좀 도와줘.

남 코브라? 아니지, 그건 아니겠다. 아, 보아 뱀! 아냐, 그건 독이 없어.

여 그것 봐! 퍼즐은 네가 생각하게 만들잖아.

남 퍼즐을 하면 너무 많이 좌절하게 돼. 퍼즐은 내가 얼마나 많은 걸 모르는지를 상기시켜 주거든.

여 아, 글쎄. 난 정답 찾는 걸 포기하겠어.

남 아, 이제 알겠다. 살모사야. 내가 뭘 타게 되는 거지?

여 내 찬사를 받지.

●●

letter 글자, 문자 **poisonous** 독이 있는 **on the contrary** 그와 반대로 **frustrate** 좌절감을 주다 **admiration** 찬사, 감탄

11 대화를 듣고, 남자의 마지막 말에 이어질 내용으로 가장 적절한 것을 고르시오.

① 맨해튼의 쇼핑 명소
② 우울증을 극복하는 방법
③ 뉴욕이 대도시가 된 이유
④ 고소공포증을 치료하는 방법
⑤ 미국에 고층 건물이 세워진 이유

M Did you just get back from New York?

W Yes, at nine this morning.

M Tell me. <u>What</u> did you <u>think</u> <u>of</u> the skyscrapers there?

W Do you mean those <u>extremely</u> <u>tall</u> buildings? As far as I could judge, they were <u>horrible</u>.

M Why?

W They are too high. The sunlight <u>can't</u> <u>reach</u> the streets below. This makes shopping in Manhattan like walking down one long, dark corridor after another.

M Do you know <u>why</u> Americans <u>built</u> <u>skyscrapers</u>?

W To make me unhappy?

M No, silly. Let me tell you about it now.

남 뉴욕에서 지금 막 돌아왔니?

여 응, 오늘 아침 9시에 왔어.

남 말해 줘. 그곳의 고층 건물들에 대해 어떻게 생각했니?

여 아주 높은 건물들 말이야? 내가 판단하기로 그것들은 끔찍했어.

남 왜?

여 그것들은 너무 높아. 햇빛이 밑에 있는 거리까지 미치지 못해. 그래서 맨해튼에서 쇼핑하는 것은 길고 어두운 복도들을 잇따라 걸어가는 것 같아.

남 왜 미국인들이 고층 건물들을 세웠는지 아니?

여 나를 불행하게 하려고?

남 아냐, 바보야. 이제 내가 그것에 대해 말해 줄게.

• •

skyscraper 고층 건물 **extremely** 몹시, 극도로 **as far as** ~하는 한 **judge** 판단하다 **corridor** 복도, 회랑

---

12 대화를 듣고, 대화 내용과 일치하지 <u>않는</u> 것을 고르시오.

① 여자는 영어 수업 시간에 대화문을 암기한다.
② 여자는 암기가 영어 회화에 도움이 된다고 생각한다.
③ 남자는 암기하는 것에 어려움을 느낀다.
④ 여자의 암기 비결은 손으로 여러 번 쓰는 것이다.
⑤ 남자는 여자가 영어 회화를 잘한다고 생각한다.

M What do you do in your English class?

W We memorize <u>dialogues</u>.

M Do you mean you <u>learn</u> them <u>by</u> <u>heart</u>?

W Yes. Lots of them.

M What good does that do?

W When you memorize something, you can <u>repeat</u> <u>it</u> <u>well</u>. I think it really helps me speak English.

M I <u>have</u> <u>a</u> <u>hard</u> <u>time</u> memorizing things. How do you do that?

W I usually write dialogues on a piece of paper, and I <u>carry</u> <u>it</u> <u>with</u> <u>me</u> all the time. Whenever I'm free, I always try to memorize them.

M That's why you are <u>quite</u> <u>good</u> <u>at</u> speaking English.

남 너희는 영어 수업 시간에 무얼 하니?

여 우리는 대화문을 암기해.

남 대화문을 외운다는 말이니?

여 응. 많이.

남 그렇게 하면 뭐가 좋으니?

여 무언가를 암기하면 그걸 잘 따라 말할 수 있어. 그렇게 하면 영어 회화에 정말 도움이 되는 것 같아.

남 난 암기하는 것은 힘들어. 너는 어떻게 그렇게 하니?

여 난 보통 대화문을 종이에 써서 항상 가지고 다녀. 시간이 날 때마다 그것들을 암기하려고 항상 노력해.

남 그래서 네가 영어 회화를 꽤 잘하는 거로구나.

• •

memorize 암기하다 **dialogue** (책 등에 나오는) 대화 **learn ~ by heart** ~을 외우다

13 대화를 듣고, 여자의 마지막 말에 이어질 남자의 말로 가장 적절한 것을 고르시오.

① Thanks a lot for your help.
② Please accept my apologies.
③ Okay, Mom. I'll be right down.
④ You're welcome. See you then.
⑤ Okay, let's cool down and think about this for a minute.

W Peter, I'm going to the grocery store. Can you come down and watch your little brother?
M Mom, I'm writing my term paper now. Can you go there later?
W No, I have to get some meat and vegetables for dinner.
M Can't Dad watch him?
W He just went to the gym to work out. I'll be gone for 30 minutes.
M But what about my paper?
W You can finish your paper after dinner.
M Then can you buy me some ice cream?
W I will. I've got to go. Come downstairs now.
M Okay, Mom. I'll be right down.

여 Peter, 난 식료품점에 가려고 해. 내려와서 남동생 좀 봐 주겠니?
남 엄마, 저는 지금 학기말 리포트를 쓰는 중이에요. 그곳에 나중에 가시면 안돼요?
여 안돼, 저녁거리로 쓸 고기와 야채를 좀 사야 한단다.
남 아빠가 동생을 보실 수는 없나요?
여 아빠는 운동하러 지금 막 체육관에 가셨어. 엄마가 30분이면 갔다 올 거야.
남 하지만 제 리포트는요?
여 넌 저녁 먹고 나서 리포트를 마무리 지을 수도 있잖니.
남 그럼 아이스크림 좀 사다 주실 수 있어요?
여 그러마. 가야겠구나. 지금 아래층으로 내려와.
남 알았어요, 엄마. 지금 내려갈게요.

•• **term paper** 학기말 리포트

---

14 대화를 듣고, 남자의 마지막 말에 이어질 여자의 말로 가장 적절한 것을 고르시오.

① I had a little trouble catching a cab.
② I'll just give you a warning this time.
③ Yeah. Then we could get to work faster.
④ Why don't you ask somebody for directions?
⑤ My car broke down on the way to work this morning.

W There is a lot of traffic at this time of day.
M It's always like this during rush hour.
W This is the heaviest traffic I've ever seen on this road.
M I'll say! We've been sitting in traffic for over an hour.
W If you look around, you'll see that in most cars, there's only one occupant, the driver.
M You're right. That makes me mad. I think people should carpool to work like us.
W You're telling me. If everyone carpooled or took other means of transportation, we could reduce traffic problems.
M We should start taking the subway to work tomorrow.
W Yeah. Then we could get to work faster.

여 하루 중 이 시간에는 교통량이 많아.
남 출퇴근 시간대에는 항상 이런 식이지.
여 이 도로에서 본 것 중에 가장 심한 교통 체증인데.
남 그러게! 우리는 한 시간 넘게 교통 체증 속에 앉아 있잖아.
여 주위를 살펴보면 대부분의 차량에 운전자 한 사람만 타고 있는 게 보일 거야.
남 맞아. 그게 열 받는 일이야. 난 사람들이 우리처럼 카풀로 출근해야 한다고 생각해.
여 네 말이 맞아. 만일 모든 사람들이 카풀을 하거나 다른 교통수단을 탄다면, 우리는 교통 문제를 줄일 수 있어.
남 내일부터 일하러 갈 때 지하철을 타야겠어.
여 그래. 그러면 우리는 더 빨리 출근할 수 있을 거야.

•• **rush hour** 출퇴근 시간대 **occupant** 타고 있는 사람 **carpool** 카풀(승용차 함께 타기)을 하다 **means of transportation** 교통수단

15 대화를 듣고, 여자의 마지막 말에 이어질 남자의 말로 가장 적절한 것을 고르시오.

① What are friends for?
② I hope to do even better next year.
③ Get on with your work while I'm away.
④ It was my pleasure to care for your parents.
⑤ Good. I was worried you wouldn't like this picture.

W Hello, Steve. Long time, no see. I came back yesterday.
M Hi. Welcome back! Did you have a nice trip, Sandy?
W Yes. It was wonderful. Fresh air, clear skies, and sunshine every day.
M Come in, and tell me more about your trip.
W I'd love to, but I have to go to the office now. I've got a lot of work to do.
M Oh, Sandy.
W I just came here to give you something. This is for you.
M Oh, thanks. It's such a beautiful picture. You shouldn't have done this.
W I really appreciate you looking after my kitty while I was away.
M What are friends for?

여 안녕, Steve. 오랜만이다. 난 어제 돌아왔어.
남 안녕. 돌아와서 반가워! 여행은 즐거웠니, Sandy?
여 응. 굉장했어. 신선한 공기, 맑은 하늘, 그리고 햇살을 매일 누렸어.
남 들어와서 여행에 대해 더 이야기해 줘.
여 그러고 싶지만 지금 사무실에 가 봐야 해. 할 일이 많거든.
남 오, Sandy.
여 단지 너에게 줄 게 있어서 여기 왔어. 이거 네 거야.
남 오, 고마워. 정말 아름다운 사진이다. 이럴 필요까지는 없는데.
여 내가 없는 동안 내 고양이를 돌봐 줘서 정말 고마워.
남 친구 좋다는 게 뭐니?

•• **look after** ~을 돌보다

▷ REVIEW TEST p. 135

A
① awake, 자지 않는, 깨어 있는 ② judge, 판단하다 ③ witness, 목격하다 ④ memorize, 암기하다
⑤ robbery, 강도, 도둑질 ⑥ describe, 설명하다, 말하다 ⑦ frustrate, 좌절감을 주다
⑧ extremely, 몹시, 극도로 ⑨ indifference, 무관심 ⑩ look after, ~을 돌보다
⑪ convenience store, 편의점 ⑫ on the contrary, 그와 반대로

B
① saw, cheating ② have, valuables ③ rush hour
④ side effects ⑤ sprained your ankle ⑥ avoid, heavy objects
⑦ reserve a table ⑧ means of transportation

문제 및 정답	받아쓰기 및 녹음내용	해석

01

대화를 듣고, 남자가 설명하고 있는 동작을 고르시오.

① ②

③ ④

⑤

W Hic! Hic!

M Uh-oh. It sounds like you <u>have the hiccups</u>.

W Help me. Hic! How do I get rid of them?

M First, hold your breath, and <u>puff out</u> your <u>cheeks</u>.

W Mm-hmm.

M Good. Now, with one hand, lightly <u>massage the back</u> of your <u>neck</u>.

W Like this? Hic!

M Don't talk! Keep <u>holding your breath</u>, or drink a glass of water.

여 딸꾹! 딸꾹!

남 이런. 너 딸꾹질하는 것 같은데.

여 도와줘. 딸꾹! 어떻게 하면 멈출 수 있지?

남 우선, 숨을 참아 봐, 그리고 뺨을 부풀려.

여 음.

남 좋아. 이제 한 손으로 가볍게 목 뒤를 안마해 봐.

여 이렇게? 딸꾹!

남 말하지 마! 계속 숨을 참아 봐, 아니면 물을 한 잔 마셔 봐.

● ●
hiccup 딸꾹질 **get rid of** ~을 끝내다, 제거하다 **breath** 숨, 호흡 **puff out** (공기를 채워) ~을 부풀리다

02

대화를 듣고, 두 사람이 대화하는 장소로 가장 적절한 곳을 고르시오.

① 공원   ② 마트
③ 세탁소   ④ 미술관
⑤ 주유소

M This is our newest piece. The <u>artist</u> is incredibly <u>talented</u>.

W It's fabulous!

M Isn't it? Of course, all his oil paintings are <u>so expressive</u>.

W Do you have any of his other pieces <u>for sale</u>?

M Certainly. In fact, the one behind you is his.

W Your showroom is <u>filled with</u> beautiful <u>paintings</u>!

M That's what we're here for: to <u>display</u> them all.

남 이것은 우리의 최근 작품입니다. 이 화가는 재능이 매우 뛰어나지요.

여 굉장하군요!

남 그렇지 않나요? 물론, 그의 모든 유화 작품은 표현이 무척 풍부해요.

여 판매하는 그의 다른 작품이 있나요?

남 물론이지요. 사실 뒤에 있는 작품이 그의 것입니다.

여 전시실이 아름다운 그림들로 가득 차 있군요!

남 그 모든 걸 전시하는 것, 그게 바로 우리가 여기에 있는 이유입니다.

● ●
piece 작품 **talented** 재능이 있는 **fabulous** 굉장한, 멋진 **expressive** 표현이 풍부한 **for sale** 판매용의 **showroom** 전시실 **display** 전시하다

03

다음을 듣고, 남자의 직업으로 가장 적절한 것을 고르시오.

① 작가
② 의사
③ 교수
④ 판매원
⑤ 컴퓨터 프로그래머

There are good parts and bad parts to this job. The pay is the best part. I was making 50,000 dollars a year straight out of college if you can believe that. I also feel like I'm on the cutting edge of computer technology. On the other hand, it is boring. All I do is write line after line of code. In addition, my eyes are getting bad from staring at the monitor all day.

이 직업에는 좋은 점과 나쁜 점이 있습니다. 임금은 가장 좋은 점입니다. 믿을지 모르겠지만 저는 대학을 나오자마자 일 년에 50,000달러를 벌었습니다. 또한 저는 컴퓨터 기술의 최첨단에 서 있는 느낌입니다. 반면에, 재미는 없습니다. 제가 하는 일은 코드를 기록하고 또 기록하는 것뿐입니다. 게다가, 하루 종일 모니터를 보면서 내 눈은 나빠지고 있습니다.

••

cutting edge 최첨단 **stare at** ~을 바라보다, 응시하다

04

대화를 듣고, 두 사람의 관계로 가장 적절한 것을 고르시오.

① 의사 - 환자
② 경찰 - 운전자
③ 변호사 - 목격자
④ 수리 기사 - 고객
⑤ 구급대원 - 운전자

W Mr. Rivers, would you please tell the court what you were doing when the accident happened and what you saw?

M Yes, I was driving to work. It was about seven thirty in the morning, and there was a silver SUV in front of me. We were both driving along Bread Street when a white car suddenly shot out from a side street. The silver SUV tried to stop, but it was impossible. It ran into the white car.

W I see. Now, how fast was the car in front of you going when the accident happened?

M The silver car? I guess 80 kilometers an hour.

W And the white car suddenly appeared without any warning or signal?

M Yes, that's right.

W Thank you, Mr. Rivers.

여 Rivers 씨, 사고가 발생했을 때 하고 있던 일과 본 것을 이 법정에 증언해 주시겠습니까?

남 예, 저는 차를 타고 출근하고 있었습니다. 대략 오전 7시 30분이었고, 제 앞에는 은색 SUV 차가 있었어요. 우리는 둘 다 Bread Street를 따라서 운전 중이었는데, 갑자기 하얀색 차가 옆 도로에서 불쑥 나타났어요. 은색 SUV는 멈추려고 했지만 불가능했어요. 그 차는 하얀색 차와 충돌하고 말았죠.

여 알겠습니다. 자, 당신 앞에 있던 차는 사고 발생 시에 주행 속도가 얼마쯤이었나요?

남 은색 차요? 시속 80km였던 것 같아요.

여 그리고 하얀색 차는 아무런 경고나 신호 없이 갑자기 나타난 겁니까?

남 예, 맞아요.

여 고맙습니다, Rivers 씨.

••

shoot out 불쑥 나타나다 **run into** ~와 충돌하다 **warning** 경고 **signal** 신호

대화를 듣고, 여자가 전화를 건 목적으로 가장 적절한 것을 고르시오.

① 피아노 가격을 물어보려고
② 피아노 레슨을 취소하려고
③ 피아노 레슨에 관해 문의하려고
④ 피아노 교사 자리를 알아보려고
⑤ 피아노 레슨 시간의 변경을 알리려고

M Hello.

W Hi. I'd like to speak to Cindy, please.

M I'm sorry. She hasn't gotten back yet. She is at lunch.

W Can I leave a message then?

M Sure, just a minute. Let me get a pen. Okay. Go ahead.

W Can you tell her that her piano lesson has changed from 3:00 to 4:00? Tell her that if she has any questions, she should feel free to call me.

M Sure. I'll tell her. Does she have your phone number?

W I guess so, but just in case, I'll give it to you. It's 734-3100.

M Okay.

남 여보세요.

여 안녕하세요. Cindy와 통화하고 싶은데요.

남 미안합니다. 그녀는 아직 돌아오지 않았어요. 점심 식사 중이거든요.

여 그럼 메시지 남겨도 될까요?

남 그럼요, 잠깐만요. 펜을 가지고 올게요. 됐어요. 말씀하세요.

여 그녀의 피아노 레슨이 3시에서 4시로 바뀌었다고 그녀에게 전해 주시겠어요? 만약에 질문이 있으면 언제든지 제게 전화하라고 그녀에게 전해 주세요.

남 네. 그렇게 전할게요. 그녀가 당신의 전화번호를 가지고 있나요?

여 그럴걸요, 하지만 만약을 위해서 제 전화번호를 드릴게요. 734-3100입니다.

남 알겠습니다.

● ●
feel free to 마음 놓고 ~해도 괜찮다

대화를 듣고, 그림에서 여자가 누구인지 고르시오.

M Is this an old class photo of yours?

W Yeah. See if you can find me. I'm in the middle row if that helps.

M Is this you with the short and curly hair?

W No, I had long hair back then.

M Did you wear glasses back then, too?

W Yes.

M Then this must be you. Wow! Look at all those curls.

W Yeah, I was the queen of big hair.

M You look better now.

남 이게 네 옛날 학급 사진이니?

여 응. 나를 찾을 수 있는지 봐 봐. 나는 가운데 줄에 있는데, 도움이 될지 모르겠네.

남 짧고 곱슬곱슬한 머리를 한 사람이 너니?

여 아니, 그때 나는 긴 머리였어.

남 그때도 안경을 썼니?

여 응.

남 그럼 이 사람이 네가 틀림없어. 와! 이 곱슬머리 좀 봐.

여 맞아, 난 크게 부풀린 머리의 여왕이었어.

남 지금이 더 나아 보여.

● ●
middle 가운데, 중앙

07 다음을 듣고, Papero의 기능으로 언급되지 <u>않은</u> 것을 고르시오.

① 얼굴 인식
② 목소리 인식
③ 숙제 돕기
④ 잘못된 행동 교정해 주기 ✓
⑤ 아이들과 놀아 주기

Papero is a childcare robot. Although it looks like a toy, Papero can <u>recognize</u> <u>faces</u> and <u>voices</u> and even respond to changing facial expressions. It can <u>help</u> kids <u>do</u> <u>their</u> <u>homework</u> and even report misbehavior to parents via a built-in mobile phone and <u>Internet</u> <u>connection</u>. This robot could be a good substitute for a pet or a friend to <u>play</u> <u>with</u> <u>kids</u>.

Papero는 육아 로봇이다. 비록 Papero가 장난감처럼 보이지만, 이 로봇은 얼굴과 목소리를 인식할 수 있고 심지어는 변화하는 얼굴 표정에 반응할 수도 있다. 이 로봇은 아이들이 숙제를 하는 것을 도와줄 수 있고, 심지어는 내장 휴대폰과 인터넷 연결을 통해 부모에게 잘못된 행동을 알릴 수도 있다. 이 로봇은 반려동물을 충분히 대신할 만한 것이 될 수 있고, 혹은 아이들과 함께 놀아 줄 친구가 될 수도 있다.

●●
recognize 인식하다 **misbehavior** 잘못된 행동 **via** ~을 통해 **built-in** (기계 등이) 내장된 **connection** 연결 **substitute** 대체물

---

08 대화를 듣고, 남자의 심정으로 가장 적절한 것을 고르시오.

① excited ② gloomy
③ nervous ④ delighted
⑤ frightened ✓

W Hey!
M Aaaaahh! You <u>scared</u> <u>me</u>!
W I got you, didn't I?
M You shouldn't do that again. Do you want to give me a <u>heart</u> <u>attack</u>?
W Sorry. I couldn't resist. You seemed <u>lost</u> <u>in</u> <u>thought</u>.
M Now I forgot what I was thinking about.
W It was funny to see your <u>reaction</u>.
M Yes, funny for you but <u>horrific</u> for me.
W Anyway, how are you?
M I'll be fine once I <u>calm</u> <u>down</u>.

여 야!
남 앗! 깜짝 놀랐잖아!
여 걸려들었다, 그렇지?
남 다시는 그러지 마. 내가 심장 마비에라도 걸렸으면 좋겠니?
여 미안해. 참을 수가 없었어. 네가 생각에 빠져 있는 것 같아서.
남 지금 내가 무슨 생각을 하고 있었는지 까먹었잖아.
여 네 반응을 보니까 웃겼어.
남 그래, 너한테는 웃기겠지만, 나한테는 끔찍하다.
여 어쨌든, 잘 지내니?
남 마음을 가라앉히고 나면 괜찮아질 거야.

●●
heart attack 심장마비 **resist** (하고 싶은 것을 하지 않고) 참다 **thought** 생각, 사고 **horrific** 끔찍한, 불쾌한

09 대화를 듣고, 두 사람이 다리를 건너기 위해 지불해야 할 왕복 요금과 이용 수단을 고르시오.

① $20 – 페리   ② $20 – 자가용
③ $40 – 페리   ④ $40 – 자가용
⑤ $80 – 자가용

W Wow. We are going to Prince Edward Island, where the writer of *Anne of Green Gables* lived.
M We're approaching the toll bridge. Can you give me some money?
W How much does it cost to cross?
M The cost to drive the car across the bridge is 40 dollars.
W That's really expensive. Why is that?
M This is the longest bridge in the world.
W Oh, really? I had no idea. How long is it?
M It's 16 kilometers long. Before the bridge was constructed, people used ferries. The cost of a ferry then was 20 dollars.
W Do we have to pay for the toll when we come back as well?
M No, we only have to pay when going to Prince Edward Island.

여 와. 우리가 '빨강머리 앤'의 작가가 살았던 Prince Edward Island에 가는구나.
남 우리는 통행료를 받는 다리로 다가가고 있어. 나 돈 좀 줄래?
여 다리 건너는 데 얼마지?
남 자가용으로 다리를 건너는 비용은 40달러야.
여 정말 비싸다. 왜 그런 거니?
남 이것이 세계에서 가장 긴 다리거든.
여 아, 정말? 몰랐어. 얼마나 긴데?
남 16km 길이야. 다리가 건설되기 전에는 사람들이 페리를 이용했어. 그 당시 페리 요금은 20달러였어.
여 우리가 돌아올 때도 통행료를 내야 하는 거야?
남 아니, Prince Edward Island로 들어갈 때만 내는 거야.

●●
approach 다가가다, 접근하다   **toll** 통행료
bridge 다리   **construct** 건설하다   **ferry** 페리, 나룻배

---

10 대화를 듣고, 남자가 여자의 말을 믿지 못했던 이유로 가장 적절한 것을 고르시오.

① 자신의 가게에서는 빵을 매일 굽기 때문에
② 빵의 유통기한이 충분히 남았기 때문에
③ 여자가 전에도 여러 번 같은 이유로 불평했기 때문에
④ 남자가 아무도 믿지 못하는 성격이기 때문에
⑤ 여자가 갖고 온 빵은 남자가 판매한 빵이 아니기 때문에

M May I help you?
W I bought a loaf of bread in your store this morning. When I took the bread home, I noticed some mold on it.
M That's impossible, ma'am. We bake fresh bread every day.
W Take a look for yourself. Do you see it?
M Well, I must admit that you're right. There is mold on the bread. We are so sorry.
W Can I take another loaf?
M Sure. Please feel free to do that.
W I'll take this one.
M Here's a coupon for a 25% discount on your next purchase here.

남 무엇을 도와드릴까요?
여 오늘 아침에 당신의 가게에서 빵 한 덩이를 샀는데요. 집에 빵을 가지고 갔는데, 빵에 곰팡이가 피어 있다는 걸 알아차렸어요.
남 그럴 리가 없는데요, 부인. 저희는 매일 신선한 빵을 굽거든요.
여 직접 보세요. 보이시죠?
남 음, 부인 말씀이 맞다는 걸 인정해야겠네요. 빵에 곰팡이가 피었군요. 정말 죄송합니다.
여 다른 빵으로 가져가도 될까요?
남 그럼요. 편안하게 고르십시오.
여 이것으로 하겠습니다.
남 여기 다음번에 구매하실 때 사용하실 수 있는 25퍼센트 할인 쿠폰입니다.

●●
loaf 덩어리   **notice** 알아채다   **mold** 곰팡이
admit 인정하다   **purchase** 구매

11 대화를 듣고, 상황에 대한 설명으로 가장 적절한 것을 고르시오.

① 여자는 응급차를 운전하던 중이었다.
② 여자가 과속으로 경찰관에게 걸렸다. ✓
③ 여자가 음주 운전으로 경찰관에게 걸렸다.
④ 여자가 경찰관의 운전면허증 제시를 거부했다.
⑤ 여자가 차선 위반으로 무인 감시 카메라에 찍혔다.

M Can I see your <u>license</u> and <u>registration</u>, please?

W What seems to be the problem, officer?

M The <u>speed</u> <u>limit</u> here is 80km <u>per</u> <u>hour</u>. You were going 110km per hour.

W I didn't realize I was going so fast.

M The computer tells me you already have two prior speeding tickets. So I <u>can't</u> <u>let</u> <u>you</u> <u>off</u> with a warning this time.

W I was <u>in</u> <u>a</u> <u>hurry</u> to go to the hospital to see my mother.

M Do you think that's an <u>excuse</u> for driving so fast? Please be mindful of the speed limit!

W Okay, officer. Here is my license.

남 당신의 면허증과 등록증을 볼 수 있을까요?

여 경관님, 무슨 문제가 있나요?

남 여기 제한 속도가 시속 80킬로미터입니다. 당신은 시속 110킬로미터로 달렸습니다.

여 제가 그렇게 빨리 달리고 있는 줄 몰랐습니다.

남 컴퓨터로 보니까 당신은 전에 이미 속도 위반 딱지를 두 번이나 떼인 적이 있군요. 그래서 이번에는 경고만 하고 봐드릴 수 없습니다.

여 어머니를 뵈러 병원에 급하게 가던 중이었습니다.

남 그것이 그렇게 빨리 운전한 것에 대한 변명이 된다고 생각하십니까? 제한 속도를 유념하세요!

여 알겠습니다, 경관님. 여기 면허증이요.

••
registration 등록증 prior 이전의 let off ~를 봐주다 be mindful of ~를 유념하다

---

12 대화를 듣고, 대화 내용과 일치하지 <u>않는</u> 것을 고르시오.

① 남자가 사용하는 욕조의 수도꼭지에 문제가 있다.
② 여자는 남자의 집에 배관공을 보내줄 것이다.
③ 남자의 집에 있는 스토브의 버너가 고장났다.
④ 남자의 전화기에서 발신음이 나지 않는다.
⑤ 여자는 전화 회사에 직접 전화할 것이다. ✓

M Mrs. Kim, this is Sung-ho, your tenant in 302.

W Hi. What's up?

M There are a few problems with the apartment. First, the <u>faucet</u> in the <u>bathtub</u> drips constantly.

W I'll ask the plumber to drop by and fix it tomorrow.

M In addition, one of the <u>burners</u> on the stove <u>doesn't</u> <u>work</u>.

W What's the matter with it?

M I can't <u>control</u> the <u>temperature</u>. I think you'll have to get an electrician.

W I'll see what I can do. Is that everything?

M Well, there's one more thing. I can't get a dial tone on the phone. It's dead.

W I'm sorry. There's <u>nothing</u> <u>I</u> <u>can</u> <u>do</u> about that. You'll have to call the phone company.

남 Mrs. Kim, 저 302호에 사는 성호예요.

여 안녕하세요. 무슨 일이죠?

남 아파트에 몇 가지 문제가 있어서요. 우선, 욕조의 수도꼭지에서 물이 계속 떨어져요.

여 배관공을 불러서 내일 그것을 고치도록 할게요.

남 게다가, 스토브의 버너 중 하나가 작동을 안 해요.

여 어떤 문제가 있죠?

남 온도를 조절할 수가 없어요. 전기 기사를 불러야 할 것 같아요.

여 제가 할 수 있는 일을 알아볼게요. 그게 전부인가요?

남 음, 문제가 한 가지 더 있어요. 전화기 발신음이 나질 않아요. 불통이에요.

여 죄송해요. 그것에 관해 제가 할 수 있는 일이 없군요. 전화 회사에 전화하셔야겠습니다.

••
tenant 세입자 faucet 수도꼭지 bathtub 욕조 drip (액체가) 똑똑 떨어지다 constantly 계속 plumber 배관공 control 조절하다 dial tone (전화) 발신음

13 대화를 듣고, 남자의 마지막 말에 이어질 여자의 말로 가장 적절한 것을 고르시오.

① Right! I've got a stomachache all the time.
② Okay. It looks like we'll have to run some tests.
③ All right, but I need to take your blood pressure.
④ Yes. I had it checked during my last physical examination.
⑤ Yes. The nurse already told me some of your symptoms.

M Good morning, Jane. I haven't seen you for a long time. Please be seated, and tell me what seems to be the trouble.
W I'm not quite sure, sir. I feel generally weak, and I had difficulty getting out of bed this morning.
M Can you tell me anything more specific than that?
W I have had a stiff neck and a headache since Saturday.
M Do you have a fever?
W I don't know as I have no thermometer, but my throat seems full of fire.
M Well, hold this thermometer in your mouth a minute while I check your pulse.
W Do I have a temperature?
M Less than a degree. But your blood pressure seems very low to me. Have you ever had it checked before?
W Yes. I had it checked during my last physical examination.

남 안녕하세요, Jane. 오랫동안 못 뵈었군요. 앉아서 무엇이 문제인 것 같은지 말씀해 보세요.
여 잘 모르겠어요, 선생님. 대체로 약해졌다는 느낌이 들고, 오늘 아침에 침대에서 일어나기가 힘들었어요.
남 그것보다 더 구체적으로 말씀해 주시겠습니까?
여 토요일 이후로 목이 뻣뻣하고 두통이 있었어요.
남 열이 있나요?
여 체온계가 없어서 모르겠지만, 목구멍이 온통 불타는 것 같아요.
남 음, 맥박을 재는 동안 잠깐 이 체온계를 입에 물고 계세요.
여 열이 있나요?
남 별로 없는데요. 하지만 제가 보기엔 혈압이 너무 낮은 것 같군요. 예전에 검사를 받으신 적이 있나요?
여 네. 지난 건강 검진 때 검사를 받았어요.

●●
generally 대체로, 일반적으로 **stiff** 뻣뻣한 **thermometer** 체온계 **pulse** 맥박 **blood pressure** 혈압 **physical examination** 건강 검진

---

14 대화를 듣고, 남자의 마지막 말에 이어질 여자의 말로 가장 적절한 것을 고르시오.

① Perhaps you are right.
② What makes you so sure?
③ She's probably not going to come.
④ Can you give me some more time?
⑤ I think you should stay away from her.

M Are you free this Saturday?
W Yes, I think so.
M Do you want to go shopping with Julia and me?
W Well... I don't know.
M You just said that you don't have anything special for this Saturday.
W To be honest, I always try to avoid Julia if I can.
M Why do you do that? I think she's fun.
W Perhaps, but she talks behind people's backs. She's nice to their faces, but she criticizes them to other people.
M I hadn't noticed that.
W I think you should stay away from her.

남 너 이번 주 토요일에 시간 있니?
여 응, 그런 것 같아.
남 Julia랑 나와 함께 쇼핑하러 갈래?
여 음… 잘 모르겠어.
남 방금 이번 주 토요일에는 특별한 일이 없다고 그랬잖아.
여 솔직히 말하면, 난 항상 가능하면 Julia를 피하려고 해.
남 왜 그러는데? 나는 그녀가 재밌다고 생각하는데.
여 그럴지도 모르지만, 그녀는 사람들 뒤에서 험담을 하거든. 사람들 앞에서는 상냥하지만, 다른 사람들에게는 그들을 비판하거든.
남 난 그런 줄 몰랐는데.
여 내 생각에 넌 그녀를 가까이하지 말아야 해.

●●
stay away from ~를 가까이하지 않다

15 대화를 듣고, 여자의 마지막 말에 이어질 남자의 말로 가장 적절한 것을 고르시오.

① I went to the wrong place.
② Are you being straight with me?
③ Then let's have lunch delivered here.
④ Really? Let's go somewhere else then.
⑤ You got it the last time. Let me get it this time.

M How about some coffee?
W That's a great idea. I <u>feel</u> dead <u>tired</u>.
M Where shall we go?
W Oh, we <u>don't</u> <u>have</u> <u>to</u> <u>go</u> anywhere. There is a coffee vending machine around that corner.
M Okay. Here is 1,000 won.
W Oh, no!
M What's the matter?
W This machine is <u>out</u> <u>of</u> <u>order</u>. And I <u>can't</u> <u>get</u> my money back.
M Forget it. Let's go to the coffee shop across the street.
W The last time I was there, it was so <u>crowded</u> that I had to <u>wait</u> <u>in</u> <u>line</u>.
M <u>Really? Let's go somewhere else then.</u>

남 커피 마실래?
여 좋은 생각이야. 피곤해 죽겠어.
남 우리 어디 갈까?
여 아, 어디 갈 필요 없어. 저 모퉁이를 돌면 커피 자판기가 있거든.
남 좋아. 여기 1,000원 있어.
여 오, 이런!
남 무슨 일이야?
여 이 기계가 고장 났어. 그리고 돈도 돌려주지 않아.
남 잊어버려. 길 건너 커피숍으로 가자.
여 내가 지난번에 그곳에 갔을 때 너무 붐벼서 줄을 서서 기다려야 했어.
남 정말? 그럼 다른 데로 가지 뭐.

●●
out of order 고장 난 **crowded** (사람들이) 붐비는

REVIEW TEST p. 143

A ① admit, 인정하다 ② display, 전시하다 ③ signal, 신호 ④ notice, 알아채다 ⑤ breath, 숨, 호흡 ⑥ warning, 경고 ⑦ recognize, 인식하다 ⑧ construct, 건설하다 ⑨ talented, 재능이 있는 ⑩ purchase, 구매 ⑪ for sale, 판매용의 ⑫ get rid of, ~을 끝내다, 제거하다

B ① approaching, bridge ② blood pressure ③ ran into ④ faucet, bathtub ⑤ staring at ⑥ Feel free to ⑦ out of order ⑧ a loaf of

문제 및 정답	받아쓰기 및 녹음내용	해석

01

대화를 듣고, 그림에서 여자의 동생이 누구인지 고르시오.

M What picture is that?

W Look. It's a picture of my friends. My sister is here.

M Your sister? Which one is she?

W <u>Take</u> a <u>guess</u>.

M Is your sister wearing a miniskirt?

W No, she isn't. She's wearing the <u>long</u> <u>dress</u> with a large <u>ribbon</u> <u>around</u> <u>her</u> <u>waist</u>.

M A ribbon? Then this lady must be your sister.

W Yes, that's right. She's a <u>famous</u> <u>fashion</u> <u>model</u>.

M Hmmm. You look like her.

W Yeah. Everybody says that.

남 저건 어떤 사진인데?

여 봐. 내 친구들의 사진이야. 내 여동생이 여기에 있어.

남 네 여동생? 누가 네 여동생인데?

여 추측해 봐.

남 네 여동생은 미니스커트를 입고 있니?

여 아니. 그녀는 긴 드레스를 입고 허리에 큰 리본을 두르고 있어.

남 리본? 그럼 이 여자가 네 여동생이 틀림없구나.

여 응, 맞아. 그녀는 유명한 패션 모델이야.

남 음. 너는 네 여동생과 닮았어.

여 응. 모두들 그렇게 말해.

●●
waist 허리

02

대화를 듣고, 두 사람이 대화하는 장소로 가장 적절한 곳을 고르시오.

① 해변　　② 숲속
③ 사막　　④ 박물관
⑤ 수족관

W It's so <u>peaceful</u> out here. I love this place.

M Yeah, me, too. I love the smell of aromatic trees.

W There's nothing like a <u>walk</u> <u>in</u> <u>the</u> <u>woods</u> to put you in a good mood.

M Shhhh! Quiet! I think I <u>see</u> <u>some</u> <u>rabbits</u> over there.

W Look! They are eating something. Wow! They are so cute.

M Oops! We <u>scared</u> <u>them</u> <u>away</u>.

W I'm hungry.

M I'm starving, too. Let's go to a rest area and have lunch.

W Good idea. Why don't we eat <u>by</u> <u>that</u> <u>stream</u> back there?

여 이곳은 정말 평화롭다. 난 이곳이 아주 좋아.

남 응, 나도 그래. 향나무 냄새가 정말 좋아.

여 숲속을 걷는 것만큼 기분을 좋게 만드는 것도 없어.

남 쉿! 조용히 해! 저기서 토끼를 본 것 같아.

여 봐! 뭔가를 먹고 있네. 와! 정말 귀엽다.

남 이크! 우리가 토끼들을 겁주어 쫓아버렸어.

여 나 배고파.

남 나도 정말 배고파. 쉼터로 가서 점심을 먹자.

여 좋은 생각이야. 저 뒤에 있는 개울 근처에서 먹으면 어떨까?

●●
aromatic 향기로운　**woods** 숲　**in a good mood** 기분이 좋은　**stream** 개울, 시내

03 다음을 듣고, Nick의 직업으로 가장 적절한 것을 고르시오.

① 군인 ② 경찰관
③ 트럭 운전사 ④ 자동차 판매원
⑤ 비행기 조종사 ✓

Did you hear about Nick? He <u>got the best job</u> after he left the Air Force. He gets full benefits, including medical and dental coverage, plus he gets to <u>fly all over the world</u>. Even his family gets to travel for free. Of course, you know what <u>commercial airlines</u> are like: they give him a lot of <u>flight hours</u>. He can handle it though. He still has one of the best safety records around.

Nick에 관한 소식 들었니? 그는 공군을 제대한 후 최고의 직장을 얻었어. 건강 보험과 치과 보험을 포함한 모든 복리 후생 혜택을 받았고, 게다가 세계 어느 곳이든 비행하게 됐어. 거기에다 그의 가족들도 공짜로 여행하게 됐어. 물론, 너도 민간 항공사가 어떤지 알겠지만 그에게 많은 비행 시간을 주고 있어. 그래도 그는 잘할 수 있어. 그는 아직도 현존하는 최고의 안전 비행 기록 중 하나를 보유하고 있어.

●●

Air Force 공군 **benefits** 복리 후생, 특전 **including** ~을 포함하여 **coverage** (보험의) 보장, 보상 범위 **commercial** 민간의 **airline** 항공사

---

04 대화를 듣고, 두 사람의 관계로 가장 적절한 것을 고르시오.

① 사장 – 비서 ✓ ② 의사 – 환자
③ 교사 – 학생 ④ 점원 – 고객
⑤ 운전사 – 승객

M Yes?

W Excuse me. There's a Mr. Smith <u>on the line</u>. He says he is your friend. Do you want to talk to him?

M No. <u>Have</u> him <u>call back</u> later. I'll be in a meeting with Dr. Cook from now until 12 o'clock.

W I see, Mr. Johnson.

M By the way, do you think you could possibly <u>work late</u> this evening? I'm afraid there's some work I really have to finish, and I can't do it <u>all by myself</u>.

W Work late? I... I suppose so if it's <u>necessary</u>.

M Thank you. You'll only have to work <u>about an hour</u> of overtime.

남 네?

여 실례합니다. Smith 씨가 연결되었습니다. 사장님의 친구라고 하던데요. 그분과 통화하시겠습니까?

남 아뇨. 나중에 다시 전화하라고 하세요. 지금부터 12시까지 Cook 박사와 회의를 할 거예요.

여 알겠습니다, Mr. Johnson.

남 그건 그렇고, 혹시 오늘 저녁 늦게까지 일할 수 있나요? 꼭 끝내야 할 일이 있는데, 그걸 나 혼자서 다 할 수는 없을 것 같군요.

여 야근이요? 저… 필요하다면 해야죠.

남 고마워요. 시간 외로 한 시간 정도만 더 일하면 될 거예요.

●●

possibly 혹시, 가능한 한 **necessary** 필요한, 필수의 **overtime** 초과 근무

05

다음을 듣고, 여자가 전화를 건 목적으로 가장 적절한 것을 고르시오.

① 남편 생일 파티에 초대하려고
② 휴가 계획에 대해 물어보려고
③ 부모님의 병문안을 부탁하려고
④ 파티 장소가 변경되었음을 알려 주려고
⑤ 생일 선물을 보내 주어 고맙다는 인사를 하려고

M Please leave a message and your phone number <u>after</u> <u>the</u> <u>beep</u>.

W Hi, Max. This is Cathy. I hope you had a <u>wonderful</u> <u>vacation</u>. Thanks for your postcard. This Sunday is <u>my</u> <u>husband's</u> <u>birthday</u>. We want you to be at the party. I told him you are my best friend. My family wants to see you, too. So I wonder if you can <u>come</u> <u>to</u> <u>the</u> <u>party</u> on Sunday afternoon. My friend really wants to see you, too. Can you call me <u>as</u> <u>soon</u> <u>as</u> <u>you</u> <u>get</u> this message?

남 삐 소리 후에 메시지와 전화번호를 남겨 주세요.

여 안녕, Max. 나 Cathy야. 멋진 휴가 보냈기를 바라. 엽서 보내 줘서 고마워. 이번 주 일요일이 우리 남편의 생일이거든. 우리는 네가 파티에 오기를 원해. 나는 그에게 네가 나의 가장 친한 친구라고 말했어. 우리 가족도 너를 만나고 싶어해. 그래서 네가 일요일 오후 파티에 올 수 있는지 궁금해. 내 친구도 너를 정말 보고 싶어해. 이 메시지를 받자마자 내게 전화해 주겠니?

●●
beep 삐 소리 **postcard** 엽서

06

다음을 듣고, 그림에서 남자의 가장 친한 친구가 누구인지 고르시오.

Today, I would like to introduce my friends. Look at the person on the <u>left</u> in the <u>front</u> <u>row</u>, wearing a baseball cap and a T-shirt. That's me, Kyle. That is my friend, Susan wearing the polka-dotted dress and sitting right next to me. Another friend, David, is right behind me. He's wearing the <u>checkered</u> shirt and glasses. The next person is Mike, who is <u>my</u> <u>closest</u> <u>friend</u>. He is the one with shoulder-length hair. He is not wearing glasses, but he has <u>sunglasses</u> <u>on</u> <u>his</u> <u>head</u>. Beside Mike, there's a girl with curly hair wearing glasses. Her name is Mickey.

오늘은 제 친구들을 소개하고 싶습니다. 앞줄 왼쪽에 야구 모자를 쓰고 티셔츠를 입고 있는 사람을 보세요. 그 사람이 저, Kyle입니다. 제 친구 Susan은 물방울무늬의 드레스를 입고서 제 바로 옆에 앉아 있습니다. 또 다른 친구 David는 제 바로 뒤에 있습니다. 그는 체크무늬 셔츠를 입고 있고 안경을 쓰고 있습니다. 그다음 사람은 Mike인데, 그는 저의 가장 친한 친구입니다. 그는 어깨 길이의 머리를 한 사람입니다. 그는 안경은 쓰고 있지 않지만 선글라스를 머리 위에 쓰고 있습니다. Mike 옆에는 곱슬머리에 안경을 쓴 여자아이가 있는데요. 그녀의 이름은 Mickey입니다.

●●
row 줄, 열(列) **polka-dotted** 물방울무늬의
checkered 체크무늬의

07 대화를 듣고, 여자가 구직 면접에서 가장 중요하다고 생각하는 것을 고르시오.

① showing off
② being likable ✓
③ listening carefully
④ describing experience
⑤ appearing knowledgeable

W Wow, you are really <u>dressed up</u> today.
M Yeah, I have a <u>job</u> <u>interview</u> today. Can you give me some advice?
W Sure. It's important to <u>appear</u> knowledgeable, but don't look like a showoff.
M Got it.
W You should also talk about your related <u>work</u> <u>experience</u> because most companies want to <u>hire</u> <u>someone</u> who already knows what they need.
M Okay. What else?
W <u>The</u> <u>most</u> <u>important</u> <u>thing</u> is to be likable. If the boss likes you, that's half the battle.
M Thanks for the tip.

여 와, 너 오늘 옷을 정말 잘 차려 입었구나.
남 응, 나 오늘 구직 면접이 있거든. 나에게 충고라도 좀 해 줄 수 있어?
여 물론이지. 아는 것이 많아 보이는 것이 중요해, 그렇지만 자랑쟁이처럼 보여서는 안 돼.
남 알았어.
여 또한 대부분의 회사들은 자신들이 필요로 하는 것을 이미 알고 있는 사람을 고용하고 싶어하기 때문에, 너는 관련된 업무 경험에 대해 이야기해야 해.
남 알았어. 또 다른 건?
여 가장 중요한 것은 호감이 가도록 행동하는 거야. 사장이 널 맘에 들어 하면, 반은 이기고 들어가는 거니까.
남 조언해 줘서 고마워.

be dressed up 옷을 잘 차려 입다
knowledgeable 아는 것이 많은
showoff 자랑쟁이 **related** 관련된
hire 고용하다 **likable** 호감이 가는

---

08 대화를 듣고, 무엇에 관한 내용인지 가장 적절한 것을 고르시오.

① 남자의 당뇨병 ✓
② 남자의 식이요법
③ 여자의 체중 감량
④ 두 사람의 장래 희망
⑤ 여자의 건강 검진 결과

W What are you doing there? Is that a <u>needle</u>?
M Yes, it is. I have to give myself an injection every day. I <u>have</u> <u>diabetes</u>.
W Do you have to do that every day?
M Yes, my body doesn't produce insulin, so I <u>have</u> <u>to</u> <u>inject</u> what my body fails to produce.
W I've never known anyone with diabetes before. It's <u>painful</u> to <u>get</u> <u>a</u> <u>shot</u> every day, isn't it?
M After a while, you don't think about it. It becomes routine.
W Do you have to do that <u>for</u> <u>the</u> <u>rest</u> <u>of</u> your life?
M Yes, I do. It's not such a big deal.

여 거기서 뭘 하고 계세요? 그거 주사 바늘인가요?
남 응, 그래. 나는 매일 주사를 놔야 하거든. 내겐 당뇨병이 있단다.
여 매일 그렇게 해야 하는 거예요?
남 그래, 내 몸이 인슐린을 생산하지 못해서, 몸에서 생산하지 못하는 것을 주입해 줘야 하거든.
여 전에 한 번도 당뇨병에 걸린 사람을 보지 못했어요. 매일 주사를 맞는 건 아프죠, 그렇지 않나요?
남 시간이 지나면 그런 건 생각 안 하게 돼. 일상 생활이 되거든.
여 평생 동안 그렇게 해야만 하나요?
남 응, 그렇단다. 그렇게 큰 일은 아냐.

needle 바늘 **injection** 주사 **diabetes** 당뇨병 **fail to** ~하지 못하다 **get a shot** 주사를 맞다 **rest** 나머지

09 대화를 듣고, 남자가 환불받게 될 금액을 고르시오.

① $50
② $350
③ $1,000
④ $1,050
⑤ $1,400

W ABC Airlines. How may I help you?

M I'd like to <u>get a refund</u> for the return portion of my ticket.

W May I see your ticket?

M Sure. I <u>wonder how much</u> I can get.

W It's not much, sir. You paid 1,400 dollars for a <u>round</u>-trip ticket last year. We can only give you the money after we deduct the full price of a one-way ticket and the <u>cancelation fee</u>.

M Then how much can I get?

W <u>350</u> dollars.

M Okay. <u>Process my request</u>, please.

여 ABC 항공사입니다. 무엇을 도와드릴까요?

남 돌아가는 표를 환불받고 싶은데요.

여 표를 좀 볼 수 있을까요?

남 그럼요. 제가 얼마나 받을 수 있는지 궁금한데요.

여 많지는 않습니다, 고객님. 작년에 왕복표 값으로 1,400달러를 내셨군요. 저희는 편도표 요금 전액과 취소 수수료를 뺀 금액만을 드릴 수 있습니다.

남 그러면 얼마를 받을 수 있나요?

여 350달러입니다.

남 알겠습니다. 제 요청을 처리해 주십시오.

●●

refund 환불(금) **portion** 몫, 부분 **deduct** 빼다, 공제하다 **one-way** 편도의 **process** 처리하다 **request** 요청, 요구

---

10 대화를 듣고, 여자가 자신이 코미디언이 되기가 어렵다고 말한 이유로 가장 적절한 것을 고르시오.

① 말을 더듬어서
② 무대 공포증이 있어서
③ 유머 감각이 전혀 없어서
④ 코미디 공연을 실패한 경험이 많아서
⑤ 부모님이 코미디언이 되는 것을 반대해서

M That joke was really funny. You really should think about <u>becoming a comedian</u>.

W Do you really think so?

M Absolutely. I don't know anyone who has <u>a sense of humor</u> like you.

W I just look at the world from a funny viewpoint. It's very natural to me.

M You really should go to a comedy club or something and <u>try to entertain</u> people.

W I don't think I can. I have stage fright. I <u>get anxious</u> when doing something <u>in front of</u> people.

M You are truly unique. I hope you can overcome your <u>stage fright</u>.

남 그 농담 정말로 웃겼어. 넌 정말 코미디언이 되는 걸 생각해 봐야 해.

여 진짜 그렇게 생각해?

남 그렇고 말고. 난 너처럼 유머 감각을 가진 사람을 알지 못해.

여 난 그냥 세상을 재밌는 관점에서 볼 뿐인데. 나한테는 매우 당연한 것이야.

남 넌 정말로 코미디 클럽 같은 데 가서 사람들을 즐겁게 해 줘야 해.

여 그럴 수 없을 것 같아. 난 무대 공포증이 있어. 사람들 앞에서 뭔가를 할 때 불안해지거든.

남 넌 정말로 독특해. 네가 무대 공포증을 극복하길 바라.

●●

joke 농담 **viewpoint** 관점, 시각 **natural** 당연한 **entertain** 즐겁게 하다 **stage fright** 무대 공포증 **anxious** 불안한 **unique** 독특한 **overcome** 극복하다

11 대화를 듣고, 두 사람이 동의한 점으로 가장 적절한 것을 고르시오.

① Einstein은 사실 천재가 아니다.
② 기술은 나쁜 용도로도 쓰일 수 있다.
③ Einstein은 음악가로서 더 소질이 있었다.
④ Einstein이 어떤 것도 발견하지 말았어야 했다.
⑤ Einstein의 발견 덕분에 많은 사람들이 치료받았다.

W What are you reading there?
M It's a book about Albert Einstein. He was truly a <u>genius</u>.
W I don't know much about him <u>except</u> <u>for</u> his famous Theory of Relativity.
M It says here in the book that after the atomic <u>bombs</u> <u>were</u> <u>dropped</u> during World War II, Einstein wished he'd never discovered anything.
W He must have <u>realized</u> <u>the</u> <u>results</u> of what he had discovered.
M Yes. In fact, he was very depressed about it.
W I guess there are <u>good</u> <u>and</u> <u>bad</u> <u>uses</u> for any type of technology.
M That's true.

여 너 거기서 무얼 읽고 있니?
남 Albert Einstein에 대한 책이야. 그는 정말 천재였어.
여 난 그 사람의 유명한 상대성 이론을 빼고는 그에 대해 잘 몰라.
남 여기 이 책에는 2차 세계대전 동안 원자 폭탄이 떨어진 후에 Einstein은 자기가 아무것도 발견하지 않았기를 바랐다고 되어 있어.
여 그는 자신이 발견한 것의 결과를 알아차렸을 거야.
남 그래. 사실, 그는 그것 때문에 매우 우울해했어.
여 어떤 종류의 기술에든 좋은 용도와 나쁜 용도가 있는 것 같아.
남 맞아.

genius 천재 Theory of Relativity 상대성 이론 atomic bomb 원자 폭탄 discover 발견하다

12 대화를 듣고, 대화 내용과 일치하지 <u>않는</u> 것을 고르시오.

① 남자는 전공을 변경했다.
② 남자의 원래 장래 희망은 회계사였다.
③ 남자는 회계학 수업을 좋아한다.
④ 남자는 음악가로서 생계를 유지하는 일이 어렵다고 생각한다.
⑤ 여자는 남자의 선택을 존중한다.

W Billy, I can't wait to hear all about your school life. Are your classes good?
M Well, yes, they are. But... I <u>changed</u> <u>my</u> <u>major</u> to music.
W To music? But I thought you were going to be an <u>accountant</u>.
M Yes, I know. I wanted to be an accountant until I took some accounting classes. I <u>hated</u> <u>them</u>.
W But if you get a degree in music, how will you support yourself?
M Well, I don't know. What I really want to do is music, but I know <u>how</u> <u>hard</u> it is to <u>earn</u> <u>a</u> <u>living</u> as a musician.
W Do you really want to do this?
M Yes. I want to be a musician.
W Well, if that's what you want to be, then that's <u>what</u> <u>you</u> <u>should</u> <u>be</u>.

여 Billy, 난 네 학교 생활에 대해 전부 듣고 싶어 기다릴 수가 없구나. 수업은 좋니?
남 음, 예, 좋아요. 그런데… 전 전공을 음악으로 바꿨어요.
여 음악으로? 하지만 난 네가 회계사가 되려 한다고 생각했는데.
남 예, 저도 알아요. 제가 회계학 수업을 듣기 전까지는 저도 회계사가 되길 원했어요. 전 그 수업들이 싫어요.
여 하지만 네가 음악으로 학위를 받으면 어떻게 생계를 유지하려고 하니?
남 음, 저도 잘 모르겠어요. 제가 진정으로 하고 싶은 것은 음악이에요, 그렇지만 음악가로서 생계를 꾸려나가는 것이 얼마나 어려운지는 저도 알아요.
여 넌 정말로 이걸 하길 원하니?
남 예. 저는 음악가가 되고 싶어요.
여 음, 그게 네가 되고 싶어하는 거라면 되어야지.

major 전공 accountant 회계사 degree 학위 living 생활비

13 대화를 듣고, 남자의 마지막 말에 이어질 여자의 말로 가장 적절한 것을 고르시오.

① I don't know where exactly.
② We need to use sunscreen at the beach.
③ I'll never forget the time I spent with you.
④ Thank you for coming here to see me off.
⑤ As a matter of fact, I went to the beach every day.

M Welcome back to San Francisco.
W Thank you for coming to the airport to meet me, Tony.
M My pleasure. Your parents and Sarah are now at home. They're busy preparing your welcome-home party. Did you have a nice trip, Alice?
W Yes, I did. Everything was wonderful.
M That's good. Where did you stay last night?
W I stayed at a hotel in Honolulu. I was in Hawaii for a week.
M I can guess how you spent that week in Hawaii. You're beautifully tanned.
W As a matter of fact, I went to the beach every day.

남 San Francisco에 돌아오신 것을 환영합니다.
여 저를 마중하러 공항까지 나와 주시다니 감사합니다, Tony 씨.
남 천만에요. 당신 부모님과 Sarah는 지금 집에 있어요. 그들은 환영 홈 파티를 준비하느라 바빠요. 여행은 즐거우셨나요, Alice?
여 예, 즐거웠어요. 모든 것이 훌륭했어요.
남 좋군요. 지난 밤에는 어디에서 묵으셨나요?
여 Honolulu의 호텔에서 묵었어요. 한 주간 하와이에 있었거든요.
남 하와이에서 어떻게 한 주를 보내셨는지 상상할 수 있겠네요. 햇볕에 멋지게 그을리셨군요.
여 사실, 매일 해변에 갔죠.

● ●
tanned 햇볕에 탄 as a matter of fact 사실은

14 대화를 듣고, 남자의 마지막 말에 이어질 여자의 말로 가장 적절한 것을 고르시오.

① See you next Monday.
② What dorm do you live in?
③ I think we should meet earlier than six.
④ We'll have to schedule these regularly.
⑤ I'm afraid I've taken up too much of your valuable time.

M Would you like to go to the campus concert with me tonight?
W I didn't know there was going to be a concert. Who's playing?
M A group called Zest will come.
W Oh, great! That group is my favorite.
M The concert starts at seven o'clock. Do you want to go out to dinner first?
W Sure, but I want to share the expenses.
M I'd really appreciate that. My funds are pretty low right now.
W Well, then I'll buy my own concert ticket, too.
M Fine with me. I'll come over to your dormitory at six o'clock.
W I think we should meet earlier than six.

남 오늘 밤에 나랑 캠퍼스 콘서트에 갈래?
여 난 콘서트가 열릴 거라는 걸 몰랐어. 누가 연주하니?
남 Zest라는 그룹이 올 거래.
여 오, 정말 잘됐다! 내가 가장 좋아하는 그룹이거든.
남 콘서트는 7시에 시작해. 일단 저녁 먹으러 나갈래?
여 물론이지, 하지만 경비는 나누어서 내면 좋겠어.
남 그렇게 하면 나야 정말 고맙지. 내가 지금은 돈이 아주 조금밖에 없거든.
여 음, 그럼 콘서트 표도 내 것은 내가 살게.
남 좋아. 6시에 기숙사로 데리러 갈게.
여 6시보다 더 일찍 만나야 할 것 같은데.

● ●
expense 경비, 비용 fund (이용 가능한) 돈, 자금

15 대화를 듣고, 여자의 마지막 말에 이어질 남자의 말로 가장 적절한 것을 고르시오.

① That sounds like a good idea.
② I wasn't expecting it to be so much.
③ I think you'd better tell your brother.
④ I didn't mean to get you in trouble. I'm sorry.
⑤ You'd better buy it some other time. It's too expensive.

M You really look down. What's the matter?

W I'm in trouble.

M What happened?

W I was going to dust the dresser. It turns out that my brother's camera was on the dresser, but I didn't see it. It fell on the floor, and it looks like the lens broke.

M That's too bad. But don't be so hard on yourself. These things happen. You didn't do it intentionally.

W Yeah, but I could have taken my time.

M Well, your brother doesn't know it yet, does he?

W No. What do you think I ought to do now?

M I think you'd better tell your brother.

남 기분이 정말 안 좋아 보이는구나. 무슨 일이니?

여 큰일 났어.

남 무슨 일인데?

여 나는 서랍장의 먼지를 털려고 했어. 서랍장 위에 오빠의 카메라가 있었는데, 난 그걸 보지 못했어. 카메라는 바닥에 떨어졌고, 렌즈가 부서진 것 같아.

남 안됐구나. 하지만 그렇게 자책하지는 마. 그럴 수도 있지. 넌 의도적으로 그렇게 한 것이 아니잖아.

여 응, 하지만 서두르지 않고 할 수도 있었을 텐데.

남 음, 네 오빠는 아직 이 사실을 모르겠구나, 그렇지 않니?

여 응. 내가 지금 뭘 해야 한다고 생각하니?

남 내 생각에는 오빠한테 말하는 게 낫겠어.

● ●
dust 먼지를 털다 **dresser** 서랍장 **turn out** ~인 것으로 드러나다[밝혀지다] **intentionally** 의도적으로, 일부러

◗ REVIEW TEST p. 151

A ❶ hire, 고용하다 ❷ waist, 허리 ❸ airline, 항공사 ❹ unique, 독특한 ❺ needle, 바늘
❻ anxious, 불안한 ❼ overcome, 극복하다 ❽ discover, 발견하다 ❾ necessary, 필요한, 필수의
❿ expense, 경비, 비용 ⓫ including, ~을 포함하여 ⓬ viewpoint, 관점, 시각

B ❶ polka ❷ Process, request ❸ dressed up
❹ front row ❺ dust the dresser ❻ get a refund
❼ related work experience ❽ in a good mood

문제 및 정답	받아쓰기 및 녹음내용	해석

01

대화를 듣고, 두 사람이 대화 직후에 할 운동으로 가장 적절한 것을 고르시오.

① ②
③ ④
⑤

W So what should we play?

M Let's play volleyball.

W How can we play volleyball with only two people?

M Oh, I didn't think of that. Well, we can play tennis.

W That's not a bad idea, but I don't have a tennis racket. Do you have an extra one?

M No, I only have one. But I do have two table tennis rackets.

W Okay. Now that sounds more like it. Follow me. My cousin has a table at her house.

M Sounds like fun.

여 그럼 우리 무슨 운동을 할까?

남 우리 배구 하자.

여 겨우 두 명이서 어떻게 배구를 할 수 있겠니?

남 아, 그건 생각하지 못했어. 그럼, 테니스는 칠 수 있겠다.

여 나쁜 생각은 아니야, 하지만 내게는 테니스 라켓이 없어. 여분의 라켓이 있니?

남 아니, 하나밖에 없는데. 하지만 탁구 라켓은 두 개가 있어.

여 좋아. 그렇다면 탁구가 더 좋을 것 같은데. 따라와. 내 사촌 집에 탁구대가 있어.

남 재미있을 것 같다.

02

대화를 듣고, 두 사람이 대화하는 장소로 가장 적절한 곳을 고르시오.

① 버스 안   ② 택시 안
③ 배의 위   ④ 기차 안
⑤ 비행기 안

W Can you hold the rudder for a while? I need to go to the restroom.

M Sure, but could you let the sail out a little first?

W Why? You want to go slower?

M Yeah. This is my first time out at sea after all.

W There's nothing to be scared of.

M I know. Hey, can you pass me the sunscreen?

W Here you go. You look a little pinkish.

M I burn so quickly with the sun reflecting off the water like this.

여 잠깐만 이 키 좀 잡아 줄 수 있어요? 저는 화장실에 가야 해요.

남 물론이죠, 하지만 우선 돛을 조금만 풀어 주시겠어요?

여 왜요? 더 천천히 가고 싶어요?

남 예. 제가 바다에 나온 것은 어쨌든 이번이 처음이거든요.

여 무서워할 것 없어요.

남 알고 있어요. 저기, 자외선 차단제 좀 건네 주시겠어요?

여 여기 있어요. 당신은 약간 벌겋게 탄 것처럼 보여요.

남 전 이것처럼 물에 반사하는 햇빛에는 정말 빨리 타요.

●●
rudder (배의) 키 **let out** ~을 풀어 주다 **sail** 돛 **pinkish** 분홍빛이 도는 **reflect** 반사하다

03 다음을 듣고, 여자의 직업으로 가장 적절한 것을 고르시오.

① 기자   ② 은행원
③ 만화가   ④ 운동선수
⑤ 실내 디자이너

I was a troublemaker when I was a kid. I used to drive my mother crazy because I <u>drew</u> silly faces <u>on the</u> <u>wallpaper</u> in my room. In high school, I caught a lucky break; the school newspaper <u>published</u> a comic strip of mine. Since then, I've done <u>comic books</u> and even some print <u>advertising</u>. I feel really lucky to be able to earn money doing exactly <u>what</u> I <u>love</u> <u>doing</u>.

어렸을 때 저는 말썽꾼이었습니다. 저는 제 방의 벽지에 우스꽝스러운 얼굴들을 그려서 어머니를 화가 나게 하곤 했습니다. 고등학교 때 저는 행운을 얻었습니다. 학교 신문에 제 만화가 게재되었던 것입니다. 그 후로 만화책과 인쇄 광고도 만들었습니다. 딱 제가 매우 좋아하는 일을 하면서 돈을 벌 수 있다니 저는 정말 운이 좋다고 느낍니다.

troublemaker 말썽꾼 **silly** 우스꽝스러운
wallpaper 벽지 **publish** (신문 등에서) 싣다,
게재하다 **comic strip** 만화 **advertising**
광고

---

04 대화를 듣고, 두 사람의 관계로 가장 적절한 것을 고르시오.

① 교사 - 학생
② 변호사 - 의뢰인
③ 경마 기수 - 기자
④ 카레이서 - 정비원
⑤ 마라톤 선수 - 코치

M Sara, can I ask you a few questions?
W Why not? But I have to be at the <u>awards</u> <u>ceremony</u> in a few minutes.
M Okay. I'll make it fast. First of all, congratulations! It's the first time a woman has <u>won</u> this <u>horse</u> <u>race</u>. How do you feel right now?
W It's hard to express how happy I am in words.
M How long <u>have</u> <u>you</u> <u>raced</u> here?
W For three years.
M But not with this horse!
W That's right. I've only been <u>riding</u> <u>this</u> <u>horse</u> since this year.
M You've done a great job in such a short time.
W Thanks. I've got to go. If you have more questions, please <u>contact</u> <u>me</u> <u>later</u>.

남 Sara, 몇 가지 질문을 해도 되나요?
여 물론이죠. 하지만 전 몇 분 후에 시상식에 가 봐야 합니다.
남 그래요. 빨리 하지요. 우선, 축하합니다! 여성이 이 경마에서 승리한 건 처음이지요. 지금 기분이 어떠신가요?
여 얼마나 행복한지 말로 표현하기 어려워요.
남 이곳에서 얼마나 오랫동안 경주하셨어요?
여 3년간 했어요.
남 그렇지만 이 말로는 하지 않았죠!
여 맞아요. 겨우 올해부터 이 말을 타 왔죠.
남 그렇게 짧은 시간에 대단한 일을 해냈군요.
여 고맙습니다. 저는 가 봐야 해요. 만약에 질문이 더 있으면 나중에 제게 연락해 주세요.

contact 연락하다

05

대화를 듣고, 남자가 전화를 건 목적으로 가장 적절한 것을 고르시오.

① 세미나 장소를 예약하려고
② Eliza와 오후에 만날 약속을 하려고 ✓
③ 행사 불참에 대한 양해를 구하려고
④ 발표 준비를 도와줄 것을 요청하려고
⑤ 세미나 시간이 변경되었음을 알려 주려고

W Hello. Eliza White's office. How may I help you?

M Hi. This is Stan Lincoln calling.

W Oh, hello, Mr. Lincoln. How have you been?

M Just fine. I was hoping I could meet with Eliza sometime this afternoon.

W I don't know, Mr. Lincoln. Her schedule is completely booked today.

M This is really important. I have to meet her before tomorrow's presentation.

W Well, how about if I ask her and then call you back?

M That sounds great. I'm looking forward to hearing from you.

여 여보세요. Eliza White의 사무실입니다. 무엇을 도와드릴까요?

남 안녕하세요. 저는 Stan Lincoln입니다.

여 오, 안녕하세요, Lincoln 씨. 어떻게 지내세요?

남 잘 지내요. 오늘 오후 중에 Eliza를 만났으면 하는데요.

여 글쎄요, Lincoln 씨. 오늘 그녀의 일정이 완전히 잡혀 있어요.

남 정말 중요한 일인데요. 저는 그녀를 내일 발표 전에 만나야 합니다.

여 그럼, 제가 물어 보고 다시 전화 드리면 어떨까요?

남 좋은 생각이군요. 소식 기다리겠습니다.

••

presentation 발표, 설명

06

대화를 듣고, 그림에서 통화 내용을 잘못 메모한 부분을 고르시오.

TICKETS FOR　① Baseball game
WHAT DAY　② Thursday
BE READY　③ By 5:30 p.m.
GAME STARTS　④ At 7:00 p.m.
WHERE　⑤ Main stadium

M Hello.

W Hi, Bobby. It's me, Linda.

M Oh, hi, Linda. What's up?

W Bobby, did you get the tickets for the baseball game?

M Yeah, I'm going to pick them up this afternoon.

W This is the first time I've ever been to a baseball game.

M It should be a lot of fun. They always are.

W I don't know a single thing about watching baseball.

M Don't worry. Leave Thursday afternoon open.

W Okay, and by what time should I be ready?

M You should be ready by no later than five thirty because the game starts an hour later, and we need to have dinner before we go.

W No problem. We're going to the main stadium, right?

M That's right.

남 여보세요.

여 안녕, Bobby. 나야, Linda.

남 오, 안녕, Linda. 잘 지내니?

여 Bobby, 야구 경기 티켓은 구했니?

남 응, 오늘 오후에 가지러 갈 건데.

여 내가 야구 경기에 가는 건 이번이 처음이야.

남 정말 재미있을 거야. 항상 그렇거든.

여 난 야구 관람에 대해서는 하나도 몰라.

남 걱정하지 마. 목요일 오후는 비워 둬.

여 알았어, 그리고 몇 시까지 갈 준비를 해야 하지?

남 너는 늦어도 5시 30분까지는 준비되어 있어야 해, 왜냐하면 한 시간 뒤에 경기가 시작되는데 가기 전에 우린 저녁을 먹어야 하거든.

여 문제 없어. 우리는 주 경기장으로 가는 거지, 그렇지?

남 맞아.

••

no later than 늦어도 ~까지는
main stadium 주 경기장

07 대화를 듣고, 여자가 할 일로 가장 적절한 것을 고르시오.

① 대학원 논문 쓰기
② 독서실에서 공부하기
③ 수학 가정 교사 구하기 ✓
④ 남자의 수학 공부 도와주기
⑤ 학교 수학 선생님에게 도움 요청하기

W Your teacher says you're <u>falling behind</u> in math.

M I know, Mom. I don't know what to do.

W What do you mean?

M I just don't get it <u>even though I spend</u> a lot of hours studying math in the library. I find math so hard.

W If I had time, I would help you, but I am also busy <u>taking</u> a <u>graduate school course</u>. Well, there's one thing I can do.

M What is that?

W I have to <u>get you</u> a <u>tutor</u>. You've fallen behind, but you can catch up.

M Do you think it will work?

W Of course, it will. Sometimes a little help can <u>go a long way</u>.

M Thank you very much, Mom.

여 너희 선생님께서 네가 수학이 뒤처지고 있다고 말씀하시더라.

남 알아요, 엄마. 저는 무얼 해야 할지 모르겠어요.

여 무슨 뜻이니?

남 도서관에서 수학을 공부하는 데 많은 시간을 보내는데도 이해를 못하겠어요. 저는 수학이 너무 어렵다고 생각해요.

여 엄마가 시간이 있으면 도와주겠는데, 엄마도 대학원 과정을 밟느라 바빠서 말이다. 음, 내가 도와줄 수 있는 한 가지 일은 있어.

남 그게 뭔데요?

여 네게 가정 교사를 구해 줘야겠어. 네가 뒤처지긴 했지만 따라잡을 수 있단다.

남 그것이 도움이 될 거라 생각하시나요?

여 물론이지, 그럴 거야. 가끔은 조금만 도와줘도 큰 도움이 될 수 있지.

남 정말 감사해요, 엄마.

●●
fall behind 뒤처지다, 낙오하다 **graduate school** 대학원 **catch up** ~을 따라잡다 **go a long way** 큰 도움이 되다

---

08 다음을 듣고, 남자의 심정으로 가장 적절한 것을 고르시오.

① lonely
② pleased
③ satisfied
④ regretful ✓
⑤ disappointed

My father is in the hospital now. He <u>suddenly collapsed</u> eight months ago due to high blood pressure. He has been in <u>intensive care</u> since then. When I got my mother's call last year, I couldn't believe what I was hearing. I <u>wasn't ready to</u> lose my father, and he was too healthy to suddenly be so ill. I <u>couldn't work</u> and eat for a while. Now I talk to my father, but he <u>doesn't respond</u>. There is one thing I <u>regret</u>: I never told him how much I love him and <u>how thankful</u> I am for him.

아버지는 지금 병원에 계신다. 8개월 전에 갑자기 고혈압으로 쓰러지셨다. 그때 이후로 중환자실에 계신다. 작년에 내가 어머니의 전화를 받았을 때, 난 내가 듣고 있는 것을 믿을 수가 없었다. 난 아버지를 보낼 준비가 되어 있지 않았고, 아버지는 갑자기 그렇게 편찮으시기에는 너무나도 건강하셨다. 난 한동안 일을 할 수도 먹을 수도 없었다. 지금 내가 아버지에게 이야기해도, 아버지는 반응이 없으시다. 내가 후회하는 것이 한 가지 있다. 그것은 내가 얼마나 많이 아버지를 사랑하고 얼마나 감사하는지를 아버지께 말하지 못한 것이다.

●●
collapse 쓰러지다 **intensive care** 중환자실

09 대화를 듣고, 여자의 성격으로 가장 적절한 것을 고르시오.

① 검소하다   ② 무례하다
③ 정직하다   ④ 사려 깊다
⑤ 욕심이 많다

M Can I ask you something, honey?

W Sure. Go ahead.

M Why don't you buy yourself a new jacket?

W What's wrong with the one I have on?

M First of all, you've had it for years.

W So what? It's still good.

M And second, it's worn out and falling apart.

W You know I never buy anything unless I absolutely need it.

M I'm telling you that you need one. Why don't you listen to me?

W I don't like to waste money. I'll buy a new jacket when I think I need one.

남 여보, 나 뭐 하나 물어 봐도 돼?

여 물론이지. 말해 봐.

남 왜 새 재킷을 사지 않는 거야?

여 내가 입고 있는 게 어때서?

남 우선, 그거 오래 입었잖아.

여 그게 왜? 아직 상태 좋은데.

남 그리고 둘째로, 닳아 해지고 너덜거리잖아.

여 나는 물건이 반드시 필요하지 않으면 그것을 결코 사지 않는다는 걸 당신도 알잖아.

남 정말로, 당신한테는 새 재킷이 필요해. 내 말 좀 듣지 그래?

여 난 돈을 낭비하고 싶지 않아. 내가 필요하다고 생각이 들 때 새 재킷을 살게.

● ●
first of all 우선   **worn out** 닳아 해진
fall apart 너덜거리다, 산산이 부서지다
unless ~하지 않는다면

---

10 대화를 듣고, 남자가 손해 본 총 금액을 고르시오.

① $10,000   ② $12,000
③ $14,000   ④ $17,000
⑤ $70,000

M Do you remember when I said you should invest in the stock market?

W Yes. Why?

M Well, forget what I told you. The value of stocks has declined so much over the last few months.

W How much did you lose?

M Around 12,000 dollars in the last two months.

W That is a lot of money. My neighbor lost 17,000 dollars in two weeks.

M I may have to sell my stocks if this trend continues.

W Maybe you should invest in something else until the economic situation becomes stable.

M I've been thinking about that, too.

남 내가 주식 시장에 투자해야 한다고 말했을 때 기억나?

여 응. 왜?

남 음, 내가 말한 건 잊어. 지난 몇 달 사이에 주식 값이 크게 떨어졌어.

여 너는 얼마나 많이 손해 봤는데?

남 지난 두 달 동안 12,000달러 정도.

여 엄청난 금액이다. 내 이웃도 2주 동안 17,000달러 손해 봤던데.

남 이런 추세가 계속된다면 내 주식을 팔아야 할지도 모르겠어.

여 경제 상황이 안정되기 전까지 아무래도 넌 다른 곳에 투자해야겠다.

남 나도 그렇게 생각하고 있어.

● ●
invest 투자하다   **stock** 주식   **value** 가치
decline 감소하다   **economic** 경제의

11 대화를 듣고, 여자가 걱정하는 이유로 가장 적절한 것을 고르시오.

① 아빠가 아끼는 꽃병을 깨뜨려서
② 친구가 빌려준 책을 잃어버려서
③ 부모님과의 약속을 못 지킬 것 같아서
④ 남자가 부모님께 자신의 실수를 말해 버려서
⑤ 엄마께 사 드리기로 한 꽃병을 구하지 못해서

M Why the long face, Janet?

W If I tell you, do you promise not to tell my parents?

M I promise. What's wrong?

W Today, I accidentally broke my father's favorite vase in the living room, and I'm afraid my parents will be angry when they get home.

M I'm sure if you tell them honestly what happened, they won't be so upset.

W Are you sure?

M I think they will understand. We all make mistakes.

W I hope you're right about that.

M Here comes your mother now. Just tell her what happened.

W Okay. Wish me luck.

남 Janet, 왜 그렇게 시무룩한 얼굴이니?

여 내가 너한테 얘기하면 너 우리 부모님한테 얘기 안 한다고 약속하겠니?

남 약속할게. 무슨 문제야?

여 오늘, 나도 모르게 그만 거실에 있는 아빠가 제일 좋아하시는 꽃병을 깨고 말았어. 그래서 부모님이 집에 오셨을 때 화내실까 봐 걱정돼.

남 네가 무슨 일이 있었는지 너희 부모님께 솔직하게 말씀드리면 부모님도 분명 그렇게 화내진 않으실 거야.

여 확신하니?

남 난 너희 부모님이 이해하실 거라 생각해. 우리 모두 실수를 하잖아.

여 네 말이 맞기를 바라.

남 지금 너희 어머님이 오시네. 무슨 일이 있었는지 그냥 말씀드려.

여 알았어. 행운을 빌어 줘.

●●
accidentally 뜻하지 않게, 우연히 **vase** 꽃병

---

12 대화를 듣고, 대화 내용과 일치하지 않는 것을 고르시오.

① 남자의 아빠는 청혼할 때 엄마를 레스토랑에 데리고 갔다.
② 남자의 아빠는 청혼할 때 긴장한 것처럼 보였다.
③ 남자의 아빠는 청혼할 때 반지를 떨어뜨렸다.
④ 남자의 엄마는 청혼 반지를 찾지 못했다.
⑤ 남자가 엄마에게서 들은 이야기는 아빠의 이야기와 다르다.

M Mom, can I ask you about something?

W Sure, what?

M What was it like when Dad proposed to you?

W Well, let me see… Your father took me to a restaurant. We had a great dinner.

M Was Dad nervous?

W Was he nervous? He certainly was!

M And he gave you a ring, didn't he?

W Yes. That was the funny part. He got the ring out, but he was shaking so much that he dropped it under the table. Anyhow, why are you so curious about that?

M Well, our teacher told us to ask both our parents about something and see if they said the same thing.

W And did we say the same thing?

M Uh, not exactly.

남 엄마, 뭐 여쭤 봐도 돼요?

여 물론이지, 뭐니?

남 아빠가 청혼할 때 어떠셨어요?

여 음, 어디 보자… 네 아빠는 나를 레스토랑으로 데리고 갔단다. 우리는 근사한 저녁을 먹었지.

남 아빠가 긴장했나요?

여 아빠가 긴장했냐고? 분명히 그랬어!

남 그리고 아빠는 엄마에게 반지를 줬고요, 그렇지 않나요?

여 맞아. 거기가 우스운 부분이었지. 아빠가 반지를 꺼냈는데 몸을 너무 많이 떨어서 반지를 식탁 아래로 떨어뜨리고 말았단다. 그런데 왜 그렇게 그것에 대해 알고 싶어 하니?

남 음, 우리 선생님이 부모들에게 어떤 것에 대해 물어보고 부모들이 똑같이 말하는지 알아보라고 하셨어요.

여 그럼 우리는 똑같은 말을 했니?

남 어, 정확히는 아니에요.

●●
curious 알고 싶어 하는

13 대화를 듣고, 남자의 마지막 말에 이어질 여자의 말로 가장 적절한 것을 고르시오.

① Yes, it was a very interesting experience.
② Those kinds of situations put me in a bad mood.
③ Yes, I have three years of experience in this field.
④ Yes, I really hit the ceiling when I heard the news.
⑤ I think I would have a better opportunity at NS Soft.

M Where is your school <u>located</u>?
W Oh, it's in Dongdaemun-gu.
M What's your major?
W I'm <u>majoring in</u> computer engineering.
M Have you taken any business classes or anything?
W Yes, I've taken accounting, programming, <u>English conversation</u>, and some others.
M Have you ever <u>worked in an office</u> before?
W Yes, I had a <u>part-time job</u> at NS Soft for six months.
M Oh, really?
W <u>Yes, it was a very interesting experience.</u>

남 학교가 어디에 위치해 있죠?
여 아, 동대문구에 있습니다.
남 전공은 무엇인가요?
여 컴퓨터 공학을 전공하고 있습니다.
남 경영 수업이나 다른 수업을 수강한 적이 있나요?
여 예, 저는 회계학, 프로그래밍, 영어 회화, 그리고 몇몇 다른 것들을 수강했습니다.
남 전에 사무실에서 일해 본 적 있나요?
여 예, NS Soft에서 6개월간 아르바이트를 했습니다.
남 오, 그래요?
여 <u>예, 아주 흥미로운 경험이었습니다.</u>

●●
computer engineering 컴퓨터 공학
conversation 회화, 대화

---

14 대화를 듣고, 여자의 마지막 말에 이어질 남자의 말로 가장 적절한 것을 고르시오.

① Of course. Just take your time, and you'll do fine.
② Cheer up! You will get good grades next semester.
③ You're telling me. I'm sick and tired of your criticism.
④ Not really! Don't you have anything nice to say to me?
⑤ It's hard to understand. I need some time to think about it.

M It looks like something is <u>bothering you</u>.
W Well, I just feel like the sun will never shine again.
M Come on! What's up with you?
W My boss has just given me my first independent <u>project to run</u>.
M That's great news. What's the problem?
W Well, I'm not sure I've got <u>enough experience</u> to do a <u>proper job</u>. I don't really think I'm good enough.
M Just relax, and everything will be all right. If he didn't think you were good enough, he <u>wouldn't have given</u> you the assignment.
W Do you really think so?
M <u>Of course. Just take your time, and you'll do fine.</u>

남 뭔가가 널 괴롭히고 있는 것 같구나.
여 음, 태양이 다시는 뜨지 않을 것 같은 느낌이 들어.
남 이봐! 무슨 일이니?
여 사장이 내가 수행할 첫 번째 독립 프로젝트를 줬어.
남 아주 좋은 소식이네. 뭐가 문제야?
여 음, 난 내가 일을 제대로 해 낼 충분한 경험을 가지고 있다고 확신하지 않아. 난 정말 내가 충분히 잘한다고 생각하지 않거든.
남 긴장 풀어, 그럼 모든 일이 잘될 거야. 사장이 네가 충분히 잘한다고 생각하지 않으면 네게 그 임무를 주지 않았을 거야.
여 정말 그렇게 생각하니?
남 <u>물론이지. 여유를 가져, 그럼 넌 잘할 거야.</u>

●●
bother 괴롭히다 **independent** 독립된
proper 제대로 된 **assignment** 임무, 과제

15 대화를 듣고, 여자의 마지막 말에 이어질 남자의 말로 가장 적절한 것을 고르시오.

① I'm sorry. I thought you were someone else.

② Sure, they respect each other as individuals.

✓③ You're right, but I think it's also kind of a generation gap.

④ My wife and I have our own separate hobbies and friends.

⑤ That's true! We should be more careful when raising our children.

W Do you feel <u>comfortable</u> with people <u>your</u> <u>own</u> <u>age</u>?

M Sure. I think I'm outgoing, so I have a lot of friends.

W How about older people?

M I can't pinpoint it, but there is something I <u>can't</u> <u>understand</u> about them.

W Have you ever <u>argued</u> with your parents because of your <u>private</u> <u>life</u>?

M Yes, I think they've put too many restrictions on me.

W Why do you think so?

M For example, they don't <u>allow</u> me <u>to</u> <u>go</u> <u>out</u> after 10 o'clock at night. And they are strict about junk food, chores, and money.

W You seem to think that older people are <u>not</u> <u>considerate</u> toward you.

M <u>You're right, but I think it's also kind of a generation gap.</u>

여 너는 네 또래들하고 지내는 게 편하게 느껴지니?

남 물론이지. 난 외향적인 것 같아, 그래서 친구가 많아.

여 나이 든 사람들과는 어떠니?

남 정확하게 꼬집어 말할 수는 없지만, 내가 그들에 대해 이해할 수 없는 무언가가 있어.

여 넌 네 사생활 때문에 부모님과 다툰 적이 있니?

남 응, 난 부모님이 나에게 너무 많은 제약을 가한다고 생각해.

여 왜 그렇게 생각하는데?

남 예를 들면, 그들은 내가 밤 10시가 지나서 외출하는 것을 허락하지 않으셔. 그리고 정크 푸드와 집안일, 돈에 대해서도 엄격하셔.

여 넌 나이 든 사람들이 너에 대해 이해심이 없다고 생각하는 것 같구나.

남 <u>맞아, 하지만 난 그것도 일종의 세대 차이라고 생각해.</u>

pinpoint 정확히 꼬집어 말하다 **private** 사적인 **restriction** 제약, 제한 **considerate** 이해심 있는

REVIEW TEST p. 159

A
① vase, 화병 ② value, 가치 ③ invest, 투자하다 ④ bother, 괴롭히다 ⑤ reflect, 반사하다
⑥ decline, 감소하다 ⑦ publish, (신문 등에서) 싣다, 게재하다 ⑧ economic, 경제의 ⑨ assignment, 임무, 과제
⑩ advertising, 광고 ⑪ accidentally, 뜻하지 않게, 우연히 ⑫ catch up, ~을 따라잡다

B
① contact ② presentation ③ unless
④ graduate school ⑤ silly, wallpaper ⑥ falling behind
⑦ no later than ⑧ and some others

문제 및 정답	받아쓰기 및 녹음내용	해석

01

대화를 듣고, 여자가 할 일로 언급되지 않은 것을 고르시오.

①   ②

③   ④

⑤

M Could you buy me some cookies at the store?

W Oh, sorry, but I'm <u>not going out</u> today.

M You're not? Well, what are you doing today then?

W The whole house is a <u>mess</u>, so I plan on wiping the windows, <u>vacuuming</u> <u>the</u> <u>floors</u>, and cleaning out the fridge.

M As long as you're cleaning, could you <u>wash</u> <u>the</u> <u>car</u>, too? As you know, I'm busy with my work.

W All right. But you have to do it the next time!

M I <u>owe</u> <u>you</u> this time.

W Don't mention it.

남 가게에서 쿠키 좀 사다 줄 수 있겠니?

여 오, 미안하지만 오늘 나는 밖에 나가지 않을 거야.

남 안 나간다고? 음, 그럼 오늘 뭘 할 건데?

여 집안 전체가 엉망이라서, 창문을 닦고 바닥을 진공청소기로 청소하고 냉장고를 청소할 계획이야.

남 청소하는 김에 세차도 해 주겠니? 네가 알다시피 나는 일하느라 바빠.

여 알았어. 하지만 다음번에는 네가 해야 해!

남 이번에 네게 신세를 지는구나.

여 천만에.

●●

mess 엉망인 상태 **vacuum** 진공청소기로 청소하다 **fridge** 냉장고 **owe** 신세를 지다

02

대화를 듣고, 두 사람이 대화하는 장소로 가장 적절한 곳을 고르시오.

① 부엌   ② 사무실
③ 미술관   ④ 커피숍
⑤ 버스 정류장

M It's really busy in here today.

W You're right. This line is taking forever.

M Why don't you <u>grab</u> <u>a</u> <u>table</u> while I wait here in line?

W Good thinking. Can you get me a mocha latte?

M Don't you <u>want</u> <u>something</u> <u>cold</u>? It's so hot today.

W You're right. I'll have a mocha milkshake, please.

M I'll <u>have</u> <u>an</u> <u>iced</u> <u>latte</u> because the mocha is too sweet for me.

W Meet me <u>on</u> <u>the</u> <u>second</u> <u>floor</u>.

M All right.

남 오늘 여기 무척 바쁘네.

여 맞아. 이 줄은 끝이 없을 것 같아.

남 내가 여기에 서서 기다리는 동안 테이블을 맡아 두는 게 어때?

여 좋은 생각이야. 내 것은 모카 라떼로 사다 주겠니?

남 차가운 음료가 좋지 않아? 오늘 무척 덥잖아.

여 네 말이 맞아. 모카 밀크셰이크를 마시겠어.

남 모카는 너무 달아서 난 아이스 라떼를 마셔야겠어.

여 2층에서 보자.

남 알았어.

●●

grab 잡다, 거머쥐다

03 대화를 듣고, 남자의 직업으로 가장 적절한 것을 고르시오.

① 교수　　② 기자 ✓
③ 작가　　④ 편집자
⑤ 아나운서

W Peter, your <u>news</u> <u>story</u> last week was very impressive.

M Thank you, Julia. At least the time that I spent researching for it <u>paid</u> <u>off</u>.

W Indeed! A lot of people like it too.

M Really? How did you know?

W Take a look at our website. You can <u>read</u> <u>the</u> <u>comments</u> from our netizens.

M Were there any negative comments?

W I read a few, but most of them were <u>positive</u>.

M That's good to hear! I hope that my next one gets the same response.

W Well, you're a <u>great</u> <u>journalist</u>. Anyway, I need you to submit your news item tomorrow.

M Oh, I <u>almost</u> <u>forgot</u> about the <u>deadline</u>!

여 Peter, 당신의 지난주 뉴스 기사는 정말 인상적이었어요.

남 고마워요, Julia. 최소한 제가 조사하느라 보낸 시간에 대해서는 보상받은 셈이네요.

여 정말 그래요! 많은 사람들도 좋아하던데요.

남 정말이요? 어떻게 알았죠?

여 우리 회사의 웹사이트를 한번 봐요. 네티즌들의 의견들을 읽어 볼 수 있어요.

남 부정적인 의견들이 있었나요?

여 몇 개를 읽긴 했지만, 대부분은 긍정적이었어요.

남 듣던 중 반가운 소리군요! 다음 기사도 같은 반응을 얻으면 좋겠어요.

여 음, 당신은 훌륭한 기자예요. 어쨌든, 내일 뉴스 기사를 제출해 주시면 좋겠군요.

남 아, 하마터면 마감 시간에 대해 잊을 뻔했네요!

●●
pay off 성과를 내다 **indeed** 정말, 아주 **comment** 의견, 논평 **negative** 부정적인 **positive** 긍정적인 **journalist** 기자 **submit** 제출하다 **deadline** 마감 시간

---

04 대화를 듣고, 두 사람의 관계로 가장 적절한 것을 고르시오.

① 배우 - 매니저
② 경호원 - 관객
③ 매표원 - 관람객 ✓
④ 수의사 - 애견 주인
⑤ 관광 가이드 - 여행객

M What do you <u>recommend</u>? There are so many good shows that I'd like to watch.

W These days, a lot of people are trying to <u>reserve</u> <u>seats</u> for the musical *Cats*. *Grease* is pretty <u>popular</u>, too.

M *Grease* sounds good. I'd like to see it.

W Let me check on the computer. We have <u>a</u> <u>few</u> <u>seats</u> <u>left</u> in the middle of the first floor and in the second row of the balcony.

M How much are the first floor seats?

W They are 50 dollars each.

M When do the <u>curtains</u> <u>go</u> <u>up</u>?

W At 8 o'clock.

M Okay. I'll take two seats on the first floor.

남 무엇을 추천하시겠어요? 제가 보고 싶은 좋은 공연이 너무 많아서요.

여 요즘 많은 사람들이 뮤지컬 'Cats'를 보려고 좌석을 예약하려고 하거든요. 'Grease'도 꽤 인기가 있어요.

남 'Grease'가 좋을 듯 하네요. 그것을 보고 싶어요.

여 컴퓨터에서 확인해 볼게요. 1층 중간과 발코니석 두 번째 줄에 몇 자리 남아 있네요.

남 1층 자리는 얼마죠?

여 각각 50달러입니다.

남 막이 언제 오르죠?

여 8시입니다.

남 알겠습니다. 1층의 두 자리로 하겠습니다.

●●
popular 인기 있는 **balcony** (2층의) 발코니석

05 대화를 듣고, 여자가 전화를 건 목적으로 가장 적절한 것을 고르시오.

① 꽃을 주문하려고
② 남자를 초대하려고
③ 스카프를 찾으려고
④ 승용차를 함께 타려고
⑤ 꽃집 위치를 물어보려고

M Hello.

W Hi. It's Emma calling. May I speak to Tom?

M This is he. Hey, Emma. What's up?

W You didn't happen to <u>see my scarf</u>, did you?

M What does it look like?

W It is blue with <u>purple</u> flowers.

M Don't worry. I think I have it.

W Where did you find it?

M I found it in my car. I was <u>wondering how</u> it got there.

W I <u>must have forgotten</u> it there when you drove me home yesterday.

남 여보세요.

여 여보세요. Emma입니다. Tom과 통화할 수 있을까요?

남 내가 Tom이야. 이봐, Emma. 무슨 일이야?

여 너 내 스카프 본 적 없지, 그렇지?

남 어떻게 생겼는데?

여 파란색에 보라색 꽃이 있어.

남 걱정하지 마. 내가 가지고 있는 것 같아.

여 어디에서 찾았는데?

남 내 자동차에서 찾았어. 어떻게 그게 거기에 들어갔는지 궁금해하고 있었어.

여 어제 네가 차로 집에 데려다 줬을 때 내가 그곳에 두고 간 것 같아.

---

06 대화를 듣고, 남자가 취하고 있는 동작을 고르시오.

①   ②
③   ④

⑤

W All right. Now we're going to try the bridge stretch.

M The bridge stretch? How do you do that?

W Start with your feet, hands, and <u>bottom on the floor</u>.

M And my knees and shoulders in the air? I feel like a zigzag.

W Right. Now <u>push your hips</u> up as high as you can.

M This is not very comfortable.

W Now walk your hands in <u>toward your feet</u>.

M Oww! I must look like an upside-down U. It's hard to do.

W Don't worry. You'll <u>get used to</u> it.

여 좋아요. 이제 다리 스트레칭을 해 보겠습니다.

남 다리 스트레칭이요? 어떻게 하는 건데요?

여 발과 손, 그리고 엉덩이를 바닥에 대고 시작하세요.

남 그리고 제 무릎과 어깨는 위로 하는 건가요? 제가 지그재그 모양이 된 것 같네요.

여 맞아요. 이제 당신의 엉덩이를 가능한 한 높이 밀어 올리세요.

남 그다지 편하지는 않네요.

여 이제 발과 가까운 곳으로 손을 이동시키세요.

남 아! U자를 거꾸로 한 모양이겠군요. 따라하기 어려워요.

여 걱정하지 마세요. 그 자세에 익숙해질 거예요.

● ●
bottom 엉덩이 **comfortable** 편안한
upside-down 거꾸로의 **get used to** ~에 익숙해지다

07

다음을 듣고, 어떤 동물에 관한 설명인지 고르시오.

① 닭 ② 소
③ 개 ④ 판다
⑤ 고양이

This is my favorite animal. Not many people like it <u>the way</u> I <u>do</u>. They say it's ugly and stupid. They use its name to mean the same as "<u>coward</u>." They don't <u>appreciate</u> it at all. In fact, it is a very important animal. The females give us <u>both</u> meat and <u>eggs</u>, and the males are very useful as natural <u>alarm</u> <u>clocks</u>. Plus, the babies are really cute. All in all, I think it <u>deserves</u> a lot more <u>respect</u>.

이것은 내가 가장 좋아하는 동물입니다. 내가 좋아하는 식으로 이 동물을 좋아하는 사람들은 많지 않지요. 사람들은 이것이 못생기고 멍청하다고 말합니다. 사람들은 '겁쟁이'와 같은 뜻으로 이 동물의 이름을 사용합니다. 사람들은 이 동물에게 전혀 감사해하지 않습니다. 사실, 이것은 매우 중요한 동물입니다. 암컷은 우리에게 고기와 알을 모두 제공하고, 수컷은 자연 자명종으로서 아주 유용합니다. 더욱이, 새끼들은 무척 귀엽습니다. 대체로, 내 생각에 그것은 훨씬 더 많은 존중을 받을 만합니다.

••

coward 겁쟁이 **female** 암컷 **male** 수컷
useful 유용한 **deserve** ~을 받을 만하다
respect 존중, 존경

08

대화를 듣고, 여자의 심정으로 가장 적절한 것을 고르시오.

① bored ② regretful
③ confused ④ delighted
⑤ frightened

M Happy Parents' Day, Mom!

W Thank you. What's this? A card?

M Yes, I <u>made</u> it <u>myself</u>. Do you like it?

W It's great. It says, "Thank you for being such a wonderful parent all these years."

M I even <u>pasted</u> a picture of our family <u>on</u> <u>it</u>.

W I see that. You spent a lot of time on this, didn't you?

M A few hours. I wanted this day <u>to</u> <u>be</u> <u>special</u>.

W Thank you for being my number-one son. I'm so glad.

M So, Mom... <u>What</u> <u>shall</u> <u>we</u> <u>do</u> this evening after Dad comes home?

W Well, let's think about it.

남 어버이날 축하드려요, 엄마!

여 고마워. 이게 뭐니? 카드니?

남 네, 제가 직접 만든 거예요. 맘에 드세요?

여 아주 좋은 걸. "지금까지 아주 멋진 부모님이 되어 주셔서 감사해요."라고 쓰여 있네.

남 제가 카드에 우리 가족 사진도 붙였어요.

여 그렇네. 너 이거 만드느라 시간 많이 들었겠다, 그렇지 않니?

남 몇 시간이요. 이날이 특별했으면 해서요.

여 최고의 아들이 되어 줘서 고맙다. 정말 기쁘구나.

남 저기 말이죠, 엄마… 아빠가 집에 오시면 오늘 저녁에 뭘 할까요?

여 글쎄, 생각 좀 해 보자.

••

paste 풀로 붙이다

09 대화를 듣고, 현재의 영화 관람료가 20년 전에 비해 얼마나 많이 올랐는지 고르시오.

① 10배   ② 14배
③ 16배   ④ 18배
⑤ 20배 ✓

M Aunt June, what is this?

W What? Oh, that? That is old money.

M I've never <u>seen</u> <u>such</u> <u>money</u> before.

W That is a 500-won bill. When I was your age, it only <u>cost</u> <u>500</u> <u>won</u> to go to the movies. That was almost <u>20</u> <u>years</u> <u>ago</u>.

M I can't believe it.

W The <u>bus</u> <u>fare</u> was only 100 won, and the most popular <u>noodles</u> were 120 won.

M Why was everything so cheap?

W It was a different time then. Now, everything is so expensive. To go to the movies now costs <u>at</u> <u>least</u> <u>10,000</u> won.

M Times have really changed, haven't they?

남 June 이모, 이게 뭐예요?

여 뭐? 아, 그거? 옛날 돈이야.

남 이전에 이런 돈을 본 적이 없는데요.

여 500원짜리 지폐야. 내가 네 나이였을 때는 영화 보는 데 500원밖에 안 들었어. 그것이 거의 20년 전이구나.

남 믿을 수가 없어요.

여 버스 요금은 단돈 100원, 그리고 가장 인기 있던 국수는 120원이었어.

남 모든 것이 왜 그렇게 쌌던 거죠?

여 그때는 시대가 달랐지. 지금은 모든 것이 너무 비싸. 지금은 영화를 보는 데 최소한 10,000원은 들잖아.

남 세월이 정말로 변했죠, 그렇지 않나요?

• •

bill 지폐   **fare** 요금, 운임   **noodle** 국수

---

10 대화를 듣고, 여자가 극장에 가지 못하는 이유로 가장 적절한 것을 고르시오.

① 친척 집에 방문하기로 해서
② 친구들과 백화점에 가기로 해서
③ 엄마가 극장에 가지 말라고 해서
④ 사촌들을 마중하러 터미널에 가야 해서
⑤ 사촌들과 시간을 보내기로 엄마와 약속 ✓
   해서

M Hey, Sarah, are you going to the movie theater tonight?

W I would love to, but <u>my</u> <u>cousins</u> <u>have</u> <u>come</u> to Seoul, and I promised my mother to <u>take</u> them to the <u>department</u> <u>store</u> this evening.

M Really? That's too bad because all our friends are going to be there.

W I know, and I feel sorry about that. But I <u>promised</u> <u>her</u> <u>weeks</u> <u>ago</u>, and they seem so excited.

M Well, a promise is a promise.

W That's true. Please tell everyone there that I'm sorry I <u>can't</u> <u>go</u>.

M I'm sure they'll understand. Besides, it's important to spend time with <u>your</u> <u>relatives</u>, too.

W You're right. I don't see them often.

M Have a good time this evening, and I'll see you soon.

W You, too.

남 안녕, Sarah, 오늘 밤에 극장에 갈 거니?

여 정말 가고 싶지만, 사촌들이 서울에 와서 오늘 저녁에 그들을 백화점에 데리고 가기로 엄마랑 약속했거든.

남 정말? 우리 친구들 모두 극장에 갈 건데 참 안됐다.

여 알아, 나도 아쉬워. 그렇지만 내가 엄마한테 몇 주 전에 약속했고, 사촌들이 매우 들떠 있는 것 같아.

남 음, 약속은 약속이니까.

여 맞아. 모두에게 내가 못 가서 미안하다고 전해 줘.

남 분명 애들도 이해할 거야. 게다가 친척들이랑 시간을 보내는 것도 중요하잖아.

여 네 말이 맞아. 사촌들은 자주 보지 못하거든.

남 오늘 저녁에 즐거운 시간 보내, 그럼 곧 보자.

여 너도.

• •

department store 백화점   **besides** 게다가
relative 친척

11 대화를 듣고, 남자가 오늘 오후에 할 일로 가장 적절한 것을 고르시오.

① 빵 굽기
② 집안 청소하기
③ 우유와 빵 사 오기
④ 텔레비전 주문하기
⑤ 저녁 식사 준비하기

M Here you go, Mom. I made you breakfast.

W Wow, what a surprise! You haven't done this for me before.

M I know. But I see you've been working very hard these days, so I thought I would give you a break. And today is Sunday.

W I really appreciate it. How about doing the same for me every Sunday?

M If you would like that, it would be my pleasure. Is there anything else I can do for you today?

W Would you please turn the television to channel four?

M No problem. Anything else?

W Not right now, but I need some milk and bread this afternoon.

M Okay. I'll do that.

남 여기 있어요, 엄마. 엄마를 위해 아침 식사를 만들었어요.

여 와, 놀랍구나! 너 전에 엄마한테 이렇게 한 적 없잖아.

남 알아요. 그렇지만 요즘 엄마가 너무 열심히 일하시는 걸 알아요, 그래서 엄마에게 휴식을 드려야겠다고 생각했죠. 그리고 오늘 일요일이잖아요.

여 정말 고맙구나. 매주 일요일마다 엄마를 위해 이렇게 해 주면 어떻겠니?

남 엄마가 원하신다면, 기꺼이 그렇게 할게요. 오늘 제가 또 엄마를 위해 할 일이 있나요?

여 텔레비전을 4번 채널로 돌려 줄래?

남 그럼요. 그 외에는요?

여 지금 당장은 없지만, 오늘 오후에 우유와 빵이 필요하긴 해.

남 알겠어요. 그렇게 할게요.

●●
break 휴식 (시간)

---

12 대화를 듣고, 대화 내용과 일치하지 <u>않는</u> 것을 고르시오.

① 남자는 어젯밤에 잠을 거의 자지 못했다.
② 남자는 잠을 자기 위해 책에 나온 방법을 시도해 보았다.
③ 남자의 옆집 이웃은 밤새도록 소음을 낸다.
④ 여자는 남자에게 이사 갈 것을 조언하고 있다.
⑤ 남자는 집주인에게 문제를 알렸지만 소용없었다.

W Are you tired? You look pale.

M Yeah, I'm exhausted. I hardly slept a wink last night.

W Again? You've been having trouble sleeping since last month.

M You're telling me. I've tried everything in the book.

W Like what?

M Counting sheep, drinking warm milk, and even wearing earplugs. Nothing has worked. I may just have to move.

W How would moving help?

M Well, the guy who lives next door blasts music all night long.

W Why don't you complain to the landlord?

M I did. Nothing helps because my neighbor is the landlord's nephew, and he thinks he can do whatever he wants.

W That's terrible.

여 피곤하니? 너 창백해 보인다.

남 응, 난 지쳤어. 난 지난밤에 거의 눈도 붙이지 못했어.

여 또? 넌 지난달 이후로 잠자는 데 문제가 있구나.

남 네 말이 맞아. 난 책에 있는 모든 것을 시도해 봤어.

여 어떤 것을?

남 양 숫자 세기, 따뜻한 우유 마시기, 심지어는 귀마개 끼기까지 말야. 아무 소용없더라. 난 그냥 이사를 가야 하나 봐.

여 이사가 어떻게 도움이 되니?

남 음, 옆집에 사는 남자가 밤새도록 음악 소리를 크게 내거든.

여 집주인에게 고충을 말해 보지 그러니?

남 말해 봤어. 옆집 사람이 집주인의 조카라서 아무 소용이 없고, 그는 자신이 원하는 것은 뭐든지 할 수 있다고 생각해.

여 끔찍하구나.

●●
pale 창백한 **count** (수를) 세다 **earplug** 귀마개 **blast** (큰 소리를) 내다 **landlord** 집주인 **nephew** 조카

13 대화를 듣고, 여자의 마지막 말에 이어질 남자의 말로 가장 적절한 것을 고르시오.

① Can I take a rain check?
② That's exactly what I believe.
③ I have to meet up with a lot of people.
④ You got it. Have you thought of anything good yet?
⑤ I think I should change my attitude toward the people I work with.

M Have you found a babysitter yet?

W No, I've decided not to work but to <u>look</u> <u>after</u> my baby <u>myself</u>.

M Why did you change your mind?

W I think babies usually <u>learn</u> <u>everything</u> from their parents.

M I think so, too.

W As you know, children are apt to learn <u>by</u> <u>watching</u> <u>others</u>. Therefore, they just imitate their parents' <u>actions</u>.

M That's true. Do you think they learn more by seeing than doing?

W Yes, children unconsciously <u>imitate</u> <u>whatever</u> <u>they</u> <u>see</u> around them.

M <u>That's exactly what I believe.</u>

남 아기 돌보는 사람은 구했니?

여 아니, 일하지 않고 내가 직접 아이를 돌보기로 결정했어.

남 왜 마음을 바꿨니?

여 난 아기들이 보통 모든 것을 부모로부터 배운다고 생각해.

남 나도 그렇게 생각해.

여 너도 알다시피, 아이들은 다른 사람들을 관찰함으로써 배우는 경향이 있잖아. 그래서 그들은 부모들의 행동을 그대로 흉내 내지.

남 맞아. 너는 아이들이 행동보다는 보는 것으로 더 많이 배운다고 생각하니?

여 응, 아이들은 무의식적으로 주변에 보이는 것은 무엇이든 흉내 내지.

남 <u>나도 바로 그렇게 믿고 있어.</u>

●●
be apt to ~하는 경향이 있다, ~하기 쉽다
therefore 그래서, 그러므로 **imitate** 흉내 내다
unconsciously 무의식적으로

---

14 대화를 듣고, 남자의 마지막 말에 이어질 여자의 말로 가장 적절한 것을 고르시오.

① It needs a bit more salt. How's your pasta?
② Skipping breakfast is really bad for your health.
③ I agree it's good, but I prefer non-greasy food.
④ Since I read those articles, I have decided to eat less meat.
⑤ I'm starving. This is the only thing I've eaten all day.

W Can you come to my house for dinner tomorrow night?

M Sure. By the way, what's the occasion?

W There is <u>no</u> <u>special</u> <u>occasion</u>. I just want to have dinner with you.

M Thanks for <u>inviting</u> <u>me</u>. What's for dinner?

W Vegetarian food.

M Vegetarian food? As far as I know, you like meat, don't you?

W Yes, but there were some <u>negative</u> <u>news</u> <u>articles</u> about cholesterol, the harmful substance that can <u>cause</u> <u>obesity</u>.

M Really? I didn't know that.

W <u>Since I read those articles, I have decided to eat less meat.</u>

여 내일 밤에 우리 집에 저녁 먹으러 올래?

남 물론이지. 그런데 무슨 일인데?

여 특별한 일은 없어. 난 그냥 너와 저녁을 함께하고 싶을 뿐이야.

남 초대해 줘서 고마워. 저녁 메뉴는 뭐니?

여 채식 요리야.

남 채식 요리? 너는 육류를 좋아하는 걸로 아는데, 그렇지 않니?

여 맞아, 하지만 비만을 일으킬 수 있는 해로운 물질인 콜레스테롤에 대한 부정적인 뉴스 기사들이 있었잖아.

남 정말? 난 몰랐어.

여 <u>그 기사들을 읽고 육류를 덜 먹기로 결정했어.</u>

●●
harmful 해로운 **substance** 물질 **obesity** 비만

15 대화를 듣고, 여자의 마지막 말에 이어질 남자의 말로 가장 적절한 것을 고르시오.

① I always take trips during vacations.

② I just stay in and watch TV on the weekends.

③ I go to the movies about three times a month.

④ I often read the newspaper, but sometimes I sleep.

⑤ I usually do oil paintings, but sometimes I work with sculptures, too.

W Do you ever drive to work?

M No, I never drive to my office. Traffic is very bad in the morning.

W Do you ever travel on the bus?

M No, I don't. I never take the bus. It takes forever to get to work.

W Well, how else do you travel in the morning?

M I usually take the train that arrives at Seoul Station at 8:45.

W Can you find a seat on the train in the morning?

M Oh, yes, I can. I always find a seat.

W So tell me... What do you do on the train in the morning?

M I often read the newspaper, but sometimes I sleep.

여 차를 타고 출근하시나요?

남 아뇨, 저는 운전해서 사무실에 가지 않아요. 아침에는 교통이 아주 나쁘거든요.

여 버스로 다니세요?

남 아뇨. 저는 버스를 타지 않아요. 출근하는 데 시간이 아주 많이 걸리거든요.

여 그럼, 아침에는 다른 어떤 수단으로 다니시나요?

남 저는 대개 서울역에 8시 45분에 도착하는 열차를 탑니다.

여 아침에 열차에 자리가 있나요?

남 아, 예, 그럼요. 저는 항상 자리를 찾아요.

여 그러면 제게 말씀해 보세요… 아침에 열차에서 무얼 하시나요?

남 저는 주로 신문을 읽지만 가끔은 잠을 자요.

REVIEW TEST p. 167

A ① grab, 잡다, 거머쥐다 ② paste, 풀로 붙이다 ③ useful, 유용한 ④ harmful, 해로운 ⑤ coward, 겁쟁이

⑥ nephew, 조카 ⑦ positive, 긍정적인 ⑧ female, 암컷 ⑨ deadline, 마감 시간

⑩ therefore, 그래서, 그러므로 ⑪ comfortable, 편안한 ⑫ substance, 물질

B ① cause obesity ② negative comments ③ deserves, respect

④ bus fare ⑤ department store ⑥ imitate, around

⑦ get used to ⑧ are apt to